First Nations, First Thoughts . . . .

First Nations, First Thoughts

The Impact of Indigenous Thought
in Canada

...... Edited by Annis May Timpson

UBCPress · Vancouver · Toronto

20 19 18 17 16 15 14 13 12 11 10   5 4 3 2

Printed in Canada on ancient-forest-free paper (100% post-consumer recycled) that is processed chlorine- and acid-free.

Library and Archives Canada Cataloguing in Publication

First Nations, first thoughts: the impact of Indigenous thought in Canada / edited by Annis May Timpson.

Includes bibliographical references and index.
ISBN 978-0-7748-1551-2 (bound); ISBN 978-0-7748-1552-9 (pbk.);
ISBN 978-0-7748-1553-6 (e-book)

1. Canada – Civilization – Indian influences. 2. Native peoples – Canada – Intellectual life. 3. Native peoples – Canada – History. 4. Native peoples – Canada – Politics and government. I. Timpson, Annis May

E78.C2F539 2008   971.004'97   C2009-901978-7

Canada

UBC Press gratefully acknowledges the financial support for our publishing program of the Government of Canada through the Book Publishing Industry Development Program (BPIDP), and of the Canada Council for the Arts, and the British Columbia Arts Council.

This book has been published with the help of financial support from the Canadian Studies Development Program at Foreign Affairs and International Trade Canada.

UBC Press
The University of British Columbia
2029 West Mall
Vancouver, BC V6T 1Z2
604-822-5959 / Fax: 604-822-6083
www.ubcpress.ca

This book is dedicated
with special thanks
to
Peter and Sue Russell
for many a warm welcome to your home
and
to
my dear friend
Jilly Jennings
for being the Elder in my life

Contents

Acknowledgments

This book's small contribution to the complex process of decolonization in Canada could not have come about without the knowledge and insight of the many Indigenous people who have taken considerable time to transmit ideas within their communities, across generations, and between cultures. As editor, I express sincere appreciation for the inspiration they have provided for this collection.

One of the joys of my academic career has been working with colleagues at UBC Press. Jean Wilson brought a wealth of professional experience to this project and helped me to make important decisions about effective ways to shape this collection. Darcy Cullen steered the book's development through its middle stage with charm, thoughtfulness, and great repartee that always made me smile. Holly Keller juggled all the elements, and all the people, involved in the editorial and production processes most efficiently. I struck gold with the appointment of Lesley Erickson as project editor, and I will always value the amount that she taught me about the intricacies of preparing text for publication. While I cannot identify everyone who has facilitated their work, I also wish to thank Megan Brand, Annette Lorek, Kerry Kilmartin, Irma Rodriguez, Martyn Schmoll, and, of course, Peter Milroy.

There is a particular dynamic involved in working with contributors who, at various points, have been located across six different time zones. I have benefited, however, from the collaboration and cooperation of a superb group of colleagues. Thank you all for your support and for providing me with the opportunity to learn so much from your research. Collectively, we benefited from the thoughtful critiques and the challenges posed by the anonymous reviewers of this collection.

I am very grateful to academic and administrative colleagues at the University of Edinburgh who helped me as director of the Centre of Canadian Studies to organize the "First Nations, First Thoughts" conference, which marked the genesis of this book. Above all, I wish to thank Elizabeth Dodds for the superb administration of a conference that brought together over one hundred scholars from nine different countries. In addition, I thank all the participants at that conference for sharing their work in Edinburgh and, since then, presenting it online. I also thank Lorraine Waterhouse, Charlie Jeffery, and Anthony Good, for their guidance, and express appreciation to Foreign Affairs and International Trade Canada for the financial support that enabled both the conference and this book.

I have been blessed throughout this project by the love and closeness of my husband, Ian Read, who has shared every stage of it with me. I have also been encouraged throughout by good friends and neighbours who have taken great interest in this work. I cannot mention them all, but I particularly want to thank Catherine Reynolds, Lindsay Davies, Mary St. Aubyn, Mandy and John Jutsum, June Sidwell, and Trevor Grosvenor, for their sustained support, and to say how good it is that Stephen Tierney and Ailsa Henderson are now close by in Edinburgh.

My concluding and profound thanks go to those on each side of the Atlantic to whom I have dedicated this book. Peter and Sue Russell have shown me many kindnesses over the years. On the occasion of this publication, I salute Peter for his extensive professional contributions to the progress of Indigenous-settler relations in Canada. Finally, as I write, just a few days away from her ninety-first birthday, I thank Jilly Jennings for her wisdom, her enthusiasm, and her love.

First Nations, First Thoughts

Introduction:
Indigenous Thought in Canada

Annis May Timpson

This book examines the impact of Aboriginal thought on Canadian public discourse. It considers how Aboriginal peoples have questioned colonial interpretations of Canadian history; challenged prevailing cultural, political, economic, and constitutional "wisdom"; called for adjustments in settler Canadian thought; and, with varying degrees of success, brought Indigenous perspectives to bear on cultural institutions, universities, governments, and the courts.

First Nations, First Thoughts explores how Aboriginal peoples have articulated ideas, visions, and perspectives within their autonomous, self-determining communities and in broader public discourse in Canada. In addition, this book considers how the ideas, innovations, and challenges that Aboriginal peoples have brought to public attention have been resisted, acknowledged, questioned, and accepted.

The scholars and practitioners who contribute to this book demonstrate how academic research, cultural narratives, governance, and constitutional discourse in Canada can be enriched by the full recognition of Indigenous thought and careful processes of Aboriginal-settler exchange. They also emphasize the complexities of integrating Aboriginal thinking into established institutions and dominant discourses, highlighting the challenges, and the responsibilities, that face Indigenous and settler nations in Canada if the potential for embracing Aboriginal perspectives in the country's public institutions is to be fully realized.

This book is designed as an interdisciplinary contribution to the broader, ongoing process of decolonization in Canada. It highlights the diverse contributions that Aboriginal thinkers have made, and continue to make, to Canadian public debate.[1] It invites readers to consider how Aboriginal self-determination could be realized and a fuller reconciliation achieved between

Aboriginal and settler communities. Although this book confirms that the process of decolonization in Canada is not yet complete, it nonetheless high-lights encouraging examples of progress toward that goal.

Oral Tradition and the Transmission of Indigenous Thought

Oral traditions in Aboriginal communities are intrinsic to the intergenerational transmission of Indigenous knowledge.[2] Aboriginal storytelling maintains the distinctness of Indigenous thought, rebalances power relations between Aboriginal peoples and settler Canadians, and, as Taiaiake Alfred has argued, reduces the alienation in Aboriginal communities that arises when people are separated from their heritage and, by implication, from themselves.[3] This book shows how Indigenous storytelling can extend the established boundaries of historical research, generate new resources for archives and museums, broaden cultural understandings of urban space, encourage retention of Indigenous languages, and rekindle community strength. It also demonstrates how these oral traditions mitigate the impact and damage of colonialism by enabling Aboriginal peoples to question research methodologies, reframe historical knowledge, challenge dominant ideas, and, above all, develop agency.

The importance of storytelling in Aboriginal communities reinforces the recognition of Elders as conveyors of deeply held Indigenous wisdom.[4] These men and women retain profound understanding and knowledge of Indigenous thought, not only for cultural reasons intrinsic to their communities but also because they often speak the endangered languages of their nations. Their stories bring nuanced understandings of Aboriginal thinking into the public domain. As John Borrows has argued, "Oral history in numerous Aboriginal groups is conveyed through interwoven layers of culture that entwine to sustain national memories over the lifetime of many generations. The transmission of oral tradition in these societies is bound up with the configuration of language, political structures, economic systems, social relations, intellectual methodologies, morality, ideology and their physical world."[5]

Indigenous storytelling generates rich oral narratives that broaden knowledge embedded in written texts, visual images, and geographical space. This book shows how such narratives enable Aboriginal people to express memories of overcoming hardship and surviving on the land. It also demonstrates how such stories sustain intergenerational knowledge within Aboriginal communities and can enhance cross-cultural understanding beyond them.

Oral traditions in Aboriginal communities reinforce awareness about profound differences between Indigenous and Western understandings of history and sovereignty. Indeed, this book clarifies how recognition and respect for Indigenous stories are important not only for intercultural communication but also for good governance, effective co-management, progressive scholarship, and, in the longer run, political and constitutional reconciliation between Indigenous and settler communities in Canada.

Integrating Indigenous Thought into Canadian Institutions

First Nations, First Thoughts not only explores ideas developed within Aboriginal communities, it also considers the impact of Indigenous thought in Canada. Contributors to this book analyze different approaches to creating and changing Canadian public institutions so that both Aboriginal and settler perspectives are embodied within them. They also consider the complexities of realizing this objective given the current under-representation of Aboriginal people on the staff and governing bodies of museums, the faculties of universities, and the bureaucracies that service public governments. Although contributors argue that the impact of Indigenous thinking on Canadian institutions will increase if the representation of Aboriginal people within these organizations is improved, they also emphasize that numerical representation alone cannot ensure the institutional absorption of Indigenous thought. More fundamental cultural shifts, inside and outside those institutions, are necessary to bring this about.

The integration of Aboriginal knowledge into Canadian public institutions that have long been shaped by Western values is complex. This book highlights alliances that have been developed to give voice to Aboriginal perspectives at the institutional level, leading in recent periods to collaboration and co-management. It also shows how these initiatives have encouraged the development of new approaches to scholarship; long-term relationships between curators, archivists, and members of Indigenous source communities; experiments in developing public agencies that prioritize Aboriginal culture; and cross-cultural initiatives by Indigenous and non-Indigenous public servants to facilitate the full absorption of Aboriginal thinking into public governance.

Nonetheless, contributors also point out the difficulties that have arisen with initiatives to integrate Indigenous thinking into Canadian institutions, including the dangers associated with appearing to pursue this objective while simultaneously absorbing Aboriginal thinking only on dominant Canadian terms. Indeed, the book raises important questions about shifts in public discourse and institutions that will have to take place if they are to be truly decolonized through the full inclusion of Aboriginal thought.

Readership

This book has been compiled with four core groups of readers in mind. First, it speaks to Indigenous and non-Indigenous scholars, and students, who are concerned with the broader impact of Aboriginal thinking in Canada and with the development of methodologies to ensure full recognition of distinct Indigenous perspectives in academic scholarship, cultural analysis, jurisprudence, and political thought. Second, it is addressed to those working with Aboriginal collections in museums and archives, both in Canada and farther afield. It highlights how an understanding of the Indigenous context of long-established collections held in these institutions can be improved through the development of co-managed projects with members of Indigenous source communities. Such initiatives not only facilitate cross-cultural understanding but also provide opportunities for Aboriginal peoples to reconnect with artifacts from their communities and, in the process, rethink and retell their histories.[6] Third, this book is aimed at activists, politicians, and officials who are concerned with developing models of governance designed to enable Indigenous communities in Canada to determine their own futures. Contributors consider how these processes might be realized through more inclusive forms of public administration, the delivery of public policies that are more effectively oriented to Aboriginal communities, and new approaches to economic development.[7]

Finally, this book offers Indigenous and non-Indigenous peoples who want to develop new approaches to Indigenous-settler relations in Canada the opportunity to consider how these relations might be grounded, as Michael Murphy notes, in "mutual respect, mutual accommodation, and consent."[8] The achievement of decolonization in Canada is still in the making, but I hope this book, published forty years after the provocative *Statement of the Government of Canada on Indian Policy*, will contribute to a broader recognition in Canada, and elsewhere, of the benefits of taking full account of Aboriginal thought.[9]

Organization

This book is divided into five core sections that, together, provide an interdisciplinary lens on Indigenous thought in Canada. Part 1 considers how

Aboriginal writers and scholars have challenged, and continue to question, dominant intellectual discourses associated with colonialism, liberalism, and a settler-oriented education system. Both chapters show how such challenges are, at times, articulated by Aboriginal thinkers working from within the frameworks of mainstream institutions established by dominant settler groups.

In Chapter 1, Robin Jarvis Brownlie considers key periods in First Nations historiography and questions how contemporary historians might respond, more effectively, to the epistemological challenges of Indigenist thought. She analyzes the earliest published work by Aboriginal authors in Canada, written by Ojibway (Anishnabe) in the mid-nineteenth century, to counter the discourse of racial inferiority in the civilizationist rhetoric of the colonial period. She then considers early twentieth-century interventions by Cree and Kainai writers who questioned the impoverishment, marginalization, and oppression of their people. Brownlie contrasts resistance to this historiography with the receptivity of non-Indigenous scholars to late twentieth-century radical Indigenous writing that challenged concepts of the "just society" encoded in the federal government's 1969 White Paper on Indian policy. She also reflects on more recent recordings of Aboriginal oral history during land claim negotiations and healing initiatives associated with settlements for the abuse suffered by Aboriginal children in residential schools. Brownlie shows how Canadian resistance to Indigenous thought shifted in the late twentieth century as academic historians addressed questions about colonization, oppression, and injustice. Nonetheless, she argues that non-Aboriginal historians could develop greater understanding of Indigenous history if they relinquished control of research agendas, became more receptive to Aboriginal narrative structures and epistemologies – including intergenerational stories of supernatural phenomena – and gave fuller recognition to Elders, as scholars, who can facilitate understanding of the history of Indigenous thought.

Drawing on her own recent experience of entering the academy as an Indigenous scholar, Margaret Kovach addresses questions about the indigenization of contemporary scholarship. In Chapter 2 she considers the vulnerability and exhaustion that Indigenous students and educators can experience within academic institutions, noting how these feelings are linked to Aboriginal experiences of education as an instrument of oppression, the underrepresentation of Aboriginal scholars in universities, and tensions generated by having to resist institutionalized racism and challenge dominant modes of thought. Kovach emphasizes how Indigenous scholars have to not only mitigate Indigenous and Western ways of knowing but also meet different expectations within Aboriginal and academic communities. She considers how academic institutions might respond, supportively, to recognize the particular forms of double duty that Indigenous scholars often undertake. Like Brownlie, she discusses how Indigenous and non-Indigenous scholars could develop research that respects Aboriginal ontology and the methodologies that flow from it.[10]

Kovach makes an important argument about the long-term advantages of nurturing Indigenous scholarship in universities to ensure that Aboriginal and non-Aboriginal students have access to a decolonized system of higher education. As she notes, this is likely to have a positive ripple effect because students who go on to become educators will be more likely to embed Aboriginal ways of knowing into their own practice as teachers. This is one of several ways, Kovach suggests, that educational institutions can contribute to the broader process of decolonization. As other contributors suggest, a decolonized education system will enhance the integration of Aboriginal perspectives into cultural and political institutions in Canada.

Part 2 focuses on the importance of Aboriginal oral traditions in the conveyance of Indigenous thought and shows how First Nations narratives provide new insight into the analysis of historical events and urban space. In Chapter 3 Leslie McCartney draws on her experience as former executive director of the Gwich'in Social and Cultural Institute to show how Gwich'in oral histories, collated and archived during the institute's Gwich'in Elders Biographies Project, highlight Indigenous thinking about the famous story of Albert Johnson, the Mad Trapper of Rat River. McCartney reinforces Brownlie's arguments regarding the value of exploring the rich tapestries of Aboriginal oral history by demonstrating that Gwich'in stories about the search for Johnson represent it not, like the mainstream media, as a hunt for an individual carried out across "a landscape that was barren, frozen, and void of people" but as an exercise that unfolded "on a rich Gwich'in cultural landscape ... alive with stories, legends, place names, trails, sacred sites, and stories of people who had, for centuries, been intimately connected with the land."[11] Moreover, she shows how these Indigenous narratives, which are missing from mainstream archives, provide insight into concerns about land, economy, treaties, and hunting practices that were shaping Gwich'in lives in 1932. McCartney also raises important concerns about the collation of Aboriginal oral histories by exposing how current copyright laws in Canada do not provide for the full recognition of those who tell these stories. Indeed, she argues that Canadian copyright law should be improved to ensure the recognition of work and insights by Aboriginal storytellers and to protect stories in their original form.

While McCartney focuses on Aboriginal narrative as oral history, Martin Whittles and Tim Patterson in Chapter 4 explore First Nations storytelling as a mechanism to indigenize urban space. Aboriginal people in Canada continue to urbanize in unprecedented numbers, and these migrations have generated much discussion about the problems of Aboriginal dislocation and urban poverty and the need for new forms of Aboriginal governance in urban centres.[12] Yet, as Whittles and Patterson note, non-Aboriginal narratives of urban environments pay limited attention to the cultural experiences of Aboriginal communities in Canadian cities and towns. Drawing on ethnographic research with members of the Blackfoot Confederacy who live in Lethbridge and Calgary, this chapter reveals the veracity of the Aboriginal urban narrative. Focusing on ways that Nápi (Old Man Creator) stories speak to geographical and architectural landmarks in these cities that are culturally specific to the Blackfoot, the chapter challenges the view that Nápi stories are "archaic legends."[13] Instead, Whittles and Patterson show how these transposive narratives [are] "fluid, situational, and responsive reflections of the world in which they are created and shared."[14] Indeed, just as Julie Cruikshank found that the "storytellers of Yukon First Nations ancestry continue to tell stories that make meaningful connections and provide order and continuity in a rapidly changing world," so Whittles and Patterson argue that Nápi narratives "are, in fact, contemporary, dynamic approaches that Siksikaitsitapi use to explain the built environment."[15] Whittles and Patterson show how these narratives recreate the city for Aboriginal people as "a place not to be headed to, but a place to be from, a place where one can be a citizen, not a transient."[16]

Part 3 focuses on the representation of First Nations in museums and highlights the importance of ensuring that significant cultural institutions renegotiate the ways in which Aboriginal peoples have been constructed in the course of the colonial project. In Chapter 5 Laura Peers and Alison Brown explore how relations between Indigenous communities and museums can be rethought through reciprocal, long-term research. They discuss the Kainai-Oxford Photographic Histories Project in which both authors were involved. This photo-elicitation initiative, co-managed by the Pitt Rivers Museum in Oxford and the Mookaakin Cultural and Heritage Foundation in Alberta, was significant not only for its findings but also because it created the first protocol agreement to be signed between an Aboriginal nation and a British museum.[17]

The project recovered cultural knowledge associated with photographs of Kainai people that had been taken by Oxford anthropologist Beatrice Blackwood in 1925. It encouraged the transmission of narratives of community strength and resistance as Kainai people interpreted the social and economic contexts of the photographs and named all the people whose images were encapsulated within them. Building upon the contributions of McCartney and Whittles and Patterson, Peers and Brown show how this project enabled the Kainai to appropriate the photographs "to fit with their own ways of inscribing the past" and pass on cultural knowledge, implicit in the names of those photographed and often preserved in the Blackfoot language, to younger generations of their tribe.[18]

Peers and Brown reinforce points made by Kovach about the importance of building and sustaining relationships to underscore community-based, Indigenous-oriented research. They show how this project has led to the development of a long-term relationship with the Kainai, and other Blackfoot peoples, to guide research on Blackfoot collections held by the Pitt Rivers Museum. In addition, echoing concerns raised by McCartney, they discuss how the project encouraged participants to rethink copyright in relation to photographic collections at the Pitt Rivers Museum. Indeed, this chapter shows how co-managed research can enhance public understanding of museum collections in which substantial Aboriginal artifacts are retained. Significantly, it also highlights how decolonization remains an international project.

In Chapter 6 Stephanie Bolton focuses on the McCord Museum of Canadian History as a case study for exploring how museums can resist, and respond to, Aboriginal perspectives. Although the museum was founded to examine the history of Aboriginal peoples and settler Canadians, as well as the relationship between them, Bolton shows that the McCord has a mixed record of engagement with Aboriginal material. This includes complex stories of institutional resistance to exhibitions focused on First Nations and, in contrast, a positive response to key recommendations of the 1992 report of the Task Force on Museums and First Peoples, an inquiry that was co-managed by the Canadian Museums Association and the Assembly of First Nations.[19]

Bolton emphasizes how the McCord Museum's founder wanted to make it "as Indian as [he] possibly [could], – a museum of the original owners of the land."[20] Nonetheless, centuries of colonial collection practices, the absence of Aboriginal people on the museum's board of trustees, and the minimal presence of Aboriginal staff at the McCord Museum complicated the realization of this goal. The implication of Bolton's argument is that the impact of Indigenous thought on Canadian cultural institutions will be incomplete if it is confined to specific projects. Indeed, it is important not only to work with Aboriginal source communities on co-managed projects but also to develop strategies that will increase Aboriginal representation in the staffing and governance of cultural institutions such as the McCord Museum. These strategies could embrace Kovach's ideas about the importance of developing more culturally sensitive educational institutions.

Part 4 focuses on the value and complexity of bringing Aboriginal cultural perspectives into public governance. It raises important questions about Aboriginal culture and autonomy and considers them in relation to broader issues of public policy delivery, government administration, and economic development in subnational jurisdictions with significant Aboriginal populations. It also highlights the need to ensure that embedded values and institutional practices do not undermine the effectiveness of achieving increased Indigenous autonomy in political, administrative, and economic spheres.

In Chapter 7 Fiona MacDonald analyzes the Manitoba government's initiative to create Aboriginal child welfare authorities in order to provide culturally relevant services for Indigenous families. She argues that although this initiative is consistent with a group autonomy approach to cultural recognition, it is also important to consider such initiatives in the context of broader, neoliberal restructuring that has enabled the provincial state to co-opt First Nations thinking about the need for Aboriginal-centred child welfare while disconnecting it from the long-term structural problems of Indigenous poverty. MacDonald demonstrates how the demand by First Nations for autonomous child welfare agencies was rooted in a concern that Aboriginal children be cared for in a manner consistent with Aboriginal culture and philosophy. However, she also questions the degree of autonomy that can be achieved through such agencies, given low funding and staffing levels, on the one hand, and the rooting of provincial child welfare policies in Anglo-Canadian cultural values, on the other. MacDonald argues that such initiatives can contribute to transformative political and cultural change for First Nations communities only if the devolution of child welfare is part of a broader, well-funded approach to Indigenous governance.

In Chapter 8, I focus on Inuit initiatives to rethink public administration in ways that facilitate the creation of an Aboriginal-oriented public service to support the new territorial government of Nunavut. This chapter analyzes the multifaceted approach that Inuit in Nunavut are developing, highlighting the combination of numerical, institutional, cultural, and linguistic initiatives involved. It highlights how Inuit public servants and Elders have worked together to identify methods of integrating Inuit knowledge into the administration of government. Nonetheless, this chapter shows that unless issues of numerical representation and cultural change are considered together, the potential to develop an Aboriginal-focused model of governance will be limited. Moreover, it presents the argument that the objective of creating a representative public service in Nunavut, one shaped by Indigenous cultural perspectives, is more likely to be realized if this project is connected to broader strategies that are designed to encourage the graduation of Inuit students from an Aboriginal-oriented education system. In addition, reflecting ideas discussed in the other two chapters in this section, it considers the extent to which it is possible to sustain Indigenous thinking about government in subnational units that are also shaped by interactions with broader frameworks of the Canadian state.

In Chapter 9 Gabrielle Slowey locates questions about Aboriginal agency in new thinking about the relationship between economic development, self-government, and cultural identity in First Nations communities. She shows how First Nations in northern Canada are challenging the foundations of development theory by re-evaluating the idea of economic development, as imposition, and expressing agency by intertwining economic development and self-determination. Slowey shows how adoption of the development paradigm by First Nations, as an act of modernization, does not preclude the retention of traditional cultural identities. She demonstrates that economic development strategies can encompass Indigenous values and culture and, simultaneously, reinforce the importance of Aboriginal participation and competition in the global economy. The significance of Slowey's analysis is that it focuses our attention on contemporary Indigenous thinking about the economic dimensions of self-sufficiency, thereby complementing discussions about political, cultural, and constitutional self-determination in other sections of this book.

The three contributions to this section emphasize the importance of embedding Aboriginal culture in new approaches to the delivery of social policy, the design of government institutions, and the promotion of economic development. Although still in their early stages, the initiatives studied highlight how public governance and economic development can be enhanced through the integration of Indigenous perspectives. The contributors also show how these innovations can be constrained by fiscal pressures, the broader influence of dominant Canadian values, and entrenched approaches to governance. At the same time, this section highlights how Indigenous communities in Canada are rethinking the extent to which the goal of Aboriginal self-determination can include selective engagements with the political, administrative, and economic frameworks of the state.

The final section of this book brings together two contributions that highlight the importance of thinking back as well as looking forward in the process of seeking political and constitutional reconciliation between Indigenous and settler nations. In Part 5 both contributors argue that it will not be possible to move toward political reconciliation between Indigenous and settler communities until we take full account of the first thoughts, and first principles, that shaped self-governing, Indigenous nations prior to the European colonization of Canada. They also argue that it is important to understand how influential political theorists, and constitutional interpretation by the courts, have failed to recognize the full significance of these fundamental principles in Indigenous thought.

In Chapter 10 Michael Murphy revisits some of the concerns raised by Brownlie in her discussion of the oppressive impact that civilizationist ideas that prevailed in the colonial period had on Indigenous people. Murphy analyzes how theorists espousing civilizationism, both in Europe during the Age of Empire and in contemporary Canada, have constructed Aboriginal nations. Murphy uses this framework to situate Tom Flanagan's book *First Nations? Second Thoughts* within a broader theoretical tradition, one that asserts that the colonization of the Americas was not only inevitable but also beneficial for Aboriginal people because it facilitated economic and human progress.[21]

Murphy focuses on critiquing Flanagan's argument that First Nations should abandon quests for self-determination and reconcile themselves to the inevitability and multiple advantages of assimilation. In so doing, he criticizes Flanagan for failing to engage with the question of consent – for constructing Aboriginal citizens as "suitable objects for assimilation" but being unable to see these same citizens as "fit subjects for self-government" who, on the basis of their prior status as members of independent, self-governing communities, have the *"right to make their own choices"* about developing *"mutually* acceptable" models of reconciliation with non-Aboriginal peoples.[22] Murphy then considers how contemporary Aboriginal thinkers, and Aboriginal nationalists, in Canada have developed routes to self-determination that are based not on "a kind of racist special pleading or a demand for extra rights that are denied to non-Aboriginal peoples" but on their "equal right to exercise choices and make decisions that for too long have been the exclusive privilege of non-Aboriginal peoples through their control of the modern state."[23]

Recognition of the precolonial status of Aboriginal nations as independent, self-governing peoples also underscores the final chapter of this book, in which Kiera Ladner considers the potential for constitutional reconciliation between Indigenous and settler communities in Canada. She emphasizes that this is important because "Indigenous people never ceded their rights and responsibilities (collective sovereignty) under their own constitutional order; nor did they consent to be ruled by the Crown or its operatives (such as Parliament)."[24] As a result, Ladner argues that "Canadians need to step beyond the myth of lawful acquisition and sovereignty" to understand that the "true magic" of the colonial period "lies in the relationships that were established between Indigenous peoples and the Crown that recognized and affirmed the sovereignty and rights of both nations and, in so doing, enabled the creation of Canada."[25]

Ladner's analysis focuses on the courts' potential for reconciling Indigenous and Canadian constitutional orders and emphasizes the importance of this project given the jurisdictional tensions and disputes about Canadian sovereignty that keep erupting on First Nations land. She has serious reservations about the Supreme Court of Canada's capacity to achieve this because she finds it to be "a colonial institution that is charged with the responsibility of defending the Crown's sovereignty."[26] Moreover, Ladner considers the possibility that the court has "framed reconciliation in a manner that is inconsistent with principles of treaty constitutionalism" by "disregard[ing] Indigenous constitutional orders (regardless of treaty) and subject[ing] Indigenous nations and their 'sovereign' constitutional orders to the sovereignty of the Crown."[27]

Nonetheless, Ladner takes some comfort in the court's 2004 decision *Haida Nation v. British Columbia (Ministry of Forests)*, which, she suggests, may have set out stepping stones that could lead to a broader debate not only about reconciliation but also about "decolonizing Canada and creating a postcolonial country based on the recognition and affirmation of Indigenous constitutional orders" and the affirmation of treaty constitutionalism in section 35 of the *Constitution Act, 1982*.[28] Thus, Ladner argues that "the courts have opened the door in making reconciliation a constitutional requirement, especially when the requirement of reconciliation is paired with the constitutional requirement to uphold not only the honour of the Crown" but also, critically, "Indigenist understandings of the Canadian Constitution, Indigenous constitutional orders, Indigenous history, and the principles of treaty constitutionalism."[29]

Murphy and Ladner both emphasize the importance of seeking political reconciliation between Indigenous and settler nations, not only because of tensions between the Crown and First Nations but also because, "as the courts have said, 'we are all here to stay'; and thus, as interdependent and intertwined people and nations, we have to find a way to live together in a mutually agreeable and mutually beneficial manner."[30] Both contributors stress that Aboriginal self-determination and a broader political commitment to a decolonized, nation-to-nation constitutional framework are essential to the achievement of reconciliation. They also highlight how such an approach could lead to enhanced "democratic dialogue," the exchange of "the best that Aboriginal and non-Aboriginal cultures have to offer each other," constitutional innovation, and more effective co-management of shared jurisdictions.[31]

Conclusion

As the title of this book suggests, its origins were triggered by the intense reaction that followed the publication, in 2000, of Tom Flanagan's book *First Nations? Second Thoughts*. In response, the first conference I organized as director of the Centre of Canadian Studies at the University of Edinburgh was titled "First Nations, First Thoughts." It invited Aboriginal and non-Aboriginal scholars to explore the significance of Aboriginal peoples to the development of cultural and intellectual thought in Canada, to consider the development and transmission of Indigenous thought, and to explore the broader impact of Aboriginal perspectives on Canadian public discourse.[32] As was the case for that conference, my goal for this book was to foster interdisciplinary analysis of the significant contribution that Aboriginal peoples have made, and continue to make, to intellectual, cultural, political, and constitutional thought in Canada.

The contributors to this book encourage us to look closely at the development of Indigenous thought, to consider its impact on Canada, to assess
current realities of integrating Indigenous thought into Canadian institutions,
and to pursue intellectual interpretations that take Aboriginal perspectives
into full account. It highlights the need for new research agendas that are not
only grounded in a recognition of the fundamental differences in Indigenous
and Western modes of thought but also acknowledge the importance of
building long-term relationships between Indigenous and non-Indigenous
communities. Such agendas would commit resources to the preservation of
Indigenous knowledge, encourage research into ways that Indigenous epistemologies might guide scholarship about Aboriginal communities, and
consider how greater space could be made to ensure that Indigenous ways of
knowing are fully embraced within Canadian public discourse.

There are consequences to overlooking Indigenous thought. Healing may
be suppressed if Indigenous thinking is not fully acknowledged or understood.
Our knowledge base will be weaker if contextual information and Aboriginal perceptions about past events are not recognized. Angry protests are more
likely to continue to erupt, and optimal organizational structures that take
account of Indigenous and non-Indigenous perspectives will not be achieved.
By contrast, Aboriginal peoples and settler Canadians stand to benefit if the
full integration of Indigenous ideas in Canadian institutions is grounded in
mutual respect and recognition of distinct histories, constitutions, cultures,
and modes of thought.

NOTES

1   See also discussions of Aboriginal contributions to civil society in Gordon Chris-
    tie, ed., *Aboriginality and Governance: A Multidisciplinary Perspective from Québec*
    (Penticton, BC: Theytus Books, 2006); Celia Haig-Brown and David A. Nock, eds.,
    With Good Intentions: Euro-Canadian and Aboriginal Relations in Colonial Canada
    (Vancouver: UBC Press, 2006); Michael Murphy, ed., *Reconfiguring Aboriginal-State
    Relations – Canada: The State of the Federation 2003* (Montreal and Kingston: McGill-
    Queen's University Press, 2005); and David Newhouse, Cora Voyageur, and Dan
    Beavon, eds., *Hidden in Plain Sight: Contributions of Aboriginal Peoples to Canadian
    Identity and Culture* (Toronto: University of Toronto Press, 2003).
2   See Julie Cruikshank, *The Social Life of Stories: Narrative and Knowledge in the Yukon
    Territory* (Vancouver: UBC Press, 1998), xii; Renée Hulan and Renate Eigenbord,
    eds., *Aboriginal Oral Traditions: Theory, Practice, Ethics* (Halifax/Winnipeg: Fernwood
    Publishing/Gorsebrook Research Institute, 2008).

3 Taiaiake Alfred, *Peace, Power, Righteousness: An Indigenous Manifesto* (Don Mills, ON: Oxford University Press, 1999), xv.

4 See also Peter Kulchyski, Don McCaskill, and David Newhouse, eds., *In the Words of Elders: Aboriginal Cultures in Transition* (Toronto: University of Toronto Press, 1999).

5 John Borrows, "Listening for a Change: The Courts and Oral Tradition," *Osgoode Hall Law Journal* 39, 1 (2001): 4.

6 See also Miriam Clavir, *Preserving What is Valued: Museums, Conservation, and First Nations* (Vancouver: UBC Press, 2002) and Laura L. Peers and Alison K. Brown, eds., *Museums and Source Communities: A Routledge Reader* (London: Routledge, 2003).

7 See also Frances Abele and Michael J. Prince, "Aboriginal Governance and Canadian Federalism: A To-Do List for Canada," in *New Trends in Canadian Federalism*, ed. François Rocher and Miriam Smith (Peterborough, ON: Broadview Press, 2003), 135-65; Graham White and Jack Hicks, "Nunavut: Inuit Self-Determination through a Land Claim and Public Government," in *Nunavut: Inuit Regain Control of Their Lands and Their Lives*, ed. Jens Dahl, Jack Hicks, and Peter Jull (Copenhagen: International Work Group for Indigenous Affairs, 2000), 30-115.

8 Michael Murphy, "Civilization, Self-Determination, and Reconciliation," in this volume, 269. See also, Alfred, *Peace, Power, Righteousness;* Patrick Macklem, *Indigenous Difference and the Constitution of Canada* (Toronto: University of Toronto Press, 2001); John Borrows, *Recovering Canada: The Resurgence of Indigenous Law* (Toronto: University of Toronto Press, 2002); Joyce Green, "Self-Determination, Citizenship and Federalism: Indigenous and Canadian Palimpsest," in *Reconfiguring Aboriginal-State Relations,* ed. Murphy, 329-52; Dale Turner, *This Is Not a Peace Pipe: Towards a Critical Indigenous Philosophy* (Toronto: University of Toronto Press, 2006).

9 Canada, *Statement of the Government of Canada on Indian Policy, 1969* (Ottawa: Queen's Printer, 1969).

10 See also Linda Tuhiwai Smith, *Decolonizing Methodologies: Research and Indigenous Peoples* (London/Dunedin: Zed Books/University of Otago Press, 1999); Renee Pualani Louis, "Can You Hear Us Now? Voices from the Margin: Using Indigenous Methodologies in Geographic Research," *Geographical Research* 45, 2 (2007): 136-37.

11 Leslie McCartney, "Respecting First Nations Oral Histories: Copyright Complexities and Archiving Aboriginal Stories," in this volume, 82.

12 See, for example, Mary Jane Norris, Martin Cooke, and Stewart Clatworthy, "Aboriginal Mobility and Migration Patterns and the Policy Implications," in *Aboriginal Conditions: Research as a Foundation for Public Policy,* ed. Jerry P. White, Paul Maxim, and Dan Beavon (Vancouver: UBC Press, 2003), 108-29; Evelyn J. Peters, "Geographies of Urban Aboriginal People in Canada: Implications for Urban

Self-Government," in *Reconfiguring Aboriginal-State Relations*, ed. Murphy, 39-76; and Alan C. Cairns, *Citizens Plus: Aboriginal Peoples and the Canadian State* (Vancouver: UBC Press, 2000), 123-26.

13 Martin Whittles and Tim Patterson, "Nápi and the City: Siksikaitsitapi Narratives Revisited," in this volume, 98.

14 Ibid., 103.

15 Cruikshank, *The Social Life of Stories*, xiii; Whittles and Patterson, "Nápi and the City," in this volume, 98.

16 Ibid., 112.

17 University of Oxford, Pitt Rivers Museum, *Annual Report*, 1 August 2005 to 31 July 2006 (Oxford: Pitt Rivers Museum, University of Oxford, 2006), 24.

18 Laura Peers and Alison K. Brown, "Colonial Photographs and Postcolonial Histories: The Kaianai-Oxford Photographic Histories Project," in this volume, 134, referencing Elisabeth Edwards, *Raw Histories: Photographs, Anthropology and Museums* (London: Routledge, 2001), 100.

19 Task Force on Museums and First Peoples, *Turning the Page: Forging New Partnerships between Museums and First Peoples* (Ottawa: Canadian Museums Association/ Assembly of First Nations, 1992).

20 Pamela Miller, "David Ross McCord," in *The McCord Family: A Passionate Vision*, ed. Pamela Miller et al. (Montreal: McCord Museum of Canadian History, 1992), 85, as quoted by Stephanie Bolton, "Museums Taken to Task: Representing First Peoples at the McCord Museum of Canadian History," in this volume, 153.

21 See Tom Flanagan, *First Nations? Second Thoughts* (Montreal and Kingston: McGill-Queen's University Press, 2000).

22 Michael Murphy, "Civilization, Self-Determination, and Reconciliation," in this volume, 264.

23 Ibid., 267.

24 Kiera Ladner, "Take 35: Reconciling Constitutional Orders," in this volume, 290.

25 Ibid., 296.

26 Ibid., 286.

27 Ibid., 283.

28 Ibid., 288.

29 Ibid., 295.

30 Ibid., 296.

31 Murphy, "Civilization, Self-Determination, and Reconciliation," in this volume, 266, 267.

32 Centre of Canadian Studies, "First Nations, First Thoughts," 30th Anniversary Conference, University of Edinburgh, 5-6 May 2005, http://www.cst.ed.ac.uk/ Events/Conferences.

WORKS CITED

Abele, Frances, and Michael J. Prince. "Aboriginal Governance and Canadian Federalism: A To-Do List for Canada." In *New Trends in Canadian Federalism*, ed. François Rocher and Miriam Smith, 135-65. Peterborough, ON: Broadview Press, 2003.

Alfred, Taiaiake. *Peace, Power, Righteousness: An Indigenous Manifesto*. Don Mills, ON: Oxford University Press, 1999.

Borrows, John. "Listening for a Change: The Courts and Oral Tradition." *Osgoode Hall Law Journal* 39, 1 (2001): 1-38.

–. *Recovering Canada: The Resurgence of Indigenous Law*. Toronto: University of Toronto Press, 2002.

Cairns, Alan C. *Citizens Plus: Aboriginal Peoples and the Canadian State*. Vancouver: UBC Press, 2000.

Canada. *Statement of the Government of Canada on Indian Policy, 1969*. Ottawa: Queen's Printer, 1969.

Centre of Canadian Studies. "First Nations, First Thoughts." 30th Anniversary Conference, University of Edinburgh, 5-6 May 2005. http://www.cst.ed.ac.uk/Events/Conferences.

Christie, Gordon, ed. *Aboriginality and Governance: A Multidisciplinary Perspective from Québec*. Penticton, BC: Theytus Books, 2006.

Clavir, Miriam. *Preserving What is Valued: Museums, Conservation, and First Nations*. Vancouver: UBC Press, 2002.

Cruikshank, Julie. *The Social Life of Stories: Narrative and Knowledge in the Yukon Territory*. Vancouver: UBC Press, 1998.

Edwards, Elisabeth. *Raw Histories: Photographs, Anthropology and Museums*. London: Routledge, 2001.

Flanagan, Tom. *First Nations? Second Thoughts*. Montreal and Kingston: McGill-Queen's University Press, 2000.

Green, Joyce. "Self-Determination, Citizenship and Federalism: Indigenous and Canadian Palimpsest." In *Reconfiguring Aboriginal-State Relations – Canada: The State of the Federation 2003*, ed. Michael Murphy, 329-52. Montreal and Kingston: McGill-Queen's University Press, 2005.

Haig-Brown, Celia, and David A. Nock, eds. *With Good Intentions: Euro-Canadian and Aboriginal Relations in Colonial Canada*. Vancouver: UBC Press, 2006.

Hulan, Renée, and Renate Eigenbord, eds. *Aboriginal Oral Traditions: Theory, Practice, Ethics*. Halifax/Winnipeg: Fernwood Publishing/Gorsebrook Research Institute, 2008.

Kulchyski, Peter, Don McCaskill, and David Newhouse, eds. *In the Words of Elders: Aboriginal Cultures in Transition*. Toronto: University of Toronto Press, 1999.

Louis, Renee Pualani. "Can You Hear Us Now? Voices from the Margin: Using Indigenous Methodologies in Geographic Research." *Geographical Research* 45, 2 (2007): 130-39.

Macklem, Patrick. *Indigenous Difference and the Constitution of Canada*. Toronto: University of Toronto Press, 2001.

Miller, Pamela. "David Ross McCord." In *The McCord Family: A Passionate Vision*, ed. Pamela Miller, Moira McCaffrey, Brian Young, Donald Fyson, and Donald Wright, 85-87. Montreal: McCord Museum of Canadian History, 1992.

Murphy, Michael, ed. *Reconfiguring Aboriginal-State Relations – Canada: The State of the Federation 2003*. Montreal and Kingston: McGill-Queen's University Press, 2005.

Newhouse, David, Cora Voyageur, and Dan Beavon, eds. *Hidden in Plain Sight: Contributions of Aboriginal Peoples to Canadian Identity and Culture.* Toronto: University of Toronto Press, 2003.

Norris, Mary Jane, Martin Cooke, and Stewart Clatworthy. "Aboriginal Mobility and Migration Patterns and the Policy Implications." In *Aboriginal Conditions: Research as a Foundation for Public Policy*, ed. Jerry P. White, Paul S. Maxim, and Dan Beavon, 108-29. Vancouver: UBC Press, 2003.

Peers, Laura L., and Alison K. Brown, eds. *Museums and Source Communities: A Routledge Reader*. London: Routledge, 2003.

Peters, Evelyn J. "Geographies of Urban Aboriginal People in Canada: Implications for Urban Self-Government." In *Reconfiguring Aboriginal-State Relations – Canada: The State of the Federation 2003*, ed. Michael Murphy, 39-76. Montreal and Kingston: McGill-Queen's University Press, 2005.

Smith, Linda Tuhiwai. *Decolonizing Methodologies: Research and Indigenous Peoples*. London/Dunedin: Zed Books/University of Otago Press, 1999.

Task Force on Museums and First Peoples. *Turning the Page: Forging New Partnerships between Museums and First Peoples*. Ottawa: Canadian Museums Association/Assembly of First Nations, 1992.

Turner, Dale. *This Is Not a Peace Pipe: Towards a Critical Indigenous Philosophy*. Toronto: University of Toronto Press, 2006.

University of Oxford, Pitt Rivers Museum. *Annual Report*, 1 August 2005 to 31 July 2006. Oxford: Pitt Rivers Museum, University of Oxford, 2006.

White, Graham, and Jack Hicks. "Nunavut: Inuit Self-Determination through a Land Claim and Public Government." In *Nunavut: Inuit Regain Control of Their Lands and Their Lives*, ed. Jens Dahl, Jack Hicks, and Peter Jull, 30-115. Copenhagen: International Work Group for Indigenous Affairs, 2000.

PART 1
Challenging Dominant Discourses

1

First Nations Perspectives and Historical Thinking in Canada

Robin Jarvis Brownlie

Racism is "fundamentally a theory of history."[1] This observation by historian Alexander Saxton illuminates an important truth about the centrality of constructions of history in racial discourses, one that is particularly relevant in white-dominated settler colonies like Canada. Theories of history based on ideas about race have provided members of colonial societies with a justification for displacing, dispossessing, and destroying Indigenous peoples. These theories explained why Europeans were entitled to engage in acts of aggression and dispossession and often went even further, erasing the agency of whites with the notion of inevitability. As literary critic Maureen Konkle has recently noted, "According to this line of thinking, it wasn't that actual white people were wreaking such havoc in Native societies but rather that the havoc wrought was inevitable when inferior met superior."[2]

Aboriginal people in North America have long produced spoken and written histories of their own that launched systematic attacks on these kinds of arguments.[3] Historical thinking and writing have been important in Aboriginal resistance to colonization for a number of reasons. First and most simply, the elucidation of historical events and processes has been essential to Aboriginal efforts to understand their own losses and the difficulties they have faced. Second, Aboriginal people who encountered the self-justifying colonial histories of white society immediately perceived what was at stake in these constructions and sought to counter them with their own understanding of what had occurred and why.

There is a third significant reason for the recurrent attention to history in Aboriginal writing, namely, the denial of historicity to "Indians" in white colonial mythology. Colonial thought in the nineteenth century increasingly constructed Aboriginal people as static, unchanging, and confined to a permanent "state of nature."[4] Such thinking placed Indigenous people outside

history and rendered them as mere relics of an earlier stage of human development that were doomed to be superseded by those who had taken their land.
Another strain of colonial discourse simply erased First Nations entirely by
dating the beginning of history from the arrival of whites.[5] Writing history,
then, became essential to the Aboriginal project of resistance and survival.
Producing their own histories has been a way for Aboriginal people to write
themselves into new societies in their lands and name and document the
wrongs of colonization. It has also allowed Aboriginal people to highlight
their own change over time and their ability to adapt like all dynamic societies.[6]

In this chapter I examine Aboriginal thinkers' interventions into historical thought and writing in Canada, and I pose the question, what was their
impact? The two earliest published Aboriginal writers in Canada, George
Copway and Peter Jones, both penned books framed as histories of the Ojibway (Anishnabe) people, a trend that continued within the sporadically
published Aboriginal works over the succeeding century.[7] More recently,
Aboriginal historical production has flourished, from confidential treaty
reports to videos and published oral and documentary histories. I will consider both early and recent manifestations of this writing to elucidate their
main points, address continuities over time, and discuss their impact (if any)
on non-Aboriginal versions of history.

Nineteenth-Century Writers

The published works of George Copway and Peter Jones, which languished
in obscurity for over a century, were recently rediscovered and are receiving
considerable attention from historians, literary critics, and others.[8] The two
men are complex and problematic in many respects, particularly in terms of
the influence that Christian ideas and their English wives had on their thinking. Both Jones and Copway were converts to Methodism (in fact, Jones spent
the rest of his life as a Methodist preacher), and this church's program and
missionary network powerfully shaped their arguments and worldviews. At
the time this set them apart from many Aboriginal people who remained
attached to their Indigenous spiritualities and had yet to acquire the literacy
skills wielded by Copway and Jones. Although Copway and Jones both argued
for assimilation, many of their compatriots were clearly pursuing a path of
cultural continuity. In addition, both men married English women who
exercised an obvious but indeterminable influence over their written work.
Finally, George Copway is an ambiguous figure because of his erratic and
opportunistic behaviour: he was charged with embezzling funds from two

Ojibway groups in Upper Canada and later became a paid recruiter of Canadian Aboriginal men for the US Civil War.[9]

These two writers employed history in their effort to defend their people from the worst effects of colonization. Copway's most historically oriented book, the second he published, bore the title *The Traditional History and Characteristic Sketches of the Ojibway Nation* and appeared in 1850. Jones' *History of the Ojebway Indians* was published posthumously in 1861 and compiled and edited by his English wife, Eliza. Without denying their assimilationism and the strong Christian influence on their goals and analyses, a sympathetic reading of their work in its historical context sees them grasping for ways to be heard, accepting some terms of the European discourse to find a voice, and then attempting to subvert it from within.

In both the United States and Canada, the mid-nineteenth-century social and geopolitical context was one of aggressive Anglo expansion into new Aboriginal territories as well as growing conflict in the United States over slavery. At the same time, the British Empire was shaken by a series of colonial wars and rebellions in Jamaica, India, and New Zealand. The resulting escalation of violence was associated with hardening racial attitudes among whites and a new insistence that colonized peoples were immutably, racially, and biologically different. According to scholar Maureen Konkle, the notion of race as inherent difference was well entrenched in North America by the 1840s, displacing the older Christian framework that saw non-white peoples as being culturally but not biologically inferior and, therefore, potentially capable of equality.[10]

This unfavourable evolution in racial thinking was among the chief factors that motivated Jones, Copway, and others to speak out; however, it also imposed narrow discursive constraints. Native intellectuals had to counter the imperialists' successful promotion of notions of racial inferiority and difference along with the Manichean ideology of civilization versus savagery. In this context it was practically impossible to argue in favour of difference and equality, since colonial discourses so vehemently linked difference (from British norms) to inferiority and, importantly, unfitness for self-government.[11] It was difficult to portray Aboriginal cultures as equally valid or valuable, given their fixed position within colonial ideology as the very definition of savagery.[12] A discourse of Aboriginal redeemability through Christianity and "civilization" allowed these spokespersons to find an audience and a voice.

Aboriginal activists also needed to foster alliances with sympathetic whites and, for the most part, these were available only among mission-oriented

Christians and certain government authorities, all of whom were intent on implementing a policy of Europeanization. By contrast, in this period the argument for leaving Aboriginal cultures unaltered was associated with the belief that First Nations were not suited to integration with whites and were doomed to extinction. For example, Sir Francis Bond Head, lieutenant-governor of Upper Canada, argued in 1836 that Aboriginal people could not adapt, died faster when converted to Christianity and agriculture, and should be segregated for their own protection so that they could live out their final days in peace: "The greatest kindness we can perform towards these intelligent, simple-minded people, is to remove and fortify them as much as possible from all communication with the Whites."[13]

All these considerations combined to compel Aboriginal intellectuals to argue for their people's ability to assimilate and, thus, earn entitlement to rights and equality. Indeed, Peter Jones wrote that his main motive for under-going his first Christian baptism, in the Mohawk Anglican church, was his desire for equality: "that I might be entitled to all the privileges of the white inhabitants."[14] After experiencing a deeper conversion at a Methodist camp meeting, Jones embraced the assimilationist approach wholeheartedly and condemned nearly every aspect of Ojibway culture. George Copway also es-poused assimilation but worked to subvert its cultural implications to some extent by denouncing the wrongs of colonization and European institutions while asserting the superiority of certain Ojibway values and practices. Both men used accounts of historical events and processes to critique certain aspects of the European presence. By arguing for their people's historicity and ability to adopt European ways, these spokesmen sought to fight colonialism's fatal linkage of "Indians" with difference, savagery, exclusion, and extinction.

Although Copway and Jones took divergent approaches to depicting Ojibway culture and society, their accounts demonstrate significant similarities in their constructions of history. Both denounced the damage wrought by colonization and the harms introduced into Ojibway and other Aboriginal societies by white traders and settlers. In both of his books, Jones repeatedly deplored the failure of white Christians to live up to their own religious rhetoric and condemned those who had harmed his people. In one sentence, which was repeated three times with only small variations in his books, he exclaimed, "Oh, what an awful account at the day of judgment must the unprincipled white man give, who has been an agent of Satan in the exter-mination of the original proprietors of the American soil!"[15] Thus, while

Jones embraced complete assimilation and worked to spread Christianity and Europeanization, he was forthright in naming colonization's history of violence and expropriation and its introduction of social problems, foremost among them being alcohol. He also mentioned the assistance that the Ojibway and other First Nations gave the British government in the War of 1812: "During the last American war the Ojebways, as well as other Indian tribes, rendered the British great assistance in fighting the Americans. In that war many of our fathers fell, sealing their attachment to the British Government with their blood."[16]

George Copway, in *Traditional History and Characteristic Sketches of the Ojibway Nation*, attacked colonization and also launched a critique of European social institutions, which he compared unfavourably with those of the Ojibway. According to Copway, Ojibway forms of law, government, and social control revealed their superior rationality: their institutions operated through the appeal to reason, not coercion, and were much more effective than European approaches for maintaining social peace. As Copway remarked about his people's means of obtaining social consensus without resort to force, "They would not as brutes be whipped into duty. They would as men be persuaded to the right."[17] Given the centrality of reason in British claims to moral superiority, such words were aimed straight at the heart of the dichotomy that opposed civilization to savagery.

Copway devoted several chapters of his book to accounts of the Ojibway's wars with the Six Nations and the Sioux (Dakota), including the Ojibway's conquest, with their allies, of the Six Nations and their lands north of Lake Ontario.[18] In a gesture that seems to be intended to evoke a parallel with empire building and expansionism in both the United States and his native Canada, Copway emphasized his people's military prowess and territorial expansion. At the same time, he mounted an outspoken critique of colonialism and commerce, for their insatiable appetite for Aboriginal lands and their willingness to acquire them unjustly. Like many other Aboriginal writers of the nineteenth century, he was particularly critical of the way alcohol was used by white traders and others to destroy Aboriginal people for personal profit. This criticism was also prominent in Jones' work.[19] Finally, Copway addressed the accusation of savagery that whites made against First Nations by reversing the direction of condemnation. Citing North American wars between Europeans as one cause of the massive decrease in the Aboriginal population, he stated, "During these wars the Indian has been called from the woods to show his fearless nature, and for obeying, and showing himself fearless, it is said of him that he is 'a man without a tear.' He has been stigmatized with the name – 'a savage,' – by the very people who called for his aid, and he gave it."[20] Not only were white readers censured for their ingratitude and hypocrisy, they also received a telling reminder of military history since the arrival of Europeans, a history in which Aboriginal people had repeatedly played a crucial role not only as opponents but also as allies.

Copway and Jones were not the only individuals to address this history of military alliance. In 1841 most of the Ojibway and Six Nations chiefs of southern Upper Canada gathered together to present donations of money to Indian Department officials. The money was donated to help rebuild the Brock Monument at Queenston Heights, which had recently been destroyed by a Canadian dissident in the tensions that followed the Upper Canada Rebellion. Sir Isaac Brock was an important figure to First Nations, having shown them respect, distinguished himself through his bravery, and fought side by side with them and one of their most important leaders, Tecumseh, in the War of 1812. The chiefs made speeches as they pledged their donations, and they emphasized the common cause they had shared with Anglo-Canadians in the fight with the Americans and also the injuries, suffering, and loss of life this had entailed. For example, Chief Canoting, who spoke for the Delaware (Lenape), Oneida, and Chippewas of the Thames, declared that their warriors had fought with Brock against the common enemy and that "it is our firm determination to retain the same zeal, loyalty, and devotion, that glowed in the bosoms of our forefathers, who bravely defended the Royal Standard, under which we have the happiness to live, and to claim the proud distinction of British subjects."[21] These speeches contained a number of central themes, including the shared suffering and danger of war, the superiority of British over American policy, and a continuing willingness to fight for the British Crown. The clear message was that the history of military alliance bound together First Nations and newcomers, creating mutual attachment and obligations, including the Crown's responsibility to reward Aboriginal people's loyalty and sacrifice. This approach was consistent with Aboriginal diplomatic practices that stressed mutual military aid as one of the pre-eminent features of cooperation and friendship between nations. Through repeated allusions to this history, First Nations people sought to keep alive a relationship of goodwill and mutual protection with the Crown that became increasingly important as their own numerical significance and political power declined.

The Early Twentieth Century

The path-breaking historical writings of men like Peter Jones and George Copway were followed by a small number of books being published in North America in the ensuing century or so. As scholar A. LaVonne Brown Ruoff has noted, the relative interest in Aboriginal writings among the white public between the 1820s and 1850s was succeeded by an unreceptive climate during the remainder of the century as Anglo-expansionists on both sides of the border (especially in the United States) fought bitter battles over land with western tribes. Thus, relatively few books appeared in the second half of the nineteenth century, and nearly all of them were published in the United States.[22] Nevertheless, the pattern of emphasis in historical writing continued: "From the 1850s to the 1890s, most of the works by Indian authors were histories of woodland tribes from the East and Midwest."[23]

Aboriginal publications were likewise scarce during the first two-thirds of the twentieth century, due in part, no doubt, to a relative lack of interest among the reading public and a general shortage of publishing opportunities in Canada. It would appear that no full-length historical books by Aboriginal authors were published in this period. Nevertheless, three men on the Prairies were painstakingly recording Aboriginal views of history: Edward Ahenakew (Cree), Joseph Dion (Cree), and Mike Mountain Horse (Kainai) wrote significant works, each of which focused on his own people.[24] These men were concerned about the poverty, marginalization, and oppression of their people and were politically active, working with the League of Indians of Western Canada and other organizations. All three were born in the 1880s and experienced both the wretched conditions of early prairie reserves and the vivid recountings of old times by those who had lived a free life on the plains before treaties and white settlement. They wrote between 1910 and 1960 and published some short pieces in newspapers and journals; they attempted to produce full-length books as well, but either did not complete them or could not find publishers for their manuscripts. All were concerned with history and sought to counter colonial representations of Aboriginal people and Native-newcomer relations through their own depictions of historical events and processes. In each case, their writings were published as books in the 1970s.[25]

Ahenakew, Dion, and Mountain Horse were all clear about their mission to correct the misrepresentations of non-Aboriginal historians, though they took different approaches to the task. Their writings share a focus on Cree and/or Kainai lifestyles and cultures, an obvious effort to invoke the reader's sympathy and understanding, and attention to at least some aspects of the harm inflicted on Aboriginal people through disease, treaties, settlement, and/or government policy. Like their predecessors, both Ahenakew and Mountain Horse drew attention to their people's military contributions, in this case the exemplary enlistment rates of Aboriginal people in the First World War. Dion briefly mentioned their role in the Second World War for the limited purpose of denouncing the Indian Department's policy of compulsory enfranchisement: "Nearly 3,000 young Indians had fought in World War Two against the power of dictators; why should a dictator be tolerated at home?"[26]

Edward Ahenakew, an ordained Anglican clergyman whose bishop forced him to cease his work with the League of Indians of Western Canada, was most circumspect in his approach.[27] The first half of his book was devoted to stories of the old days from his friend Chief Thunderchild. The stories beautifully conveyed the tenor of a young Cree man's life before treaties and simultaneously preserved these important oral traditions before they died out.[28] The second half created a character known as Old Keyam, which meant in Cree "I don't care," that allowed him to speak about important issues such as education and government policies. Ahenakew used the voice of Old Keyam to make a key intervention into the construction of history: to defend the Cree who took part in the killings at Frog Lake during the 1885 Northwest Rebellion. Old Keyam explained these events as acts of vengeance against unpopular officials and also as an expression of frustration and rage at the misery and degradation of reserves. He concluded, "Looking back now, we can recognize that the massacre at Frog Lake was the last effort of the Indian to register in letters of blood his opposition to the ever-increasing and irresistible power of another race in the land that had been his."[29]

Mike Mountain Horse was more direct in expressing his objection to the depictions of Aboriginal people in histories authored by whites. The first words of his book asserted his need to tell the Aboriginal side of the story: "Often, in perusing supposedly authentic historic[al] volumes, I have read of the Indians as being bloodthirsty individuals, yelling, whooping, and seeking to destroy. I have become increasingly aware, as I continued reading, that very few of the good points of the Indians were chronicled. Hence it became my desire to narrate as accurately as possible some of the true facts concerning my people."[30] Mountain Horse's book recounts stories of his childhood and upbringing intermingled with descriptions of the Kainai worldview and customs. He also tells specifically historical tales such as "The Great Battle," which recounts the last bloody battle between the Blackfoot Confederacy and the Plains Cree. Mountain Horse's central goal seems to be to evoke sympathy and empathy in his non-Aboriginal target audience.

Of the three authors, Joseph Dion most explicitly offered a corrective to dominant versions of history: "A great deal has been written by various white historians in their own style dealing with the western Indians. A lot of these writers have been carried away with themselves and mixed fiction with the truth."[31] He was also the most forthright in naming the negative impact of the European invasion on his people, explaining that "the white man" brought "new and wicked weapons" and "set to work to destroy everything where ever he went." This destructiveness, combined with European diseases and "plain cruel selfishness" resulted in "untold misery" and "ultimate degradation" for the Plains Cree.[32] Dion discussed at length the smallpox epidemics, and he included some vivid first-hand accounts of the treaty and the violence of 1885, both at Frog Lake and at Poundmaker's and other reserves. Although Dion had begun writing as early as 1912, much of his book was written in the 1950s. It is possible that the anti-colonial spirit of the postwar era, as well as his own maturity and experience, permitted him the freedom to criticize the dominant society more directly than his predecessors.

Work since 1969

Aboriginal history writing did not flourish fully until the last three decades of the twentieth century. The current phase of Aboriginal intellectual production relating to history began in around 1969, when the federal government's *Statement of the Government of Canada on Indian Policy, 1969* (better known as the White Paper) sparked major political mobilization.[33] This movement took root with the publication of Harold Cardinal's *The Unjust Society*.[34] His scathing response to the White Paper was aimed at a wide audience and garnered considerable attention, which helped to begin the process of educating mainstream, non-Aboriginal Canadians about the injustices of the past. Framing his well-aimed polemic around Trudeau's proclaimed goal of building a just society, Cardinal outlined the features of Canadian history that he considered central to the unjust society that Aboriginal people experienced. He emphasized dispossession, deception, failed educational policy, and the injustice of forced assimilation. He also lambasted the government for its history of smothering control, bureaucratic red tape, indifference, and incompetence. The very first sentence declared Cardinal's historical focus: "The history of Canada's Indians is a shameful chronicle of the white man's disinterest, his deliberate trampling of Indian rights and his repeated betrayal of our trust."[35] Cardinal declared his intention to provide a more accurate version of history: "I intend to document the betrayals of our trust, to show step by step how a dictatorial bureaucracy has eroded our rights, atrophied our culture and robbed us of simple human dignity."[36]

Howard Adams' *Prison of Grass*, published in 1975, took a similar approach, indicting Canadian society and the federal government, and attaining bestseller status.[37] He too began with statements about the inaccuracy of mainstream history: "I attempt to examine history and autobiography and their intersection with colonization. The intentions of the book are to unmask the white supremacy that has dominated native history, and to construct an authentic Indian/Métis history."[38] Adams began with a Marxist analysis of racism and its economic and psychological impact; he then devoted considerable space to exploring the history of the Métis from the founding of Red River to 1885. Like Cardinal, Adams highlighted many of the same issues that Jones and Copway had raised a century before, especially the history of deceptive and/or forcible land seizure, the social ills created by colonization, and Aboriginal people's exclusion from mainstream society. Like the other writers, he excoriated the Department of Indian Affairs for the bureaucratic control that smothered all initiative and freedom: "All activities of the native community were completely under the control of the colonizing officials, who made all the decisions affecting the daily operations of native people ... This grinding paternalism and prison-like authority has persisted to this day."[39]

Aboriginal writers of this period confronted a new sociopolitical context in which the overt racism and paternalism of previous eras were rejected by many Canadians. Nevertheless, in practice, the same colonial relations and pervasive racist assumptions and practices prevailed. Nothing made this more obvious than the process that surrounded the Trudeau government's attempts to revamp federal Indian policy in 1968-69. Having proclaimed its commitment to a just society and participatory democracy, the government embarked on an unprecedented process of consultation, only to produce a set of policy proposals that directly opposed Aboriginal goals.[40] The more liberal political climate made the contradictions of government policy and rhetoric more glaring and provided a more accommodating set of discourses from which to assail colonialism. Harold Cardinal was able to use the Liberal Party's rhetoric of justice and democracy to denounce the authoritarian Indian Affairs system and demonstrate the exclusion of First Nations from society. Howard

Adams had access to Marxist analyses of exploitation and colonization to ground his own critique of Canadian society.

In a climate where questions of sexual discrimination were again being addressed, it was also possible to raise an old colonial issue, the sexual abuse of women. Thus, some Aboriginal writers revisited the problem of violence, which had been present in nineteenth-century Aboriginal writings. The Pequot Methodist William Apes, who was the first published Aboriginal writer to produce a full-length life history, had voiced this theme in 1829, when he wrote that whites had "committed violence of the most revolting kind upon the persons of the female portion of the tribe."[41] It is also worth noting that Peter Jones quietly attacked the use of the racist term "squaw" by stating in a footnote in his *History of the Ojebway Indians*, "The Indians generally consider this word a term of reproach."[42] Sarah Winnemucca, the first Aboriginal woman to publish her life story, referred repeatedly to rapes and attempted rapes of Aboriginal women and noted, "The mothers are afraid to have more children, for fear they shall have daughters, who are not safe even in their mother's presence."[43] She also added a strong assertion about her determination to resist any such attacks: "If such an outrageous thing is to happen to me, it will not be done by one man or two, while there are two women with knives, for I know what an Indian woman can do."[44]

Both Howard Adams and Harold Cardinal also took the opportunity to name this kind of ongoing colonial violence. Adams approached the issue by means of an anecdote about racist taunting he experienced at the hands of some Mounties who offered him a ride, seemingly for the opportunity to bait him by insulting Métis women. He cited a series of sexualized racist slurs directed particularly at women but also at men and his own person.[45] Cardinal wrote more forthrightly about the impact of constant sexual insults and organized sexual assault by pointing out the pervasiveness of these practices and double standards within the justice system, which Aboriginal people perceived as condoning white violence against them. He confronted his readers with a reverse scenario: "Turn the tables and see what would happen. Imagine a carousing invasion of one of your suburbs by roistering young Indian males in search of white girls for easy conquest."[46]

Cardinal and Adams are the earliest and best-known authors of a small group of writers who have written openly polemic works that critique the present situation partly by expressing Aboriginal understandings of historical events and processes. Daniel Paul is one later writer who has written in a similar manner. In his book *We Were Not the Savages*, Paul positions his work more squarely as an academic, historical study that is carefully supported with research into written documents.[47] Yet this sort of overt criticism is less common than deploying autobiography as a means of taking on historical injustice and discrimination. A series of autobiographies published in Canada since the 1970s has raised these issues in more subtle language, though clearly with the same intent to expose and critique. Some of the better-known examples of this genre include Eleanor Brass' *I Walk in Two Worlds*, Basil Johnston's *Indian School Days*, and Jane Willis' *Geniesh: An Indian Girlhood*.[48]

Since the 1970s several developments have had major implications for the publication of Aboriginal historical interpretations. One is the gradual increase in Aboriginal postsecondary and postgraduate education, which has produced a small but important group of Aboriginal academics. Some of the better-known Aboriginal academics whose work relates to the history of colonization include Howard Adams, Taiaiake Alfred, Marie Battiste, John Borrows, Olive Dickason, James (Sákéj) Youngblood Henderson, Emma LaRocque, Patricia Monture, Georges Sioui, Blair Stonechild, and Sharon Venne. Of this group, Olive Dickason, Blair Stonechild, and Georges Sioui are academic historians, while many of the other scholars address historical themes in their works on law, politics, culture, self-government, and literature.[49] The Royal Commission on Aboriginal Peoples (RCAP), which was established in 1991 and reported in 1996, was another major venue for Aboriginal historical analysis and interpretations.[50]

A third significant development was the federal government's establishment of a land claims process that has produced a large historical research industry. Aboriginal people have participated extensively in the claims process, helping to generate a vast new body of historical research that often represents a collaboration between non-Aboriginal researchers and First Nations researchers and governments. Revelations of widespread physical and sexual abuse in Canada's Indian residential schools have also spurred research into the schools and many lawsuits against the government and the churches that ran them.[51] The establishment and steady expansion of the claims system has involved academic historians, anthropologists, and other scholars in claims-related research with significant implications for academic research in general.[52] In the discipline of history, for example, the hitherto almost ignored treaties had begun by the 1980s to receive more serious scholarly treatment, along with general issues related to land, law, and the *Indian Act*.[53] More attention was devoted to accessing Aboriginal perspectives, imagining history from Aboriginal points of view, and comprehending the ways in which First Nations people were able to exercise agency. The academic literature on residential schools postdates Aboriginal initiatives to publicize the harm these institutions inflicted, and scholars working in this area have tended to work with Aboriginal people in their research.[54]

The last decade or so has witnessed a noticeable trend toward more widespread Aboriginal involvement in the recording and interpretation of their own history. In addition to works directly produced through the land claims process, there are books such as Treaty 7 Elders and colleagues' *The True Spirit and Original Intent of Treaty 7*, Ila Bussidor and Üstün Bilgen-Reinhart's *Night Spirits*, the Glenbow Museum and Blackfoot Elders' *Nitsitapi-isinni: The Story of the Blackfoot People*, and *Ahtahkakoop*, written by Deanna Christensen, with the Ahtahkakoop First Nation.[55] All of these books represent collaborations between Aboriginal and non-Aboriginal people that are designed to facilitate the publication of and access to Aboriginal people's own historical interpretations. There are also more Aboriginal historians in the academy, including Winona Wheeler, Heather Devine, and Susan Hill.[56] Growth in this area remains slow, however, and the preponderance of works appearing outside the academic fold is noteworthy.

Aboriginal People and Academic History Writing

What are we to make of the fact that so many Aboriginal people interested in history disseminate their ideas outside the academy? This fact poses epistemological, political, and paradigmatic questions for university historians. Does this choice relate in part to the mode of Western academic inquiry and to the Western knowledge project in general? When investigation of the conditions, attitudes, and experiences of First Nations has been a central component of the colonial project in Canada, some effort is required to reclaim academic inquiry and strip it of its oppressive connotations. Make no mistake – Aboriginal people did not have to read Michel Foucault to understand the meaning of "hierarchical observation" and the ways that knowledge collection underpinned the control exercised over them by the Department of Indian Affairs.[57] Given these historical realities, there are some challenges for First Nations people who seek a place for their own forms of knowledge and their own emancipatory political projects in the Western-oriented academy that our universities represent. I believe that non-Aboriginal scholars can help advance this process by displaying more openness, innovation, and willingness to take risks, both in their own work and in their interactions with Aboriginal scholars. For their part, Aboriginal scholars have voiced many concerns about racism and colonialism within the academy.[58]

Another problem is the translation process that is required for many Aboriginal students to engage in the type of intellectual debate and inquiry that is pursued in academic institutions. Some of the barriers are linguistic: in Manitoba, for example, some students speak an Aboriginal language as their mother tongue. Other obstacles relate to distinct Aboriginal epistemological premises and intellectual concerns that are not reflected in university curricula. Anthropologist Julie Cruikshank has made perhaps the greatest contribution to explaining these epistemologies to the non-Aboriginal world through her work on storytelling and Aboriginal people's use of stories.[59] When Cruikshank first began to record the life stories of Tlingit and Tagish women in Yukon, she found that, instead of talking about their personal life experiences, the women insisted on telling traditional stories about cultural figures.[60] She finally grasped that the women were giving her cultural training to prepare her to engage with their society's form of historical analysis, which centred on the tropes, thematic concerns, and narrative structures of such stories. The women understood their lives in terms of the traditional stories they told, and they constantly reconfigured and reconstituted the stories to make sense of their own life experiences and larger historical events such as the Yukon Gold Rush and the construction of the Alaska Highway.[61] Such an understanding of history and meaning differs radically from those disseminated in the academy.

In academic communities it is important to ask whether there is room to expand the category of scholar. Aboriginal people frequently observe that their Elders are the equivalent of libraries. Why do we not consider Aboriginal Elders with historical and/or cultural knowledge to be scholars, too? Such people have interpretations and analyses that have been partly passed down from their own teachers and partly developed through many years of thought and study. In most Aboriginal societies, oral history and tradition are evaluated rigourously through a process that compares the comments and stories of several Elders and affirms as certain only those that correspond with the others.[62] So the question can be posed: Should we always require university degrees to bestow recognition on scholarship?

Clearly, Aboriginal people are increasingly interested in having access to publishing as a way to relate and interpret their own history – and they are not always turning to the academy to do so. In fact, there is considerable suspicion in many communities that academic research is simply another form of colonial exploitation.[63] This perception is founded on the notion that non-Aboriginal people who seek information from First Nations are there only to take something away, that their research is, in effect, a form of theft that robs the people of something valuable. In part, this is a response to the fact that, in the past, researchers often disappeared after doing their research, and the communities gained nothing from their participation – a phenomenon that has not ceased entirely. In part, it reflects the view that researchers should conform to Aboriginal cultural protocols regarding access to the community and its knowledge.[64] In many Aboriginal societies, some form of payment often accompanied the transfer of valuable knowledge to non-kin. Elders expect to receive something in return for their stories, which normally means offering meaningful monetary payments as well as adhering to cultural protocols.[65] Beyond this, there is a strong feeling in many communities that First Nations knowledge is valuable and should not be given away to outsiders.[66] When a community is involved in any kind of treaty or land negotiation, there is a fear that community research could be used against them to affect their negotiations adversely. Thus, there are political barriers to collaborative research, and there are also competing knowledge paradigms: a Western, academic one that views knowledge essentially as a common good and an Aboriginal one that views knowledge as valuable individual or family property that should be retained more intimately within the kinship network.

There is another set of unresolved questions concerning the validity and uses of oral history and tradition. In the field of Aboriginal history, the belief that oral history is important has come to be almost universally accepted, and many academic historians are making greater efforts to conduct this sort of research. It is becoming almost a platitude to state that oral history is essential, but oral history is difficult to do. If anything, it is getting more difficult as First Nations become empowered to protect and claim their own knowledge and are increasingly cautious about vouchsafing that knowledge into an outsider's hands. The academic evaluation and reward system also militates against the pursuit of oral history. Oral history takes far longer than conventional documentary history, and it demands teamwork and community-relations skills that are not part of a historian's academic training and take considerable time and effort to develop. Approaching oral history ethically and sustainably means relinquishing control over the content and timing of the end product, if there is one. Probably one of the most valuable things to do at this particular historical conjuncture is to put academic funding and resources into projects that record and preserve the knowledge of Aboriginal communities – regardless of whether they contribute directly to academic researchers' publication records. But to do so is risky for academic scholars because success in institutional evaluation processes and grant competitions has much to do with the number of publications they can produce. The Social Sciences and Humanities Research Council of Canada has recently instituted an Aboriginal Research Program that seems calculated to address concerns of this sort, but more change is required to facilitate new approaches to Aboriginal research in the academy.[67]

Within the discipline of history, some efforts have been made to respond to Aboriginal concerns. Despite Aboriginal people's misgivings about academic historians, Aboriginal interpretations of history have been influential in some respects. Although an analysis of oppression and colonization did not originate solely with Aboriginal people, the strong emphasis on these interpretive frameworks by Aboriginal writers from Harold Cardinal onward has shaped the writing of two generations of academic historians and other scholars who have followed. Aboriginal history and anthropology in Canada have focused since the 1969 White Paper extensively on various aspects of colonization and oppression. This is perhaps most apparent in the literature on residential schools, where non-Aboriginal contributors to the literature have clearly been responding to public and private condemnations of the system issued by First Nations.[68] The literature concerning treaties has likewise been shaped powerfully by these sorts of research collaborations and infused with an Aboriginal understanding that emphasizes the spirit and intent of treaties, presses governments and the courts to interpret them broadly, and sees these agreements as founding documents of Canadian history.[69]

Not surprisingly, academic history has been most receptive to Aboriginal influences that are easy to accommodate in the existing forms, epistemologies, methodologies, and interpretive frameworks. Understandings that do not fit neatly into these have had less impact. For instance, traditional stories are an integral part of Aboriginal historical understandings, as Julie Cruikshank has demonstrated in her work with Yukon Elders. The centrality of storytelling was also revealed, for example, in *Ahtahkakoop*, which was commissioned by the Ahtahkakoop First Nation of Saskatchewan and incorporates traditional stories into its narrative flow to show the integrated cultural world of the Plains Cree by underlining values and self-understandings.[70] While Cruikshank's work has deservedly received a good deal of attention, the publication of *Ahtahkakoop* passed virtually unnoticed, and the book appears to have had little impact on academic history.

There is also a fundamental cleavage between the way Aboriginal writers such as Howard Adams and Daniel Paul and non-Aboriginal historians approach issues of responsibility and agency. Adams and Paul place a strong emphasis on the wrongs of colonialism and white society and tend to portray Aboriginal people historically as more or less powerless victims. Even Harold Cardinal, who generally depicts First Nations as intelligent and self-confident, approvingly quotes David Courchene, president of the Manitoba Indian Brotherhood, who stated in 1968 that nineteenth-century Aboriginal treaty negotiators were "uneducated people" who were "impressed by the pomp and ceremony and the authority of the officials" and "really did not know or understand fully the meaning and implications" of the treaties.[71] This image of Aboriginal treaty participants as unsophisticated and unaware, as tricked or coerced into signing treaties by the officials of a powerful state, is common in Aboriginal public discourse. In contrast, non-Aboriginal writers on this subject tend to stress treaty negotiations in which chiefs like Mawedopenais, Peau de Chat, Mistawasis, and Ahtahkakoop demonstrated an awareness of coming changes such as mass immigration and their own inability to halt the invasion.[72] Both sets of perspectives accurately reflect historical realities, but they present the treaty process in distinctly different lights. Nonetheless, all parties agree on the deceptive language used by government negotiators, the pressure they placed on First Nations to sign, the prevalence of "outside promises" made verbally but left out of written treaties, and the excessively narrow, legalistic interpretations that the federal government applied in implementing them.[73]

Conclusion

The observations in this chapter will, I hope, contribute to the mapping out of new terrain in which academic history could be more responsive to Aboriginal historical thinking. Perhaps the most difficult challenge is the effort to expand our categories of what constitutes history, what constitutes a scholar, and even what constitutes reality. For example, Aboriginal histories often include stories of "supernatural" phenomena and "magical" transformations in which beings move from the human to the animal world and back again, stories that are not deemed to be "history" and for which the English language is sadly lacking a useful vocabulary and corresponding concepts.[74] Native origin stories often conflict with Western science's insistence on its theory of Asian origins and migration across the Bering Strait. Few scholars have resisted the temptation to endorse Western epistemology and, thus, perpetuate science's exclusive truth claim. Few of us have been willing to abandon our diachronic time scales and our chronological narrative structures for alternative formats. Finally, it remains a challenge for academic historians to contemplate a research agenda shared with or even determined by Aboriginal collaborators or to surrender control of crucial decisions such as the uses and end products of research. Until we take more steps in these directions, we will continue to maintain significant barriers between ourselves and the Aboriginal people whose histories we attempt to understand.

ACKNOWLEDGMENTS

I would like to thank the Social Sciences and Humanities Research Council of Canada for the Standard Research Grant that made possible the research for this study.

NOTES

1 Alexander Saxton, *The Rise and Fall of the White Republic: Class Politics and Mass Culture in Nineteenth-Century America* (London: Verso, 1990), 14, quoted in Matthew Frye Jacobson, *Whiteness of a Different Color: European Immigrants and the Alchemy of Race* (Cambridge, MA: Harvard University Press, 1998), 6.

2 Maureen Konkle, *Writing Indian Nations: Indian Intellectuals and the Politics of Historiography, 1827-1863* (Chapel Hill: University of North Carolina Press, 2004), 43.

3 In addition to those cited throughout this chapter, other early writers/speakers include Samson Occom (Mohegan), who preached and spoke in the 1770s, and nineteenth-century writers Andrew J. Blackbird (Ottawa), William W. Warren (Ojibway), E. Pauline Johnson (Mohawk), and John Rollin Ridge (Cherokee). For oral literature, see Penny Petrone, *First People, First Voices* (Toronto: University of Toronto Press, 1983) and *Native Literature in Canada: From the Oral Tradition to the Present* (Don Mills, ON: Oxford University Press, 1990).

4 Konkle, *Writing Indian Nations*, 6, 36. See also Colin M. Coates and Cecilia Morgan, *Heroines and History: Representations of Madeleine de Verchères and Laura Secord* (Toronto: University of Toronto Press, 2002), 257-74.

5 This is particularly evident, for example, in Upper Canadian newspapers in the first half of the nineteenth century, in which histories of towns and settlements are constructed as though First Nations people did not exist by denoting the place before the arrival of Europeans "a howling wilderness." See R.J. Brownlie, "Settlement, 'Indianness,' and Whiteness in Upper Canadian Discourses, 1820-1860"

(paper presented at the annual meeting of the Canadian Historical Association, Toronto, 29 May 2006).

6   Maureen Konkle has written on this subject, "For Native writers, to claim modern time is to claim the history of European depredations on Native peoples and to refute EuroAmericans' insistence that racial difference is the explanation for everything that happened to Native peoples, as well as for their eventual doom. To claim to progress through time, to argue that Native peoples can and will persist into the future, is to claim political standing and to insist on recognition," *Writing Indian Nations*, 37.

7   George Copway, *The Traditional History and Characteristic Sketches of the Ojibway Nation* (London: Gilpin, 1850). The book later appeared under the title *Indian Life and Indian History, by an Indian Author, Embracing the Traditions of the North American Indian Tribes Regarding Themselves, Particularly of That Most Important of All the Tribes, the Ojibways* (1858; repr., New York: AMS, 1977). Peter Jones (Kahkewaquonaby), *History of the Ojebway Indians: With Especial Reference to Their Conversion to Christianity* (London: A.W. Bennett 1861).

8   Relevant works include Donald B. Smith, "Kahgegagahbowh: Canada's First Literary Celebrity in the United States," in *Life, Letters, and Speeches*, by George Copway, ed. A. LaVonne Brown Ruoff and Donald B. Smith (Lincoln: University of Nebraska Press, 1997), "The Life of George Copway or Kah-ge-ga-gah-bowh (1818-1869) – and a Review of His Writings," *Journal of Canadian Studies* 23, 3 (1988): 5-38, and *Sacred Feathers: The Reverend Peter Jones (Kahkewaquonaby) and the Mississauga Indians* (Lincoln: University of Nebraska Press, 1987); Konkle, *Writing Indian Nations*; A. LaVonne Brown Ruoff, "Three Nineteenth-Century American Indian Autobiographers," in *Redefining American Literary History*, ed. A. LaVonne Brown Ruoff and Jerry W. Ward (New York: Modern Language Association of America, 1990), 251-69; Cheryl Walker, *Indian Nation: Native American Literature and Nineteenth-Century Nationalisms* (Durham, NC: Duke University Press, 1997).

9   Smith, "The Life of George Copway," 16, 27.

10   Konkle, *Writing Indian Nations*, 40. Catherine Hall places the date for a similar transition in England toward the end of the 1840s and the beginning of the 1850s: see *Civilising Subjects: Metropole and Colony in the English Imagination 1830-1867* (Chicago: University of Chicago Press, 2002), 20.

11   For an instructive analysis of the concept of "fitness for self-government" and its imbrication with notions of race, see Matthew Frye Jacobson, *Whiteness of a Different Color*, 7-8, 14, 22-31, and passim.

12   Scientist Stephen Jay Gould, upon analyzing nineteenth-century attitudes toward race, stated, "I cannot identify any popular position remotely like the 'cultural relativism' that prevails (at least by lip service) in liberal circles today." Stephen Jay Gould, *The Mismeasure of Man* (1981; repr., New York: W.W. Norton, 1996), 63, quoted in Celia Haig-Brown and David A. Nock, introduction to *With Good*

Intentions: Euro-Canadian and Aboriginal Relations in Colonial Canada, ed. Celia Haig-Brown and David A. Nock (Vancouver: UBC Press, 2006), 10.

13 United Kingdom, *British Parliamentary Papers*, vol. 12, *Correspondence, Returns and Other Papers relating to Canada and to the Indian Problem Therein, 1839* (Shannon: Irish University Press, 1969), 353; Bond Head to Glenelg, no. 32, 20 November 1836, quoted in Robert J. Surtees, "Treaty Research Report: Manitoulin Island Treaties," Treaties and Historical Research Centre, Indian and Northern Affairs Canada, 1986.

14 Peter Jones, *Life and Journal of Kah-ke-wa-quo-na-by (Rev. Peter Jones), Wesleyan Missionary* (Toronto: Missionary Committee, Canada Conference, 1860), 7.

15 Jones, *History of the Ojebway Indians*, 29-30.

16 Ibid., 129.

17 Copway, *Traditional History and Characteristic Sketches of the Ojibway Nation*, 144.

18 The Ojibway's military history was also one of the main preoccupations of the other famous Ojibway-authored work of the nineteenth century, William W. Warren's *History of the Ojibways, Based upon Traditions and Oral Statements* (St. Paul: Minnesota Historical Society, 1885).

19 See Ruoff, "Three Nineteenth-Century American Indian Autobiographers," 253; see also Walker, *Indian Nation*, 96.

20 Copway, *Traditional History*, 263.

21 "Chief Canoting, speaking at conference held at Colborne-on-Thames on Jan. 27, 1841, in presence of Supt of IA [Superintendent of Indian Affairs]; Rev Richard Flood; Rev. Solomon Waldron; and the Chiefs of the Delawares, Oneidas, and Chippewas," quoted in Jones, *History of the Ojebway Indians*, 272-73.

22 For a bibliography of works by Aboriginal authors that focuses mainly on the United States (but with some works published by authors born in Canada), see A. LaVonne Brown Ruoff, "American Indian Literature," in *Redefining American Literary History*, ed. A. LaVonne Brown Ruoff and Jerry W. Ward Jr. (New York: Modern Language Association of America, 1990), 327-52.

23 Ruoff, "Three Nineteenth-Century American Indian Autobiographers," 260.

24 Many thanks to my colleague at the University of Manitoba, Dr. Kathleen Buddle-Crowe, for sharing with me her research on Aboriginal media activism, which includes a most informative section on these three men. See Kathleen Buddle-Crowe, "From Birchbark Talk to Digital Dreamspeaking: A History of Aboriginal Media Activism in Canada" (PhD diss., McMaster University, 2002).

25 Edward Ahenakew published "Cree Trickster Tales" in *The Journal of American Folk-lore* 42, 166 (1929): 309-53; Joseph Dion published articles in the *Bonnyville Tribune* and other newspapers, while Mike Mountain Horse published in the *Lethbridge Herald*. Edward Ahenakew and Joseph Dion were unable to complete their planned books before their deaths; Mike Mountain Horse was unable to find a publisher in the 1930s. See Hugh A. Dempsey, introduction to Joseph F. Dion, *My Tribe the Crees*,

ed. Hugh A. Dempsey (Calgary: Glenbow Museum, 1979), vii; Hugh A. Dempsey, introduction to *My People the Bloods*, by Mike Mountain Horse (Calgary/Standoff: Glenbow-Alberta Institute/Blood Tribal Council, 1979), vii; Ruth M. Buck, "Introduction to the 1973 Edition," in Edward Ahenakew, *Voices of the Plains Cree*, ed. Ruth M. Buck, rev. ed. (Toronto: McClelland and Stewart, 1973; Regina: Canadian Plains Research Center, 1995), 1, 3. Citations are to the 1995 edition.

26 Dion, *My Tribe the Crees*, 176.

27 Stan Cuthand, "Introduction to the 1995 Edition," in Ahenakew, *Voices of the Plains Cree*, ed. Buck, xviii.

28 Ahenakew's niece, Christine Wilna (Willy) Hodgson, states that he was aware of the threat to Cree oral tradition and understood that its transmission would have to change in order to preserve it; that is, that it would have to be committed to writing. Christine Wilna (Willy) Hodgson, foreword to Ahenakew, *Voices of the Plains Cree*, ed. Ruth M. Buck, vii.

29 Ahenakew, *Voices of the Plains Cree*, 73.

30 Mountain Horse, *My People the Bloods*, xiii.

31 Dion, *My Tribe the Crees*, ix.

32 Ibid., 65.

33 Canada, *Statement of the Government of Canada on Indian Policy* (Ottawa: Queen's Printer, 1969).

34 Harold Cardinal, *The Unjust Society: The Tragedy of Canada's Indians* (Edmonton: M.G. Hurtig, 1969).

35 Ibid., 1.

36 Ibid., 2.

37 Howard Adams, *Prison of Grass: Canada from the Native Point of View*, rev. ed. (Toronto: New Press, 1975; Saskatoon: Fifth House, 1989).

38 Adams, *Prison of Grass*, 6, from the preface to the 1989 edition.

39 Ibid., 37.

40 For a thorough analysis of the events surrounding the *Statement of the Government of Canada on Indian Policy, 1969* (the White Paper), see Sally M. Weaver, *Making Canadian Indian Policy: The Hidden Agenda, 1968-1970* (Toronto: University of Toronto Press, 1981).

41 William Apes, *Son of the Forest: The Experience of William Apes, a Native of the Forest* (1829), cited in A. LaVonne Brown Ruoff, "Three Nineteenth-Century American Indian Autobiographers," in *Redefining American Literary History*, ed. A. LaVonne Brown Ruoff and Jerry W. Ward Jr., 253.

42 Jones, *History of the Ojebway Indians*, 164.

43 Sarah Winnemucca Hopkins, *Life Among the Piutes: Their Wrongs and Claims* (New York: G.P. Putnam, 1883; repr., Reno: University of Nevada Press, 1994), 48.

44 Ibid., 228.

45 Adams, *Prison of Grass*, 38-39.

46 Cardinal, *The Unjust Society*, 77.

47 Daniel N. Paul, *We Were Not the Savages: A Micmac Perspective on the Collision of European and Aboriginal Civilizations*, 2nd ed. (Halifax: Nimbus, 1993; Halifax: Fernwood, 2000).

48 Eleanor Brass, *I Walk in Two Worlds* (Calgary: Glenbow Museum, 1987); Basil H. Johnston, *Indian School Days* (Toronto: Key Porter Books, 1988); Jane Willis, *Geniesh: An Indian Girlhood* (Toronto: New Press, 1973).

49 Howard Adams, *Prison of Grass* and *Tortured People: The Politics of Colonization* (Penticton, BC: Theytus Books, 1995); Taiaiake Alfred, *Wasa'se: Indigenous Pathways of Action and Freedom* (Peterborough, ON: Broadview Press, 2005), *Peace, Power, Righteousness: An Indigenous Manifesto* (Don Mills, ON: Oxford University Press, 1999), and *Heeding the Voices of Our Ancestors: Kahnawake Mohawk Politics and the Rise of Native Nationalism* (Don Mills, ON: Oxford University Press, 1995); Marie Battiste and James (Sákéj) Youngblood Henderson, *Protecting Indigenous Knowledge and Heritage: A Global Challenge* (Saskatoon: Purich, 2000) and Marie Battiste, ed., *Reclaiming Indigenous Voice and Vision* (Vancouver: UBC Press, 2000). John Borrows, *Recovering Canada: The Resurgence of Indigenous Law* (Toronto: University of Toronto Press, 2002); John Borrows and Leonard Rotman, *Aboriginal Legal Issues: Cases, Material, and Commentary* (Toronto: Butterworths, 1998); Olive Dickason, *Canada's First Nations: A History of Founding Peoples from Earliest Times* (Don Mills, ON: Oxford University Press, 1992, 1996, 2002) and *The Myth of the Savage and the Beginnings of French Colonialism in the Americas* (Edmonton: University of Alberta Press, 1997); James (Sákéj) Youngblood Henderson, *First Nations Jurisprudence and Aboriginal Rights: Defining the Just Society* (Saskatoon: Native Law Centre, University of Saskatchewan, 2006) and *The Mi'kmaw Concordat* (Halifax: Fernwood, 1997); Emma LaRocque, "Native Writers Resisting Colonizing Practices in Canadian Historiography and Literature" (PhD diss., University of Manitoba, 1999) and *Defeathering the Indian* (Agincourt, AB: Book Society of Canada, 1975); Patricia Monture, *Journeying Forward: Dreaming First Nations' Independence* (Halifax: Fernwood, 1999) and Patricia Monture-Angus, *Thunder in My Soul: A Mohawk Woman Speaks* (Halifax: Fernwood, 1995); Georges Sioui, *Huron-Wendat: The Heritage of the Circle* (Vancouver: UBC Press, 1999) and *For an Amerindian Autohistory: An Essay on the Foundations of a Social Ethic* (Montreal and Kingston: McGill-Queen's University Press, 1992); Blair Stonechild, *The New Buffalo: The Struggle for Aboriginal Postsecondary Education in Canada* (Winnipeg: University of Manitoba Press, 2006) and Blair Stonechild and Bill Waiser *Loyal Till Death: Indians and the North-West Rebellion* (Calgary: Fifth House, 1997); Sharon Venne, *Our Elders Understand Our Rights: Evolving International Law Regarding Indigenous Peoples* (Penticton, BC: Theytus Books, 1998) and *Indian Acts and Amendments, 1868-1975: An Indexed Collection* (Saskatoon: Native Law Centre, University of Saskatchewan, 1981).

50 Canada, Royal Commission on Aboriginal Peoples, *Report of the Royal Commission on Aboriginal Peoples*, 5 vols. (Ottawa: Canada Communications Group, 1996).

51   See, for example, John Milloy, *A National Crime: The Canadian Government and the Residential School System, 1879 to 1986* (Winnipeg: University of Manitoba Press, 1999); J.R. Miller, *Shingwauk's Vision: A History of Native Residential Schools* (Toronto: University of Toronto Press, 1996); and Agnes Grant, *No End of Grief: Indian Residential Schools in Canada* (Winnipeg: Pemmican Publications, 1996).

52   Major examples include John Milloy's book on residential schools, *A National Crime*, which was originally a report for the Royal Commission on Aboriginal Peoples, and two treaty reports that became published books: Harold Cardinal and Walter Hildebrandt, eds. *Treaty Elders of Saskatchewan: Our Dream Is That Our Peoples Will One Day Be Clearly Recognized as Nations* (Calgary: University of Calgary Press, 2000), which documents the oral history record, and Arthur J. Ray, Jim Miller, and Frank Tough, *Bounty and Benevolence: A Documentary History of Saskatchewan Treaties* (Montreal and Kingston: McGill-Queen's University Press, 2000), which documents and analyzes the written record.

53   For Ontario, historical writing related to treaties began a little earlier, with a series of unpublished doctoral theses in the 1970s: Anthony J. Hall, "The Red Man's Burden: Land, Law, and the Lord in the Indian Affairs of Upper Canada, 1791-1858" (PhD diss., University of Toronto, 1984); Douglas Leighton, "The Development of Federal Indian Policy in Canada, 1840-1890" (PhD diss., University of Western Ontario, 1975); and Robert J. Surtees, "Indian Land Cessions in Ontario, 1763-1862: The Evolution of a System" (PhD diss., Carleton University, 1983).

54   John Milloy's *A National Crime* has already been cited and is the most obvious example, but the other major survey on the topic, J.R. Miller's *Shingwauk's Vision*, included a substantial number of interviews with survivors.

55   Treaty 7 Elders and Tribal Council, with Walter Hildebrandt, Sarah Carter, and Dorothy First Rider, *The True Spirit and Original Intent of Treaty 7* (Montreal and Kingston: McGill-Queen's University Press, 1996); Ila Bussidor and Üstün Bilgen-Reinhart, *Night Spirits: The Story of the Relocation of the Sayisi Dene* (Winnipeg: University of Manitoba Press, 1997); Blackfoot Gallery Committee, *Nitsitapiisinni: The Story of the Blackfoot People* (Toronto: Key Porter Books, 2001); Deanna Christensen, *Ahtahkakoop: The Epic Account of a Plains Cree Head Chief, His People, and Their Struggle for Survival, 1816-1896* (Shell Lake, SK: Ahtahkakoop Publishing, 2000).

56   Winona Wheeler, "'Ethnic' Assimilates 'Indigenous': A Study in Intellectual Neo-colonialism," *Wicazo Sa Review* 13, 1 (Spring, 1998): 33-51, Winona Stevenson (Wheeler), "The Journals and Voices of a Church of England Native Catechist: Askenootow (Charles Pratt), 1851-1884," in *Reading Beyond Words: Contexts for Native History*, ed. Jennifer S.H. Brown and Elizabeth Vibert (Peterborough, ON: Broadview Press, 1996), 237-62, and Winona Wheeler, ed., "Indigenous Voices from the Great Plains," special issue, *Oral History Forum*, 19-20 (1999-2000); Heather Devine, *The People Who Own Themselves: Aboriginal Ethnogenesis in a Canadian Family, 1660-1990* (Calgary: University of Calgary Press, 2004); Susan M. Hill,

"'The Clay We Are Made Of': An Examination of Haudenosaunee Land Tenure on the Grand River Territory" (PhD diss., Trent University, 2005).

57   Michel Foucault, *Discipline and Punish: The Birth of the Prison*, trans. Alan Sheridan (New York: Vintage Books, 1995).

58   See, for example, Monture-Angus, *Thunder in My Soul*; Emma LaRocque, "The Colonization of a Native Woman Scholar," in *Women of the First Nations: Power, Wisdom, and Strength*, ed. Christina Miller and Patricia Chuchryk (Winnipeg: University of Manitoba Press, 1996), 11-18. For the United States, see Devon A. Mihesuah and Angela C. Wilson, eds., *Indigenizing the Academy: Transforming Scholarship and Empowering Communities* (Lincoln: University of Nebraska Press, 2004).

59   Julie Cruikshank, *Life Lived Like a Story: Life Stories of Three Yukon Native Elders* (Lincoln/Vancouver: University of Nebraska Press/UBC Press, 1990) and *The Social Life of Stories: Narrative and Knowledge in the Yukon Territory* (Lincoln/Vancouver: University of Nebraska Press/UBC Press, 1998).

60   Cruikshank, *Life Lived Like a Story*, 2, 14-15, 19-20.

61   See also Julie Cruikshank, "Discovery of Gold in the Klondike: Contributions from Oral Tradition," in *Reading Beyond Words: Contexts for Native History*, ed. Jennifer S.H. Brown and Elizabeth Vibert (Peterborough, ON: Broadview Press, 1996), 433-59.

62   See, for example, Julie Cruikshank, "Oral History, Narrative Strategies, and Native American Historiography: Perspectives from the Yukon Territory, Canada," in *Clearing a Path: Theorizing the Past in Native American Studies*, ed. Nancy Shoemaker (New York: Routledge, 2002), 15-16.

63   See Linda Tuhiwai Smith, *Decolonizing Methodologies: Research and Indigenous Peoples* (London/Dunedin: Zed Books/University of Otago Press, 1999), 1-6.

64   Ibid., 15-16.

65   Jonathan H. Ellerby, *Working with Aboriginal Elders: An Introductory Handbook for Institution-Based and Health Care Professionals Based on the Teachings of Winnipeg-Area Aboriginal Elders and Cultural Teachers* (Winnipeg: Native Studies Press, 2001), 28-36, 50-54.

66   I experienced this in my own research, while organizing a local Elders' gathering at a Dene community in northern Manitoba.

67   The Social Sciences and Humanities Research Council of Canada (SSHRC) launched its Aboriginal Research Program in 2004. It seeks to help foster more direct Aboriginal involvement in research and more culturally appropriate approaches. In 2007-8 an evaluation was completed that recommended continuation of the program, with minor adjustments. For a summary of the evaluation results, see Social Sciences and Humanities Research Council of Canada, "Management Response Summary: Aboriginal Pilot Program," SSHRC, http://www.sshrc.ca/site/about-crsh/publications/arpp_evaluation_response_e.pdf.

68   In addition to the books by J.R. Miller and John S. Milloy cited previously, many other works show this influence, including Roland Chrisjohn and Sherri Young,

with Michael Maraun, *The Circle Game: Shadows and Substance in the Indian Residential School Experience in Canada* (Vancouver: Theytus Books, 2006); Celia Haig-Brown, *Resistance and Renewal: Surviving the Indian Residential School* (Vancouver: Tillacum Library, 1988); Isabelle Knockwood, *Out of the Depths: The Experiences of Mi'kmaw Children at the Indian Residential School at Shubenacadie, Nova Scotia*, rev. ed. (Lockeport, NS: Roseway, 2001).

69 See, for example, Ray, Miller, and Tough, *Bounty and Benevolence*. Cole Harris' book *Making Native Space: Colonialism, Resistance, and Reserves in British Columbia* (Vancouver: UBC Press, 2002) is also strongly shaped by BC First Nations century-long struggle for their land.

70 Christensen, *Ahtahkakoop*.

71 David Courchene, president of the Manitoba Indian Brotherhood, speaking during the regional consultation meeting with the federal government in December 1968, quoted in Cardinal, *The Unjust Society*, 36.

72 See, for example, Ray, Miller, and Tough, *Bounty and Benevolence*.

73 Ibid. See also Jean Friesen, "Magnificent Gifts: The Treaties of Canada with the Indians of the Northwest, 1869-76," *Transactions of the Royal Society of Canada* series 5, 1 (1986): 41-51; Richard T. Price, ed., *The Spirit of the Alberta Indian Treaties* (Edmonton: University of Alberta Press, 1999); Sharon Venne, "Treaty 6: An Indigenous Perspective," in *Aboriginal and Treaty Rights in Canada: Essays on Law, Equality, and Respect for Difference*, ed. Michael Asch (Vancouver: UBC Press, 2002), 173-207; J.R. Miller, "'I will accept the Queen's hand': First Nations Leaders and the Image of the Crown in the Prairie Treaties," in *Reflections on Native-Newcomer Relations: Selected Essays*, ed. J.R. Miller (Toronto: University of Toronto Press, 2004), 242-66.

74 See, for example, Louis Bird's delightful book, produced in collaboration with academic historians Jennifer S.H. Brown, Paul W. DePasquale, and Mark F. Ruml, eds., *Telling Our Stories: Omushkego Legends and Histories from Hudson Bay* (Peterborough, ON: Broadview Press, 2005).

WORKS CITED

Adams, Howard. *Prison of Grass: Canada from the Native Point of View*. Rev. ed. Toronto: New Press, 1975; Saskatoon: Fifth House, 1989.

–. *Tortured People: The Politics of Colonization*. Penticton, BC: Theytus Books, 1995.

Ahenakew. Edward. "Cree Trickster Tales." *The Journal of American Folklore* 42, 166 (1929): 309-53.

–. *Voices of the Plains Cree*. Ed. Ruth M. Buck. Rev. ed. Toronto: McClelland and Stewart, 1973; Regina: Canadian Plains Research Center, 1995.

Alfred, Taiaiake. *Heeding the Voices of Our Ancestors: Kahnawake Mohawk Politics and the Rise of Native Nationalism*. Don Mills, ON: Oxford University Press, 1995.

–. *Peace, Power, Righteousness: An Indigenous Manifesto*. Don Mills, ON: Oxford University Press, 1999.

–. *Wasa'se: Indigenous Pathways of Action and Freedom*. Peterborough, ON: Broadview Press, 2005.

Battiste, Marie, ed. *Reclaiming Indigenous Voice and Vision*. Vancouver: UBC Press, 2000.

Battiste, Marie, and James (Sákéj) Youngblood Henderson. *Protecting Indigenous Knowledge and Heritage: A Global Challenge*. Saskatoon: Purich, 2000.

Bird, Louis, with Jennifer S.H. Brown, Paul W. DePasquale, and Mark F. Ruml, eds. *Telling Our Stories: Omushkego Legends and Histories from Hudson Bay*. Peterborough, ON: Broadview Press, 2005.

Blackfoot Gallery Committee. *Nitsitapiisinni: The Story of the Blackfoot People*. Toronto: Key Porter Books, 2001.

Borrows, John. *Recovering Canada: The Resurgence of Indigenous Law*. Toronto: University of Toronto Press, 2002.

Borrows, John, and Leonard Rotman. *Aboriginal Legal Issues: Cases, Material, and Commentary*. Toronto: Butterworths, 1998.

Brass, Eleanor. *I Walk in Two Worlds*. Calgary: Glenbow Museum, 1987.

Brownlie, J.B. "Settlement, 'Indianness,' and Whiteness in Upper Canadian Discourses, 1820-1860." Paper presented at the annual meeting of the Canadian Historical Association, Toronto, 29 May 2006.

Buck, Ruth M. "Introduction to the 1973 Edition." In Edward Ahenakew, *Voices of the Plains Cree*, ed. Ruth M. Buck, 1-8. Rev. ed. Toronto: McClelland and Stewart, 1973; Regina: Canadian Plains Research Center, 1995.

Buddle-Crowe, Kathleen. "From Birchbark Talk to Digital Dreamspeaking: A History of Aboriginal Media Activism in Canada." PhD diss., McMaster University, 2002.

Bussidor, Ila, and Üstün Bilgen-Reinhart. *Night Spirits: The Story of the Relocation of the Sayisi Dene*. Winnipeg: University of Manitoba Press, 1997.

Canada. *Statement of the Government of Canada on Indian Policy*. Ottawa: Queen's Printer, 1969.

–. Royal Commission on Aboriginal Peoples. *Report of the Royal Commission on Aboriginal Peoples*. 5 vols. Ottawa: Canada Communications Group, 1996.

Cardinal, Harold. *The Unjust Society: The Tragedy of Canada's Indians*. Edmonton: M.G. Hurtig, 1969.

Cardinal, Harold, and Walter Hildebrandt, eds. *Treaty Elders of Saskatchewan: Our Dream Is That Our Peoples Will One Day Be Clearly Recognized as Nations*. Calgary: University of Calgary Press, 2000.

Chrisjohn, Roland, and Sherri Young, with Michael Maraun. *The Circle Game: Shadows and Substance in the Indian Residential School Experience in Canada*. Vancouver: Theytus Books, 2006.

Christensen, Deanna. *Ahtahkakoop: The Epic Account of a Plains Cree Head Chief, His People, and Their Struggle for Survival 1816-1896*. Shell Lake, SK: Ahtahkakoop Publishing, 2000.

Coates, Colin M., and Cecilia Morgan. *Heroines and History: Representation of Madeleine de Verchères and Laura Secord*. Toronto: University of Toronto Press, 2002.

Copway, George. *The Traditional History and Characteristic Sketches of the Ojibway Nation.* London: Gilpin, 1850.

Cruikshank, Julie. "Discovery of Gold in the Klondike: Contributions from Oral Tradition." In *Reading Beyond Words: Contexts for Native History,* ed. Jennifer S.H. Brown and Elizabeth Vibert, 433-59. Peterborough, ON: Broadview Press, 1996.

–. *Life Lived Like a Story: Life Stories of Three Yukon Native Elders.* Lincoln/Vancouver: University of Nebraska Press/UBC Press, 1990.

–. "Oral History, Narrative Strategies, and Native American Historiography: Perspectives from the Yukon Territory, Canada." In *Clearing a Path: Theorizing the Past in Native American Studies,* ed. Nancy Shoemaker, 3-27. New York: Routledge, 2002.

–. *The Social Life of Stories: Narrative and Knowledge in the Yukon Territory.* Lincoln/ Vancouver: University of Nebraska Press/UBC Press, 1998.

Cuthand, Stan. "Introduction to the 1995 Edition." In Edward Ahenakew, *Voices of the Plains Cree,* ed. Ruth M. Buck, ix-xxii. Rev. ed. Toronto: McClelland and Stewart, 1973; Regina: Canadian Plains Research Center, 1995.

Dempsey, Hugh A. Introduction to *My People the Bloods,* by Mike Mountain Horse, v-xi. Calgary/Standoff: Glenbow-Alberta Institute/Blood Tribal Council, 1979.

–. Introduction to *My Tribe the Crees,* by Joseph F. Dion, ed. Hugh A. Dempsey, v-viii. Calgary: Glenbow Museum, 1979.

Devine, Heather. *The People Who Own Themselves: Aboriginal Ethnogenesis in a Canadian Family, 1660-1990.* Calgary: University of Calgary Press, 2004.

Dickason, Olive. *Canada's First Nations: A History of Founding Peoples from Earliest Times.* Don Mills, ON: Oxford University Press, 1992, 1996, 2002.

–. *The Myth of the Savage and the Beginnings of French Colonialism in the Americas.* Edmonton: University of Alberta Press, 1997.

Dion, Joseph F. *My Tribe the Crees,* ed. Hugh A. Dempsey. Calgary: Glenbow Museum, 1979.

Ellerby, Jonathan H. *Working with Aboriginal Elders: An Introductory Handbook for Institution-Based and Health Care Professionals Based on the Teachings of Winnipeg-Area Aboriginal Elders and Cultural Teachers,* Winnipeg: Native Studies Press, 2001.

Foucault, Michel. *Discipline and Punish: The Birth of the Prison.* Trans. Alan Sheridan. New York: Vintage Books, 1995.

Friesen, Jean. "Magnificent Gifts: The Treaties of Canada with the Indians of the Northwest, 1869-76." *Transactions of the Royal Society of Canada,* Series 5, 1 (1986): 41-51.

Gould, Stephen Jay. *The Mismeasure of Man.* 1981. Reprint, New York: W.W. Norton, 1996.

Grant, Agnes. *No End of Grief: Indian Residential Schools in Canada.* Winnipeg: Pemmican Publications, 1996.

Haig-Brown, Celia. *Resistance and Renewal: Surviving the Indian Residential School.* Vancouver: Tillacum Library, 1988.

Haig-Brown, Celia, and David A. Nock. "Introduction." In *With Good Intentions: Euro-Canadian and Aboriginal Relations in Colonial Canada,* ed. Celia Haig-Brown and David A. Nock, 1-31. Vancouver: UBC Press, 2006.

Hall, Anthony J. "The Red Man's Burden: Land, Law and the Lord in the Indian Affairs of Upper Canada, 1791-1858." PhD diss., University of Toronto, 1984.

Hall, Catherine. *Civilising Subjects: Metropole and Colony in the English Imagination 1830-1867*. Chicago: University of Chicago Press, 2002.

Harris, Cole. *Making Native Space: Colonialism, Resistance, and Reserves in British Columbia*. Vancouver: UBC Press, 2002.

Henderson, James (Sákéj) Youngblood. *First Nations Jurisprudence and Aboriginal Rights: Defining the Just Society*. Saskatoon: Native Law Centre, University of Saskatchewan, 2006.

–. *The Mi'kmaw Concordat*. Halifax: Fernwood, 1997.

Hill, Susan M. "'The Clay We Are Made Of': An Examination of Haudenosaunee Land Tenure on the Grand River Territory." PhD diss., Trent University, 2005.

Hodgson, Christine Wilna (Willy). Foreword to Edward Ahenakew, *Voices of the Plains Cree*, ed. Ruth M. Buck, vii-viii. Rev. ed. Toronto: McClelland and Stewart, 1973; Regina: Canadian Plains Research Center, 1995.

Hopkins, Sarah Winnemucca. *Life Among the Piutes: Their Wrongs and Claims*. New York: G.P. Putnam, 1883. Reprint, Reno: University of Nevada Press, 1994.

Jacobson, Matthew Frye. *Whiteness of a Different Color: European Immigrants and the Alchemy of Race*. Cambridge, MA: Harvard University Press, 1998.

Johnston, Basil H. *Indian School Days*. Toronto: Key Porter Books, 1988.

Jones, Peter. *Life and Journal of Kah-ke-wa-quo-na-by (Rev. Peter Jones), Wesleyan Missionary*. Toronto: Missionary Committee, Canada Conference, 1860.

–. (Kahkewaquonaby). *History of the Ojebway Indians: With Especial Reference to Their Conversion to Christianity*. London: A.W. Bennett, 1861.

Knockwood, Isabelle. *Out of the Depths: The Experiences of Mi'kmaw Children at the Indian Residential School at Shubenacadie, Nova Scotia*. Lockeport, NS: Roseway, 2001.

Konkle, Maureen. *Writing Indian Nations: Indian Intellectuals and the Politics of Historiography, 1827-1863*. Chapel Hill: University of North Carolina Press, 2004.

LaRocque, Emma. "The Colonization of a Native Woman Scholar." In *Women of the First Nations: Power, Wisdom, and Strength*, ed. Christina Miller and Patricia Chuchryk, 11-18. Winnipeg: University of Manitoba Press, 1996.

–. *Defeathering the Indian*. Agincourt, AB: Book Society of Canada, 1975.

–. "Native Writers Resisting Colonizing Practices in Canadian Historiography and Literature." PhD diss., University of Manitoba, 1999.

Leighton, Douglas. "The Development of Federal Indian Policy in Canada, 1840-1890." PhD diss., University of Western Ontario, 1975.

Mihesuah, Devon A., and Angela C. Wilson, eds. *Indigenizing the Academy: Transforming Scholarship and Empowering Communities*. Lincoln: University of Nebraska Press, 2004.

Miller, J.R. "'I will accept the Queen's hand': First Nations Leaders and the Image of the Crown in the Prairie Treaties," in *Reflections on Native-Newcomer Relations: Selected Essays*, ed. J.R. Miller, 242-66. Toronto: University of Toronto Press, 2004.

–. *Shingwauk's Vision: A History of Native Residential Schools.* Toronto: University of Toronto Press, 1996.

Milloy, John. *A National Crime: The Canadian Government and the Residential School System, 1879 to 1986.* Winnipeg: University of Manitoba Press, 1999.

Monture, Patricia. *Journeying Forward: Dreaming First Nations' Independence.* Halifax: Fernwood, 1999.

Monture-Angus, Patricia. *Thunder in My Soul: A Mohawk Woman Speaks.* Halifax: Fernwood, 1995.

Mountain Horse, Mike. *My People the Bloods.* Calgary/Standoff: Glenbow-Alberta Institute/Blood Tribal Council, 1979.

Paul, Daniel N. *We Were Not the Savages: A Micmac Perspective on the Collision of European and Aboriginal Civilizations.* 2nd ed. Halifax: Nimbus, 1993; Halifax: Fernwood, 2000.

Petrone, Penny. *First People, First Voices.* Toronto: University of Toronto Press, 1983.

–. *Native Literature in Canada: From the Oral Tradition to the Present.* Don Mills, ON: Oxford University Press, 1990.

Price, Richard T., ed. *The Spirit of the Alberta Indian Treaties.* Edmonton: University of Alberta Press, 1999.

Ray, Arthur J., Jim Miller, and Frank Tough. *Bounty and Benevolence: A Documentary History of Saskatchewan Treaties.* Montreal and Kingston: McGill-Queen's University Press, 2000.

Ruoff, A. LaVonne Brown. "American Indian Literature." In *Redefining American Literary History,* ed. A. LaVonne Brown Ruoff and Jerry W. Ward Jr., 327-52. New York: Modern Language Association of America, 1990.

–. "Three Nineteenth-Century American Indian Autobiographers." In *Redefining American Literary History,* ed. A. LaVonne Brown Ruoff and Jerry W. Ward Jr., 251-69. New York: Modern Language Association of America, 1990.

Saxton, Alexander. *The Rise and Fall of the White Republic: Class Politics and Mass Culture in Nineteenth-Century America.* London: Verso, 1990.

Sioui, Georges. *For an Amerindian Autohistory: An Essay on the Foundations of a Social Ethic.* Montreal and Kingston: McGill-Queen's University Press, 1992.

–. *Huron-Wendat: The Heritage of the Circle.* Vancouver: UBC Press, 1999.

Smith, Donald B. "Kahgegagahbowh: Canada's First Literary Celebrity in the United States." In *Life, Letters, and Speeches, by George Copway,* ed. by A. LaVonne Brown Ruoff and Donald B. Smith, 23-60. Lincoln: University of Nebraska Press, 1997.

–. "The Life of George Copway or Kah-ge-ga-gah-bowh (1818-1869) – and a Review of His Writings." *Journal of Canadian Studies* 23, 3 (1988): 5-38.

–. *Sacred Feathers: The Reverend Peter Jones (Kahkewaquonaby) and the Mississauga Indians.* Lincoln: University of Nebraska Press, 1987.

Smith, Linda Tuhiwai. *Decolonizing Methodologies: Research and Indigenous Peoples.* London/Dunedin: Zed Books/University of Otago Press, 1999.

Social Sciences and Humanities Research Council of Canada. "Management Response Summary: Aboriginal Pilot Program." SSHRC. http://www.sshrc.ca/site/about-crsh/ publications/arpp_evaluation_response_e.pdf.

Stevenson, Winona. "The Journals and Voices of a Church of England Native Catechist: Askenootow (Charles Pratt), 1851-1884." In *Reading Beyond Words: Contexts for Native History*, ed. Jennifer S.H. Brown and Elizabeth Vibert, 237-62. Peterborough, ON: Broadview Press, 1996.

Stonechild, Blair. *The New Buffalo: The Struggle for Aboriginal Postsecondary Education in Canada*. Winnipeg: University of Manitoba Press, 2006.

Stonechild, Blair, and Bill Waiser. *Loyal Till Death: Indians and the North-West Rebellion.* Calgary: Fifth House, 1997.

Surtees, Robert J. "Indian Land Cessions in Ontario, 1763-1862: The Evolution of a System." PhD diss., Carleton University, 1983.

–. "Treaty Research Report: Manitoulin Island Treaties." Treaties and Historical Research Centre, Indian and Northern Affairs Canada, 1986.

Treaty 7 Elders and Tribal Council, with Walter Hildebrandt, Sarah Carter, and Dorothy First Rider. *The True Spirit and Original Intent of Treaty 7*. Montreal and Kingston: McGill-Queen's University Press, 1996.

United Kingdom. *British Parliamentary Papers.* Vol. 12, *Correspondence, Returns and Other Papers relating to Canada and to the Indian Problem Therein, 1839.* Shannon: Irish University Press, 1969.

Venne, Sharon. *Indian Acts and Amendments, 1868-1975: An Indexed Collection*. Saskatoon: Native Law Centre, University of Saskatchewan, 1981.

–. *Our Elders Understand Our Rights: Evolving International Law Regarding Indigenous Peoples.* Penticton, BC: Theytus Books, 1998.

–. "Treaty 6: An Indigenous Perspective." In *Aboriginal and Treaty Rights in Canada: Essays on Law, Equality, and Respect for Difference*, ed. Michael Asch, 173-207. Vancouver: UBC Press, 2002.

Walker, Cheryl. *Indian Nation: Native American Literature and Nineteenth-Century Nationalisms*. Durham, NC: Duke University Press, 1997.

Warren, William W. *History of the Ojibways, Based Upon Traditions and Oral Statements.* St. Paul: Minnesota Historical Society, 1885.

Weaver, Sally M. *Making Canadian Indian Policy: The Hidden Agenda, 1968-1970*. Toronto: University of Toronto Press, 1981.

Wheeler, Winona. "'Ethnic' Assimilates 'Indigenous': A Study in Intellectual Neocolonialism," *Wicazo Sa Review* 13, 1 (1998): 33-51.

–, ed., "Indigenous Voices from the Great Plains." Special issue, *Oral History Forum* 19-20 (1999-2000).

Willis, Jane. *Geniesh: An Indian Girlhood.* Toronto: New Press, 1973.

2
Being Indigenous in the Academy: Creating Space for Indigenous Scholars

Margaret Kovach

I am of Plains Cree and Saulteaux ancestry and a member of the Pasqua First Nation located in the Qu'Appelle Valley of southern Saskatchewan. I was not raised in Pasqua but in a small rural community nearby. I view myself as a facilitator for Indigenous knowledges. I am not a knowledge keeper, for that has not been my training. Rather, I have worked to challenge established norms so as to open windows, possibly doors, for alternative ways of being. This has led me on a life journey within education. Education is powerful in its ability to stifle or, conversely, spark the social transformation necessary for a society to respect the diversity it holds. I have many years within post-secondary education, as a student, sessional lecturer, and curriculum developer. Recently, though hesitantly, I accepted a position as an assistant professor within a Western university. This caution, and pause, has arisen from observing Indigenous academic friends deal courageously with the inherent problems of this place and the struggle of simply being here, period. This chapter integrates my experiences of being Indigenous within the academy, though I trust that I am not alone. Furthermore, the thoughts shared herein emerge from a critical perspective on matters that require attention, not solely by Indigenous academics but also by the entire academic community.

This chapter moves beyond an analysis of why Western universities, as colonial spaces, may be problematic to focus on institutional aspects that, given an anticolonialist response, can support Indigenous scholars and the knowledge systems they bring. It is recognized that Indigenous postsecond-ary studies exist within tribal universities, colleges, and programs.[1] Indigen-ous academics who work under the auspices of tribal authorities and Western enterprises share common ground but have distinctive struggles. Although a comparative study of these groups would indeed be insightful, the focus here is on Indigenous academics within Western institutions.

This chapter is structured to align with four ways of being that influence Indigenous academic life in Western universities: mind, heart, spirit, and body. Although this textual arrangement cannot escape its linearity, the intention is to offer a snapshot of the various contradictions that reverberate in the self. The terms "Indigenous academic" and "Indigenous scholar" are used interchangeably throughout the analysis. The terms not only indicate personal identity, they also refer to Indigenous people who conduct scholarship that advances tribal knowledge and/or a decolonizing perspective. Hence, I also use the term "Indigenous academic/scholar."

Several years ago Indigenous scholar Eber Hampton wrote of the interconnection between memory, research, and scholarship and advised a return to the sacred medicine bundle of memory to understand motivation and purpose.[2] It is a perspective that honours experience as a valid form of knowledge and reflects a holistic epistemology found within tribal cultures. Furthermore, it stresses accountability to tribal knowledge systems that expect a clear purpose in the pursuit of scholarly activities, particularly when they impact on the collectivity of tribal peoples. The inclusion of narrative in this commentary aligns with the pre-eminence of story within Indigenous knowledge systems. Indigenous scholar Jo-ann Archibald situates story as a means for reflection and action; both its form and content are associated with specific knowledge systems that respect particular, subjective understandings.[3] Increasingly, Indigenous scholarly writing integrates – at minimum, acknowledges – narrative; thus, such scholarship can be identified by the recognition of this form of knowing.

A further motivation for threading narrative into this commentary is the dearth of literature that recounts the experience of Indigenous academics. Given the short history of Indigenous people in academia, this does not surprise – reasons for this under-representation can be found within colonial environments. In Canada historical, legislative barriers imposed by the Canadian state played a role. Prior to 1951 the price of a postsecondary education for a status Indian was the loss of identity. Before the *Indian Act* was revised in 1951, a status Indian who wished to attend university was automatically enfranchised.[4] The relinquishment of Indian status meant the individual lost the ability to live among kith, kin, community, and culture.[5] Such laws, in conjunction with myriad colonial obstacles, including residential school curricula that streamed students into trades, ensured low Indigenous participation in postsecondary education. Department of Indian Affairs (DIA) statistics show that between 1934 and 1976 only 2 PhD degrees and an overall total of 750 higher education degrees were awarded to Status Indians in Canada.[6] This history of structural detainment of Indigenous people's "democratic" right to pursue higher education is now manifest in the under-representation of Indigenous postsecondary educators within Canadian universities. Multiple oppressions, including those of race and class, are the hidden curricula of this colonial strategy, with the educational mechanisms sorting and stratifying efficiently. Given this history, it is no wonder that our presence, and our story, as Indigenous academics is largely missing.

My contention is that Indigenous scholars (as a collective entity) are vulnerable. This is not due to any flaw within the scholars themselves but because there are not many of us, and we are working in a tough environment. A recent 2007 statistic tells us that less than 1 percent of academic postsecondary faculty in Canada is Aboriginal.[7] Yet there is a growing trend toward the postsecondary recruitment of Indigenous students. In 1986, 23 percent of non-Registered Indians and 36 percent of on-Registered Aboriginal people were participating in postsecondary education. Ten years later these proportions had increased to 37 and 47 percent, respectively.[8] A more recent study, published in 2005, on the educational aspirations of First Nations residing in on-reserve communities found that 72 percent of individuals between the ages of sixteen and twenty-four believe they will obtain advanced education. Moreover, 70 percent of their parents hold the belief that their children will achieve a postsecondary education.[9] This suggests a growing population of Indigenous postsecondary students who will require a relevant education. Furthermore, non-Indigenous students are increasingly requesting Indigenous content within their programs. This is placing a demand upon universities to recruit and retain Indigenous postsecondary educators to meet this emerging expectation.

Although this is positive, I fear we are on the precipice of a dilemma that begs us to remember the assimilative effects of Western education without Indigenous knowledges. Furthermore, expecting Indigenous people within the academy to counter the assimilative tendencies of Western educational spaces without assistance is problematic. Hence my worries about the situation. Although such concerns warrant thought from a variety of perspectives, specific attention ought to be paid to Indigenous academics because of their specific role within postsecondary institutions, not least of which is their role as human holding dams who resist the flood of Western indoctrination that is surging through their respective academic establishments. Arguably, Indigenous academics have options; they can refuse to engage with these dominions of Western culture. Personally, this is not much of a choice for me; I would rather acknowledge (and live with) the complicity intrinsic to this identity and stay on floodgate duty. This is more about being pragmatic than virtuous, for Indigenous people have a right to participate in post-secondary education that does not violate them spiritually or culturally. Indigenous academics are uniquely positioned to serve as advocates for such space, but we need support from a number of places.

Thus, the overarching concern of this critical reflection is to ask Indigenous scholars, students, and communities and non-Indigenous university folk (including administrators) the question: What is the plan for recruiting, supporting, and retaining Indigenous academics and for ensuring that the institutions do not diminish the distinctive Indigenous scholarship that they bring? Before delving into specifics, it is useful to consider how Indigenous academics hold a distinctive location within academia, for the question lingers, are Indigenous scholars *really* different from other marginalized groups? When focusing solely upon the marginalized identity of Indigenous groups, one grapples with how Indigenous scholarship differs from that concerned with other marginalized people who struggle for representation and voice. Assuredly, there are similarities; yet Indigenous scholars' experience is unique: it rests largely within epistemology but also emerges from the historical relationship between Aboriginal peoples and the land upon which settler institutions of higher learning reside. This question is of significance because it situates the specific experience of Indigenous scholars (and scholarship), and it is vital to any effective response to this issue.

Indigenous higher education is not ahistorical; it has roots borne of the imposing presence of settler society. Colonial contextualized conversations demand a historical preface, for as Rauna Kuokkannen writes, when it comes to Indigenous peoples, "there is a peculiar and common attitude that fundamentally dissociates the past from the present."[10] This attitude is borne of a colonial majority's distaste for dredging up the past, which lends itself to a denial, or at best a peripheral assessment, of the social tensions that surge from imperial histories; furthermore, it impedes a useful, progressive response that is capable of acknowledging, but not repeating, colonial patterns of the past. For First Nations in Canada, the formal involvement of the Canadian state in their people's lives can be traced to the Royal Proclamation of 1763 and subsequent treaties that were signed between Indian nations and Canada.[11] The *British North America Act* of 1867 outlined the jurisdictional arrangement of federal and provincial authority, and the *Indian Act* assumed regulatory power over the lives of Status Indians (as defined by that Act). This overarching framework provided a context in which educational systems and colonial strategies, which included Christian missionaries and boarding and public schools, intersected with curricula that actively diminished Indigenous people and cultures. Historically, the Canadian state used education either to assimilate Indigenous people into mainstream culture or to eradicate their cultures. Educational policy for Status Indians, evoked through the *Indian Act*, consistently, and unashamedly, served this objective. In 1973 the National Indian Brotherhood released a position paper that responded to educational policy and called for Indian control of Indian education. It resulted in the formation of Indian-controlled schools in communities.[12] While the principal concern of the Indian Brotherhood was K-12 education, the organization recognized the need for adequate learning opportunities for adult Indian people. Since 1973 studies have been commissioned that reference Indigenous education (including postsecondary education), notably, the 1996 report of the Royal Commission on Aboriginal Peoples.[13] Advocacy efforts have resulted in local control of education, demand for Indigenous content within public school systems, and an increasing number of Indigenous students obtaining their high school diplomas and entering into postsecondary studies.

To access higher learning, Indigenous people are entering into colonial spaces, an experience akin to living in another's house. Such a metaphor suitably, and poignantly, encapsulates what it means for Indigenous people to participate in Western academia. Although universities sit upon ancestral land, the shape of these institutions and the ideas they hold are not Indigenous. Western academies borne of Indigenous-settler societies are the inheritors of an empirical history and are aptly described as "colonial universities."[14] Within these institutions of higher learning, rules are established and decisions are made as to what counts as knowledge and how that knowledge is generated. The governance implied and the knowledge claims made within such institutions stand at a paradigmatic distance from Indigenous ways of being. These structures and claims characterize a hegemonic relationship between the dominant and the subordinate.[15] Social theorist Antonio Gramsci was concerned with how the development and maintenance of particular "relations within and between hegemonic and subaltern classes" occurred within Italian society.[16] His theory of hegemony was later used to explain how the dominant engaged the subordinate in its own oppression, and it is useful for highlighting the manipulative-complicit dynamic evoked by colonial relations.[17] Within a Canadian context, Kulychyski proposes that the hegemony experienced by Indigenous peoples comes in the form of totalitarian actions by the state, which result in assimilation policies and practices that undermine Indigenous cultures. He argues that Indigenous politics substantively involve an assertion of distinctiveness that is tied to "land-based subsistence economy as well as to the languages, spiritualities and culture."[18] This assertion, which is based on identity, has worked powerfully to defy the totalitarian strategy of colonial politics found in the imposition of Eurocentric beliefs, religion, laws, and policy, thus moving the relationship from impartial subservience to negotiation, albeit of a compromised kind, for Indigenous peoples. Considering that Indigenous "domestication" is not, nor has it ever been, total and that Indigenous people were not conquered, the omnipresent potentiality of Indigenous self-determination remains a perpetual fly in the colonial "ointment." The early treaties, though arguably borne of coercive circumstances, provide an example of the recognition of distinct status in imperial law; the entrenchment of Aboriginal rights within the Canadian Constitution is another.[19] Indigenous involvement within contested sites suggests a strategic awareness by Indigenous people of the utility of formal arrangements for future generations. Although Indigenous mandates in these early (or subsequent) deliberations do not detract from the pervasive homogeneity of settler privilege, they do complicate it. It is not only ideology, power, and privilege but also the tacit matter of the land and what it represents that evokes discomfort by the water cooler and in the boardroom and classroom. Indigenous people have never relinquished stewardship responsibilities for their ancestral homelands, and settler society, by its own recognition, has not been able to fully dismiss the Indigenous imperative.

In colonial relations our ability to negotiate the "other" is exasperated by systems that prohibit relational opportunities and, equally, by "inclusionary" spaces that only allow the physicality of being with one another without recognizing the historical, psychological, epistemological, or spiritual complexities of being in the presence of those whom we do not fully trust. The result is inhospitable environments in which Indigenous people, as the minority, experience the cool chill. Indigenous people have always been a threat to settler society: the sharp teeth of colonially motivated racism is evidence of this. It is a racism shared by minority groups who have racial, ethnic, and cultural differences that distinguish them from the Eurocentric norm; in colonial sites, it is also a racism that specifically targets *Indigenous* identity. The 2008 report of Toronto's School Community Safety Advisory Panel found that within one large Toronto-based school only 0.3 percent of students in Grades 7 to 11 identify as Aboriginal, which was an under-representation of the actual proportion of Aboriginal students in those grades. In this same study, 2 percent of children in Grades 7 to 11 reported that they had experienced victimization because of their Aboriginal ancestry. The re-searchers assert that self-identifying as Aboriginal is a risk factor for young people and that Aboriginal students are not self-identifying because of the victimization potential of declaring their cultural identity.[20] Such studies document the heightened tensions experienced by Indigenous peoples living in colonial spaces, tensions that are intensified in co-racial educational in-stitutions such as universities. Yet educational sites continue to be places of reckoning, places where we can re-examine our colonial history and re-vision future relationships. Where once Indigenous people were excluded from higher learning and struggled simply to get in the door, the landscape has now changed. Indigenous people are entering postsecondary environments, and our presence demands that academia examine a plethora of issues to create a holistically inclusive learning environment. The infusion of Aborig-inal content into academic programming, the emergence of tribal universities, and the merging of distributed learning and Indigenous communities are ways in which the shift is taking place. A revitalization of national interest in Aboriginal education with a specific focus on postsecondary education is warranted. Such a development would help us to revisit the historical back-drop from which Indigenous postsecondary education has emerged, and postsecondary education will remain a natural extension of colonial educa-tion if it is not monitored vigilantly.

It is this complex Indigenous-settler history and their independent pos-ition within it that differentially situates Indigenous scholars. This is a chal-lenge for those who engage with intellectual questions, including Indigenous academics, and who, by necessity, must grapple with epistemological con-siderations. Within the Indigenous-settler relations of Western universities, this challenge is particularly complex.

Mind

In this rumination on the relationship between Indigenous scholars and tribal knowledges in an academic setting, I address the contradictions experienced by Aboriginal scholars who serve distinctive thought paradigms, the emergent response of non-Indigenous scholars, and strategies for supporting both

scholars and epistemologies of tribal knowledge systems. Indigenous knowledges are community-based, contextual, holistic, and interpretative. They
cannot be objectified or commodified, nor can they be held within institutional spaces. The knowledges sit in story, history, place, and with people.
They defy theoretical categorization and exist on their own terms. Indigenous
knowledges are imbued with a fluidity that is bound to place but can never
be fully captured within an institutional net. Although they do not dismiss
the empirical knowledges that accompany observational methods, tribal
knowledge systems do decentre empirical objectivism. Indigenous scholar
Gregory Cajete explains the rationale within research and education: "Objective research has contributed a dimension of insight, but it has substantial
limitation in the multidimensional, holistic, and relational reality of the
education of Indigenous people."[21] Within Western academia, there is a growing recognition of these two differing knowledge paradigms but less discussion
about how the structures of the institution support a co-epistemological
foundation. Such difficulties are evident in research frameworks that seek to
incorporate Indigenous knowledge perspectives.

Research methodologies are the place where theory meets practice in the
creation of new knowledge. In this context, Indigenous epistemologies have
far-reaching ripples. Within research frameworks, there exists an exacting
worldview; regardless of whether the epistemology is overt or hidden, the
choices we make in research design reflect assumptions about knowledge.
Indigenous knowledge systems arise from a distinctive knowledge paradigm
with its own methods. If one proposes an Indigenous research framework
situated in tribal knowledge, it will not mirror grounded theory and participatory action research, it will involve the development of a research methodology, congruent with tribal epistemologies, that reflects the distinctive
approach of Indigenous knowledge systems to the generation of new knowledges. Many non-Indigenous scholars, for a number of reasons, cannot assess
tribal knowledges on their own terms; a more pervasive difficulty is that they
cannot recognize tribal methodologies.

More often, the approach to Indigenous epistemology (either in research
or pedagogy) is a form of "Indianism" that – as David Newhouse, Don
McCaskill, and John Milloy observe – involves an anthropological explica-
tion of Indigenous perspectives without the incorporation of Indigenous
voices and ideas.[22] This is slowly starting to shift because of a role displace-
ment among non-Indigenous scholars that coincides with an increasing

responsibility to be accountable to and conversant with Indigenous knowledges in an anticolonial manner. Non-Indigenous scholars have responded to the uncertainty of living in new territory in a variety of ways, including frustrated backlash or despondency, respectful disengagement, or significant outreach to Indigenous scholars. Non-Indigenous scholars can, however, come to understand Indigenous knowledges and tribal epistemologies by forming community relationships with Aboriginal communities outside the academy. These relationships will demand a more organic, non-institutional approach to knowledge-seeking. If Indigenous knowledges are to flourish, there must be room for story, purpose, place, holism, and protocol, for the ceremonial, relational, and spiritual aspects of life, all of which demand a natural, non-institutional learning environment.

Indigenous academics are being asked to subsume an overarching responsibility that coincides with the infusion of Indigenous knowledges into academia, a task that demands skills in addition to those used by decolonizing, anti-oppressive scholars. This involves a layered approach that begins with decolonization and moves to deeper waters to explore what it means to be in accord with tribal philosophy. The stewardship responsibilities that this process will demand of Indigenous academics are great. Respected Indigenous scholars have acknowledged contradictions inherent in bringing our knowledges into the academy.[23] Even if we were to reconcile ourselves with the perils of bringing Indigenous knowledges into a colonial space, along with all of the ethical considerations inherent in this proposition, the knowledges themselves will never fully find a home in another's house. As Angela Cavender Wilson has argued, we are starting at a compromised place.[24] Yet, as the academy shifts to involve Indigenous participation, it must include rather than diminish, subsume, overpower, or disrespect tribal epistemologies. How can this be accomplished; where should we start? Devon Abbott Mihesuah suggests that taking Indigenous knowledges seriously means pushing at the gates that protect the ontological, epistemological, and ideological assumptions that power the academy.[25] There is no doubt that academia includes gated communities: Who gets hired and why? What gets taught and why? Who gets published and why? Who gets to be principal investigator and why? and so on. From practical reasons, Mihesuah proposes multiple strategies to uphold Indigenous knowledges in Western universities. Her plan includes supporting the interdisciplinary nature of Indigenous scholarship; maintaining the distinctive nature of Indigenous pedagogy; seeking out sources of funding to assist individual scholarships and programs; supporting one another as Indigenous peoples and recognizing gender disparities between Indigenous men and women in the academy; pushing for more Indigenous faculty in higher education; serving as advocates for social justice and not letting racism, sexism, or any other "ism" slide; using more Indigenous theories; and using Indigenous knowledges and language in a respectful fashion.[26] I would add that gatherings at the local, territorial, provincial and/or state, and national levels should be held to call upon Indigenous communities, scholars, postsecondary students, and allies to respond to the needs of Indigenous higher education.

Given that academia is about the production of knowledge, it is no wonder that matters pertaining to thought are of primary importance to Aboriginal scholars. In the academy, the method of producing new knowledge, in conjunction with the knowledge itself, has been normalized, rendered acultural, and decontextualized. Once it has been accepted by the community of Western scholars, this knowledge becomes "truth." While alternative systems of knowledge are entertained, and possibly tolerated, they live in marginal places within the institution. However, if, as the academy claims, it is interested in Indigenous ways of knowing, what it means "to know" must be reconsidered. As was mentioned previously, this poses an intellectual conundrum: non-Indigenous academics may have analytical insights into the socio-political circumstances of Indigenous peoples, but they do not have equal insight into Indigenous knowledges. Appreciating Indigenous knowledges requires engaging with a relationally imbued form of scholarship, which is quite different from the norm. Indigenous knowledges exist beyond the parameters of what established Western knowledge systems can grapple with, given the current fragmentation of Western thought. And before this work can begin, there needs to be a recognition that Indigenous knowledges matter.

Body

To express my thoughts about the physicality of experience, I want to return to numbers, because numbers are tangibles that can tell a story. Numbers, on their own, are malleable and can be bent at the storyteller's convenience. Take, for example, my home province, Saskatchewan. Statistical projection tells us that the population of Indigenous students in Saskatchewan schools will increase to 35 percent by 2017.[27] This statistic can be interpreted to suggest that more Indigenous children are entering the school system, building a critical mass, and it could possibly indicate a socio-economic upswing for Indigenous communities. Conversely, this statistic could be interpreted to suggest that more Indigenous children are entering an ill-prepared school system that is facing an emerging crisis. To respond to the projected numbers, the Saskatchewan education system must train and hire more Indigenous teachers. This will require more support for the existing Indigenous post-secondary teacher education programs and the recruitment of Indigenous teachers into the mainstream teacher education program. Furthermore, non-Indigenous teachers, who will potentially have a profound impact on Indigenous children's lives, must be introduced to decolonizing pedagogies. Within education faculties, Indigenous academics have the best odds of attracting, training, and retaining Indigenous student teachers and incorporating decolonizing pedagogies into the education of non-Indigenous teachers.

However, there are a number of specific institutional stressors placed upon Indigenous academics that will complicate the experience of being an Indigenous scholar. First, it is difficult simply being an individual of Indigenous identity in the academy for a variety of reasons, many of which have already been identified in this chapter. Second, Indigenous academics are, for the most part, fully cognizant of the Indigenous-settler dynamic and are actively engaged in decolonizing scholarship. This renders both Aboriginal and non-Aboriginal scholars hyperalert to the ideological and political residues of colonialism that float through the postsecondary work environment and rouse internal and external conflicts on a daily basis. Given the discomfort, most Indigenous scholars find purpose in being here – in the academy. In 1969 Indigenous scholar Vine Deloria Jr. foresaw that, because the problems of Indigenous peoples are primarily ideological, the arena of confrontation would be the academy.[28] To disengage from postsecondary universities is to forfeit possibilities for the next generation. Indigenous people are participating in postsecondary education; they wish to be there and are voting with their feet by walking into these sites. If Indigenous people are not represented at all institutional levels, we will lose our ability to advocate effectively for meaningful education. Yet, I am reminded of Russell Means and a question he asked of Indigenous people entering postsecondary institutions: What are *you* doing *there*?[29] His question served as a warning about the manipulative force of Western institutions and the danger of losing one's tribal sense of self.

What am *I* doing *here*? My sense is that Indigenous academics are intricately connected to the goal of upholding Indigenous communities. However, the fact that each Indigenous academic could interpret this goal differently heightens the complexity of decolonizing the academy and creates new internal Indigenous politics. Mohawk scholar Taiaiake Alfred suggests that there are Indigenous academics who "walk in beauty on the peaceful path to irrelevance," those who cave in too quickly to the colonial construct of university relations by acquiescing to knowledge paradigms that are not their own.[30] Not being aware of the hegemonic conditions of this livelihood, and the complicity it implies, is to be manipulated into serving the status quo. Choosing not to see the perils of being Indigenous in Western universities is a way of resisting the decolonization of the academy. However, heightened awareness, along with a consistent sense that our utility is being evaluated daily (internally and externally), and often at cross-purposes, is challenging and is not necessarily compatible with tenure.

Hyper-vigilance toward the manipulative forces of hegemonic institutions is complicated by the fact that Indigenous scholars are held accountable to two divergent interests. Indigenous scholars who uphold decolonizing scholarship reverberate with the contradictions of serving the Indigenous community from inside the academy. Dual accountability is not new to Indigenous people or academic settings. In a former life, as a training manager for First Nations child welfare, this was a consistent theme in my career and those of my co-workers. The tension of serving two diverging authorities, and dealing with value conflicts, heightened the level of workers' stress. It is not so much the physical demand of involving oneself in tasks associated with each authority (though that can be a challenge); rather, it is the emotional toil of serving conflicting worldviews that engenders physical discomfort. In academia this is manifested in simple, tedious, daily encounters that range from linear classroom-seating arrangements, which symbolize a distinctly Western approach to learning, to the dismissal of Indigenous knowledges as legitimate ways of knowing. Indigenous scholars must also sit in circle with community members, many of whom distrust the Western knowledges that Indigenous scholars represent simply because they are employed by Western universities. Indigenous academics find ways to negotiate dual accountabilities, but it takes a toll.

Returning to the discussion of numbers, universities that wish to hire more Indigenous faculty are increasingly becoming aware that there is no proverbial Indigenous PhD garden patch from which they can pick job candidates. What can be done? We have a good sense of why there are so few candidates, but how can we change this? One development has been the creation of the Supporting Aboriginal Graduate Enhancement (SAGE) program.[31] The goal of this program is to increase the number of Indigenous academics; however, the issue is not simply a numbers game. The spirit of the program is to ensure that Indigenous people can participate in doctoral studies that provide opportunities to integrate, infuse, consider, and explore decolonizing and tribal knowledges. Emerging Indigenous scholars with doctorates from SAGE programs will be well placed to engage with the academy. Similiar initiatives are needed to prepare Indigenous scholars for the dual, often conflicting, responsibilities that he or she has to the community and the academy. A critical mass of Indigenous academics prepared for the particular demands of Indigenous scholarship will be a tool to work toward parity, of a critical kind, between Indigenous and non-Indigenous scholars within the academy. If one believes that the overuse of scant resources will lead to depletion, then the need for more Indigenous academics is apparent. What we are doing here is deeply purposeful, given that we are few and the needs of the next generation are many. That being said, it ain't easy street.

Heart

Given that the human condition comprises an interconnected web of experiences, I am hard pressed to isolate any one specific experience that evokes deep feeling. Yet, if asked, I know my response: it is racism. These days in universities, racial privilege takes a more covert and less confrontational form. It reveals itself in more sophisticated, institutional manifestations. It may be less tangible, but it is no less personal. And it exists. Frances Henry and Carol Tator argue that Eurocentricism continues to pervade the academy. "How can you tell?" they ask. "One important indicator of this is the under-representation of Aboriginal people and people of color in the system."[32] This under-representation is a clear indicator that systemic racism, of which, arguably, most Western academic institutions are guilty, persists in the academy. Knowing this generates in me a great sadness, because it suggests that social relations in academia will continue to mirror those of the larger society. In my experience, the emotional toll has not been so much from the experience of direct racism but rather from the ache of decolonizing colonial spaces.

Instruction goes hand in hand with scholarship, and, for Indigenous faculty, instruction is a central task. I have taught an introductory course on Indigenous issues for many years. It is a core course that all students in the department have to take to get their degree. The majority of students are of European ancestry, and, for many, the course is the first time they have had to examine their stereotypical assumptions about Indigenous peoples. The course is really about decolonizing people's mind, hearts, and spirits. These introductory decolonization courses are common and seem to follow a consistent pattern. Daniel Heath Justice, an Indigenous faculty member who teaches Aboriginal literature, outlines the two-pronged process that is involved in their instruction. Initially, these courses focus on "deconstructing the hackneyed stereotypes [that students have] absorbed in seventeen-plus years of life"; they then require students to consider Indigenous ways in a respectful manner.[33] Personally, I find dealing with the stereotypes quite painful. For example, students inevitably feel the need to express negative stereotypes of Indigenous peoples as they explain how they used to think (or how others think), and as they assure the class that they now know better. I tell students that free speech does not mean racist expression, even if it is done with good intentions, as is the inevitable claim. It is difficult because academic classrooms are contradictory places where many racist stereotypes about Indigenous people were born in the form of empirical, anthropological research. It is no wonder that students absorb the old energies that resonate in these rooms. It is an effort to stay vigilant on this front, for people want to slip back. The expectation that students will confront stereotypes angers students who see decolonizing, respectful communication as work they did not necessarily sign up for. To decolonize classrooms is emotionally taxing, yet it is in the classroom that I find purpose. As bell hooks so appropriately declared in the title of one of her books, we are "teaching to transgress."[34] If postsecondary institutions are a site of struggle for Indigenous faculty, classrooms are the front line. When you peel through enough of the layers, it becomes apparent that much of colonialism is driven by people acting out of fear.

The deep feelings that accompany being Indigenous in a bastion of Western privilege are felt in the hallways as well as in the classrooms. Increasingly, attracting Indigenous students is being identified as a priority, and, as universities allocate resources to this end, quiet resentments reveal themselves in many different ways: exclusion, chilly climate, and so forth. After all, taking space is taking space, and it is not always appreciated. In this context, I can understand some Indigenous scholars' desire to retreat from it all, but, given our small number, this should not be an option. We are all needed on the decolonizing front. To assist, there are strong arguments in favour of the settler doing his or her own work to hasten decolonization. To unsettle the settler, non-Indigenous scholar Paulette Regan challenges those of settler origin to undertake their own decolonizing work in four thematic areas:

responsibility, identity and myth, history, and truth telling.[35] But how should non-Indigenous scholars, who work on Indigenous questions, deal with the contradictions they face? While I cannot answer this question in full, because I am Indigenous, I can offer some places to begin. First and foremost, it is important for non-Indigenous scholars to recognize that the scene has shifted over the past five to ten years. In a non-static world, decolonization is ongoing, and the question that needs to be re-evaluated frequently is whether one is making space or taking space. There are a few non-Indigenous scholars who have made this shift effectively and become essential resource people. They have figured out how to serve Indigenous communities in a respectful way by being honest, humble, helpful, and relevant. This is a tall order, given that there is the temptation (or perhaps the habit?) of applying totemic window dressing to Indigenous research activities and calling them "consultation," a word that makes me twitch. Respected non-Indigenous scholars tend to focus not on consultation but rather on relationship building, the two processes being substantively different.

Within the academy non-Indigenous scholars and researchers who are committed allies use their positions and networks to serve Indigenous peoples. They have skills borne of relationships with Indigenous communities; they know when to step up and when to step back. How did they come by this awareness, and what are the unique contradictions they face? I do not have the answers, but my experience tells me that these folks have humility, a sense of humour, and are attuned – all of which are relational skills. The answer is not a formulaic response; rather, it derives from intuitive knowledge about specific situations that can emerge during a lengthy relationship with Indigenous communities. There is no short cut: the non-Indigenous scholars who maintain a successful relationship with Indigenous scholars and scholarship have gone to communities, and they keep going back. I encourage non-Indigenous scholars who have worked effectively with Indigneous communities to share their stories.

For all academics, the work of decolonization continues to be central, unsettling, and pervasive. Vine Deloria Jr. wrote with concern about Indigenous scholars who want to sidestep the distasteful politics of our plight. In effect, he said to us, "Don't kid yourself, every bit of who you are as an Indigenous scholar is political in this place. It is unlikely that meritocracy, hard work and fair play are going to serve you well."[36] His point is that, for Indigenous academics, universities do not provide a level playing field. Emotionally, this section is hard to write, because it traces the overt and insidious ways that institutional mandates can devalue Indigenous ways of being. Given the epistemological, practical, and emotional challenges of Indigenous scholarship, why would Indigenous scholars stay in the academy? I want to leave this chapter on a hopeful note, so I turn to my thoughts on spirit.

Spirit

To me, spirit is that which uplifts and gives hope. In my work, I find spirit manifests itself consistently in meaningfulness. Participating in higher education holds much purpose for Indigenous peoples and communities. As Indigenous scholars, our work matters, and we need to keep pushing at the edges on several fronts.

The connection between Indigenous academics and their communities nourishes spirit. This means honouring the values of respect, reciprocity, and relevance, which manifest themselves in a variety of ways; but the bottom line is that we must engage with community. This is done through our familial and community service relationships and through our connections to Indigenous students, staff, and faculty who represent community within the academy. As Indigenous academics, we integrate these relationships into our work with students by taking educational programs to communities. I was involved in the development and instruction of an Indigenous research course. One goal of the curriculum was to encompass the varied knowledges that influence knowledge construction. The course included an experiential field trip that gave instructors and students the opportunity to be in community and culture. We were able to walk the ancestral trails on Coast Salish territory with a cultural guide. As we were walking by the river, among the ancient trees, we embraced a way of knowing that cannot be replicated in the classroom. Recently, I was able to join an Indigenous group of instructors and students for a cultural ceremony led by a community healer in a First Nations community. After the ceremony, we gathered to share food and laughter and simply be in relation to one another. My doctoral defence was held at an urban Friendship Centre amid community, family, and friends. I integrated an honouring and food into the proceedings for those who came to witness this significant milestone in my life. It took extra effort, but it was a small way to honour community relationships.

Carrying out these activities in good ways is but one indication of the time that must be invested to build relationships. Certainly, if relationship building and research activities were given the same amount of value in the academy, this would not be problematic. However, relationship building does not show the same structured output as research; it cannot be measured in terms of Western efficiency. It is here that worldviews conflict. When cultural activities are listed beside publications, awards, and conference presentations in a curriculum vitae, Western universities do not give them equal weight. In a certain cultural context, the power-packed academic curriculum vitae appears to be little more than self-aggrandizement, which contradicts the value of humbleness. Indigenous scholars who have attained a high level of education do experience a certain amount of backlash from some (not all) Indigenous community members. Although these are seemingly small matters, they add to the value contradictions that cause a rub.

The academy that will benefit Indigenous peoples (and society more generally) will be one that openly accepts a more holistic, broader range of knowledges. It will require a shift from clinging to one approach to fit all to valuing knowledge-creation approaches for what they contribute toward curiosity. In both research and instruction, perspectives as divergent as Indigenous knowledges require due space. In tandem, the academy needs to provide evidence that it supports Indigenous scholarship. Evidence includes increasing the number of Indigenous faculty, revitalizing curricula to mirror a commitment to Indigenous issues, persevering in community engagement, putting in place promotional policies to acknowledge community work, and instituting university ethical reviews that reflect Indigenous protocols and resource allocation. There are multiple ways to approach these changes, many of which are at the structural level and will require planning, the more comprehensive the better. For everyone involved, the responsibility of listening to Indigenous postsecondary needs implies moving toward action that expands and strengthens the Indigenous presence within the academy. This shift will help to ease some of the contradictions experienced by Indigenous scholars, and it will revitalize the academy so it remains relevant to society. Furthermore, such a shift will make the academy a more hospitable environment, one that nourishes all of our spirits.

Conclusion

In this chapter I have referenced several avenues for change, but this is not a manifesto. A manifesto would imply that creating space in academia is solely up to Indigenous peoples. It is not. It is a social responsibility that demands the attention of all who seek a more respectful way of being in the world, if not for a deep love of Indigenous peoples, then for a love of the land that is stewarded by Indigenous people. I need to point no further than

the ecological fiasco toward which Western society is heading. For all their
potential to move sideways, universities continue to be a haven for the sacred
possibility of ideological shifts that can lead us out of our collective disarray.
From its earliest incarnation, the academy has been a protective grove for
great minds (and hearts) to stoke the embers of wisdom and justice. We must
remember that this place is a powerful sanctuary for visioning and change.

In concluding this commentary on being an Indigenous academic in
Western universities, my mind flashes back to a memory and a sign that suggests that divergent voices may be nurtured in the academy. A number of years
ago, during my doctoral journey, I had the task of identifying possible super-
visors for my committee and made an appointment with a non-Indigenous
faculty member. I remember walking into her office. It was a typical academic office, with books set out on a wall shelf, a filing cabinet with articles
piled on top, and a bulletin board above the desk. As I sat down, my eyes
focused on the fully laden corkboard, in the left-hand corner of which was
a crisp white sheet of paper on which I could see the Leonard Cohen lyrics:
"There is a crack in everything, / That's how the light gets in."[37] These words
on a wall were not particularly Indigenous-relevant, yet I have held them in
memory because they stir a sense of possibility. I believe increasingly, though
with a cautious faith, that Indigenous scholarship is being taken seriously in
postsecondary education. However, the challenges facing Indigenous scholars require attention for the light to fully enter the academy. In closing, I
return to Eber Hampton's reminder to value memory and story. I think about
the pushpin note with the Leonard Cohen lyrics on it. I have listened to
Cohen's ragged, strained voice crooning these lines time and again in my
mind. As I write about Indigenous scholarship and our relationships with
allies in the academy, I hear him reassuring me, "There is a crack in everything,
/ That's how the light gets in," and I think it is not impossible to create space
for Indigenous scholarship in the academy ... it is only hard.

NOTES

1   Tribal postsecondary institutions include the First Nations University of Canada
    and Nicola Valley Institute of Technology (where university credit programs are
    offered). The Indian Teacher Education Program (ITEP) and the Saskatchewan
    Urban Native Teacher Education Program (SUNTEP) are examples of programs
    that have relationships with Western universities but operate independently from
    them.

2   Eber L. Hampton, "Memory Comes before Knowledge: Research May Improve if Researchers Remember Their Motives," *Canadian Journal of Native Education* 21 (1995): S46-S54.

3   Jo-ann Archibald, "Editorial: Sharing Aboriginal Knowledge and Aboriginal Ways of Knowing," *Canadian Journal of Native Education* 25, 1 (2001): 1-5.

4   Blair Stonechild, *The New Buffalo: The Struggle for Aboriginal Post-Secondary Education in Canada* (Winnipeg: University of Manitoba Press, 2006).

5   Canada, House of Commons, Standing Committee on Aboriginal Affairs and Northern Development, *No Higher Priority: Aboriginal Post-Secondary Education in Canada*, February 2007, 39th Parliament, 1st Session.

6   Stonechild, *The New Buffalo*, 42.

7   Helen Brelauer, "Academic Restructuring and Equality," *Journal of Higher Education – Academic Matters* (April 2007): 20-22.

8   R.A. Malatest, *Aboriginal Peoples and Post-Secondary Education: What Educators Have Learned* (Montreal: R.A. Malatest & Associates, 2004), 7.

9   Canada, Millennium Scholarships Foundation, *Changing Course: Improving Access to Post-Secondary Education in Canada*, September 2005, Millennium Research Note no. 2, http://www.millenniumscholarships.ca/en/research/OthePublications.asp.

10 Rauna Kuokkanen, "Towards a New Relation of Hospitality in the Academy," *American Indian Quarterly* 27, 1 and 2 (2003): 267-95.

11 I use the term "First Nation" in this context to reference this group specifically, as opposed to Indigenous people in general.

12 Jean Barman, Yvonne Hébert, and Don McCaskill, eds., *Indian Education in Canada*, vol. 1, *The Legacy* (Vancouver: UBC Press, 1986), 16.

13 Canada, Royal Commission on Aboriginal Peoples, *Report of the Royal Commission on Aboriginal Peoples*, vol. 3, *Gathering Strength* (Ottawa: Canada Communications Group, 1996).

14 Linda Tuhiwai Smith, *Decolonizing Methodologies: Research and Indigenous Peoples* (London/Dunedin: Zed Books/University of Otago Press, 1999), 65.

15 R.W. Connell, "Knowledge, Objectivity and Hegemony," in *Schools and Social Justice*, ed. R.W. Connell (Toronto: Our Schools Ourselves, 1993), 30-42.

16 Andrew Wells, "Imperial Hegemony and Colonial Labor," *Rethinking Marxism* 19, 2 (2007): 181.

17 See, for example, Peter Kulchyski, "Aboriginal Peoples and Hegemony in Canada." *Journal of Canadian Studies* 30, 1 (1995): 60-68; Wells, "Imperial Hegemony," 181.

18 Kulchyski, "Aboriginal Peoples and Hegemony," 63.

19 On imperial law, see Sheila Carr-Stewart, "A Treaty Right to Education," *Canadian Journal of Native Education* 26, 2 (2001): 125-43.

20 School Community Safety Advisory Panel, *The Road to Health: A Final Report on School Safety*, vol. 3, 2008, http://www.schoolsafetypanel.com/finalReport, 526.

21 Gregory Cajete, *Look to the Mountain: An Ecology of Indigenous Education* (Skyland, NC: Kivaki Press, 1994), 21.

22 David Newhouse, Don McCaskill, and John Milloy, "Culture, Tradition and Evolution: The Department of Native Studies at Trent University," in *Native American Studies in Higher Education: Models for Collaboration between Universities and Indigenous Nations*, ed. Duane Champagne and Jay Strauss (Walnut Creek, CA: AltaMira Press, 2002), 78.

23 See, for example, Marie Battiste and James (Sákéj) Youngblood Henderson, *Protecting Indigenous Knowledge and Heritage* (Saskatoon: Purich, 2000); Leroy Little Bear, "Jagged Worldviews Colliding," in *Reclaiming Indigenous Voice and Vision*, ed. Marie Battiste (Vancouver: UBC Press, 2004), 77-88; Richard Atleo, *Tsawalk: A Nuu-chah-nulth Worldview* (Vancouver: UBC Press, 2004); Gregory Cajete, *Native Science: Natural Laws of Interdependence* (Santa Fe: Clear Light Publishing, 1997); Anne Water, *American Indian Thought: Philosophical Essays* (Malden, MA: Blackwell Publishing, 2003).

24 Angela Cavender Wilson, "Reclaiming Our Humanity: Decolonization and the Recovery of Indigenous Knowledges," in *Indigenizing the Academy: Transforming Scholarship and Empowering Communities*, ed. Devon Abbott Mihesuah and Angela Cavendear Wilson (Lincoln: University of Nebraska Press, 2004), 73.

25 Devon Abbott Mihesuah, "Academic Gatekeepers," in *Indigenizing the Academy*, ed. Mihesuah and Wilson, 32-33.

26 Devon Abbott Mihesuah, "Indigenizing the Academy: Keynote Talk at the Sixth Annual American Indian Studies Consortium Conference," *Wicazo Sa Review* 21, 1 (2006): 131-37.

27 Vivian Hajnal, "The Changing Face of Saskatchewan Schools," unpublished report prepared for the College of Education, University of Saskatchewan, 2007, 1.

28 Vine Deloria Jr., *Custer Died for Your Sins: An Indian Manifesto* (New York: Macmillan, 1969), 251-52.

29 Russell Means, "The Same Old Song," in *Marxism and Native Americans*, ed. Ward Churchill (Boston: South End Press, 1989), 32.

30 Taiaiake Alfred, "Indigenizing the Academy? An Argument Against?" *Journal of Higher Education: Academic Matters* (February 2007): 22.

31 David Holmes, *Redressing the Balance: Canadian University Programs in Support of Aboriginal Students* (Ottawa: Canadian Association of Universities and Colleges, 2006), 15.

32 Frances Henry and Carol Tator, "Through a Looking Glass," *Journal of Higher Education: Academic Matters* (February 2007): 24.

33 Daniel Heath Justice, "Seeing (and Reading) Red: Indian Outlaws in the Ivory Tower," in *Indigenizing the Academy*, ed. Mihesuah and Wilson, 111.

34 bell hooks, *Teaching to Transgress: Education as the Practice of Freedom* (New York: Routledge, 1994).

35 Paulette Regan, "Decolonizing Dialogues and Historical Conflicts" (paper presented to First Nations Symposium, Royal Roads University, Victoria, 22 November 2006).

36 Vine Deloria Jr., "Marginal and Submarginal," in *Indigenizing the Academy*, ed. Mihesuah and Wilson, 27.

37 Leonard Cohen, "Anthem," *The Future*, © 1992 Leonard Cohen and Sony/ATV Music Publishing Canada Company.

WORKS CITED

Alfred, Taiaiake. "Indigenizing the Academy? An Argument Against?" *Journal of Higher Education – Academic Matters* (February 2007): 22-23.

Archibald, Jo-ann. "Editorial: Sharing Aboriginal Knowledge and Aboriginal Ways of Knowing." *Canadian Journal of Native Education* 25, 1 (2001): 1-5.

Atleo, Richard. *Tsawalk: A Nuu-chah-nulth Worldview*. Vancouver: UBC Press, 2004.

Barman, Jean, Yvonne Hébert, and Don McCaskill, eds. *Indian Education in Canada*. Vol. 1, *The Legacy*. Vancouver: UBC Press, 1986.

Battiste, Marie, and James (Sákéj) Youngblood Henderson. *Protecting Indigenous Knowledge and Heritage*. Saskatoon: Purich, 2000.

Brelauer, Helen. "Academic Restructuring and Equality." *Journal of Higher Education: Academic Matters* (April 2007): 20-22.

Cajete, Gregory. *Look to the Mountain: An Ecology of Indigenous Education*. Skyland, NC: Kivaki Press, 1994.

–. *Native Science: Natural Laws of Interdependence*. Santa Fe: Clear Light Publishing, 1997.

Canada. House of Commons. Standing Committee on Aboriginal Affairs and Northern Development. *No Higher Priority: Aboriginal Post-Secondary Education in Canada*. February 2007, 39th Parliament, 1st Session.

–. Millennium Scholarships Foundation. *Changing Course: Improving Access to Post-Secondary Education in Canada*. Millennium Research Note no. 2. http://www.millenniumscholarships.ca/en/research/OthePublications.asp.

–. Royal Commission on Aboriginal Peoples. *Report of the Royal Commission on Aboriginal Peoples*. Vol. 3, *Gathering Strength*. Ottawa: Canada Communications Group, 1996.

Carr-Stewart, Sheila. "A Treaty Right to Education." *Canadian Journal of Native Education* 26, 2 (2001): 125-43.

Cohen, Leonard. "Anthem." *The Future*. © 1992 Leonard Cohen and Sony/ATV Music Publishing Canada Company.

Connell, R.W. "Knowledge, Objectivity and Hegemony." In *Schools and Social Justice*, ed. R.W. Connell, 30-42. Toronto: Our Schools Ourselves, 1993.

Deloria, Vine, Jr. *Custer Died for Your Sins: An Indian Manifesto*. New York: Macmillan, 1969.

–. "Marginal and Submarginal." In *Indigenizing the Academy: Transforming Scholarship and Empowering Communities*, ed. Devon Abbott Mihesuah and Angela Cavender Wilson, 16-30. Lincoln: University of Nebraska Press, 2004.

Hajnal, Vivian. "The Changing Face of Saskatchewan Schools." Unpublished report for the College of Education, University of Saskatchewan, 2007.

Hampton, Eber L. "Memory Comes before Knowledge: Research May Improve if Researchers Remember Their Motives." *Canadian Journal of Native Education* 21 (1995): S46-S54.

Henry, Frances, and Carol Tator. "Through a Looking Glass." *The Journal of Higher Education: Academic Matters* (February 2007): 24-25.

Holmes, David. *Redressing the Balance: Canadian University Programs in Support of Aboriginal Students*. Ottawa: Canadian Association of Universities and Colleges, 2006.

hooks, bell. *Teaching to Transgress: Education as the Practice of Freedom*. New York: Routledge, 1994.

Justice, Daniel Heath. "Seeing (and Reading) Red: Indian Outlaws in the Ivory Tower." In *Indigenizing the Academy: Transforming Scholarship and Empowering Communities*, ed. Devon Abbott Mihesuah and Angela Cavender Wilson, 100-23. Lincoln: University of Nebraska Press, 2004.

Kulchyski, Peter. "Aboriginal Peoples and Hegemony in Canada." *Journal of Canadian Studies* 30, 1 (1995): 60-68.

Kuokkanen, Rauna. "Towards a New Relation of Hospitality in the Academy." *American Indian Quarterly* 27, 1 and 2 (2003): 267-95.

Little Bear, Leroy. "Jagged Worldviews Colliding." In *Reclaiming Indigenous Voice and Vision*, ed. Marie Battiste, 77-85. Vancouver: UBC Press, 2004.

Malatest, R.A. *Aboriginal Peoples and Post-Secondary Education: What Educators Have Learned*. Montreal: R.A. Malatest & Associates Ltd, 2004.

Means, Russell. "The Same Old Song." In *Marxism and Native Americans*, ed. Ward Churchill, 19-33. Boston: South End Press, 1989.

Mihesuah, Devon Abbott. "Academic Gatekeepers." In *Indigenizing the Academy: Transforming Scholarship and Empowering Communities*, ed. Devon Abbott Mihesuah and Angela Cavender Wilson, 31-47. Lincoln: University of Nebraska Press, 2004.

–. "Indigenizing the Academy: Keynote Talk at the Sixth Annual American Indian Studies Consortium Conference." *Wicazo Sa Review* 21, 1 (2006): 131-37.

Newhouse, David, Don McCaskill, and John Milloy. "Culture, Tradition and Evolution: The Department of Native Studies at Trent University." In *Native American Studies in Higher Education: Models for Collaboration between Universities and Indigenous Nations*, ed. Duane Champagne and Jay Strauss, 61-82. Walnut Creek, CA: AltaMira Press, 2002.

Regan, Paulette. "Decolonizing Dialogues and Historical Conflicts." Paper presented to First Nations Symposium, Royal Roads University, Victoria, 22 November 2006.

School Community Safety Advisory Panel. *The Road to Health: A Final Report on School Safety*, Vol. 3, 2008. http://www.schoolsafetypanel.com/finalReport.

Smith, Linda Tuhiwai. *Decolonizing Methodologies: Research and Indigenous Peoples*. London/Dunedin: Zed Books/University of Otago Press, 1999.

Stonechild, Blair. *The New Buffalo: The Struggle for Aboriginal Post-Secondary Education in Canada*. Winnipeg: University of Manitoba Press, 2006.

Water, Anne. *American Indian Thought: Philosophical Essays*. Malden, MA: Blackwell Publishing, 2003.

Wells, Andrew. "Imperial Hegemony and Colonial Labor." *Rethinking Marxism* 19, 2 (2007): 180-94.

Wilson, Angela Cavender. "Reclaiming Our Humanity: Decolonization and the Recovery of Indigenous Knowledges." In *Indigenizing the Academy: Transforming Scholarship and Empowering Communities*, ed. Devon Abbott Mihesuah and Angela Cavender Wilson, 69-87. Lincoln: University of Nebraska Press, 2004.

PART 2

Oral Histories and Narratives

3
Respecting First Nations Oral Histories: Copyright Complexities and Archiving Aboriginal Stories

Leslie McCartney

This chapter addresses two related issues: the lack of recorded oral history in Canadian archives of events perceived, witnessed, and experienced by Canada's First Nations and the problems that arise once such oral histories are deposited into the archives, particularly as oral forms of history are not given the same protection and respect as literary works under the *Copyright Act*.

My background in the legal and archival fields proved to be beneficial when I served as executive director of the Gwich'in Social and Cultural Institute (GSCI) in Northwest Territories between 2002 and 2004. The GSCI was set up in 1992 as a non-profit registered charity, partly in response to Gwich'in people's concerns about the erosion of their language and culture. Save for the Inuit, the Gwich'in are the most northerly Aboriginal people in North America. Many Gwich'in still live on their traditional lands, which border the boreal forest from the Mackenzie Valley in Northwest Territories, through Yukon, and into the interior of Alaska. Originally Athapaskan speakers, the Gwich'in now speak predominantly English and number approximately 2,400.[1] Anthropologically, the Gwich'in are considered to be part of the Dene.[2] In 1992 the Canadian federal government and the Gwich'in signed a Comprehensive Land Claim Agreement, which created the Gwich'in Settlement Region.

The mandate of the GSCI is "to document, preserve and promote the practice of Gwich'in culture, language, traditional knowledge, and values."[3] In its effort to accomplish this task, the GSCI has amassed an extensive archival collection that includes at least one thousand hours of oral history audio tape. As I worked with the GSCI and thought about its future, including the operation of a publicly accessible archive, the legal issues and implications of recording and archiving Aboriginal oral history became apparent, and they remain issues of concern.

A Story of Firsts: The Albert Johnson Story

To introduce the issues addressed in this chapter, I will tell an abridged version of the Albert Johnson story that has been grafted together from files in various archives across the country. The story takes place in 1932, in the dim, arctic light of Canada's Yukon and Northwest Territories.

A strange man arrived in Fort McPherson in the summer of 1931 via the Peel River and a handmade log raft. He barely spoke to anyone, bought a canoe from a local man and several rounds of ammunition and supplies in the local store, and then made his way to the Rat River, where he built himself a cabin. On New Year's Eve the Royal Canadian Mounted Police (RCMP) at the Arctic Red River detachment received complaints from some Gwich'in men that a man by the name of Albert Johnson had been springing their traps. A constable and a special constable were dispatched to investigate. When they reached the cabin, the man inside refused to open the door. The police patrol made its way to Aklavik to obtain a search warrant. Two RCMP officers and two special constables returned to the cabin with a search warrant. As one officer knocked on the door, the man inside shot through it and lodged a bullet in the officer's chest. The officer managed to crawl a short distance away, where his colleagues settled him into their dog sled and then travelled back to Aklavik. This incident led to the formation of a full police party made up of members of the RCMP, the Royal Canadian Corps of Signals, local trappers, and Gwich'in. The party returned to the cabin, and despite its effort to blast the cabin with dynamite, which they first had to thaw in a frying pan over an open fire, Johnson escaped. He managed to elude police for fifty-three days in bone-chilling weather, and during this chase he killed an RCMP officer. Once Johnson crossed the mountains into Yukon, the RCMP from the Old Crow detachment became involved. The Canadian government also called in pilot Wop May, a hero of the First World War, to assist in locating Johnson's trail from the air and, more importantly, to ferry supplies to the police party and their dog teams. Johnson continued to elude the posse until noon on 17 February 1932, when it caught up with him on Yukon's Eagle River. Before he was killed, Johnson shot and wounded another man from the police party. Johnson's body was taken back to Aklavik for burial. Over $2,000 in Canadian and American bills, five pearls, some pieces of gold dental work (not his), and some alluvial gold were found on his body. There was nothing on the body to identify the man, and the real identity of the man known as Albert Johnson has never been established, although there are several theories in many publications that speculate as to who he really was.

Established Archival Record

The story of the Mad Trapper has been well documented in archives through-out Canada, not only because it combines a number of "firsts" but also because of the mystery of Johnson's true identity. Library and Archives Canada has an extensive file that contains newspaper clippings, paperwork that illustrates the bureaucratic process of burying an unknown criminal and distributing his possessions, clips of radio programs about the story, and a few audio tapes of some of the men who were involved in the case or who discussed it over the years.[4] The Johnson files in the RCMP archives in Ottawa contain police reports and an array of correspondence from people attempting to identify Johnson between 1932 and the 1960s.[5] The Johnson file in the Northwest Territories Archives contains newspaper clippings and notes about the case.[6] Files in the Yukon Archives hold similar material, as well as draft screenplays based on the story.[7] Various author notes by writers such as Dick North, who lived in Whitehorse and published several books on Johnson, are also in-cluded.[8] Significantly, all the documents in these archival holdings were created either by representatives of the RCMP or by newspaper columnists, screenwriters, or authors of popular literature. The documents produced by each group have embedded within them distinctive ways of telling and know-ing the story of Albert Johnson.

RCMP Versions

The RCMP stories of Albert Johnson are distinctive in the sense that they have embedded within them a story of Canadian sovereignty in the North, one that includes the government's role in maintaining peace, law, and order through the RCMP and an analysis of the impact of government policy on the North's social and political landscape. The RCMP documents note how those Mounties involved in the case overcame blizzards and kept going until they got their man; they endured unparalleled hardships in their duty to maintain the peace, all the while following proper procedure. For the RCMP, the mad trapper case represented several Canadian "firsts": it was the first large-scale manhunt carried out in the Canadian north; coined the "Arctic Circle War" by the press, it was the country's first live, play-by-play, national broadcast of a police event; and it constituted the first time an airplane was used in an attempt to locate and apprehend a criminal.[9] The use of these technologies expanded the borders of the northern landscape, bringing with them profound and lasting changes to the region and the way law was enforced in it and elsewhere. Symbolically, the Johnson case served as an example of what can happen to those who choose to challenge the law of the land and threaten peace and security. For the RCMP, Johnson's death was evidence that the force could maintain peace in the area. After an inquest was held and Johnson's estate was handled, the case was closed. The files were then placed in various archives around the country, and the story was told from time to time in RCMP-related journals and retrospective articles and touted as one of the incidents in which the Mounties did indeed get their man, in the harshest of conditions.[10]

POPULAR VERSIONS
Popular literature about Johnson – poems, plays, screenplays, films, short stories, novels, and magazine articles – and songs about the Mad Trapper of Rat River share common symbolic themes that make this group of stories distinctive from those told by the RCMP, and, as I will discuss later, by the Gwich'in.[11] National ideologies or cultural symbols subtly distinguish Canadian stories, which explore the theme of survival, from American stories, which explore the role of the frontier. Layered onto these themes are others: the myth of the North; stereotypes of "Indians" as either victims or heroes; stereotypes of "real men" who are self-reliant, tough, and determined; and depictions of the North as a massive geographical place, an untouched and uninhabited wilderness where you have to rely on your wits and endure freezing temperatures and unrelenting blizzards to survive.[12] Johnson may have been killed, but the Mad Trapper survives as a legend, and the mystery of his identity has been the inspiration for much of the popular literature about him since his demise over seventy years ago.

Investigating the Johnson story in the archives sources involves sifting through an overwhelming amount of material that can lead to the assumption that this event has been well documented and told in its entirety. This assumption is far from accurate.

Unheard Johnson Stories
As I researched the Johnson case in various archives around the country, I reflected on the two meanings of "history": the past as it actually happened and the past as it has been represented.[13] The Johnson story has been told in two ways: in the European tradition of the written text and in the Aboriginal tradition of oral storytelling. Julie Cruikshank notes that the European scientific tradition and the Aboriginal oral tradition present very different models for thinking about the world and speaking from different perspectives.[14]

Whereas a scientific report will use grid numbers to refer to the land, Aboriginal oral tradition will speak of the land in a story form that flows like a stream. Such a story will contain more than one message, and it will encompass a lifetime of experience. The Johnson story was represented differently in RCMP and popular versions; why were the stories of Gwich'in Elders not included in the archival record?

Paul Thompson states that "all history depends ultimately upon its social purpose."[15] Each version of a story represents an interpretation by a different group, and each version situates them within a particular time and place.[16] With each act of interpretation, each group reinforces its cultural values.[17] Written text is one way to document a historical event, but oral history is another. However, as both Elizabeth Tonkin and Julie Cruikshank point out, the oral history process is profoundly social: in it, the historical and social perspectives are not separate, they merge into one.[18] To understand the Gwich'in stories as "history-as-lived," as something that is connected to but distinct from the Johnson stories as "history-as recorded," the perspective of Gwich'in Elders who tell the Johnson story as a people living and developing in times of change must be taken into account.[19] It must be recognized that when the Gwich'in Elders tell this story, they are speaking about their lives as lived in the 1920s and 1930s. I also contemplated that most of the written records reflected the point of view of people in authority and, as a consequence, became the leading voice in the story.[20] Foucault posed that knowledge is indissociable from powerful regimes and can be acquired for purposes of social control.[21] The Gwich'in versions of the Johnson story provide examples of how Aboriginal oral accounts have been marginalized by more powerful knowledge systems.[22] What has not been understood is that the Gwich'in do have stories about Johnson that symbolize how they interpreted the manner in which they were living at the time the events occurred. The Gwich'in stories of Johnson are not so different, in fact or in the chain of events, from those found in RCMP and popular versions; however, for the Gwich'in, the "true" story is the importance of the land, the process of telling the story, and the relationships that are integral to their story. Thus, the Gwich'in experience of the story is different from other versions because of their distinctive way of knowing.[23]

According to several Gwich'in Elders, many Gwich'in assisted the police in their hunt for Johnson because the chase took place on land long inhabited by their people. It was Gwich'in special constables who enabled the police party to find their way by using centuries-old trails; it was the Gwich'in who assisted the police by providing them with food and lodgings at their camps along the posse trail; it was the Gwich'in who made it possible for the police party to survive. None of these stories were or have been written down, as those directly involved still used the oral tradition of telling stories rather than committing them to paper. Instead of this story unfolding on a landscape that was barren, frozen, and void of people, as the archival records seem to indicate, it unfolds on a rich Gwich'in cultural landscape, a landscape alive with stories, legends, place names, trails, sacred sites, and stories of people who had, for centuries, been intimately connected with the land, with a cultural landscape the Gwich'in called home.[24]

The land is central in Gwich'in stories of Johnson, and, as the following extracts illustrate, the story was used to teach Gwich'in Elder Pierre Benoit traditional hunting techniques and trapping trails. Benoit was about nine years old when his uncle told him the story of Johnson the winter that Pierre's family camped at Campbell Creek. Benoit underscores the importance of how "he got that story":

> We listen by people telling story, travelling among themselves.
> That was in 1932 it happened. February. We stayed at Campbell
> Creek, and that Paul Niditchie and all his family went to Sitidgi
> Lake and, then, from there when they run out of grocery ... Well,
> that time, at Big Rock, about more than ten miles there, there's a
> trader there, call him Billy Phillip. He's trading there, and there's
> John Niditchie and Amos Niditchie – them two brothers – they go
> and get the groceries and what they need, you know, from there.
> That's where they get the story, and, when they pass us, they tell us
> that story too. I was about nine year old that time. Boy, big year,
> that year! That was lots of news! Gee it was [some] kind of excite-
> ment! One of the guys was telling the story about it when I was
> listening to his story, you know. That was [Special Constable] Joe
> Bernard, [my uncle]. He was the one right there [with Johnson],
> and he was telling this story. He was telling this story, and I listen
> to him good, and that's how come I got that story.[25]

Another Elder, Annie Benoit, continues to live in Aklavik but spends as much time as she can at her fish camp. She tells her version of the Johnson story:

Oh, good many times we travel in cold winter, I tell you. Over the mountain – no tree, no willow – we go over. Six miles over. That's where they were working with Albert Johnson. Oh, really scared. Even that, we have to go 'cause lots of caribou over there. We're scared of him. We went over; we just think he was just going to get shot! They're working with Albert Johnson down that way. It's bare ground, bare hill. No nothing. We go over. We took this trail this way, but not this way. We all travelling – my father, mother, brother Charles – all of us. Big family going over. And then, after that, we put up a tent. We march up the snow with snowshoe – press it, press it, press it down. And then we take our snowshoe off and just put snow out. We put all the branches around the wall in there. We tie stick together like this and put the tent pole like this. We tie it both side, outside. And then we bank it with snow. And somebody make fire already. They warm up the place and bring all this stuff in, put the caribou on the branches. As soon as [the] stove start[s] getting warm up, everything frozen is just thaw out, and everything get warm up. Right away, they bring that fresh meat, they put caribou skin, they spread it, spread all that caribou skin, and we put our fresh meat. We cook something. First thing we fry: meat. Oh, we eat good! We just eat anything of caribou. Boy! We eat good! Healthy. We never made, never take, no medicine, no nothing. Nothing. Them days, people never get sick. Oh, cold, flu went through sometime. Just about forty below, he still travel around it. Oh, bad, everybody cry for him. We feel sad for him because they suffer him too long, and they never even eat nothing. Why they bother him? ... Why? He don't pay for his licence? That time, that police, Millen, that one he shot, Millen he ask him question. He don't talk too much, too. He just look over his mosquito [net]. And Millen, him, told him, "You should get your licence," his trapping licence. He never did. He just went on his own. That's where they're after him. Gee, that's a good story, and, the same time, I feel sad when they shot him. He was just starving. He never eat for long time, he never sleep right. They suffer him. At the end, they shot him. They say he just skin and bone. I don't like to talk about it.[26]

The late Sarah Peters describes how she and her husband benefited from the Johnson manhunt:

> I was staying at the mouth of the Rat River with my sick husband.
> Those who were staying near us all moved to the mountains. In
> the meantime, early in the fall before freeze-up, Albert Johnson
> had moved up the Rat River to trap. All at once, the police from
> Arctic Red River and Aklavik came by our place to look for Albert
> Johnson ... It took a lot of grub and dog feed [for all the men
> in the hunt]. All this was done by airplane, and planes always
> landed at our place because we were staying near a big river.
> When they landed, I would haul the stuff up the bank and store
> it away for the police until they came back again to keep on
> their search for Albert Johnson ... After everything was over, we
> still were keeping lots of grub for the police. It was all given to
> me, which was a great help to us, for helping them when they
> went by my place. My husband was very sick and there was no
> way for us to get grub. All winter we stayed at the mouth of the
> Rat River. I trapped a bit sometime. I would get a few mink and
> foxes. Also, I snared rabbits so that we could eat, and I had to
> cut wood for our house. It was getting towards spring – the water
> was just starting to run on the river. It was about the first part
> of April when my husband passed away. He was sick for a long
> time, and, all that time, I look after him the best I could. In this
> story, I am telling out about Albert Johnson. It happened when
> we were staying at the Rat River, and this is the end of my story.[27]

When I served as a researcher for the GSCI, on a project interviewing and recording the life histories of Gwich'in Elders, the story of Johnson surfaced many times as Elders discussed memories and experiences on the land in their younger years. The stories told by Pierre and Annie Benoit illustrate how the Gwich'in Elders used the Johnson story to mark time and place. Many Elders referred to "that Albert Johnson year," "that time they were hunting Johnson, February, 1932," or "that year we stay at [certain place name] when we heard about Johnson." I came to realize that stories of this event, for many Gwich'in Elders, were analogous to questions I had heard many times in southern Canada: for instance, do you remember where you were and what you were doing when Kennedy was assassinated or, more recently, on 11 September 2001? In the interviews, everyone remembered where they were on the land when they became aware of the Johnson events. Locations on the land served as mnemonic aids, or pegs, upon which myriad associations and oral narratives were hung; they indicated intrinsic ties between personal history and concept of self that are anchored to places on the landscape.[28]

Many Gwich'in Elders insisted that what had been written about the Johnson story (their observation was based primarily on popular books and movies) was not completely true. They would then tell me the story as they knew it. The basic framework and facts of the story were similar to those disclosed at the beginning of this chapter, but the story was really a story about how the Gwich'in were living their lives in 1932. It was evident that there were distinct differences between what their narratives were saying on the surface and the deeper meanings that were embedded within the Johnson stories that the Gwich'in told.[29] The stories told are rich in Gwich'in social and cultural history. Listening to the stories, which sound more like travelogues than factual stories, one realizes that they tell where families were staying on the land, where they were travelling and hunting, what they were trapping, and the intricacies of relationships between the various people and the entire Gwich'in nation. Johnson appears as a mere shadow in the background. In the foreground are the social, political, and economic realities that were impacting their lives. For example, Treaty 11 had been signed only ten years earlier, in 1921, and shortly thereafter the Gwich'in discovered they were not exempt, as promised, from game laws and regulations that made it illegal to hunt traditional food-source animals (notably, caribou and moose) in certain seasons. Licensed hunting, time frames for legal hunting, and quotas were being imposed to limit the number of animals that could be harvested.[30]

The stories refer to the economic realities of their lives and how the decline of fur prices, due to the Depression, was affecting their way of life. Pierre Benoit's narrative hints at the shortage of animals that winter and the growing dependence, for some, on purchased groceries. Sarah Peters talks about the poor state of health of some of the people. A flu epidemic swept through the area in 1928, taking with it most of the young and the old.[31] Many survived, only to cope with the residual effects of tuberculosis. Rich details found in Annie Benoit's story describe the camps that were set up and the trails that were used. The stories denote Gwich'in place names and their associated meanings and connected stories. Even names of the people involved carry with them gems of the Gwich'in kinship history.

Thus, in "that Albert Johnson Story," as many Gwich'in refer to it, Johnson is merely one thread in a rich tapestry of Gwich'in social history for 1932. Symbolically, this story is a vehicle for the Gwich'in to embed their stories within other histories. This social history speaks of social interruption, upheaval, dislocation, and survival, not only physical survival on the land but also spiritual and cultural survival as people embrace and adapt to a changing world around them. While the Johnson story, as recorded in the archives, is told from the perspective of the police or those who write popular literature, the Gwich'in versions are recounted from a perspective steeped with cultural meanings that are derived from the people's relationship to the hunt, land, resources, property, and kinship. Disregarding the stories because Johnson is not in the foreground would discredit the story and its tellers – for it is the historical, political, economic, and social realities experienced by the Gwich'in in 1932, and cultural constructions of those experiences, that *is* the story.

The Addition of Oral Histories to Archival Holdings

If these oral histories about Johnson, as told by the Gwich'in, were to be collected and deposited in an archive, they would provide a more holistic and balanced record of the past. The oral histories would present yet another approach to "knowing" or, in other words, add another perspective to a Canadian historical event. Cruikshank notes that "narrative recollections and memories about history, tradition and life experience represent distinct and powerful bodies of local knowledge that have to be appreciated in their totality, rather than fragmented into data."[32] Depositing these stories in archives can also fulfill several secondary purposes. If they are recorded in the Gwich'in language, more spoken records of a language that is on the brink of extinction will be preserved.[33] The stories can also serve as cultural and historical records for the Gwich'in themselves. Very few young Gwich'in now live on the land, and only a few know the stories behind traditional personal and place names or the stories connected to those places.

Although it would be logical for researchers to collect oral histories of the Johnson story and deposit them into an archive, there are many issues to consider if this task is to be undertaken. Many Gwich'in Elders, and other Aboriginal people I have worked with, have become increasing concerned about copyright protection, and, given their treatment in the past, these concerns are justified. "I'm not giving my story so someone else can make money off it" is a common response, yet Elders realize that if they do not tell the stories, the stories will die with them. The transmission of stories from one generation to the next has broken down, not simply in the Gwich'in community but in many Aboriginal communities across Canada. Elders realize that, by recording their stories, they will be preserved and can be used in the future as a heritage resource for the next generation, especially if the stories are told in their own language.

Issues pertaining to copyright and preservation are not exclusive to the Gwich'in. Many Aboriginal people in Canada have voiced concerns about the cultural appropriation and commercial exploitation of traditional cultural expressions such as art, songs, and stories. They have drawn attention to the unauthorized use of sacred symbols, stories, and songs; to the fragmentation of cultural expressions that results when they are used outside the context and intent of their original creation; and to the fact that the original creators rarely receive thanks or economic benefit from the use of these expressions.[34] It is of paramount importance that, for deep appreciation, these cultural expressions be preserved, and promoted, within the cultural context in which they were created and intended. Thus, we must consider issues of copyright.

The Complexities of the 1985 Copyright Act

"Copyright" is a term used to define a number of legal rights that are attached to "works" that, although not defined by law, "are best understood as intellectual creations such as books, films and art."[35] Copyright exists to protect the creator's right to control the use of his or her work and payment for it. The counterbalance to copyright is public access to protected works.[36] There are seven categories of material protected by the 1985 Copyright Act. Literary materials – that is, anything that is written down – are defined as "works," whereas sound recordings are defined as "other subject matter" and their creators are, consequently, accorded fewer rights and a shorter term of protection. The common characteristic shared by materials that are defined as other subject matter is that they are new creations based on works protected by copyright; for example, a literary work that has been made into a sound recording.[37]

The Government of Canada defines folklore as "traditional forms of artistic expression of a people, group or community"; examples include songs, dances, and old stories that have been handed down for generations.[38] If, today, I were to go out and collect the Johnson story from members of the Gwich'in community, I would, according to Canadian legislation, be collecting folklore because the original Gwich'in members who participated in the events are no longer living and the stories have been handed down.

However, let us operate on the assumption that I did collect oral history with Gwich'in who were involved in the story. Copyright only protects materials that are original; therefore, historical facts, such as those found in the Johnson story, are not protected by copyright. An expression of these facts in an original form, such as a literary story or a sound recording of an interview, would be protected. For literary works, copyright remains with the creator; for sound recordings, copyright remains with the maker of the sound recording; that is, the person who arranged the first fixation of the sounds.[39] This is usually the interviewer or producer. Oral histories, under the *Copyright Act*, are considered to be and protected as sound recordings.[40] Consequently, the interviewee has no copyright protection. Section 14.1(1) of the *Copyright Act* states that authors of works have the right to the integrity of the work; thus, any changes to the work are prejudicial.[41] In the case of oral history recordings, storytellers have no recourse if the story is appropriated or used in such a way as to prejudice his or her reputation. A storyteller has no legal recourse if his or her name is not used and no legal recourse if the work is distorted, modified, misinterpreted, or changed. In other words, the storyteller has no moral rights. By contrast, in the case of literary works, the author-creator enjoys both the copyright and moral rights.

The issue of translation adds even more complexity to copyright considerations. If the oral history is told, for reasons outlined above, in a mother tongue, it would need to be translated into another language (probably English) for it to be understood by most Gwich'in and the general public. The *Copyright Act* includes the sole right to produce or reproduce the work via translation, as long as the original owner – in the case of an audio recording, the interviewer or producer – gives permission for the translation to occur.[42] The translated work, however, becomes a separate piece of work; that is, the author of the translated work is now the first owner of copyright unless, of course, there is agreement to the contrary.[43] Copyright for a sound recording is for the remainder of the calendar year in which the recording was made plus fifty years.[44] It is not surprising, therefore, that the Royal Commission on Aboriginal Peoples recommended that "the federal government, in collaboration with Aboriginal peoples, review its legislation on the protection of intellectual property to ensure that Aboriginal interests and perspectives, in particular collective interests, are adequately protected.[45]

The Government of Canada has initiated the process of copyright reform. Lawmakers are beginning to realize that the current legislation does not take into consideration that oral traditions embedded within folklore, songs, dances, and legends cannot be traced to a single person and that, because their authorship is not "fixed," these items are not protected under the *Copyright Act*. Moreover, as ownership of these traditions has been handed down for generations, an expiry date of fifty years is not applicable. However, the federal government has not yet introduced legislation to address this range of issues.[46]

The theory behind the provisions of the *Copyright Act* is based on the concept of private ownership of property. Traditional knowledge, stories, and folklore do not always fit this theory. A story takes many forms. Pierre Benoit illustrates perfectly how he "got that story" from his uncle Joe Bernard. Because Bernard was involved in the Johnson events, he had the right to tell the story and "give" it to Benoit, who, in turn, had the right to give it to others. Stories can be shared with a special person or group, they can be meant for certain people's ears alone, or, if they are in songs, they can rest with a certain person, not to be retold, or resung, by others.[47]

There has been debate about whether the *Copyright Act* should be amended to alter existing rights that protect works of traditional knowledge or whether it should be amended to create a new class of rights that take into account the special circumstances surrounding the creation and use of these works.[48] Perhaps what is needed is a completely different perspective or approach. Instead of trying to fit Aboriginal traditional knowledge and folklore into the existing Western legal paradigm and the philosophy upon which it was constructed, perhaps another "landscape" or "way of knowing" needs to be seen and understood. In the end, I believe members of Aboriginal communities should decide how they want to see their oral histories preserved, used, and accessed.

Conclusion

All stories are constructed by reading the past selectively. As I have illustrated with the Johnson example, there are ways of knowing a story that extend beyond the evidence that currently exists in archival holdings. But when we record oral histories, we need to be aware that narratives or stories may not only be locally grounded, culturally specific, and highly particular, they may also become frames of reference, or ways of knowing, to further experience the world. Stories reflect larger historical, social, and political process and, thus, their inclusion in archival holdings is important.[49] We have much to learn from the traditional knowledge and folklore of Aboriginal communities, especially regarding social history.[50] Because they are framed within a particular understanding of land as the centre of the world, rather than something to be conquered, oral histories such as "that Albert Johnson story" have been marginalized by more powerful systems of knowledge.[51] The inclusion of these oral histories in our holdings is long overdue, particularly given that these histories reflect the diversity of Canada's peoples and bring new perspectives to bear on past events. The stories cannot be fragmented. The importance of Aboriginal people's histories must be recognized. Their sophisticated stories, which embody distinct cultural and historical contexts, can make important contributions to the historical record for all people; consequently, they demand as much respect as other holdings in archives. Unfortunately, the issue of how these oral forms of history can be given the same protection and respect as literary works has not yet been resolved through legislation.

ACKNOWLEDGMENTS

I thank Wanda Noel for introducing me to the complex issue of oral history and the *Copyright Act* and for her helpful comments on points of law raised in this chapter. I also thank Ingrid Kritsch, research director and first executive director of the Gwich'in Social and Cultural Institute, for her suggestions, comments, and assistance in reviewing earlier versions of this chapter.

NOTES

1   Northwest Territories, Education, Culture and Employment, *Revitalizing, Enhancing, and Promoting Aboriginal Languages: Strategies for Supporting Aboriginal Languages* (Yellowknife: Government of the Northwest Territories, 2001), 11.

2   The term "Dene" means "people" and refers to various groups of Northern Athapaskan speakers.

3   Gwich'in Social and Cultural Institute, *Into the Next Millennium: The Five-Year Plan of the Gwich'in Social and Cultural Institute, 1996-2001* (Tsiigehtchic: Gwich'in Social and Cultural Institute, 1996), inside cover.

4   Library and Archives Canada, Northern Administration Branch, RG 85/12.

5   Royal Canadian Mounted Police Headquarters Archives, Ottawa, Mad Trapper Case, vol. 3, Yukon and NWT 1931/32, files 1, 2, and 3.

6   Northwest Territories Archives, Yellowknife, Royal Canadian Mounted Police fonds.

7   Yukon Archives, Whitehorse, Albert Johnson (The Mad Trapper), general file.

8   Dick North, *The Saga of the Mad Trapper* (Yukon: Midnight Arctic Series 1, 1969), *The Mad Trapper of Rat River* (Toronto: Macmillan of Canada, 1972), and *Track-*

down: The Search for the Identity of the Mad Trapper (Toronto: Macmillan of Canada, 1989).

9 Robert Knuckle, "No. 51 – Millen, Edgar – Cst. Regimental No. 9669. January 30, 1932 – Rat River, Northwest Territories Age: 31. The Mad Trapper of Rat River," in *In the Line of Duty: The Honour Roll of the RCMP since 1873* (Burnstown, ON: General Store Publishing House, 1974), 151-54; T.E.G. Shaw, "Who Was Albert Johnson?" in Frank W. Anderson, *The Death of Albert Johnson: Mad Trapper of Rat River* (Surrey, BC: Heritage House, 1986), 46-53.

10 Constable Eric Rebiere, "Revisiting Our Storied Past (Part 1)," *RCMP Quarterly* 63 (1998): 21-28; "Revisiting Our Storied Past (Part 2)," *RCMP Quarterly* 63 (1998): 37-43. Artifacts, including Johnson's rifle, are on display at the Royal Canadian Mounted Police Museum, Regina, Saskatchewan.

11 Wilf Carter, "The Capture of Albert Johnson," song, RCA 1932-33; *Death Hunt*, directed by Peter Hunt, screenplay by Michael Grais and Mark Victor (Hollywood, CA: 20th Century Fox, 1981); Chuck D. Keen, "Story Line: The Mad Trapper of the Yukon," unpublished manuscript, no date, Yukon Archives, MSS 004 – Keen, Chuck – Acc. 82/74; *Mad Trapper of Rat River*, produced and directed by Dan Wood, written by Paul Kligman and Ed. McNamara (Ottawa: Canadian Broadcasting Corporation, 1972); Robert Kroetsch, "Poem of Albert Johnson," in *The Stone Hammer Poems: 1960-1975* (Nanaimo, BC: Oolichan Books, 1975), 48-49; Howard O'Hagan, "The Man Who Chose to Die," in *Wilderness Men* (Vancouver: Talonbooks, 1976), 63-80; Rudy Wiebe, *The Mad Trapper: A Novel* (Toronto: McClelland and Stewart, 1980); "The Outeredge News from the Frontier: 'Mad Trapper' Gun?" *Up Here* 18, 2 (2002): 13.

12 Robert Brannon, "The Male Sex Role: Our Culture's Blueprint of Manhood and What It's Done for Us Lately," in *The Forty-Nine Percent Majority*, ed. Deborah S. David and Robert Brannon (Reading, UK: Addison-Wesley, 1976), 1-45.

13 See Elizabeth Tonkin, *Narrating Our Pasts: The Social Construction of Oral History* (Cambridge: Cambridge University Press, 1989); John Tosh, *The Pursuit of History: Aims, Methods and New Directions in the Study of Modern History* (London: Longman, 1999), viii.

14 Julie Cruikshank, *Reading Voices = Dän Dhá Ts'edenintth'ę: Oral and Written Interpretations of the Yukon's Past* (Vancouver: Douglas and McIntyre, 1991).

15 Paul Thompson, *The Voice of the Past: Oral History* (New York: Oxford University Press, 2000), 1.

16 See Mark Freeman, *Rewriting the Self: History, Memory, Narrative* (London: Routledge, 1993), 9; Scott Rushforth, "The Legitimation of the Beliefs in a Hunter-Gatherer Society: Bearlake Athapaskan Knowledge and Authority," *American Ethnologist* 19, 3 (1992): 484; Tonkin, *Narrating Our Pasts*, 3.

17 See Tonkin, *Narrating Our Pasts*, 3.

18 See Cruikshank, *Reading Voices* and Tonkin, *Narrating Our Pasts*.

19 See Tonkin, *Narrating Our Pasts*, 12.

20 See Thompson, *Voice of the Past*, 6, 7, 34.

21 See Steven Best and Douglas Kellner, *Postmodern Theory: Critical Interrogations* (New York: Palgrave Macmillan, 1991), 50.

22 See Julie Cruikshank, *The Social Life of Stories: Narrative and Knowledge in the Yukon Territory* (Vancouver: UBC Press, 1998), xiii.

23 See Jean-Guy A. Goulet, *Ways of Knowing: Experience, Knowledge, and Power among the Dene Tha* (Vancouver: UBC Press, 1998).

24 For more on the Gwich'in cultural landscape, see Michael Heine et al., *Gwichya Gwich'in, Googwandak: The History and Stories of the Gwichya Gwich'in as Told by the Elders of Tsiigehtchic* (Tsiigehtchic and Yellowknife: Gwich'in Social and Cultural Institute, 2001).

25 Pierre Benoit, Gwich'in Elder, interview by Leslie McCartney, 2000, Tsiigehtchic, Gwich'in Elders Biographies Research Project, Gwich'in Social and Cultural Institute Archives, Tsiigehtchic. Joe Bernard's sister married Pierre Benoit's father.

26 Annie Benoit, Gwich'in Elder, interview by Leslie McCartney, 2001, Aklavik, Gwich'in Elders Biographies Research Project, Gwich'in Social and Cultural Institute Archives, Tsiigehtchic. Annie Benoit (née Koe) married Pierre Benoit in the 1950s. At the time of the Johnson events, she was only a child.

27 Canadian Broadcasting Corporation, Sarah Peters (Speaker), "A Long Time Ago/ Spruce Gum Man/The Two Women/Albert Johnson," original sound recording made for Committee for Original People's Entitlement, no. L27-11, audio cassette, Northwest Territories Archives, Yellowknife, 1973.

28 See also Thomas D. Andrews and John B. Zoe, "The Idaa Trail: Archaeology and the Dogrib Cultural Landscape, Northwest Territories," in *At a Crossroads: Archaeology and First Peoples in Canada*, ed. George P. Nicholas and Thomas D. Andrews (Burnaby, BC: Archaeology Press, Simon Fraser University, 1997), 10, 161-77; Ingrid Kritsch and Alestine M. Andre, "Gwich'in Traditional Knowledge and Heritage Studies in the Gwich'in Settlement Area," in *At a Crossroads*, ed. Nicholas and Andrews, 8, 126-44.

29 See Paul Ricoeur, "The Model of the Text: Meaningful Action Considered as a Text," in *Interpretive Social Science: A Reader*, ed. Paul Rabinow and William M. Sullivan (Berkeley: University of California Press, 1979), 73-101.

30 See Usher's discussion of the legislation of 1916 and 1917, Peter Usher, "The Growth and Decay of Trading and Trapping Frontiers in the Western Canadian Arctic," *Canadian Geographer* 19, 4 (1975): 308-20. See also Fumoleau, who discusses how the enforcement of these laws against the Gwich'in (who depended on game for their existence) caused extreme hardship: René Fumoleau, *As Long as This Land Shall Last: A History of Treaty 8 and Treaty 11, 1870-1939* (Toronto: McClelland and Stewart, 1973), 226.

31　Kerry Abel, *Drum Songs: Glimpses of Dene History* (Montreal and Kingston: McGill-Queen's University Press, 1993), 197, 198, 208.

32　Julie Cruikshank, "Uses and Abuses of Traditional Knowledge: Listening for Different Stories" (paper presented at "Relations between Traditional Knowledge and Western Science: A Northern Forum," Carleton University, Ottawa, 7 March 2003).

33　The Gwich'in language is the most endangered of the Dene languages in Northwest Territories. According to the 1996 Census of Canada, less than 2 percent of the Gwich'in regularly speak their mother tongue in the home. See Northwest Territories, Education, Culture and Employment, *Revitalizing, Enhancing, and Promoting Aboriginal Languages*, 11.

34　Canada, Department of Canadian Heritage, "A Framework for Copyright Reform," 2001, Copyright Reform Process, Archives, http://strategis.ic.gc.ca/epic/site/crp-prda.nsf/en/rp01101e.html; Peter Kulchyski, "From Appropriation to Subversion: Aboriginal Cultural Production in the Age of Postmodernism," *American Indian Quarterly* 21, 4 (1997): 605-20.

35　Wanda Noel, *Staff Guide to Copyright: National Archives of Canada* (Ottawa: Her Majesty the Queen in Right of Canada, 1999), 7.

36　Ibid., 8.

37　Other subject matter is of three types: sound recordings, performers' performances, and communication signals. The more limited protection for other subject matter is set out in sections 15 to 22 of the 1985 *Copyright Act*.

38　Canada, Department of Canadian Heritage, "A Framework for Copyright Reform."

39　*Copyright Act*, R.S.C. 1985, c. C-42.

40　Noel, *Staff Guide to Copyright*, 74.

41　Ibid., 46.

42　*Copyright Act*, R.S.C. 1985, c. C-42, s. 3.1(a).

43　Noel, *Staff Guide to Copyright*, 35.

44　*Copyright Act*, R.S.C. 1985, c. C-42, s. 6.

45　Canada, Royal Commission on Aboriginal Peoples, *Report of the Royal Commission on Aboriginal Peoples*, vol. 3, *Gathering Strength* (Ottawa: Canada Communications Group, 1996), 15.

46　Wanda Noel, e-mail message to author, 2 April 2007.

47　See Cruikshank, *The Social Life of Stories*, 36-38.

48　See Canada, Industry Canada, *Supporting Culture and Innovation: Report on the Provisions and Operation of the Copyright Act, Section 92 Report* (Ottawa: Minister of Supply and Services, 2002), 23.

49　See Cruikshank, *Social Life of Stories*, xii.

50　See Cruikshank, "Uses and Abuses of Traditional Knowledge," 1.

51　See Cruikshank, *Social Life of Stories*, xiii, 4.

WORKS CITED

Abel, Kerry. *Drum Songs: Glimpses of Dene History.* Montreal and Kingston: McGill-Queen's University Press, 1993.

Andrews, Thomas D., and John B. Zoe. "The Idaa Trail: Archaeology and the Dogrib Cultural Landscape, Northwest Territories," in *At a Crossroads: Archaeology and First Peoples in Canada,* ed. George P. Nicholas and Thomas D. Andrews, 10, 161-77. Burnaby, BC: Archaeology Press, Simon Fraser University, 1997.

Best, Steven, and Douglas Kellner. *Postmodern Theory: Critical Interrogations.* New York: Palgrave Macmillan, 1991.

Brannon, Robert. "The Male Sex Role: Our Culture's Blueprint of Manhood and What It's Done for Us Lately." In *The Forty-Nine Percent Majority,* ed. Deborah S. David and Robert Brannon, 1-45. Reading, UK: Addison-Wesley, 1976.

Canada. Department of Canadian Heritage. "A Framework for Copyright Reform," 2001, Copyright Reform Process, Archives. http://strategis.ic.gc.ca/epic/site/crp-prda.nsf/en/rp01101e.html.

–. Industry Canada. *Supporting Culture and Innovation: Report on the Provisions and Operation of the Copyright Act, Section 92 Report.* Ottawa: Minister of Supply and Services, 2002.

–. Royal Commission on Aboriginal Peoples. *Report of the Royal Commission on Aboriginal Peoples.* Vol. 3, *Gathering Strength.* Ottawa: Canada Communications Group, 1996.

Canadian Broadcasting Corporation. Peters, Sarah (Speaker). "A Long Time Ago/Spruce Gum Man/The Two Women/Albert Johnson." Original sound recording made for Committee for Original People's Entitlement, no. L27-11, audio cassette. Northwest Territories Archives, Yellowknife, 1973.

Carter, Wilf. "The Capture of Albert Johnson." Song. RCA 1932-33.

Cruikshank, Julie. *Reading Voices = Dän Dhá Ts'edenintth'ę: Oral and Written Interpretations of the Yukon's Past.* Vancouver: Douglas and McIntyre, 1991.

–. *The Social Life of Stories: Narrative and Knowledge in the Yukon Territory.* Vancouver: UBC Press, 1998.

–. "Uses and Abuses of Traditional Knowledge: Listening for Different Stories." Paper presented at "Relations between Traditional Knowledge and Western Science: A Northern Forum," Carleton University, Ottawa, 7 March 2003.

Death Hunt. Directed by Peter Hunt. Screenplay by Michael Grais and Mark Victor. Hollywood, CA: 20th Century Fox, 1981.

Freeman, Mark. *Rewriting the Self: History, Memory, Narrative.* London: Routledge, 1993.

Fumoleau, René. *As Long as This Land Shall Last: A History of Treaty 8 and Treaty 11, 1870-1939.* Toronto: McClelland and Stewart, 1973.

Goulet, Jean-Guy A. *Ways of Knowing: Experience, Knowledge, and Power among the Dene Tha.* Vancouver: UBC Press, 1998.

Gwich'in Social and Cultural Institute. *Into the Next Millennium: The Five-Year Plan of the Gwich'in Social and Cultural Institute, 1996-2001.* Tsiigehtchic: Gwich'in Social and Cultural Institute, 1996.

Heine, Michael, Alestine Andre, Ingrid Kritsch, and Alma Cardinal. *Gwichya Gwich'in Googwandak: The History and Stories of the Gwichya Gwich'in as Told by the Elders of Tsiigehtchic*. Tsiigehtchic and Yellowknife: Gwich'in Social and Cultural Institute, 2001.

Knuckle, Robert. "No. 51 – Millen, Edgar – Cst. Regimental No. 9669. January 30, 1932 – Rat River, Northwest Territories Age: 31. The Mad Trapper of Rat River." In *In the Line of Duty: The Honour Roll of the RCMP since 1873*, 151-54. Burnstown, ON: General Store Publishing House, 1994.

Kritsch, Ingrid D. and Alestine M. Andre. "Gwich'in Traditional Knowledge and Heritage Studies in the Gwich'in Settlement Area." In *At a Crossroads: Archaeology and First Peoples in Canada*, ed. George P. Nicholas and Thomas D. Andrews, 8, 126-44. Burnaby, BC: Archaeology Press, Simon Fraser University, 1997.

Kroetsch, Robert. "Poem of Albert Johnson." In *The Stone Hammer Poems: 1960-1975*, 48-49. Nanaimo, BC: Oolichan Books. 1975

Kulchyski, Peter. "From Appropriation to Subversion: Aboriginal Cultural Production in the Age of Postmodernism." *American Indian Quarterly* 21, 4 (1997): 605-20.

Mad Trapper of Rat River. Produced and directed by Dan Wood. Written by Paul Kligman and Ed McNamara. Ottawa: Canadian Broadcasting Corporation, 1972.

Noel, Wanda. *Staff Guide to Copyright: National Archives of Canada*. Ottawa: Her Majesty the Queen in Right of Canada, 1999.

North, Dick. *The Saga of the Mad Trapper of Rat River*. Yukon: Midnight Sun Arctic Series 1, 1969.

–. *The Mad Trapper of Rat River*. Toronto: Macmillan of Canada, 1972.

–. *Trackdown: The Search for the Identity of the Mad Trapper*. Toronto: Macmillan of Canada, 1989.

Northwest Territories. Education, Culture and Employment. *Revitalizing, Enhancing, and Promoting Aboriginal Languages: Strategies for Supporting Aboriginal Languages*. Yellowknife: Government of the Northwest Territories, 2001.

O'Hagan, Howard. "The Man Who Chose to Die." In *Wilderness Men*, 63-80. Vancouver: Talonbooks, 1976.

"The Outeredge News from the Frontier: 'Mad Trapper' Gun?" *Up Here* 18, 2 (2002): 13.

Rebiere, Constable Eric. "Revisiting Our Storied Past (Part 1)." *RCMP Quarterly* 63 (Winter 1998): 21-28.

–. "Revisiting Our Storied Past (Part 2)." *RCMP Quarterly* 63 (Spring 1998): 37-43.

Ricoeur, Paul. "The Model of the Text: Meaningful Action Considered as a Text." In *Interpretive Social Science: A Reader*, ed. Paul Rabinow and William M. Sullivan, 73-101. Berkeley: University of California Press, 1979.

Rushforth, Scott. "The Legitimation of the Beliefs in a Hunter-Gatherer Society: Bearlake Athapaskan Knowledge and Authority." *American Ethnologist* 19, 3 (1992): 483-500.

Shaw, T.E.G. "Who Was Albert Johnson?" In Frank W. Anderson, *The Death of Albert Johnson: Mad Trapper of Rat River*, 46-53. Surrey, BC: Heritage House, 1986.

Thompson, Paul. *The Voice of the Past: Oral History*. New York: Oxford University Press, 2000.

Tonkin, Elizabeth. *Narrating Our Pasts: The Social Construction of Oral History*. Cambridge: Cambridge University Press, 1989.

Tosh, John. *The Pursuit of History: Aims, Methods and New Directions in the Study of Modern History*. London: Longman, 1999.

Usher, Peter. "The Growth and Decay of the Trading and Trapping Frontiers in the Western Canadian Arctic." *Canadian Geographer* 19, 4 (1975): 308-20.

Wiebe, Ruby. *The Mad Trapper: A Novel*. Toronto: McClelland and Stewart, 1980.

4
Nápi and the City:
Siksikaitsitapi Narratives Revisited

Martin Whittles and Tim Patterson

The Canadian city has been popularly understood as a dynamic place, a hub that attracts talent of all varieties. As an urban heartland that is perceived to be overflowing with opportunity, the metropolis has, characteristically, attracted people who are enthusiastic about the assurance of expected affluence and the promise of excitement. However, the city is not always a welcoming and promising place: Aboriginal people in Canada, among others, are often excluded from the social opportunities and prosperity of urban life.[1] Kevin Lee and Cheryl Engler have shown that, in 1995, 56 percent of Aboriginal people in Canadian cities were living in poverty, compared to 24 percent of non-Aboriginal people.[2]

The cultural and physical dislocation that many Aboriginal people experience with urbanization is often compounded by a lack of sufficient marketable skills to ensure gainful employment. All of these factors combine to make for difficult, if not impossible, transitions to urban life. Less obvious is the fact that Aboriginal people's introduction to, experience of, and inclusion in the fabric of city life is often painted in a negative light. As a result of the extreme dislocation and poverty that they commonly experience, urban Aboriginal people are often perceived as culturally dead, as people who left the remaining elements of their culture back on the reserve.[3] Nevertheless, Aboriginal people in Canada continue to urbanize in unprecedented numbers. Although it is often ignored, one aspect of the urban experience that remains significant to urban Aboriginal people is storytelling. We show that Aboriginal stories and storytelling continue to reflect a uniquely Aboriginal sense of the world, even though, to many non-Aboriginal urbanites, the city is a place alien to all things Native.

To better understand the role of urban Aboriginal storytelling, members of the Treaty 7 Blackfoot Confederacy who call themselves Siksikaitsitapi (Blackfoot-speaking real people) agreed to participate in an ethnographic research project that focused on the production and continuance of *Siksikait-sitapi sopoksistotsi* (superior knowledge about an activity through one's experience) within two Albertan cities.[4] We conducted place-based interviews with Siksikaitsitapi individuals who resided in Lethbridge (*siko-ko-to-ki*, Black Rock) and Calgary (*moll-inistsis-in-aka-apewis*, Elbow Many Houses). Drawing inspiration from Howard Morphy's work with the Yolngu-speaking peoples of eastern Arnhem Land in Australia, where landscape(s) and "traditional narratives" are indivisible, we discovered the veracity of *Siksikaitsitapi akaitapiit-sinikssiistsi* (ancient stories) as instruments of cultural representation – not only within their former reserve communities but also in their more recent urban homes.[5]

This chapter addresses aspects of the urban Blackfoot experience in Albertan cities as reflected through Blackfoot oral traditions. Our goal in collecting these stories was to describe and lend context to the considerable legacy of storytelling as it relates to the shifting reality of Blackfoot peoples. We collected stories between 2002 and 2005 through ethnographic and personal contact with numerous Siksikaitsitapi. With the exception of the two storytellers presented here, many Siksikaitsitapi did not give permission for their stories to be included in this publication because they feared that their stories would be subject to non-Aboriginal textual expropriation and cultural appropriation. As ethnic and political markers of identity, many stories are nothing short of sacred. The risk of stories being circulated without the appropriate level of cultural context and respect led many Siksikaitsitapi participants to see themselves at risk for some level of cultural and political jeopardy. Indeed, the increased recognition and use of oral traditions has led John Borrows to describe the "shifting purposes of oral tradition" as being from individual and family narratives that are contextual and localized to grand narratives that appear to be simplistic and overgeneralized.[6]

While the Nápi (Old Man Creator) stories presented in this chapter hold a distinct place within Blackfoot culture, they do not include all Blackfoot ways of knowing, nor do they include the more complex sets of *akaitapiitsiniks-siistsi* (ancient stories).[7] Beyond demonstrating the overall significance of Siksikaitsitapi narrative in the city, this chapter echoes David Newhouse's call to recognize Aboriginal people's significant contributions to Canadian history and culture.[8] This chapter shows how stories of Nápi typically depicted as archaic legends are, in fact, contemporary, dynamic approaches that Siksikaitsitapi use to explain the built environment. We illustrate how Nápi stories speak to geographical and architectural landmarks culturally specific to the Siksikaitsitapi in two Alberta cities. We also demonstrate how narrative help to explain all manner of contemporary urban issues, including domestic violence, homelessness, alienation, and poverty.

David Newhouse and Evelyn Peters note that "Aboriginal people live in cities ... [Yet] this simple declarative statement hides a complex reality. Life in small towns and large cities is part of Aboriginal reality as is life on reserves."[9] The urban Aboriginal population forms a distinctive cultural amalgam, as evinced in Tim Patterson's description of Canadian urban Indian, Métis, and Inuit as a city population without compare.[10] For many Native people, the city is a place both exclusionary and enigmatic, a place where they are simultaneously "excluded from much of the prosperity enjoyed by non-aboriginal Canadians ... [and] where simple notions are never as they appear."[11] Yet, as we have argued, for many Aboriginal people, "the bright lights and glare of the city can be overshadowed: cities can also be artificial, restrictive, and exploitative places, polarized by class and ethnicity, as alien to people freshly arrived from rural communities and recent immigrants, as they are to an often permanent under-class of long-time residents – most specifically, Aboriginal city-dwellers."[12] Yet, as daunting as urban life can be, in this chapter we assert that Aboriginal narrative mediates the contradictions of being urban and being Aboriginal but does not resolve them.[13]

Historically, the Siksikaitsitapi are thought to have numbered between thirty and forty thousand.[14] Their traditional territory ranged from the "North Saskatchewan River [Ponoká'sisaahtaa] to Yellowstone [Otahkoiitahtayi] and from the Rocky Mountains [Miistakistsi] to the present Alberta-Saskatchewan border [Kaayihkimikoyi], or more commonly, Cypress Hills."[15] Then as now, the Siksikaitsitapi included members of four constituent communities: North Piikani (Aapatohsipiikani), South Piikani (Aamsskaapipiikani), Blood (Aapaitsitapi), and Blackfoot (Siksika). Prior to European contact in 1691, the Siksikaitsitapi were nomadic buffalo hunters and warriors. By the middle of the eighteenth century, they were perhaps the most powerful and affluent nation on the Canadian prairies.[16] Following the arrival of the horse (*Ponokaomita*, elk-dog), perhaps as early as 1700, and firearms, traded from the east and south, the Siksikaitsitapi enjoyed a profound cultural fluorescence.[17] As Esther Goldfrank noted, "Their country was well stocked with the buffalo upon which they depended for food, shelter, and clothing; their early possession of the horse and the gun, and their comparative freedom from white pressure gave ample opportunity for effective hunting and substantial profit from an expanding fur trade."[18]

Following extensive European contact in the nineteenth century, the Siksikaitsitapi suffered near total decimation by successive waves of smallpox, measles, and influenza: smallpox epidemics in 1837 and 1869, in addition to measles and scarlet fever in 1819 and 1864, struck down a population that is estimated to have been 11,200 in 1823 to about 6,000 within one generation.[19] If that were not enough, by the late 1860s successive waves of American traders opened whisky posts throughout the region. Offering an almost unlimited supply of liquor at places like Akaisakoyi (Many Dead, commonly known as Fort Whoop-Up), Standoff, and Slideout. The whisky forts soon became places where the Siksikaitsitapi tragically fell victim to white avarice, poisoned liquor, and violence without compare. Following the arrival of the North West Mounted Police, which was dispatched in 1874 to what would become southern Alberta with the remit to dismantle the illegal liquor trade, the Siksikaitsitapi were forcibly settled under Treaty 7 in 1877 and relocated to reserves in the expectation that they would be assimilated into a sedentary, Christian, and agricultural lifestyle. By 1880 the buffalo herds that had provided a rich staple had been all but exterminated by whites, Cree, and mixed-blood Aboriginal hunters from the east, leaving the Siksikaitsitapi little choice but to settle on reserves east of Calgary, south and west of Fort Macleod, and east of Pincher Creek.

Today members of the three First Nations live throughout traditional Siksikaitsitapi territory, including the cities of Lethbridge (population 75,000) and Calgary (population 1 million), where the Aboriginal populations are 3.5 percent and 2.3 percent, respectively.[20] Aboriginal urbanization is as old as the city in Canada.[21] However, the large-scale migration of Aboriginal people to cities began only in the 1960s, not as "a sign of growing readiness to join the majority society, but rather [as] a desperate response, on the part of a people most unready to leave the security of the reserve, to the shrinking demand in rural job markets."[22] Urbanization among Indigenous people in Canada has since increased to the point where nearly one-half of all Aboriginal people currently reside in urban areas. In the half-century that followed the 1951 census, the proportion of urban Aboriginal people increased from 6.7 percent to 49 percent. In Calgary the Aboriginal population increased 41.2 percent from 1996 to 2001, compared to a general population increase of only 15.5 percent. Additionally, as Pruegger demonstrates, the city's Aboriginal population is young, with one-third under the age of fourteen. Finally, while nearly half of Aboriginal Calgarians own their own home (44.5 percent), urban Aboriginal people continue to be over-represented in the homeless population, constituting 14.7 percent of the total.[23]

As alien as the city can be for the Siksikaitsitapi, their culture and history is not far away. In addition to their proximity to three Siksikaitsitapi reserves, Calgary and Lethbridge each have a network of roadways, buildings, landmarks, and public parks that have Aboriginal origins. They include the Apikaiees (Scabby Dried Meat, commonly known as the Deerfoot) expressway and Isapo-muxika (Crow Indian's Big Foot, commonly shortened to Crowfoot) boulevard, the Calf Robe Bridge, the Elbow River, and Nosehill Park in Calgary; and the Napi-tahta (Old Man River), Ishiktakmiska (Slough or Where it Flows Across), Asinaawa-iitomottsaawa (Were We Slaughtered the Crees, now called Indian Battle Park), and Aksiiksahko (Clay Banks or Steep Banks) in Lethbridge. For the Siksikaitsitapi, these places are profoundly significant as cultural representations that have been long fixed in *Inahkotait-sinik-a'-topi* (what we pass on through the generations, through storytelling).

Whether oral or written, narrative can be understood as a sequence of relayed temporal events that record, recount, define, frame, order, structure, shape, schematize, and connect human experiences.[24] Narrative concisely helps us to make sense of the world by defining and asserting shared significance, while it reaffirms or transforms power relationships intrinsic to a social system. Additionally, as Julie Cruikshank observes, narrative includes meaningful accounts that people transmit in word or gesture that are extraordinarily distinctive, whether in the complexity of subjectivity or in the nuances between form and meaning.[25] Poet and novelist Ben Okri notes that "we live by [narratives, yet] we also live in them. One way or another we are living the stories planted in us early or along the way."[26] In this way, the embodiment and emplacement of narratives illustrate their flexibility and the ways in which cities and reserves can (and do) generate different narrative structures or styles.

Yi-Fu Tuan, a leading scholar of the cultural geography of place and space, recognized the historical, academic neglect of speech – in which we include narrative – that occurred when geographers, historians, and the general public failed to see or hear speech that surrounded city planning and place making.[27] For Aboriginal people in Canada, one of the most persistent arguments against urbanization is the real or perceived loss of language, for although the "loss of language doesn't necessarily lead to the death of a culture, it can severely handicap [the] transmission of that culture."[28] At present, only 24 percent of the people who identify themselves as Aboriginal in Canada possess language competency in their mother tongue; among the Siksikaitsitapi, only 4,415 are conversant in Blackfoot.[29] This loss of language (and, subsequently, of narratives themselves) appears to be consistent with recent personal and collective narrative forms that originate from urban Aboriginal dwellers who portray profound subjectivity as well as embody stories that are generally pre-ordained by urban theory.[30] When we investigated this further, we sought the counsel of Stanley Knowlton, a member of the Siksikaitsitapi who lives in Lethbridge but also maintains a home on the Kainai Nation south of Fort Macleod. Stanley, who recently completed a postgraduate degree at the University of Lethbridge and focused on Siksikaitsitapi entho-archaeology, related to us: "The people have lost the Niitis'powahsinni [Blackfoot language], so they have lost the stories. Many Blackfoot people in cities ... don't speak ... or have [not] been taught ... or have forgotten their language. See, every place ... in Lethbridge ... as well as in southern Alberta, our traditional land ... has a Blackfoot name. These places also have stories – Blackfoot stories. Some are about Nápi, while some are family or personal stories. These stories in our language pass on our history ... pass on our culture ... that is why language is so important."[31]

In surveying storytelling and seeking context and meaning for Siksikaitsitapi stories, we identify four principal varieties of contemporary Aboriginal narrative and develop a fifth model. The first variety is anchored in urban theory. Often temporal and a vehicle for delivering metaphorical notions of the metropolis, this type of narrative describes the clash between modern and postmodern, rural and urban, while frequently depicting the individual in a continuous struggle for identity.[32] These stories become linked specifically with urban theories and remain key features in "myth making" or the telling and retelling of urban legends as folklore, which can generally shape the perception of city life.[33] Such narratives often register powerful markers in theory. However, stories linked with urban theory are often inconsistent with everyday experiences. The clarity in their linguistic grammar, the weight of social context, and the overall description tend "to drive rival and complementary interpretations and explanatory sketches out of mind, with the result that the object of study – a human experience, which is almost always ambiguous and complex – turns into something schematic and etiolated."[34]

Perceptional and family narratives, developed and maintained by individuals and family groups, are the second identifiable group of narratives. As subjective stories, they are guided temporally but rooted in family histories and the personal life stories of urban dwellers.[35] For ethnic minorities in the urban environment, narrative links past and present, allowing for cultural congruency as well as the marking of place in a new environment. Aboriginal narratives in Canada, by contrast, are generally rural in origin and nature and have little tolerance for these urban narratives beyond the victimization, assimilation, and enculturation of Aboriginals who have "lost their way" in the bright lights of the city.[36]

A third range of narratives includes those best defined as colonial in nature and originating from non-Native interpretations of rural Native life. In response to this discourse, Aboriginal writer Thomas King suggests that the often stereotypical notions of Aboriginal people in such narratives are incomplete, and he notes that they "trust easy oppositions ... [and are] suspicious of complexities, distrustful of contradictions, [and] fearful of enigmas."[37]

A fourth variety of narrative, also non-Native in origin and broadcast, is the racist story, delivered either as a bigoted joke or as an ethnocentric aside.

We propose a fifth, alternative approach. Although our aim is not to scrutinize narrative form in general, we recognize that narratives take a distinctive form among urban Siksikaitsitapi. We argue that, as cultural anchors, Siksikaitsitapi narratives enrich life with the "language, stories and experiences of everyday life," and thereby expand Siksikaitsitapi life beyond the "traditional" into the "modern."[38] In this way, Siksikaitsitapi stories frame what we define here as "transponsive narratives" – narratives that are fluid, situational, and responsive reflections of the world in which they are created and shared. At one level, our model of transponsive narratives identifies them as ongoing expositions of the philosophy and science of creation as well as discourses with an Aboriginal worldview. However, transponsive narratives are more than expressions of a given worldview. They help to make sense of the world, but they are, in a sense, the world itself, presented in a culturally meaningful and value-laden package. Transponsive narratives are indicators of location and situation: they are dialogues, not monologues, that are neither chronologically static nor extemporaneous. Nor are they entirely ancient; rather, they remain malleable, at times embryonic, as they continue to inform and frame daily life as events require. As a kind of reflective dialogue, stories in our model of transponsive narrative become culturally insightful mirrors of day-to-day realities that, in turn, lend explanatory weight to the stories themselves. They offer a series of explanations and elaborations on the here-and-now world of the contemporary city, as well as delivering dialogues that speak to the importance of stories and storytelling in general. As the 1996 *Report of the Royal Commission on Aboriginal Peoples* noted, "In Aboriginal historical traditions the particular creation story of each people, although it finds its origins in the past, also and more importantly, speaks to the present. It invites listeners to participate in the cycle of creation through their understanding that as parts of a world that is born, dies and is reborn in the observable cycle of days and seasons, they too are part of a natural order, members of a distinct people who share in that order."[39]

Elsewhere, this purposive use of transponsive narrative is illustrated in Martina Tyrrell's observations about Inuit traditional ethno-zoological knowledge at Arviat, Nunavut: "Stories not only link a person to the past, but give guidance for present and future actions. Stories have practical meaning, other than being good for passing the time. Through the performance of stories, identity is reconfirmed and ideas and suggestions for practical action are presented, either consciously or subconsciously on the part of the narrator."[40]

Beyond the everyday, Leroy Little Bear – Siksikaitsitapi scholar and former professor of Native American studies at the University of Lethbridge – illustrates the expansive purpose of transponsive narratives in a research paper prepared for the Royal Commission on Aboriginal Peoples: "Creation is continuity, and if creation is to continue, then it must be renewed. Renewal ceremonies, songs and stories are the human's part in the maintenance of the renewal of creation. Hence the Sundance, the societal ceremonies and the unbundling of medicine bundles at certain phases of the year are all interrelated aspects of happenings that take place on and within Mother Earth."[41]

Our model of transponsive narrative illuminates Siksikaitsitapi stories as beacons of First Nations identity. Additionally, they broadcast an unambiguous sense of cultural legitimacy by employing stories to mark the identity of urban Aboriginal narrators who superimpose Siksikaitsitapi culture and meaning over more recent developments – like the expanding urban stretch of Calgary or Lethbridge, as is explained in the following narrative:

> I do a lot of walking ... As I walk, [my] *Kakyosin isstaokaki'tsotsp* [observation that gives us intelligence, knowledge, and wisdom] of the landmarks speak about our *Kipaitapiwahsinnooni* [traditional knowledge]. I see Nápi; I see the Old Man's belly [pointing to the river]. I see where the three brothers went ... [pointing to the eastern horizon]. These markers remind me that I am *ookóówa* [at home]; whether I am on the reserve or here in Lethbridge, I can still see them.[42]

Siksikaitsitapi transponsive narratives not only claim the city as an Aboriginal place, they reclaim it. They do not create but rather recreate urban spaces as Siksikaitsitapi spaces – as they were originally. This recognition of Aboriginal places and narrative portrays *Niipaitapiiwahin* (culture, way of life) and is best exemplified in narratives we have been told a number of times through the course of the present research. What follows are the reflections of Narcisse Blood, a member of the Siksikaitsitapi who teaches Kainai studies at Red Crow Community College on the Kainai Reserve south of Fort Macleod:

Once there was a hunter who was hungry and needed to feed his family and himself, so he went hunting in the foothills and mountains. He was poor and only had one horse; he could not trade or buy another. Back then, men had two or more horses, one to ride and others or another to pack the meat. This hunter only had one horse. He was a poor man. He was very happy this day as he had a successful hunt. So he cut up the meat and put it on his only horse, leaving some meat for coyotes, wolves and other animals. While he was on his way home, a pack of wolves ran by him to get to the meat he had left for them he supposed; the wolves did not bother him. A while later, the hunter came across Old Wolf slowly making his way up the trail in the direction of the other wolves and the meat the hunter had left. The hunter stopped his horse and proceeded to take out a choice cut to offer to the Old Man. The hunter told the Old Man, by the time you get to the kill, there will be nothing for you, here take this meat so you will not starve. The Old Man, thanked the hunter and replied, I am in a hurry as those that ran ahead will be hungry, I need to get there as they will not start without me, I am their grandfather. Before the Old Wolf left, he told the hunter, you will be rewarded for your generosity. That hunter never had any problems with hunting ever again and as a result had many horses.[43]

Narcisse Blood's story, told from the point of view of someone who has spent much of his life living in Alberta's cities, is set in what is currently southern Alberta and, thus, plays out in territory that includes the cities of Lethbridge and Calgary. It speaks to and teaches about Blackfoot reciprocity and the importance of respecting all that surrounds us – a landscape that now includes urban regions. Although seemingly describing an event from the past, the story, as a transponsive narrative, indigenizes the landscape, not to make sense of the built environment but rather to continue the practice of *taking up a view in* the world.[44] Put simply, transponsive narratives further a sense of belonging and connection to southern Alberta for all Siksikaitsitapi people.

If, as Thomas King observes (citing Anishinabe writer Gerald Vizenor in *The Truth about Stories*), "You can't understand the world without telling a story ... there isn't any centre to the world but a story," then Nápi narratives are stories of great importance to the Siksikaitsitapi.[45] Yet, to many non-Natives, Nápi, or Old Man, remains enigmatic. Contemporary and conventional perspectives misrepresent Nápi in a number of ways. Nápi is often presented as merely a traditional icon – fixed to the labels of long-lost mythology or quaint oral history. Non-Aboriginal people often characterize Nápi stories as little more than trickster tales.[46] To define Siksikaitsitapi stories in this way, as other than transponsive narratives, not only limits their significance, it also reduces them to archaic relics and frames Aboriginal people's experiences as merely contingent and negotiated.[47] This tendency to misrepresent reflects what Cree scholar Loraine Le Camp defines as "the 'terranullism' of critical theory – the habit on the part of academics from all backgrounds to adopt a post-conquest set of assumptions, that the Americas are originally empty lands, devoid of any valid Indigenous presence."[48]

The first written account of Nápi appeared over a century ago, after anthropologist George Grinnell was told the following:

> In the beginning there was water everywhere; nothing else was to be seen. There was something floating on the water, and on this raft were Old Man and all the animals. Old Man wished to make the land, and he told the beaver to dive down to the bottom of the water and try to bring up a little mud. The beaver dived and was under the water for a long time, but he could not reach the bottom. Then the loon tried, and after him the otter, but the water was too deep for them. At last, the muskrat was sent down, and he was gone for a long time; so long that they thought that he must have drowned, but at last he came and floated almost dead on the water, and when they pulled him up and looked at his paws, they found a little mud in them. When Old Man had dried this mud, he scattered it over the water and land was formed.[49]

Later, in a chapter entitled "Blackfoot Genesis," Grinnell described Nápi as a creator who "made the mountains, prairies, timber, and brush ... fixing-up the world as we see it to-day. Old Man covered the plains with grass for the animals to feed on ... He put trees in the ground. He put all kinds of animals on the ground."[50] Later, Nápi made the first woman and child and gave the Siksikaitsitapi gifts of clothing, tools, and the land on which they live.[51] Elsewhere, Walter McClintock described Nápi as "a strange and mythical character ... he was a sort of creator and teacher, but at the same time a trickster who played evil pranks. Some of the tales about him were brutal and obscene."[52]

A later generation of anthropologists virtually ignored the central importance of Nápi to the Siksikaitsitapi: Oscar Lewis, in 1942, and Ester Goldfrank, in 1945, made no mention of Old Man in their seminal ethnographies.[53] Following McClintock, John Ewers identified the Old Man River that flows through the Aapatohsipiikani (North Piikani) Reserve as the Old Man's Gambling Place.[54] More recently, Alice Kehoe has identified specific locations in southern Alberta associated with Nápi, including, Old Man's Sliding Place, Rolling Stone Creek, and Tongue Flag River.[55] David Peat argues that "Nápi is not cast in the Western heroic mold; rather, he performs foolish acts, turns things upside down, and makes people laugh."[56] Elsewhere, Peat describes him as "always manifesting himself in a different form; sometimes he's an old man, at other times, he's an animal or baby."[57] More importantly,

> Nápi is the creator, the one hero who brought the land into being, the one who gave it its shape and form. Nápi created the animals and gave the Blackfoot their home. Nápi also allowed The People to choose death over continual life and in this way provided for balance on earth. But Nápi is also the trickster, the Clown, the Old Man who transcends the laws of nature ... Yet in no way is Nápi a mythic person or anthropological hero figure. As an actual being he walked across the earth teaching the Blackfoot.[58]

However, it is the Siksikaitsitapi themselves who offer the most complex and compelling descriptions of Nápi, ones that are framed within the context of transponsive narratives. Siksikaitsitapi Elder Stanley Knowlton describes Nápi as "the maker of the land, animals, and people. He is responsible for the placement of all the plants, rivers, lakes, and mountains."[59] In *Nitsitapi-isinni: The Story of the Blackfoot People*, Nápi is described variously as "rude, mean, and stingy. He often lied and played dirty tricks. He was always getting into trouble and suffering the consequences of his bad behavior. And yet, he did not act out of malice. He merely overdid things and caused chaos as a result."[60] Siksikaitsitapi scholar Betty Bastien speaks of Nápi as being "representative of the fallibility of man. He reminds us that to do things that are wrong will result in negative consequences. He is the subject of our legends in which he is always getting himself into difficult situations because he doesn't do the 'right thing.' If something bad or humorous happens as a result of our in-attention, etc., we might say 'That is Nápi, he is all around us.'"[61]

To some Siksikaitsitapi, Old Man stories mark the significant link that Nápi continues to hold in the here and now:

> I see our stories – stories of Nápi – not in time, like it is under-
> stood when isolated to categories of oral history or mythology,
> but as stories that speak of distance. When we speak of Nápi, the
> stories do not move you back in time, but they transport you to
> the places where the stories occur. See ... Nápi stories are still alive;
> they still are part of us, so to speak of them as they were of another
> time ... makes these stories and [Blackfoot peoples] an artifact like
> those in the museum. [Placing] stories in terms of distance, you
> recognize the land and the stories and the places that are real and
> already there.[62]

Cleary more than archaic and somewhat quaint trickster tales, Napi stories convey Siksikaitsitapi membership, a clear sense of place and belonging in the urban environment, and a series of fluid philosophical reflections.

Linking Blackfoot and Nápi stories to the landscape raises the question of how one might identify the ways in which traditional narratives speak about, or add to, the modern Canadian city. Beyond challenging static classifications, Siksikaitsitapi transponsive narratives advance the Aboriginal struggle for recognition and, by continuing to tell Aboriginal stories, link the "contemporary" and the "traditional," as a Siksikaitsitapi Elder outlined recently:

> While the land and all that live on [it] ... are covered with concrete
> ... and the buffalo hunt is replaced with rush hour traffic ... and
> traditional stories are [supplanted] by news broadcast ... [our
> memory] is limited to what yesterday's headlines were ... It is
> the stories, Nápi and others that speak about those places that

were once open prairie ... [and] even the grasslands and bush is replaced with office towers and houses. It is our stories that keep us alive ... [as] they are not forgotten ... [and in this way, we as a people can be] on equal footing in these places ... because the stories are still there.[63]

In light of sustained existence, the Old Man defies conventional Western labelling and moves Siksikaitsitapi transponsive narratives from the realm of the archaic and invariable to that of the vigorous and variable. Therefore, while Nápi remains uneasily defined, to some, the label of trickster is hard to ignore, as is illustrated here:

See Nápi – he arrives at the time between thought and the physical form. That time just before an action takes place. In this way, Nápi is the city ... he is said to live there because of all the many different things happening ... the constant change ... the constant movement. Nápi is a funny one; he is never happy with what he creates. He continually goes back and changes things. This is why the city changes its form, a road here, houses there, next year, the house gets torn down for a shop, etc.[64]

More often than not, Aboriginal trickster stories have been interpreted as functioning as an adaptive tool that serves to buffer and mitigate the ill effects of life in a "hostile" city environment.[65] Conversely, Susan Lobo argues that Aboriginal Elders are an important segment of the urban population, and the stories they tell maintain, in part, tribal traditions.[66] Nonetheless, these interpretations – regardless of whether they are viewed as arguments that recognize functional adaptation or as arguments that recognize cultural preservation and maintenance – typically prevent Siksikaitsitapi knowledge and narrative from being perceived as moving beyond folklore in popular thought and, therefore, confine Indigenous knowledge, of which Blackfoot transponsive narratives are a part. Nevertheless, Siksikaitsitapi knowledge continues to resist identification as an ethnographic artifact or minority adaptive strategy:

Many assume Nápi is gone – people say that he moved north after he was done here [at Lethbridge]. He turned west near what is now Nanton and went into the trees ... some say he is there, but

he was not done yet. He told the people before he moved north
that he would be coming back from this way [pointing east]. The
Siksika used to have their camps in rows with the entrances facing
this way [pointing east]. When the Siksika first encountered ...
[European explorers], the Siksika assumed [they were] Nápi, so
[the Siksika] put their camp back into a circle ... So Nápi is here
somewhere [making a circle with his hand].[67]

While the dynamic nature of Nápi may appear dubious for non-Aboriginal
city dwellers, for many Siksikaitsitapi, Nápi stories are not interpreted in the
same light; they are seen to be set into motion by and through Elders who
"know when it is right to release those stories."[68] The recent circulation of
Nápi stories about the city may also be a cautionary statement by the *Iipom-
mowaiksi* (old people) about the perils of losing sight of *Niisitapi Oopai-
tapiiyssoowaiyi* (the lifeway of Niitsitapi, or all First Nations).[69] Regardless of
their rationale or purpose, "these stories are out there, but many don't believe
... Nápi doesn't fit into western notions."[70] This apprehension is illustrated
with a description of a contemporary Aboriginal performance:

Nápi also changes the people in the city – there was a play [I
recently saw] ... that used Nápi ... It begins with a Nápi story –
he has many wives – the play then moves to depict a man and a
woman who have a child; the man and woman fight, he leaves the
woman and child for another woman, they drink, and [the play]
ends with the man leaving that woman to live on the street for
awhile. The play ends with the last part of the Nápi story. As
uncomfortable as it was for many of the people present, the
play illustrates that Nápi is here today. He interacts, moves, and
attempts to assist [in his creation]. Sometimes it works, and sometimes it doesn't. The point is that Nápi is said to be the city.[71]

Beyond the cynicism that some may feel is inherent in the previous narrative, the recent adventures of Nápi do more than exemplify a description
of the harsh realties of life for many Siksikaitsitapi in the city; rather, they
describe the ways that Old Man assists people in understanding modern-day
topics. Elsewhere, Nápi helps to decipher the unfamiliar architecture of the
contemporary city, where the physical world appears contentious because of
its significance to Siksikaitsitapi peoples living on or off the reserve:

The city is seen by more Blackfoot to be the centre [not only because of the city's great potential, resources and lifestyle], but the centre is where Nápi brings things together. Take a building for example – a tree is chosen and then cut down; it then goes to the sawmill and becomes a board, which is brought to the city to build a house; the wood is joined with other materials – metal in nails, which come from rocks; oil in plastic, which come from the ground; concrete, which is made of stone and sand – and on it goes.[72]

Yet, as Garrett Tailfeathers, himself a Siksikaitsitapi who has lived both on the Blackfoot Reserve and in a city, told us, the connection to the physical world is always present and clear:

The earth is never far; in fact, it is at our feet as I speak to you ... We do lose some connection to our mother [earth] because every place we go in the city appears to be covered with concrete, covering our mother's power. But, look over there [pointing to the sidewalk]. See those weeds? They are able to break the sidewalk and live. So, if a weed can grow, so can I. My father says that I will lose my Nativeness; others tell me that I am becoming white. To me, I am like that weed: I still belong to the earth, even if I am an annoyance to those that only see me as altered.[73]

A final narrative combines the self and the environment through stories that are created in the city:

The house is further joined with thought, which humans bring, [and soon this building] becomes a home, a place of stories, and the stories are built up and become special. But Nápi gets jealous and tries to destroy those places and build new ones that he wants. In the end, the city and Nápi are one.[74]

With the creation of the physical landscape that began with Nápi's movement through what is now recognized as southern Alberta, Nápi remains in the stories and the lessons imprinted on the land and remembered and lived by Siksikaitsitapi individuals, families, and communities. As cultural anchors, Siksikaitsitapi narratives enrich life, telescope time and space, and extend beyond the traditional into the modern:

> We want new words to describe our presence; we don't want to be considered [as] vanishing ... [or] invisible ... We are part of this country. We don't want ... to be considered as [merely traditional], our people are well versed in society in general; [therefore, we are in fact] contributing to [the greater urban] society, [as well as to our] own [culture, making us] ... modernists.[75]

As transponsive narratives that remain fluid, situational, and responsive reflections of the world in which they are created and shared, Siksikaitsitapi stories inform and frame daily life in the city – just as they do on the reserve – as the dynamism of events require. For those who seek it, they provide salient philosophical and scientific discourses that reflect the Siksikaitsitapi worldview. Finally, they remain self-referential, illuminating the importance of stories and storytelling in general.

Ultimately, through Nápi stories, the city becomes a gathering place for some Siksikaitsitapi. The metropolitan landscape becomes not only a collection of individuals but also a collective of Aboriginal communities, landscapes, and institutions. Consequently, the city becomes a different kind of public space for Aboriginal people, a place not to be headed to, but a place to be from, a place where one can be a citizen, not a transient. In this fashion, far from a being a "vanishing race," the Siksikaitsitapi move forward in a manner that is consistent and congruent with both the old (the traditional) and the new (the modern). Put another way, through the use of transponsive narrative, Siksikaitsitapi culture is not something that is simply abandoned at Alberta's city limits.

ACKNOWLEDGMENTS

The authors wish to thank Cameron Reid, Ryan Heavy Head, Dawn Farough, and three anonymous reviewers for their valuable input to earlier drafts of the present work. We would also like to express our sincere gratitude to those Siksikaitsitapi who shared their stories, insights, and wisdom with us and afforded us fresh opportunities to think about stories and the people who tell them.

NOTES

1   Jeremy Hull, *Aboriginal People and Social Classes in Manitoba* (Winnipeg: Canadian Centre for Policy Alternatives, 2001), 53.

2   Kevin Lee and Cheryl Engler, *A Profile of Poverty in Mid-Sized Canadian Cities* (Ottawa: Canadian Council on Social Development, 2000), 1, http://www.ccsd.ca/pubs/altapov/2.htm.

3   Edgar J. Dosman, *Indians: The Urban Dilemma* (Toronto: McClelland and Stewart, 1972), 8.

4   We use Blackfoot terminology, wherever possible, out of respect for the Blackfoot language and its speakers, and as further evidence of the persistence of Blackfoot culture in urban Alberta.

5   Howard Morphy, "Landscape and the Reproduction of the Ancestral Past," in *The Anthropology of Landscape: Perspectives on Place and Space,* ed. Eric Hirsch and Michael O'Hanlon (Oxford: Clarendon Press, 1995), 184-209.

6   John Borrows, "Listening for Change: The Courts and Oral Tradition," *Osgoode Hall Law Journal* 39, 1 (2001): 1-38.

7   Ryan Heavy Head (Kainai Studies Department, Mi'kaistoo Community College) in discussion with the authors, Lethbridge, May 2004.

8   David Newhouse, "Hidden in Plain Sight: Aboriginal Contributions to Canada and Canadian Identity Creating a New Indian Problem" (paper presented at "First Nations, First Thoughts," 30th Anniversary Conference, Centre of Canadian Studies, University of Edinburgh, 5 May 2005), http://www.cst.ed.ac.uk/2005conference/archiveN-Z.html.

9   David Newhouse and Evelyn Peters, introduction to *Not Strangers in These Parts: Urban Aboriginal Peoples,* ed. David Newhouse and Evelyn Peters (Ottawa: Policy Research Initiative, 2003), 5.

10 Tim W. Patterson, "The 'Other' Aboriginal: Reconsidering the Urban Aboriginal Image," *Opinion Canada* 6, 3 (2004): 1-2.

11 Ibid., 1.

12 Tim W. Patterson and Martin J. Whittles, "Reclaiming Cities: Canadian Aboriginal Urban Stories in Context," *Opinion Canada* 6, 38 (2004): 1.

13 See Evelyn Peters, "'Urban' and 'Aboriginal': An Impossible Contradiction?" in *City Lives and City Forms: Critical Research and Canadian Urbanism,* ed. Jon Caulfield and Linda Peake (Toronto: University of Toronto Press, 1996), 47-62.

14 Walter McClintock, *The Old North Trail: Life, Legends, and Religion of the Blackfeet Indians* (Lincoln: University of Nebraska Press, 1999), 5.

15 Ibid., 5.

16 Diamond Jenness, *The Indians of Canada* (Ottawa: E. Cloutier, Queen's Printer, 1932), 317.

17 Hugh A. Dempsey, "The Blackfoot Nation," in *Native Peoples: The Canadian Experience,* ed. R. Bruce Morrison and C. Roderick Wilson (Don Mills, ON: Oxford University Press, 2004), 275-96.

18   Esther S. Goldfrank, *Changing Configurations in the Social Organization of a Blackfoot Tribe during the Reserve Period: With Observations on Northern Blackfoot Kinship*, Monographs of the American Ethnological Society 8-9 (Seattle: University of Washington Press, 1945), 5.

19   Dempsey, "The Blackfoot Nation," 429.

20   Statistics Canada, "Aboriginal Peoples in Canada: A Demographic Profile," 2001 Census, Statistics Canada, http://www12.statcan.ca/english/census01.

21   See also *The Rossdale Flats Aboriginal Oral Histories Project* (Edmonton: Edmonton Aboriginal Urban Affairs Committee, 2004), 4.

22   Helen Buckley, *From Wooden Ploughs to Welfare: Why Indian Policy Failed in the Prairie Provinces* (Montreal and Kingston: McGill-Queen's University Press, 1992), 6.

23   Valerie Pruegger, "Aboriginal People: Diversifying Calgary's Communities," *Perspectives: Calgary's Window on Social Issues* (Spring 2005): 3.

24   Nigel Rapport and Joanna Overing, *Social and Cultural Anthropology: Key Concepts* (London: Routledge, 2000), 283-84.

25   Julie Cruikshank, *Life Lived Like a Story: Life Stories of Three Yukon Native Elders* (Vancouver: UBC Press, 1991), 2-4.

26   Ben Okri, *A Way of Being Free* (London: Phoenix House, 1997), 46.

27   Yi-Fu Tuan, "Language and the Making of Place: A Narrative Descriptive Approach," *Annals of the Association of American Geographers* 81, 4 (1991): 684.

28   Mary Jane Norris, "Canada's Aboriginal Languages," *Canadian Social Trends* 51 (1998): 8.

29   Statistics Canada, "Aboriginal Peoples in Canada: A Demographic Profile."

30   Ruth Finnegan, *Tales of the City: A Study of Narrative and Urban Life* (Cambridge: Cambridge University Press, 1998), 15.

31   Stanley Knowlton (Siksikaitsitapi Elder), in discussion with the authors, Lethbridge, July 2002.

32   See Finnegan, *Tales of the City*, 19.

33   See also Alan Dundes, *Folklore Matters* (Knoxville: University of Tennessee Press, 1993), 8.

34   Tuan, "Language and the Making of Place," 686.

35   Dolores Hayden, *The Power of Place: Urban Landscapes as Public History* (Cambridge, MA: MIT Press, 1997), 46-47.

36   See also Mylène Jaccoud and Renée Brassard, "The Marginalization of Aboriginal Women in Montréal," in *Not Strangers in These Parts*, ed. Newhouse and Peters, 131; Thomas Biolsi, "The Anthropological Construction of 'Indians': Haviland Scudder Mekeel and the Search for the Primitive in Lakota Country," in *Indians and Anthropologists: Vine Deloria, Jr., and the Critique of Anthropology*, ed. Thomas Biolsi and Larry J. Zimmerman (Tucson: University of Arizona Press, 1997), 134.

37   Thomas King, *The Truth about Stories: A Native Narrative* (Toronto: House of Anansi Press, 2003), 25.

38 Knowlton, in discussion with the authors, Lethbridge, July 2002.

39 Canada, Royal Commission on Aboriginal Peoples, *Report of the Royal Commission on Aboriginal Peoples*, vol. 1, *Looking Forward, Looking Back* (Ottawa: Canada Communications Group, 1996), pt. 1, chap. 3, s. 1.

40 Martina Tyrrell, "Knowledge and Enskillment in a Northern Marine Environment" (paper presented at "First Nations, First Thoughts," 30th Anniversary Conference, Centre of Canadian Studies, University of Edinburgh, 6 May 2005), http://www.cst.ed.ac.uk/2005conference/archiveN-Z.html.

41 Leroy Little Bear, James Youngblood Henderson, and Tony Hall, "The Relationship of Aboriginal People to the Land and the Aboriginal Perspective on Aboriginal Title," research paper prepared for the Royal Commission on Aboriginal Peoples, 1993, quotation cited in Canada, Royal Commission on Aboriginal Peoples, *Report of the Royal Commission on Aboriginal Peoples*, vol. 1, pt. 1, chap. 4.

42 Knowlton, in discussion with the authors, Lethbridge, July 2002.

43 Narcisse Blood, "Indigenous Knowledge" (paper presented at "First Nations, Métis and Inuit Education" conference, Calgary, Alberta, 8 March 2005; see also Betty Bastien, *Blackfoot Ways of Knowing: The Worldview of the Siksikaitsitapi* (Calgary: University of Calgary Press, 2004), 35–36.

44 Tim Ingold, "Human Worlds are Culturally Constructed: Against the Motion," in *Key Debates in Anthropology*, ed. Tim Ingold (London: Routledge, 1996), 117.

45 King, *The Truth about Stories*, 32.

46 Vine Deloria Jr., *Custer Died for Your Sins: An Indian Manifesto* (Norman: University of Oklahoma Press, 1988), 13; see also, Ralph Maud, *A Guide to BC Indian Myth and Legend* (Vancouver: Talonbooks, 1982), 9.

47 Bonita Lawrence, *"Real" Indians and Others: Mixed-Blood Urban Native Peoples and Indigenous Nationhood* (Lincoln/Vancouver: University of Nebraska Press/UBC Press, 2004), 2.

48 Ibid., citing Lorraine Le Camp, "Terra Nullius/Theoria Nullius – Empty Lands/Empty Theory: A Literature Review of Critical Theory from an Aboriginal Perspective," unpublished manuscript, Department of Sociology and Equity Studies, Ontario Institute for Studies in Education, 1998.

49 George Bird Grinnell, *Blackfeet Indian Stories* (New York: Charles Scribner's Sons, 1913), 145-46.

50 Ibid., 137-38.

51 Ibid., 139-44.

52 McClintock, *The Old North Trail*, 171.

53 Oscar Lewis, *The Effects of White Contact upon Blackfoot Culture with Special Reference to the Role of the Fur Trade*, Monographs of the American Ethnological Society 6 (Seattle: University of Washington Press, 1942) and Goldfrank, *Changing Configurations in the Social Organization of a Blackfoot Tribe*.

54 John Canfield Ewers, *The Blackfeet: Raiders on the Northwestern Plains* (Norman: University of Oklahoma Press, 1958), 4.

55 Alice Beck Kehoe, introduction to *Mythology of the Blackfoot Indians*, by Clark Wissler and D.C. Duvall (Lincoln: University of Nebraska Press, 1995), ix.

56 F. David Peat, *Blackfoot Physics: A Journey into the Native American Universe* (York Beach, ME: Phanes Press, 1996), 304.

57 Ibid., 284.

58 Ibid., 24-25.

59 Knowlton, in discussion with the authors, Lethbridge, July 2002.

60 Blackfoot Gallery Committee, *Nitsitapiisinni: The Story of the Blackfoot People* (Buffalo, NY: Firefly Books, 2001), 10.

61 Bastien, *Blackfoot Ways of Knowing*, 226.

62 Knowlton, in discussion with the authors, Lethbridge, July 2002.

63 Blood, "Indigenous Knowledge," 5.

64 Knowlton, in discussion with the authors, Lethbridge, June 2005.

65 Jeanne Guillemin, *Urban Renegades: The Cultural Strategy of American Indians* (New York: Columbia University Press, 1975); see also, Mary Lea Meadows, *Adaptation to Urban Life by Native Canadian Women* (Ottawa: National Library of Canada, 1981).

66 Susan Lobo, "Urban Clan Mothers: Key Households in Cities," *American Indian Quarterly* 27, 3 and 4 (2003): 505.

67 Knowlton, in discussion with the authors, Lethbridge, July 2002.

68 Ibid.

69 Sees also, Bastien, *Blackfoot Ways of Knowing*, 226.

70 Betty Bastien, "Transcending Trauma among First Nations" (paper presented at "First Nations, Métis and Inuit Education" conference, Calgary, 8 March 2005).

71 Knowlton, in discussion with the authors, Lethbridge, July 2002.

72 Ibid.

73 Garrett Tailfeathers (Siksikaitsitapi), in discussion with the authors, Lethbridge, 2005.

74 Knowlton, in discussion with the authors, 2005.

75 Darrell Kipp, "Darrel Kipp Speaks about Traditional and Modernist Values," 2002, Trailtribes.org, http://www.trailtribes.org/greatfalls/home.htm.

WORKS CITED

Bastien, Betty. *Blackfoot Ways of Knowing: The Worldview of the Siksikaitsitapi*. Calgary: University of Calgary Press, 2004.

–. "Transcending Trauma among First Nations." Paper presented at "First Nations, Métis and Inuit Education" conference, Calgary, 8 March 2005.

Biolsi, Thomas. "The Anthropological Construction of 'Indians': Haviland Scudder Mekeel and the Search for the Primitive in Lakota Country." In *Indians and Anthropologist: Vine Deloria, Jr., and the Critique of Anthropology*, ed. Thomas Biolsi and Larry J. Zimmerman, 133-59. Tucson: University of Arizona Press, 1997.

Blackfoot Gallery Committee. *Nitsitapiisinni: The Story of the Blackfoot People.* Buffalo, NY: Firefly Books, 2001.

Blood, Narcisse. "Indigenous Knowledge." Paper presented at "First Nations, Métis and Inuit Education" conference, Calgary, 8 March 2005.

Borrows, John. "Listening for Change: The Courts and Oral Tradition." *Osgoode Hall Law Journal* 39, 1 (2001): 1-38.

Buckley, Helen. *From Wooden Ploughs to Welfare: Why Indian Policy Failed in the Prairie Provinces.* Montreal and Kingston: McGill-Queen's University Press, 1992.

Canada. Royal Commission on Aboriginal Peoples. *Report of the Royal Commission on Aboriginal Peoples.* Vol. 1, *Looking Forward, Looking Back.* Ottawa: Canada Communications Group, 1996.

Cruikshank, Julie. *Life Lived Like a Story: Life Stories of Three Yukon Native Elders.* Vancouver: UBC Press, 1991.

Deloria, Vine, Jr. *Custer Died for Your Sins: An Indian Manifesto.* Norman: University of Oklahoma Press, 1988.

Dempsey, Hugh A. "The Blackfoot Nation." In *Native Peoples: The Canadian Experience,* ed. R. Bruce Morrison and C. Roderick Wilson, 275-96. Don Mills, ON: Oxford University Press, 2004.

Dosman, Edgar J. *Indians: The Urban Dilemma.* Toronto: McClelland and Stewart, 1972.

Dundes, Alan. *Folklore Matters.* Knoxville: University of Tennessee Press, 1993.

Ewers, John Canfield. *The Blackfeet: Raiders on the Northwestern Plains.* Norman: University of Oklahoma Press, 1958.

Finnegan, Ruth. *Tales of the City: A Study of Narrative and Urban Life.* Cambridge: Cambridge University Press, 1998.

Goldfrank, Esther S. *Changing Configurations in the Social Organization of a Blackfoot Tribe during the Reserve Period: With Observations on Northern Blackfoot Kinship.* Monographs of the American Ethnological Society 8-9. Seattle: University of Washington Press, 1945.

Grinnell, George Bird. *Blackfeet Indian Stories.* New York: Charles Scribner's Sons, 1913.

Guillemin, Jeanne. *Urban Renegades: The Cultural Strategy of American Indians.* New York: Columbia University Press, 1975.

Hayden, Dolores. *The Power of Place: Urban Landscapes as Public History.* Cambridge, MA: MIT Press, 1997.

Hull, Jeremy. *Aboriginal Peoples and Social Classes in Manitoba.* Winnipeg: Canadian Centre for Policy Alternatives, 2001.

Ingold, Tim. "Human Worlds are Culturally Constructed: Against the Motion." In *Key Debates in Anthropology,* ed. Tim Ingold, 112-18. London: Routledge, 1996.

Jaccoud, Mylène, and Renée Brassard. "The Marginalization of Aboriginal Women in Montréal." In *Not Strangers in These Parts: Urban Aboriginal Peoples,* ed. David Newhouse and Evelyn Peters, 131-46. Ottawa: Policy Research Initiative, 2003.

Jenness, Diamond. *The Indians of Canada*. Ottawa: E. Cloutier, Queen's Printer, 1932.

Kehoe, Alice Beck. Introduction to *Mythology of the Blackfoot Indians*, by Clark Wissler and D.C. Duvall, v-ix. Lincoln: University of Nebraska Press, 1995.

King, Thomas. *The Truth about Stories: A Native Narrative*. Toronto: House of Anansi Press, 2003.

Kipp, Darrell. "Darrel Kipp Speaks about Traditional and Modernist Values," 2002. Trailtribes.org. http://www.trailtribes.org/greatfalls/home.htm.

Lawrence, Bonita. *"Real" Indians and Others: Mixed-Blood Urban Native Peoples and Indigenous Nationhood*. Lincoln/Vancouver: University of Nebraska Press/UBC Press, 2004.

Le Camp, Lorraine. "Terra Nullius/Theoria Nullius – Empty Lands/Empty Theory: A Literature Review of Critical Theory from an Aboriginal Perspective." Unpublished manuscript, Department of Sociology and Equity Studies, Ontario Institute for Studies in Education, 1998.

Lee, Kevin, and Cheryl Engler. *A Profile of Poverty in Mid-Sized Canadian Cities*. Ottawa: Canadian Council on Social Development, 2000. http://www.ccsd.ca/pubs/altapov/2.htm.

Lewis, Oscar. *The Effects of White Contact upon Blackfoot Culture with Special Reference to the Role of the Fur Trade*. Monographs of the American Ethnological Society 6. Seattle: University of Washington Press, 1942.

Little Bear, Leroy, James Youngblood Henderson, and Tony Hall. "The Relationship of Aboriginal People to the Land and the Aboriginal Perspective on Aboriginal Title." Research paper prepared for the Royal Commission on Aboriginal Peoples, 1993.

Lobo, Susan. "Urban Clan Mothers: Key Households in Cities." *American Indian Quarterly* 27, 3 and 4 (2003): 505-22.

Maud, Ralph. *A Guide to BC Indian Myth and Legend*. Vancouver: Talonbooks, 1982.

McClintock, Walter. *The Old North Trail: Life, Legends, and Religion of the Blackfeet Indians*. Lincoln: University of Nebraska Press, 1999.

Meadows, Mary Lea. *Adaptation to Urban Life by Native Canadian Women*. Ottawa: National Library of Canada, 1981.

Morphy, Howard. "Landscape and the Reproduction of the Ancestral Past." In *The Anthropology of Landscape: Perspectives on Place and Space*, ed. Eric Hirsch and Michael O'Hanlon, 184-209. Oxford: Clarendon Press, 1995.

Newhouse, David. "Hidden in Plain Sight: Aboriginal Contributions to Canada and Canadian Identity Creating a New Indian Problem." Paper presented at "First Nations, First Thoughts," 30th Anniversary Conference, Centre of Canadian Studies, University of Edinburgh, 5 May 2005. http://www.cst.ed.ac.uk/2005conference/archiveN-Z.html.

Newhouse, David, and Evelyn Peters. Introduction to *Not Strangers in These Parts: Urban Aboriginal Peoples*, ed. David Newhouse and Evelyn Peters, 5-13. Ottawa: Policy Research Initiative, 2003.

Norris, Mary Jane. "Canada's Aboriginal Languages." *Canadian Social Trends* 51 (1998): 8-16.

Okri, Ben. *A Way of Being Free*. London: Phoenix House, 1997.

Patterson, Tim W. "The 'Other' Aboriginal: Reconsidering the Urban Aboriginal Image." *Opinion Canada* 6, 3 (2004): 1-2.

Patterson, Tim W., and Martin J. Whittles. "Reclaiming Cities: Canadian Aboriginal Urban Stories in Context." *Opinion Canada* 6, 38 (2004): 1-3.

Peat, F. David. *Blackfoot Physics: A Journey into the Native American Universe*. York Beach, ME: Phanes Press, 1996.

Peters, Evelyn. "'Urban' and 'Aboriginal': An Impossible Contradiction?" In *City Lives and City Forms: Critical Research and Canadian Urbanism*, ed. Jon Caulfield and Linda Peake, 47-62. Toronto: University of Toronto Press, 1996.

Pruegger, Valerie. "Aboriginal People: Diversifying Calgary's Communities." *Perspectives: Calgary's Window on Social Issues* (Spring 2005): 3.

Rapport, Nigel, and Joanna Overing. *Social and Cultural Anthropology: Key Concepts*. London: Routledge, 2000.

The Rossdale Flats Aboriginal Oral Histories Project. Edmonton: Edmonton Aboriginal Urban Affairs Committee, 2004.

Statistics Canada. "Aboriginal Peoples in Canada: A Demographic Profile." 2001 Census, Statistics Canada. http://www12.statcan.ca/english/census01.

Tuan, Yi-Fu. "Language and the Making of Place: A Narrative Descriptive Approach." *Annals of the Association of American Geographers* 81, 4 (1991): 684-96.

Tyrrell, Martina. "Knowledge and Enskillment in a Northern Marine Environment." Paper presented at "First Nations, First Thoughts," 30th Anniversary Conference, Centre of Canadian Studies, University of Edinburgh, 6 May 2005. http://www.cst.ed.ac.uk/2005conference/archiveN-Z.html.

PART 3
Cultural Heritage and Representation

5
Colonial Photographs and Postcolonial Relationships: The Kainai-Oxford Photographic Histories Project

Laura Peers and Alison K. Brown

Between 1924 and 1927 Beatrice Blackwood, an anthropologist from the Pitt Rivers Museum (PRM) in Oxford, conducted research on First Nations and African American communities in North America.[1] In the course of her fieldwork, Blackwood spent two days at the Kainai Nation in southern Alberta, where she took thirty-three photographic portraits.[2] Like many anthropological field collections, these photographs and Blackwood's other papers were eventually transferred to the PRM, where they became part of an extensive body of documentation that has been used in different ways to create narratives about Indigenous peoples, largely for Western audiences. Some eighty years later, copies of these photographs have been returned to the Kainai Nation through a visual repatriation project that takes into consideration the contemporary meanings of the images to Kainai people. The photographs, taken within intersecting anthropological and colonial perspectives on "traditional" and "acculturating" Aboriginal peoples, are the kind of colonial legacy that makes up ethnographic museum collections.

At the PRM, where such collections are exhibited within a deliberately retained Victorian mode of display, the shift to a postcolonial mode of intellectual curation might be thought to be especially challenging. The Kainai-Oxford Photographic Histories Project is, however, contributing to this shift, in part by exploring the meanings and shifting intellectual contexts of one collection. More importantly, and as a result of the project's outcomes, it is prompting the museum to develop new ways of working with source communities in which long-term partnerships are key.[3] The community-centred research process that has shaped the project has been crucial to uncovering – and challenging – the meanings, knowledge, and discursive formations attached to this collection of images.

Beatrice Blackwood's Research

Blackwood's research, funded by the Laura Spelman Rockefeller Foundation, concerned issues of culture, intelligence, and "race," broadly defined. She conducted psychological tests, gathered genealogies, and collected physical measurements from Native American and African American communities to try to understand which behaviours and physical appearances were inherited, which were responses to social and economic circumstances, and which were learned. By the time she reached the Blood Reserve in August 1925, she had realized that prejudice and poverty, as well as political forces, constrained the lives of First Nations far more than any physical factor. She was shown around the reserve by Joseph Faunt, the Indian agent, and recorded observations on the community's response to their economic situation and to restrictions on ceremonies imposed by the government, as well as comments about education and health care. Blackwood's photographs record what she thought depicted "traditional" or "modern" aspects of First Nations cultures; many are also referentially anthropometric in their paired front and side poses. Her Kainai images show men in the fields, women collecting rations, a family group beside a tipi, and children with their mothers. They also include photographs of girls at residential school who were forbidden by the staff to return home from the time they reached puberty until they married. The photographs thus show both the pressures the community faced at the time of Blackwood's visit and the strength of Kainai people. They make a remarkable portrait of a strong community in transition.

Process

The Kainai-Oxford Photographic Histories Project has demonstrated that research methodology is crucial to uncovering knowledge, meanings, and discursive formations surrounding artifacts, especially those that were acquired in circumstances of intellectual and political control during the colonial period. Over the years, many Aboriginal people have talked to us about the legacy of mistrust of museums and anthropologists that exists in their communities. We have been told about times when researchers have made promises that were not fulfilled or published sensitive information without permission. We have also been told about misinterpretations and errors within ethnographic texts and archival sources that are still drawn upon by researchers, Aboriginal and non-Aboriginal. It has been patiently explained to us that communities need to reinterpret historical documents and photographs in their own way, for their own purposes, to ensure that their histories

Kainai men, August 1925. *Left to right:* Kiaayo (Bear), Isstsstsiimi (Rough Hair), Aatso'to'aawa (Shot Both Sides), and Aasainio'tokaani (Crying Head), Blood Reserve, August 1925. *Photograph by Beatrice Blackwood / Pitt Rivers Museum, University of Oxford, PRM.BB.A3.74.*

are presented in their own words.[4] As this project has progressed, we have learned that historical photographs – including those produced by anthropologists – can be used by communities to recover histories that have been submerged by mainstream academic analyses and to prompt memories that challenge received interpretations.[5]

The Kainai-Oxford Photographic Histories Project has aimed to produce outcomes for both Kainai people and outside researchers. Together we have developed a kind of analysis that reflects both Aboriginal and Western understandings of how histories are constructed and how visual images serve as a focus for understanding the past. In addition, we have written a book geared

toward museum professionals and academics that considers the potential of
photographs to recover cultural and historical information for community
use and recognizes the importance of community consultation.[6] From the
beginning, however, we insisted that Kainai people frame the project and that
the results be accessible to them in a format of their choice.

When we began the project in 2001, we contacted the Mookaakin Cultural and Heritage Foundation, a voluntary organization that is for the most
part made up of spiritual advisers from the Kainai community who have
worked with museums throughout North America, primarily to negotiate
repatriation claims.[7] The role of the Mookaakin Foundation is not to grant
permission to researchers but to ensure that research is undertaken in a culturally appropriate manner that respects community-held values and serves
community needs. Several board members of the Mookaakin Foundation are
also educators, and they immediately saw great potential for using Blackwood's photographs in community schools. They also expressed interest in
Blackwood's motives and our own. From the outset the Mookaakin Foundation has supported our goal to emphasize to museum and archival professionals the importance of consulting with Aboriginal peoples. However, while
its members strongly wished to see Blackwood's photographs utilized to teach
history and recover voices and knowledge, they made it clear that the project
should proceed on Kainai terms to meet Kainai needs and not simply academic interests. Narcisse Blood, chair of the Mookaakin Foundation, explained his perspective, which had been shaped by many years of listening
to, observing, and working with researchers from outside the community:

> We want people to look at us more as people rather than as just
> another item or archival material in the museum. This is what we
> endured. This is what our ancestors went through. Just the fact
> that you're talking to a descendant of those is a testimony to the
> resilience, the spirit of those people and what they went through.
> And we still have challenges even today that we're facing. For us,
> it's inspirational too, to see the kind of hardships that they went
> through. If they could make it, we certainly can too ... Now, if we
> can convince you that we can do a lot more to reach some better
> understanding than in the past, that we're not just relics, you
> know, for somebody else's benefit, to earn a degree, or write
> about, or so forth.[8]

To meet their concerns, board members of the Mookaakin Foundation suggested that we write a protocol agreement that outlined the project goals and, to ensure that these goals were reached, spelled out the responsibilities of the museum staff and the Mookaakin Foundation. Verbal assurances that we would share the information were not enough. The Foundation wanted an agreement that extended beyond us as individual researchers to include the PRM itself. They envisaged a long-term relationship that would be upheld by future museum staff in the years ahead. The protocol agreement we developed states that the Mookaakin Foundation will help to facilitate interviews and will provide cultural guidance; in return, we agreed that a set of Blackwood's photographs would be given to the tribe and that copies of all interview tapes and transcripts would be sent to interviewees for review and, with their permission, deposited with the community. Furthermore, it was agreed that the board of the Mookaakin Foundation would see drafts of all oral or written presentations about the project. Several Kainai mentors, for instance, have read and commented on drafts of this chapter.[9]

Working Together

Working with the Mookaakin Foundation allowed us to learn about the community's views on research ethics and opened up connections within the community that we have been able to draw upon for assistance in the research process – whether this took the form of suggesting people whom we should approach for interviews or explaining cultural rules for behaviour. Although the protocol agreement was certainly a crucial starting point, its importance shifted as the project developed. Mookaakin Foundation members have since commented that they were willing to participate not only because we brought materials to them (without having to be asked) but also because of the way we approached them and tried to respect cultural rules of behaviour throughout the project. For example, Alison Brown met with the Red Crow Community College Elders Advisory Board early in the process to inform Elders about the nature of the project and seek their guidance on it, as is expected with any new cultural and educational project, and Kainai Elders have been an important source of guidance and support throughout the research.

The fact that we had made a commitment to ensure that the research would be available to the community was extremely important to those who shared their knowledge during interviews. Trust building proceeded differently across the community: for some, the protocol agreement was important

Andy Blackwater and Annie Bare Shin Bone examine Beatrice Blackwood's photographs,
27 November 2001. *Photograph by Alison Brown.*

as a formal codification of expectations; for others, making sure that every
interviewee had the opportunity to comment on how his or her information
would be used was far more important than any written document. It is also
important to emphasize that all those who assisted us did so for their own
reasons and to benefit future generations of Kainai in various ways.

The first phase of interviews, which Brown undertook from September
to December 2002, concentrated on identifying the people Blackwood photographed; people then began to share contextual biographical and historical
information. During the interviews the photographs were presented in clear
plastic wallets in a folder that also contained contact details for the PRM staff
who were responsible for the North American collections, Photograph and
Manuscript collections, and Marketing (the department responsible for au-
thorizing reproductions of images in the museum's collections); a short
biography of Blackwood and her research; and copies of the diary entries and
field notes that pertained to Blackwood's visit to the Blood Reserve. Sticky
notes were used to attach the identifications that Blackwood had provided
for some individuals, and these were added to as the interviews progressed

and names were remembered. The interviews were quite open, as we hoped people would talk freely about what the images meant to them, rather than being directed to particular topics. However, some general questions were asked of each interviewee that concerned the ways in which he or she thought the images might be used to talk about history and how they could be used within the community.

Many older people contributed to the project, but younger people were also interviewed. Although the youth did not necessarily know the people photographed personally, it was important for us to explore generational responses to the photographs and for younger Kainai to have an opportunity to express their views about the potential of the images to promote under-standing about the past. On one occasion a class of students at Kainai High School also viewed the photographs, and its members were invited to think about the relevance of the images to their own history. This added another perspective to the readings of the images, that of Kainai teenagers. Afterwards, their teacher spoke about how amazed she had been at the response of her students to images of their great-great-grandparents, as she had often found it difficult to get them to engage with other forms of history.[10]

This first phase of research was followed by a second field trip in the summer of 2002, when Brown revisited all those interviewed previously to review the transcripts and make any necessary changes. Progress reports were made to the Mookaakin Foundation and to the Red Crow Elders Advisory Council, and they were invited to comment on a proposed book outline. During this period many participants recorded consent statements, mostly in Blackfoot, in which they explained why they had contributed to the project and what they hoped future generations might learn from it. Mary Stella Bare Shin Bone, for example, made the following remarks:

> The way I see things, this is going to help us preserve our know-ledge of our people in the past ... In a lot of cases, what we cannot recall about us we tend to rely on the white man's version of us [the written version]. I, for myself, do not rely on or have the white man's perception. I strongly rely on our own perception in respect to our view of our way of life ... Today we have lost a great deal of our ways; it is important that this project takes place so that it may help our people, especially the young, to recall more of our history ... If I thought and believed that it is not to the benefit of our people, then I will not share my knowledge.[11]

Following this second visit, and prior to a further short field trip in May 2003, we drafted the book manuscript and sent chapters to the Mookaakin Foundation and other interested community members. On this visit each interviewee was shown the draft manuscript, we explained the context in which their quotations had been used, and asked for their approval and suggestions for any changes. It was also during this trip that copies of all the tapes, transcripts, and Blackwood's photographs were presented to Red Crow Community College for community use and we hosted a supper at the college to which everyone who had participated was invited. At this event we put copies of the photographs up on the wall, with the identifications in Blackfoot and English, so that other people who were in the building at the time and who had not previously had an opportunity to see them were able to do so. It was at this event that the one individual who had yet to be recognized was finally identified as Piaana (Falling over the Cutbank). Although this man's face was familiar to many of the people who had seen the photograph, his name had not been recalled. There was considerable discussion among the guests as to who he might have been and some concern that he might remain "nameless." However, when Sylvia Weasel Head, the wife of one of our advisers, Frank Weasel Head, arrived, she recognized the man almost immediately, and her identification of him as Piaana was then confirmed by several other guests.

Meanings and Knowledge Revealed

Museums are repositories of knowledge that can transcend existing narratives and ways of thought, and Blackwood's photographs are a very good example of this. As Elizabeth Edwards has noted of anthropological photographs more generally, "even the most dense of colonial documents can spring leaks" if one looks carefully at the images themselves and at "the points of fracture" provided by their details and their implications.[12] Theory and narratives by dominant-society scholars about Indigenous peoples have, of course, a long history of entanglement with relations of power between these groups. Challenging these existing narratives and theories is similarly entangled with altering the relations of power that surround artifacts in museum collections, especially those artifacts that have been important in the formulation of theory. In our case, negotiating issues of power that are embedded in research proved to be vital to understanding the meanings that the Kainai attached to Blackwood's images and to challenging existing anthropological understandings of these photographs.

In the process of interviewing community members about Blackwood's photographs, a great deal of information was recovered – but this would not have been the case if we had taken a less community-based approach to research. Indeed, had we not been willing to frame the research and outcomes according to community expectations, it is likely that the project would not have proceeded at all. We emphasize, however, that we are not simply saying, "We were sensitive ethnographers, and, therefore, people spoke to us." By trying to understand the community's concerns about the research process, we actually began to understand what these images mean to Kainai people. Their concern that we adhere to cultural protocols for the proper transmission of information had much to do with the nature of the information they saw encoded in the photographs, and with the culturally based intellectual framework within which Kainai people interpreted the images. This Kainai framework emphasizes biography and family history as lenses through which one understands community history as well as the fluid dynamics between past and present.

This relationship between method and theory can perhaps be best understood as a parallel register of meaning to that often used in the analysis of ethnographic photographs, which are "read" at both the surface level of forensic detail and at the deeper level of the historical, intellectual, social, and political contexts that went into their composition.[13] Only by working in a community-based manner could we begin to understand the nature and importance of the deeper level of conjunctive knowledge associated with the photographs and the attendant social responsibilities attached to such information.

This model of parallel registers of meaning is also useful for understanding Kainai responses to the photographs. The portraits elicited a great deal of biographical and associated family information about the people shown. As a result of our early discussions with members of the Mookaakin Foundation and the Red Crow College Elders Advisory Board, it was decided, collectively, that such personal, family histories did not belong in an academic publication. Should Kainai people themselves wish to publish or use this kind of information in educational projects, they would need to negotiate its use with the families concerned. In addition to genealogical knowledge, interviewees shared information that clustered into several broad themes about Kainai history and survival, which we agreed could be written about for external audiences. These themes include the period of transition represented by the photographs; the survival of Kainai people and culture in the face of such change; and the cultural knowledge and values embedded in the photographs, which were "read" by Kainai people from surface details that they saw in the images. This kind of information acts as a frame of reference and is needed to enable younger people – who may lack other sources of such knowledge – to learn about the strength of ancestors who survived this period, dominated as it was by assimilation policies that were imposed by colonial agencies.

One especially striking example that shows these different layers of meaning concerns naming practices and the importance Kainai people have placed on restoring both the Blackfoot and English names of individuals whom Blackwood photographed. Although Blackwood recorded some English names, her images were intended as "type" shots, and within this analytical framework the personal names of her subjects were not important. For the Kainai, however, recovering the Blackfoot names was central to the project. Older people related how important identification is to sharing clan and family histories that are linked to those individuals and promoting an understanding of the historical knowledge embedded in the names. In addition, younger people suggested that the photographs could be used to reconstruct part of the community's history that has not been passed down. As Betty Bastien observed, biographies of Blackwood's subjects that have not been transmitted to succeeding generations may yet come to be told because the individuals are known to community members whose lives overlapped with them. These reflections can be used to help younger people understand the realities of their ancestors' lives and the importance of the contributions that their former leaders made: "These kinds of pictures give us our connections in terms of the generations. And the history ... about our people and the kind of people they were, their personality, perhaps their accomplishments, what they did for the tribe ... like Shot Both Sides ... that's a history that we don't have, in terms of our own history of the generations before us."[14] Indeed, Aatso'to'aawa (Shot Both Sides) (1873-1956), who became a lifetime head chief of the Kainai in 1913 and can be seen on page 125, is remembered today as an extremely strong leader who defended the land and rights of his people against severe opposition from the Canadian government.[15]

Visual anthropologist Roslyn Poignant has noted that photographs, memories, and histories intersect with one another and, in combination with other ways of articulating perspectives about the past, can prompt "inside ways of responding to culturally specific actualities, which are not necessarily available to outsiders."[16] Kainai responses to Blackwood's photographs reveal

Schoolgirls under the age of fifteen at St. Mary's Roman Catholic Residential School, Blood Reserve, August 1925. *Back row, left to right:* Kimmata'pssii (Lily Shot Both Sides), Iinakay (Annie Good Rider), Mini (Minnie Snake [or Bug] Eater), Rosine Two Flags, Antonia Hairy Bull, Mini (Minnie Sun Going Up the Hill). *Front row, left to right:* Aistaayohtowa (Eva or Emma Mills), Mini (Minnie Chief Moon), Josette Melting Tallow, Mary MacDonald, Bibian Sun Dance, Mary A. Skipper, Nancy Many Bears, Susan Crazy Bull, Adeline Fox, Lizzie Standing Alone. *Photograph by Beatrice Blackwood / Pitt Rivers Museum, University of Oxford, PRM.BB.A3.79.*

an acute concern among some community members that each successive generation's knowledge of community-focused histories and genealogies has been disrupted or cut off. Access to photographs allows people to share "inside" readings of the images, which successive generations can then reincorporate into their understanding of the community's collective history or into individual family histories.

Kainai insistence on recovering the names of individuals in Blackwood's photographs, then, is by no means a narrow focus on surface details. The names themselves, which are family and clan-based, are central to how Kainai construct and use history. Most importantly, their responses to the photographs made it very clear that the images can have dual sets of meaning: one familiar to anthropologists and one familiar to the Kainai. These are not simply anthropometric photographs; they are photographs of Kainai people, lives, and histories. By reattaching names, the Kainai appropriated these photographs to fit with their own ways of inscribing the past.[17]

A second theme addressed by many interviewees concerned the notion of historical transition. Blackwood's photographs were taken during a time when the differences in experience and expectation between community members who had grown up on the reserve and those who recalled the pre-treaty era were becoming starkly apparent. The introduction of new systems of education, politics, religion, and health care, combined with agricultural developments, fostered an environment in which the Kainai embraced and adapted to these changes at varying levels. As visual indicators of people's responses to their changing circumstances, the forensic details in photographs enable them to be read in ways that complement documentary sources and confirm oral histories. As a result, the photographs can be used to broaden understanding of a period of Kainai history that has not been the subject of extensive research.[18]

The notion of survival was related to this theme. Some people spoke of the images in terms of the negative experiences of disruption and loss; at the same time, they saw within the images strength and contentment, from which they felt people today could learn. Frank Weasel Head, for example, spoke forcefully and eloquently about what he saw in the images:

> I'm proud to see these pictures of our people. And to me, it's sort of an educational thing. I see those people; I know some of these people personally. I met them. I talked to them. And some of them are still alive; the younger ones, they are still alive. I know them and I can see how they struggled in those times. And they struggled. They were caught in between the old ways and the new ways, and they struggled. They adapted, but yet they wanted us to keep our old ways, our old values. And yet, they knew we had to sort of change in order for us to succeed. I always say we can never go back fully to the old days, the physical way we lived, but we can keep, as they kept, their values and traditions. They kept their values; we can keep those values and still live in the modern way of living, in our homes, everything. As long as we keep our traditional values of what those people lived through. And they managed. They managed, and we can keep our traditional ways, and we can keep within our own values and traditions – our language, our

spirituality, our respect, our sharing, caring, and loving of other
people, and respecting all people, all things; and I mean things
that nature provides for us, respecting those. They coexisted; we
can learn to coexist with each other. And that's sort of the way
I look at these pictures.[19]

Even though the community had been confined to a reserve for fifty years,
for many Kainai the images show the connections that the people depicted
in the photographs still had with their traditional culture and worldview. As
they discussed the transitions that their ancestors had experienced, many
individuals commented on their ability to adapt, survive, and maintain their
identity as Kainai, despite extreme hardships and being subject to the destructive impact of colonial rule.

This sense of survival and pride in identity, and in history, was remarked
upon with great admiration and respect. Even though the photographs held
many mixed messages for viewers, the theme of survival and awe at what
their ancestors had endured for the benefit of their children and grandchildren
was articulated repeatedly, in terms that emphasized the importance of
understanding their ancestors' struggles and experiences, and learning from
them today. This point was, perhaps, best summed up by Andy Blackwater:

[This] was perhaps almost the lowest point in our history. When
the buffalo was all gone. Not having the kind of industrial skills
and farming, ranching ... And it's reflected even in the faces of the
pictures. But being a First Nation people, your priorities are different. Of course we joke about ourselves, character-wise, but the
richness of our people is on the inside rather than on the outside.
And you look at these pictures, and even though they are going
through some hardship, you can see people are somewhat content. Still content. Some are able to laugh. They are not completely
succumbed to the outside forces; still have their liberty, freedom at
least to facial and other expressions. It shows the diversity and the
ability to adapt to new situations. We are very adaptable.[20]

Kainai in Oxford

Working collaboratively, under the guidance of the protocol agreement and
in the knowledge that this methodology would have important outcomes for
the Kainai Nation and the Pitt Rivers Museum, we considered it essential that

some of our core advisers from the Mookaakin Foundation have the opportunity to see the other context of the photographs project: the Pitt Rivers
Museum, with its Victorian-style displays. We also thought that it was important for a broad range of the museum's staff to meet some Kainai who had
been involved in the project so that there would be a stronger institutional
understanding of the importance of working with source communities. These
goals echo those of much recent work in museums with Indigenous people
because source community members often express their frustration with finite,
project-based consultations and their desire for broader relationships to support long-term mutual agendas.[21] Although many museums have worked
hard in recent years to develop closer relationships with community groups,
particularly in the area of exhibitions development, this work rarely extends
to full co-management of collections in instances where the museum and
the community are located at considerable distance from each other.[22]

After we had multiple trips to the Blood Reserve to work on various aspects of the project, we were finally able to welcome Kainai visitors to the Pitt
Rivers Museum in the spring of 2004. Frank Weasel Head and Andy Blackwater, with whom we had worked closely during the entire project, spent
several days in Oxford, meeting staff, looking at collections, and seeing the
museum.[23] To extend the relationship we had formed, we asked Weasel Head
and Blackwater to help museum staff identify and understand Blackfoot
material in the PRM collections. We thought that our relationship and our
obligations, as set out in the protocol agreement, extended to assisting our
advisers to locate and examine material heritage held in overseas museums.
Moreover, we recognized that, reciprocally, they could add greatly to the
museum's knowledge of its collections, just as they had with Blackwood's
photographs. In order to allow their voices to be heard directly by the museum's staff and students, we also invited them to give a lecture on the work
they had done to repatriate sacred material. Although we had not anticipated such opportunities or obligations when we began working with the
Kainai, the implications of collaboration and partnership were making themselves clear: they extended beyond the life of the photographs project to other
Blackfoot collections in the PRM and other UK museums. Collaboration, and
the mutual respect on which it is founded, led onward, into the future, in
sometimes unexpected ways. That the PRM staff and the Kainai found that
they had things to say to one another beyond the scope of the photographs
project, and could find other ways of assisting each other, was a natural out-
growth of this process.

The most exciting part of the visit by Weasel Head and Blackwater was a session that examined mid-nineteenth-century Blackfoot ceremonial shirts in the PRM collections. These shirts, acquired in 1841 or 1842 by Hudson's Bay Company officials, came to the PRM in the 1890s and have seldom been exhibited; they have largely been inaccessible to Blackfoot people since their collection. Knowing that these were important heritage objects, we asked our advisers to examine them in the museum's storeroom and tell us their responses. Upon examining one shirt in detail, Weasel Head and Blackwater taught us to look for traces of body paint left by the wearers and described their ceremonial use. When Weasel Head saw a drawer with another five of these shirts, though, he said, "I have never even seen one of these kinds of shirts. Not a single one."[24] In his lecture to PRM staff and students the following day, he asked not only why he had never seen these shirts before but also why not a single Kainai child in the past century and a half had ever seen them. Blackwater subsequently reminded us why such visits are difficult for Aboriginal people: "You are holding part of us there. We don't alienate ourselves from those items. We continue to include them in our prayers. In our community we don't have one of those at all, at the present time.[25]"

Andy Blackwater has since explained that providing access to historic artifacts, such as the photographs and the shirts, is a way of looking beyond the items themselves to consider the possibility of knowledge regeneration and revival within source communities.[26] As is the case with responses to Blackwood's photographs, tribal perspectives on historic artifacts are important to the consolidation and transmission of cultural knowledge and, thus, can encourage the process of community healing: the stories told about objects, and the knowledge embodied in them, are important to the construction of strong cultural identity today. Many collections made in North America are held in British museums, where they are largely unknown to First Nations people. Providing physical access to such material is expensive and difficult but extremely important, as part of the responsibility that museums have in caring for their collections is interpreting them and making them accessible. On the basis of Weasel Head's and Blackwater's responses to these early shirts – and our subsequent discussions with representatives from the Kainai, Piikani, and Siksika Nations and the Blackfeet Tribe in Montana – we have begun to plan a temporary exhibition of the shirts, which will travel to the Glenbow Museum in Calgary and the Galt Museum in Lethbridge in 2010. This will be followed by conservator-led handling workshops for tribal members and outreach activities for schoolchildren and youth groups in Blackfoot communities. As a bridge between the two projects, and in order to begin the process of thinking about the shirts and their meanings in the community, we have also circulated sets of detailed images of the shirts in all Blackfoot communities. In addition, we have promised to consult with, and involve, Blackfoot people in the grant-writing, exhibition, and workshop-planning processes, as well as in the writing of publications derived from the project. We see this as a direct extension of the spirit of the photographs project in which we learned so much from bringing tribal members together with their material heritage, thereby enabling stories associated with these items to emerge and circulate within the community.

Implications and Conclusion

At its deepest level, this project has turned out to be not about photographs or artifacts, at all, but about relationships – the relationships documented in the photographs and the relationships that can be developed around such materials in the present. The knowledge generated and recovered in this project has taken many forms. We have learned that although community members welcomed the opportunity to use the knowledge elicited by the photographs to create counternarratives to external impressions of Kainai people and history for a broad audience, they were primarily interested in using the images to bridge knowledge gaps within their *own* community. We should emphasize that this is a common situation in projects that bring together museum collections, curators, and Indigenous source communities: there is not simply a multiplicity of narratives and counternarratives but usually a multiplicity of agendas and goals for such projects, which differ greatly for museum, scholarly researcher, and source community members. Like the narratives themselves, these competing agendas and goals are not always reconcilable.

For the Kainai, historical and cultural information has been retrieved, recorded, transcribed, and deposited for community use in the library at Red Crow Community College. The photographs that were given to individuals for personal use are also circulating throughout the community and, in many cases, have taken their place alongside other family photographs on display in people's homes. Beatrice Blackwood's intended meaning, to document racial "types" and examples of cultural purity, is being subverted, and the photographs will serve as prompts for conversations, across generations, about Kainai cultural values and behaviour. The interview tapes are already being listened to, and we have received messages from college staff about the richness of the information recorded in Blackfoot specifically for the community. This material is being used not only for teaching purposes but also to help staff members clarify aspects of their own genealogies. For example, Duane Mistaken Chief, an instructor at the college, explained that looking at the photographs and listening to the interview tapes has cleared up a number of questions that surrounded his own history and that of his children's family: "They actually do have a lot contained in them and knowing the language; the context; and the background of the speakers really enriches what I have heard on the tapes. It's kind of like having a different kind of conversation going on in my head, other than what is being said on tape."[27]

For the PRM staff, the process of learning how to work within a community-based research paradigm has been challenging but rewarding. We have had to rethink the issue of copyright attached to photograph collections, our obligations to source communities, and the ways in which source communities are (and generally are not) represented in displays, research grant applications, and institutional policies. The protocol agreement has provided the basis for policy documents within several departments of the museum. Most significantly, we have gained a sense that collections really do belong, at one level, to their communities of origin, that they have meanings, memories, and knowledge attached to them that are tremendously empowering in places other than the museum or scholarly arena. We also learned that the collaborative research process, and the relationships it creates, are not limited to the end of a grant-funded project: mutual obligations and the desire to assist one another continue into the future and, like other kinds of social relationships, continue to evolve.

One of the most important lessons the PRM staff learned was about the nature of repatriation. Intriguingly, none of the Kainai we worked with raised the issue of bringing the original images home: establishing access to the images was crucial, and the museum needs to ensure that these images are accessible to community members over time and in various formats and locations. It was equally intriguing that many Kainai viewed the development of knowledge, rather than repatriation, as the project's primary concern. That there are possibilities, rather than simply problems and losses, within the concept of repatriation has been a powerful lesson for the museum staff.

It has taken almost eighty years for the Kainai community to have access to Blackwood's photographs, and one of the questions posed by the Kainai at the outset of the project was, why had it taken the museum so long to bring these images to them? In trying to answer that direct and necessary question, we have had to articulate our own understanding of why museums need to operate differently within the postcolonial era and how they might do so. As the PRM redefines itself as a relational museum, by exploring social and material relationships in the present as well as the past, we look forward to fostering an ongoing relationship with the Kainai Nation. This will help us to understand more fully how the meanings they bring to museum collections can foster new perspectives on colonial interactions and contribute to debates about the responsibilities of museums to source communities.

ACKNOWLEDGMENTS

We would like to thank the Centre of Canadian Studies, University of Edinburgh, for giving us the opportunity to present at the "First Nations, First Thoughts" conference and are most grateful to participants in our panel for their feedback. We also appreciate the thoughtful editorial suggestions of Annis May Timpson. We would also like to thank the Arts and Humanities Research Council for funding the Kainai-Oxford Photographic Histories Project and our PRM colleagues for their suggestions and practical assistance. Most especially, we would like to thank the people of the Kainai Nation for agreeing to work with us on the project and for supporting us every step of the way.

NOTES

1   Beatrice Blackwood's photographs and papers are in the Photograph and Manuscript collections of the PRM, http://www.prm.ox.ac.uk.

2   The Kainai (Aakainaiwa or Aapaitsitapi, in their own language) are a Blackfoot-speaking people who were referred to at the time of Blackwood's visit, and often still are, as the Blood Tribe. The traditional territory of the Blackfoot people runs from the North Saskatchewan River south to the Yellowstone River and from the Rocky Mountains east to the Cypress Hills in present-day Saskatchewan. The Blackfoot recognize three tribes among themselves: the Kainai; the Piikani (Peigan), who comprise the Aapatohsipiikani (or Northern Piikani in southern Alberta) and the Aamsskaapipiikani (Blackfeet or Southern Piikani), whose reservation is in Montana; and the Siksika (also referred to as Blackfoot or Northern Blackfoot), whose reserve is located approximately 100 kilometres east of Calgary. See Blackfoot Gallery Committee, *Nitsitapiisinni: The Story of the Blackfoot People* (Buffalo, NY: Firefly Books, 2001), 4-5.

3   The term "source communities" refers to the peoples and their descendants from whom artifacts in museums were collected. See Laura Peers and Alison K. Brown,

introduction to *Museums and Source Communities: A Routledge Reader*, ed. Laura Peers and Alison K. Brown (London: Routledge, 2003), 1.

4   See also Wayne Warry, "Doing unto Others: Applied Anthropology and Native Self-Determination," *Culture* 10, 1 (1990): 61-73.

5   For other photograph projects that explore these themes, see Joshua A. Bell, "Looking to See: Reflections on Visual Repatriation in the Purari Delta, Gulf Province, Papua New Guinea," in *Museums and Source Communities*, ed. Peers and Brown, 111-22; Judith Binney and Gillian Chaplin, "Taking the Photographs Home: The Recovery of a Maori History," in *Museums and Source Communities*, 100-10; Roslyn Poignant with Axel Poignant, *Encounter at Nagalarramba* (Canberra: National Library of Australia, 1996); Elizabeth Edwards, *Raw Histories: Photographs, Anthropology and Museums* (London: Routledge, 2001).

6   Alison K. Brown and Laura Peers with members of the Kainai Nation, *Sinaakssiiksi aohtsimaahpihkookiyaawa/Pictures Bring Us Messages: Photographs and Histories from the Kainai Nation* (Toronto: University of Toronto Press, 2006).

7   Dr. Gerald Conaty, director of curators, Glenbow Museum, is also on the board. Conaty is not Blackfoot himself, however, he has extensive experience working in the areas of repatriation and the traditional care of First Nations collections. Institutions with which the Moohaahin Foundation has worked include the National Museum of the American Indian, the Royal Alberta Museum, Glenbow Museum, the Canadian Museum of Civilization, and Parks Canada.

8   Interview between Narcisse Blood and Alison Brown, Red Crow Community College, Kainai First Nation, 6 December 2001.

9   The text of the protocol agreement is reproduced in Brown and Peers with members of the Kainai Nation, *Sinaakssiiksi aohtsimaahpihkookiyaawa*, Appendix 3.

10 Alvine Mountain Horse to Alison Brown, personal communication, Kainai First Nation, 6 December 2001. For comparative remarks concerning the responses of Blackfeet students to historical photographs, see William E. Farr, *The Reservation Blackfeet, 1882-1945* (Seattle: University of Washington Press, 1984), xiii.

11 Interview between Mary Stella Bare Shin Bone and Alison Brown, Kainai First Nation, 14 August 2002, translated from the Blackfoot by Andy Blackwater.

12 Edwards, *Raw Histories*, 12.

13 See, for example, Elizabeth Edwards, "Visualizing History: Diamond Jenness's Photographs of D'Entrecasteaux Islands, Massim, 1911-1912 – A Case Study in Re-engagement," *Canberra Anthropology* 17, 2 (1994): 1-26.

14 Interview between Betty Bastien and Alison Brown, Sunset Motel, Fort Macleod, 27 November 2001.

15 Brown and Peers with members of the Kainai Nation, *Sinaakssiiksi aohtsimaahpihkookiyaawa*, 21-22.

16 Poignant with Poignant, *Encounter at Nagalarramba*, 8.

17 See Edwards, *Raw Histories*, 100.

18 Although the Blackfoot nations have been the subject of numerous ethnographies and popular accounts, there are few scholarly works that address in detail Kainai experiences during the 1920s. Historical literature that provides context for the early twentieth century includes Lucien M. Hanks and Jane Richardson Hanks, *Tribe under Trust: A Study of the Blackfoot Reserve of Alberta* (Toronto: University of Toronto Press, 1950); Hugh Dempsey, *Tom Three Persons: Legend of an Indian Cowboy* (Saskatoon: Purich Publishing, 1997); Farr, *The Reservation Blackfeet*; Mary Eggermont-Molenaar, ed. with contributions by Alice Kehoe, Inge Genee, and Klaus van Berkel, *Montana 1911: A Professor and His Wife among the Blackfeet* (Lincoln: University of Nebraska Press, 2005), Keith Regular, *Neighbours and Networks: The Blood Tribe in the Southern Alberta Economy, 1884-1939* (Calgary: University of Calgary Press, 2008). Four volumes of Elders' recollections produced by the Blood tribe have also been extremely valuable to this project: Flora Zaharia and Leo Fox, eds., *Kitomahkitapiiminnooniksi: Stories from Our Elders*, vols. 1-3. (Edmonton: Donahue House Publishing/Kainai Board of Eduation, 1995) and Flora Zaharia, Leo Fox, and Marvin Fox, eds., *Kitomahkitapiiminnooniksi: Stories from Our Elders*, vol. 4 (Edmonton: Duval House Publishing/Kainai Board of Education, 2003).

19 Interview between Frank Weasel Head and Alison Brown, Shot Both Sides Administrative Building, Standoff, Kainai First Nation, 28 November 2001.

20 Interview between Andy Blackwater and Alison Brown, Continuing Care Centre, Standoff, Kainai First Nation, 26 November 2001.

21 On such shifts in museological praxis, see Ruth Phillips, "Community Collaboration in Exhibitions: Toward a Dialogic Paradigm," in *Museums and Source Communities*, ed. Peers and Brown, 155-70.

22 In countries such as Canada, New Zealand, and Australia, there have been concerted efforts to find ways to co-curate collections that extend beyond exhibition work. Constrained as they are by distance and the political implications of serving primarily the needs of local people above those of overseas audiences, museum staff in Europe generally have far less experience addressing traditional care and co-management practice as these relate to the material heritage of Indigenous communities. For a notable UK exception, however, see Anita Herle, "Museums and Shamans: A Cross-Cultural Collaboration," *Anthropology Today* 10, 1 (1994): 2-5.

23 The visit followed from Frank Weasel Head and Andy Blackwater participating in the opening of the Glenbow Museum's travelling exhibition, "Nitsitapiisinni: The Blackfoot Way of Life," Manchester Museum of Science and Industry, 30 January to 6 June 2004. Weasel Head and Blackwater were accompanied to Oxford by Beth Carter, curator of ethnology at the Glenbow Museum.

24 Frank Weasel Head, personal communication to Alison Brown and Laura Peers, Pitt Rivers Museum, Oxford, 2 February 2004.

25 Andy Blackwater, telephone interview with Laura Peers, 5 May 2004.

26   Andy Blackwater, telephone interview with Alison Brown, 5 December 2006.

27   Duane Mistaken Chief to Alison Brown, e-mail communication, 15 April 2004.

WORKS CITED

Bell, Joshua A. "Looking to See: Reflections on Visual Repatriation in the Purari Delta, Gulf Province, Papua New Guinea." In *Museums and Source Communities: A Routledge Reader*, ed. Laura Peers and Alison K. Brown, 111-22. London: Routledge, 2003.

Binney, Judith, and Gillian Chaplin. "Taking the Photographs Home: The Recovery of a Maori History." In *Museums and Source Communities: A Routledge Reader*, ed. Laura Peers and Alison K. Brown, 100-10. London: Routledge, 2003.

Blackfoot Gallery Committee. *Nitsitapiisinni: The Story of the Blackfoot People*. Buffalo, NY: Firefly Books, 2001.

Brown, Alison, and Laura Peers, with members of the Kainai Nation. *Sinaakssiiksi aohtsimaahpihkookiyaawa/Pictures Bring Us Messages: Photographs and Histories from the Kainai Nation*. Toronto: University of Toronto Press, 2006.

Dempsey, Hugh. *Tom Three Persons: Legend of an Indian Cowboy*. Saskatoon: Purich Publishing, 1997.

Edwards, Elizabeth. *Raw Histories: Photographs, Anthropology and Museums*. London: Routledge, 2001.

–. "Visualizing History: Diamond Jenness's Photographs of D'Entrecasteaux Islands, Massim, 1911-1912 – A Case Study in Re-engagement." *Canberra Anthropology* 17, 2 (1994): 1-26.

Eggermont-Molenaar, Mary, ed., with contributions by Alice Kehoe, Inge Genee, and Klaus van Berkel. *Montana 1911: A Professor and His Wife among the Blackfeet*. Lincoln: University of Nebraska Press, 2005.

Farr, William E. *The Reservation Blackfeet, 1882-1945*. Seattle: University of Washington Press, 1984.

Hanks, Lucien M., and Jane Richardson Hanks. *Tribe under Trust: A Study of the Blackfoot Reserve of Alberta*. Toronto: University of Toronto Press, 1950.

Herle, Anita. "Museums and Shamans: A Cross-Cultural Collaboration." *Anthropology Today* 10, 1 (1994): 2-5.

Peers, Laura, and Alison K. Brown. Introduction to *Museums and Source Communities: A Routledge Reader*, ed. Laura Peers and Alison K. Brown, 1-16. London: Routledge, 2003.

Phillips, Ruth B. "Community Collaboration in Exhibitions: Toward a Dialogic Paradigm." In *Museums and Source Communities: A Routledge Reader*, ed. Laura Peers and Alison K. Brown, 155-170. London: Routledge, 2003.

Poignant, Roslyn, with Axel Poignant. *Encounter at Nagalarramba*. Canberra: National Library of Australia, 1996.

Regular, Keith. *Neighbours and Networks: The Blood Tribe in the Southern Alberta Economy, 1884-1939*. Calgary: University of Calgary Press, 2008.

Warry, Wayne. "Doing unto Others: Applied Anthropology and Native Self-Determination." *Culture* 10, 1 (1990): 61-73.

Zaharia, Flora, and Leo Fox, eds. *Kitomahkitapiiminnooniksi: Stories from Our Elders*. Vols. 1-3. Edmonton: Donahue House Publishing/Kainai Board of Education, 1995.

Zaharia, Flora, Leo Fox, and Marvin Fox, eds. *Kitomahkitapiiminnooniksi: Stories from Our Elders*. Vol. 4. Edmonton: Duval House Publishing/Kainai Board of Education, 2003.

6

Museums Taken to Task: Representing First Peoples at the McCord Museum of Canadian History

Stephanie Bolton

> Museums are not innocent, neutral institutions that evolve outside
> of sociopolitical struggles. Rather, they are shelters for the flotsam
> of a bygone past. Windows that open on the Other and mirrors
> of a collective Us, they are the living cells of a social memory that
> repeatedly creates and recreates a past that corresponds to what
> we think we are.
> > –Jean Hamelin, Le Musée du Québec[1]

The underlying sociopolitical imperatives of museum collections, exhibitions, and administrative policies with regard to Aboriginal peoples were brought into the spotlight in Canada in the late 1980s. In 1988 Calgary's Glenbow Museum presented an exhibition entitled "The Spirit Sings: Artistic Traditions of Canada's First Peoples" as the highly publicized showpiece of the Winter Olympic Games' Arts Festival.[2] The exhibition featured Aboriginal art and artifacts, from the period of early contact between Aboriginal peoples in Canada and European explorers and traders.

Response to "The Spirit Sings" was mixed; many critics deplored the exhibition for being insensitive to the present condition of Indigenous people and went so far as to suggest that the exhibition presented Aboriginal cultures as the vestiges of a prehistoric past. Moreover, presentation of "The Spirit Sings" coincided with negotiations between the Albertan, Canadian, and Lubicon Lake First Nation governments regarding traditional land titles and the treaty rights of the Lubicon people. The Glenbow Museum impoliticy granted exclusive corporate sponsorship for "The Spirit Sings" to Shell Canada, one of the companies that was, at the time, commercially exploiting land claimed by the Lubicon Nation. To protest the indifference and autocratic attitude of governments and corporations, and in reaction to the lack of respect accorded to First Nations, the Lubicon Nation called for a boycott of both the 1988 Winter Olympics and "The Spirit Sings."[3]

The boycott and the subsequent political, academic, and artistic debates were instrumental in effecting changes to federal museum policy. They familiarized a wider general audience with the issues of Aboriginal representation and cultural appropriation, making it impossible for governments or cultural institutions to trivialize or dismiss these issues. Of particular significance to this debate was the decision by the Canadian Museums Association (CMA) and the Assembly of First Nations (AFN) to organize a conference entitled "Preserving Our Heritage: A Working Conference for Museums and First Peoples." This was held at Carleton University in 1988 and led to the creation of the nationwide Task Force on Museums and First Peoples.[4]

This chapter investigates the influence of the Task Force on Museums and First Peoples on museum practices in Canada. It analyzes the problem of unequal social representation in museums, explains how the task force was formed, and describes the task force's objectives. It then introduces the McCord Museum of Canadian History as a case study that demonstrates the significant impact of the task force on exhibition practices in Canadian museums.

Museums Creating Culture

Regarded traditionally as neutral sites of historical commemoration, museums are currently being re-evaluated as producers of history that help to shape our understandings of cultural memory. Public memory, we now accept, is hardly objective: it is created and operates to unite (or divide) society and to form images that, through repetition, attain the value of truth, even if they deviate from fact.[5]

Because interactions between European settlers and Aboriginal peoples underpin Canadian history, Aboriginal objects are central elements in the collections of Canadian museums that tell stories of Canada since the early days of European immigration. The histories of Aboriginal peoples have been told by voices that have appropriated and distorted the past, often exploiting Aboriginal symbols, art, and culture to foster a specific perception of Canadian identity. Alternative histories are now redefining what constitutes a valid historical record, and, as a result, audiences are reconsidering which versions of that record merit a hearing. Moreover, dedicated efforts are being made to preserve – and therefore remember – a wider, more inclusive record of the past for future generations.

Political geographer James Anderson argues that successful identity construction involves ongoing reinforcement of both internal cohesion and external distinctiveness. In other words, we form a community because we share certain past events and commonalities and because others do not.[6] Producing a common social memory is an ongoing process that is reinforced through many sources, including, though not restricted to, academic history taught in public schools. Several participants at the "Preserving Our Heritage" conference noted how "museums are intended to preserve the past, but they also unwittingly preserve stereotypes."[7] In addition, they reflected on how "the stereotyping does not necessarily start in museums, it begins with teaching those who work in museums ... schools, universities, literature, the media, films, and television."[8] Changing inculcated inaccuracies that are embedded in the national consciousness requires a concerted effort on the ground. In her work as an Aboriginal educator in the Native Programs division of the McCord Museum, Dolorès Contré Migwans spent the last decade actively reviewing and revising educational programming.[9] This work has included the integration of a personal discourse into tours of the collection by school groups to diminish the objectification of Aboriginal peoples and cultures. She also helped to create a team of Aboriginal guides and workshop facilitators to eliminate archaic stereotypes that impede the development of an authentic understanding of contemporary Indigenous people.[10]

The role that museums play in attaching historical meaning to displayed artifacts is problematic. Selection policies often foster the presentation of an incomplete historical picture, and the inherent subjectivities of the individuals who decide what goes into the display case also affect this outcome. "Because of their partial nature," writes David Fleming, "museum collections have an inbuilt set of biases, and even when curators are keen to give pictures of life in the round ... they are handicapped by the range of material they have to hand."[11] Accumulating and displaying artifacts present more challenges. Fleming explains: "*What* we collected cannot be dissociated from *who* did the collecting. And this is where it starts becoming difficult, because our history collections, for example, reflect not the make-up of society at large, but the make-up of the collectors."[12]

Examining the McCord Museum during the transition period of the 1990s – when museums, the academic world, and public heritage organizations were deciding how to integrate the task force report into their operations (or whether to do so) – shows how an important cultural institution adapted to changing ideas about museum theory and to the expectations of historical accuracy, and representational fairness, provided by the task force. The Mc-Cord Museum's location in Montreal also made it the ideal subject of a case study that explores changing priorities in ethnographic and historical discourse. With pronounced social and spatial divisions based on language, religion, ethnicity, and wealth, the city of Montreal has long been confronted with acute tensions over the construction of public identities and, in particular, the commemoration of a contested past.[13]

The experience of the McCord Museum provides a valuable perspective on the issue of museums and cultural heritage because it has one foot in both the museum and academic worlds and benefits greatly from its close link to McGill University and the contributions of renowned scholars.[14] Moreover, as the McCord Museum was founded in order to create a museum of Canadian history and culture that embraced Anglo-Canadian, Franco-Canadian, and Aboriginal histories and relations, it acts as a barometer for changes in Canadian social attitudes toward Aboriginal people.[15]

Preserving Aboriginal Heritage

Before turning our attention to the McCord Museum, it is worth considering the origins of the task force itself. The primary objective of Carleton University's 1988 "Preserving Our Heritage" conference was the "establishment of ongoing mechanisms for exchange both between and amongst the Aboriginal and museum communities," in part to determine the best ways for non-Aboriginal institutions to represent Aboriginal cultures, arts, and histories sensitively to Aboriginal and non-Aboriginal communities in Canada.[16]

In his opening remarks at the conference, the AFN leader, Georges Erasmus, thanked the museum specialists who had dedicated their professional lives "to showing what they believe is the accurate picture of Indigenous peoples" and also expressed the desire of Aboriginal people to move beyond exhibitions in which non-Aboriginal experts analyze and represent Aboriginal peoples and subjects.[17] Integrity of expression and creative control of representations of the Aboriginal historical and cultural record by Aboriginal people were also important concerns for participants. As Chris McCormick, the representative of the Native Council of Canada, stated: "The project of reconquest [of our homeland] must extend to the task of interpretation. We must affirm control and sovereignty over our cultures; if we do not, we will remain guests and onlookers in the museum world. To be sure, we will be asked to consult and cooperate but we will not be in control. A culture that is controlled, owned, or housed under another roof is at most a refugee, at worst a dead thing. My culture has survived, but ... it must cease to be a refugee."[18]

While the "Preserving Our Heritage" conference was generally optimistic, and sparked enthusiasm for the creation of a task force to identify concrete measures and strategies for solving troublesome issues between museums and Aboriginal peoples, Barbara Tyler, then president of the CMA, acknowledged in her closing remarks that the people gathered at the conference were largely "the converted." No museum board trustees, and few institutional directors or government delegates, were present, and, in addition, many Aboriginal leaders were absent.[19] Understandably, some Aboriginal groups were reluctant to deepen their involvement with public cultural institutions. As cultural studies scholar Lola Young writes: "There are many who wish to remain 'excluded' because they do not wish to be a part of a system that promotes inequality and injustice throughout its structures. Any publicly funded organization may stand accused of reproducing the problems that it is supposedly attempting to resolve since it is, necessarily, part of the system and thus part of the problem."[20] Lee-Ann Martin, curator of Contemporary Canadian Aboriginal Art at the Canadian Museum of Civilization, concurs, and she notes that Aboriginal curators and cultural workers may feel some ambivalence about working in an institution in which they see Aboriginal cultures and histories misrepresented or dealt with summarily.[21] A common consensus still exists that until Aboriginal people gain representation in the power infrastructures of institutions controlled by the non-Aboriginal majority – representation commensurate with the importance of Aboriginal collections in those institutions – they must regard the policy decisions of museum board members with some suspicion. Despite these misgivings, the CMA and AFN decided at the closing of the conference that they would jointly organize and fund a task force to investigate the points raised at the conference and make specific recommendations for museums and Aboriginal groups.

Task Force on Museums and First Peoples
Building upon public debate surrounding "The Spirit Sings," and questions raised by museologists about the appropriate representation of Aboriginal arts and cultures in museums, the CMA and the AFN jointly set up the 1990 Task Force on Museums and First Peoples. It was designed to identify strategies that would help resolve deeply ingrained differences between cultural institutions and Aboriginal communities.

The first coordinator of the task force was Lee-Ann Martin, who was then a freelance curator and researcher, and the two co-chairs were Tom Hill of the Woodland Cultural Centre and Trudy Nicks of the Royal Ontario Museum. To round out the task force, the chairs chose Aboriginal and non-Aboriginal members of the museum and arts communities as well as representatives from Aboriginal communities across Canada.[22]

After two years of national consultations, the Task Force on Museums and First Peoples published its 1992 report, which emphasized the need for "the increased involvement of Aboriginal peoples in the interpretation of their culture and history by cultural institutions."[23] In the many discussions, reports, and submissions recorded by the task force, "interpretation" referred to "all facets of museum administration, research, public program and exhibition planning, and the presentations that result from such planning."[24] The task force identified access to museum collections as another important factor that would increase interpretive control.[25] "Access" was defined as "not only physical access ... for purposes of viewing, research, making reproductions and ceremonial use, but also access to funding sources, policy development and implementation activities, as well as training and employment in museums and other cultural institutions."[26]

National and International Influence

The task force report influenced the *Ethics Guidelines*, which were drafted by the Canadian Museums Association. The CMA updated its code of ethics in response to "a number of significant changes to Canadian society and in museum theory and practice," citing its support for the *ICOM Code of Professional Ethics 1986*.[27] At its 1986 conference, the International Council of Museums had called for museums to listen more attentively to the wishes and needs of Indigenous groups and publicly supported the Lubicon boycott of "The Spirit Sings."[28] The CMA shares this ICOM mandate, and its ethics handbook contains sections titled "Respect for Traditional Customs" and "Culturally Sensitive Objects and Human Remains."[29]

Although the current Canadian Museums Association handbook does not specifically mention the Task Force on Museums and First Peoples or single out First Nations issues, the spirit of the task force is present: the CMA ethics committee warns that the board of directors will not hesitate to deal with violations of the *Ethics Guidelines*.[30] This document differs significantly from the CMA's previous statement on ethical behaviour, published in 1979, which focused on potential conflicts of interest among museum workers.[31]

Because CMA board members are established cultural workers in Canadian institutions, documents produced by CMA boards of directors reveal the changing priorities of Canadian museum professionals in a practical and dynamic manner.

Similar changes are also evident on the federal front. The 1990 *Canadian Museum Policy: Temples of the Human Spirit*, unlike the 1986 *Report and Recommendations of the Task Force Charged with Examining Federal Policy concerning Museums*, explains the importance of "our understanding of the roles played by the Aboriginal people ... in the development of our country" and pledges support "for the professional development of Aboriginal museum personnel ... in close consultation with the Aboriginal and museum communities."[32] The federal government has followed up on this pledge by increasing its funding for Aboriginal cultural workers and introducing measures to incorporate Aboriginal museums and cultural institutions into the Museums Assistance Program.[33]

Canadian Heritage provides funding for Aboriginal museums through its Museums Assistance Program, and the Canada Council for the Arts also offers different grants through the Aboriginal Arts Secretariat to aid Aboriginal curators and artists with their projects and research.[34] These are important initiatives that recognize the need to hire more Aboriginal people in cultural institutions. As Lee-Ann Martin has stated, research on Aboriginal cultural issues is still mostly done by non-Aboriginal people, which contributes to the exclusion of Aboriginal scholars.[35] In 2002 the Social Sciences and Humanities Research Council of Canada (SSHRC) identified the representation and participation of Aboriginal peoples in research initiatives as a major priority and began to encourage Aboriginal research in designated SSHRC areas through a pilot program.[36] This sponsorship of research on Aboriginal issues, especially research by Aboriginal people, was important because it was designed to both enhance public understanding of cultural change affecting Aboriginal peoples and promote Aboriginal participants' engagement in identifying research priorities in areas of importance to Aboriginal communities.[37]

Nearly twenty years after the formation of the Task Force on Museums and First Peoples, however, funding priorities are still a source of frustration for Aboriginal cultural workers trying to break into the perpetually cash-strapped museum world. The general feeling is that there is never enough money to buy art by Aboriginal artists or to develop the training to encourage the appointment of Aboriginal people to fill full-time, permanent positions in museums and galleries.[38] The majority of museums with collections of

Aboriginal ethnographic material hire Aboriginal people, but, too often, only in contractual positions – as guides, workshop leaders, or researchers and guest curators. According to Martin, "there are still few Aboriginal people in powerful positions of authority and decision-making within these institutions ... Such temporary and subordinate positions cannot adequately influence those structures and policies which most directly exclude the arts of Native peoples from these institutions."[39]

Since the task force reported in 1992, what changes have occurred in Canadian museums with regard to the representation of Aboriginal cultures and histories? The recommendations were bold and innovative, but did the task force have a real impact on the way museums approach the issue of the representation and participation of Aboriginal peoples in cultural institutions in Canada? Was the task force report a well-meaning but ultimately limited gesture of appeasement to Aboriginal communities and their supporters? Did its recommendations alter subsequent museum practices and administrative policies? Were these revisions a result of changes in government regulations or increasing demands for inclusive and equitable exhibitions by modern museum audiences? Lee-Ann Martin believes that the most significant effect of the task force was the development of a framework to help non-Aboriginal museums work with Aboriginal communities. According to Martin, the task force broke new ground by overcoming barriers to collaboration built up by both museums and Aboriginal groups, the latter hesitating to work with the former because of the history of colonialist anthropological and archaeological interventions in their communities.[40] The task force also helped to encourage a climate of trust necessary for a true partnership between museums and Aboriginal communities.

The McCord Museum: A Case Study

Conceived as a national museum by its founder, David Ross McCord (1844-1930), the McCord Museum of Canadian History has an exceptionally broad collection for a mid-sized institution. Because of the economic, political, and cultural centrality of Montreal in the early history of Canada, the museum houses an extensive record of Canada's past, and it reflects the liberal interests of its founder. The museum was originally a gift from McCord to McGill University that was accepted ungraciously in 1919. The collection mouldered for decades in dingy quarters and was used almost exclusively for academic research. After moving to its current location on Sherbrooke Street in 1968, the museum remained virtually unchanged until it closed for major renovations and expansion in 1989.[41] McGill University was initially hesitant about assuming the burden of caring for and administering McCord's collection. There was also an awkward period in the 1980s and early 1990s that was plagued by frequent administrative changes. However, with a will to keep abreast of changing priorities in research and public access becoming manifest in the late 1990s, the McCord now seems to have established its permanent mandate.[42] Because it is determined to reflect and record the many changes that are occurring socially, politically, and in the field of museum theory, the McCord Museum is an appropriate institution on which to base a case study of the impact of the Task Force on Museums and First Peoples.

The McCord Museum claims to be a museum of *Canadian* history that, from its earliest days, assumed that accurate preservation of Canada's historical record must include representations of British, French, and Aboriginal communities. David McCord clearly stated his ambition to create a collection with national scope, and he repeatedly stated the vision for his museum: "I am not going to make a Protestant or a Catholic museum. I will ... make it as Indian as I possibly can, – a museum of the original owners of the land."[43] More than a mere Victorian curio collector, David McCord, through his close association with various tribes, collected objects and documents that he believed reflected the changing times. Throughout its history the McCord Museum has added to its important collection of Aboriginal material culture. It is particularly relevant to this study that the McCord Museum was directly associated with the controversy surrounding "The Spirit Sings": it refused to support the boycott of the Calgary exhibition and lent several items to the Glenbow Museum. This participation led to the resignation of Professor Bruce Trigger from his position as honorary curator of the McCord Museum. He remained vocal in his denunciation of the Museum's attitude toward Aboriginal rights over their own cultural property.[44]

An examination of the McCord Museum immediately before the conflicts of the late 1980s and the appearance of the task force report reveals a museum with exhibitions focused on nineteenth-century Canadian decorative arts, photography, and portraiture. Despite the remarkable breadth of its ethnographic collection and its often-stated ambition to "reach out to welcome and serve everyone: Anglophones, Francophones, the Native peoples and our main cultural groups," the vast majority of the McCord Museum's exhibitions in the 1980s either described the commercial history of Montreal and its surrounding area or focused on aspects of Victorian culture that have been central to the writing of traditional Canadian history.[45]

Throughout the latter half of the 1980s, Aboriginal subjects were dealt with explicitly in only a few exhibitions, including "The Métis: A Glenbow Museum Exhibition" (1986) and "Ivalu: Traditions of Inuit Clothing" (1988), which was organized by the McCord Museum and guest-curated by Betty Kobayashi Issenman and Catherine Rankin.[46] The latter was the only large-scale presentation concerning Aboriginal peoples mounted by the McCord Museum itself in the three-year period before the museum closed for renovations in 1989.

IVALU: TRADITIONS OF INUIT CLOTHING (1988)

The "Ivalu" exhibition was envisioned, and most of the planning was completed, before the Lubicon boycott. The curators of "Ivalu" would not, therefore, have been much influenced by the task force report or even by the 1988 "Preserving Our Heritage" conference that led to its creation. Nonetheless, "Ivalu" emerges in a positive light when it is evaluated according to the criteria set out by the task force to ensure cultural sensitivity toward Aboriginal concerns, particularly regarding interpretation and access. Even so, the Lubicon Nation wanted to stop "Ivalu" from being presented at the museum, leading Issenman to consult with members of McGill University's Centre for Northern Studies and with Inuit cultural workers, who all agreed – even though they were in full sympathy with the Lubicon – that the exhibition was too important to be aborted.[47] According to Issenman, communication between the curators and members of various Inuit communities was open throughout the duration of the exhibition.[48] Moreover, Inuit and other Arctic residents helped with the research and planning processes of the exhibition, and several Inuit were involved in public educational programs.[49] The exhibition described Inuit clothing production, from prehistoric times to the present, in meticulous detail and discussed the future impact of Inuit clothing and materials on the fashion industry. Although its main purpose was to "emphasize the role of clothing as identifier and culture bearer embodying Inuit spiritual, social, and artistic conventions," "Ivalu" affirmed the currency and vibrancy of the contemporary Inuit clothing industry.[50] In addition, the object labels in the exhibition and catalogue were all written in English, French, and Inuktitut, an important inclusionary gesture to Inuit audiences.

The idea for "Ivalu" came from a research project that was undertaken by Betty Issenman while she was working in the Costume and Textiles division of the McCord Museum. Asked to write about a donation of Inuit clothing to the museum, Issenman found no existing reference material that adequately

discussed Inuit clothing. "Ivalu" grew out of her own research to gain a better understanding of the McCord Museum's collection of Inuit ethnographic
material.[51]

Issenman hoped that Inuit cultural experts would participate in all aspects
of the planning and implementation of "Ivalu," but she and associate curator
Catherine Rankin encountered stiff opposition from the administration of
the McCord Museum to any suggestion of collaboration. Moreover, the meeting that Issenman set up between the museum and representatives from the
North to discuss collaboration on the exhibition went badly. Some museum
staff showed the northern attendees little respect and were indifferent to the
purpose of the meeting.[52]

Issenman, who has been involved with the McCord Museum for thirty
years as an independent researcher and volunteer, is careful to point out that
the atmosphere of the McCord Museum today in no way resembles the attitudes of the 1980s. Despite constant disagreements with the administration
and its criticism of her ideas, Issenman was not dissuaded from completing
her research or going ahead with "Ivalu."[53]

Looking at "Ivalu" in retrospect, Issenman sees many areas where improve-
ments could have been made, noting particularly that more Aboriginal people
could have been encouraged to participate in the exhibition. Issenman states
further that she would have rewritten parts of the exhibition catalogue, which
she criticizes for situating Inuit culture in the past.[54] However, in her effort
to make revisions, Issenman extensively debated nearly every aspect of the
catalogue with the museum's administration, without noticeable success.
Both curators were dissatisfied with the layout and the images that were
chosen by museum staff to illustrate the exhibition, and several names of
artists and contributors were either omitted or inaccurate. The curators were
not shown the final draft of the catalogue before it was sent to the printer,
although the catalogue was delayed and not published until months after
the exhibition opened. Despite repeated attempts by Issenman and Rankin
to revise the catalogue, the final version contained many mistakes, and several requests to include errata slips in the catalogues were ignored. Even when
such slips were inserted, the lists of works and contributors continued to
contain errors and omissions until only weeks before the exhibition was
scheduled to close. In short, the tone of the catalogue matched neither the
curators' vision of the exhibition nor the message they had hoped to communicate through their work.[55] This was shabby treatment of an exhibition
that the McCord Museum claimed was "a long-standing dream."[56]

"Ivalu" was in its final planning stages when the boycott of "The Spirit Sings" was raging in Calgary. The timing of these exhibitions that dealt with Aboriginal cultures, combined with bad press over Professor Bruce Trigger's resignation as honorary curator of ethnology, confronted the McCord Museum's management with the need to reconsider its position regarding the representation of Aboriginal cultures within its walls. The museum's closure for major renovations in 1989 offered a three-year opportunity for theoretical contemplation. Administrative changes occurred as well, with Moira McCaffrey, an associate member of the Task Force on Museums and First Peoples, joining the team at the McCord Museum in 1990 as its first curator of ethnology and archaeology. During these years the task force was also preparing its report in the hope that it would influence policy in museums across the country.

The "New" McCord

When the McCord Museum reopened in 1992, it was a revitalized institution: it was more accessible to the general public and had a new emphasis on the interpretation of Aboriginal cultures and histories. Of the five inaugural exhibitions, three dealt with Aboriginal cultures: "A Village Called Hochelaga," "Names and Lives in Nunavik," and "Marks of the Micmac Nation." The curatorial team had decided to mount three separate exhibitions that depicted different Aboriginal groups "in order to better represent the diversity of Native cultures in Canada."[57] In his introductory comments to the catalogue for these exhibitions, then-director Luke Rombout sent a clear message that almost mirrored the recommendations of the task force report. "At a time when Native issues figure prominently in the political debates of this country," wrote Rombout, "it is clear that our Museum has an increasingly important role to play in making accessible the cultural heritage and contemporary visions of the First Nations and, in so doing, generating in-depth dialogue with Native people. In our discussions with representatives of Native communities," he continued, "we came to realize that a new museological approach to the display of Native artifacts was called for. We were asked repeatedly to ensure that our displays link the past to the present and acknowledge the ongoing vitality of Native cultures."[58]

These inaugural exhibitions, as well as the dozens of displays that have focused on Aboriginal history since the appearance of the task force, clearly show the willingness of the McCord Museum to represent Aboriginal cultures and histories more sensitively and in concert with Aboriginal groups. The year Moira McCaffrey was hired as curator of ethnology and archaeology, the McCord introduced its plan for a permanent Ethnology and Archaeology Gallery, "through [whose] in-depth examinations the McCord Museum will be making valuable contributions to scholarly research."[59]

ACROSS BORDERS: BEADWORK IN IROQUOIS LIFE (1999)

The McCord Museum's altered approach to the presentation of Aboriginal cultures can be seen not only in its post-1992 programming but also in one of its high-profile exhibitions, "Across Borders: Beadwork in Iroquois Life" (1999).[60] "Across Borders" was curated by Moira McCaffrey in concert with Kanatakta, executive director of the Kanien'kehaka Raotitiohkwa Cultural Centre in Kahnawá:ke Mohawk Territory, Quebec; Sandra Olsen and Kate Koperski of the Castellani Art Museum, Niagara University; Trudy Nicks of the Royal Ontario Museum (co-chair of the Task Force on Museums and First Peoples); Ruth Phillips of the Museum of Anthropology at the University of British Columbia; and Jolene Rickard of the University of Buffalo. Representatives of the Iroquois were involved in all aspects of the exhibition, and approval of different facets of the exhibition was reached by consensus. Two members of the curatorial team were from nations of the Iroquois Confederacy, and beadworkers from Kahnawá:ke and the Tuscarora Nation in New York, two historical centres of commercial beadwork production, were instrumental in shaping the exhibition.[61] "Across Borders" was a successful collaboration between stakeholders in the museum world, academia, and First Nations communities, all of which were aware of the recommendations of the task force report and were determined to follow them.

"Across Borders" presented a brief history of early Iroquois beadwork before approaching the main topic of the exhibition: commercial beadwork production. Consisting largely of historical tourist art such as souvenirs and beaded art, the exhibition also included current trends in beading and beaded clothing. McCaffrey noted that "To create an exhibition that even attempted to explain the importance of beadwork in the lives of the Iroquois, we had to explore the spiritual, social, cultural, and economic significance of making beadwork."[62] The exhibition was divided into six thematic rather than chronological displays. The introduction, while explaining the historical significance of beadwork to the Iroquois, also included contemporary photos of Iroquois and was anchored by a signed statement from the curatorial team that explained the process of collaboration that led to the exhibition. The next section, the Iroquois Universe, detailed the iconography of objects displayed repeatedly throughout the exhibition. The universe was set under a starlit dome, with a soundtrack of the Iroquois Thanksgiving Address, in the Mohawk and Tuscarora languages, playing in the background. The Development of Beadwork section traced the transition of materials that were used for embroidery from traditional moosehair and porcupine quills to postcontact glass beads, with use of the latter being linked to the precontact propensity to use reflective, translucent materials such as mother-of-pearl. The Creating section described the technical and stylistic developments of historical souvenir art and contemporary beadwork designs, complete with contemporary photos of beadworkers in their workshops and excerpts from interviews with Iroquois beadworkers. The Marketing section reviewed the entrepreneurial ventures of past and present beadworkers and the economic importance of beadwork in Iroquois communities. Finally, the Continuing section stressed the place of beadwork in Iroquois cultural identity and featured work by well-known contemporary artists Shelley Niro and Jeffrey Thomas.[63]

Although the exhibition was collaborative in spirit and developed with input and participation from Aboriginal communities, it was not without its controversies. One of the most hotly debated decisions of the curatorial team was whether to display a wampum belt in the exhibition. Despite arguments from some Iroquois communities that wampum is sacred and should not be displayed in public, the curatorial team for "Across Borders" included the wampum belt after "[drawing] on the knowledge and expertise of a number of Iroquois historians and elders" and consulting the Mohawk community of Kahnesatà:ke, where the belt originated.[64]

The McCord Museum's discursive shift regarding representations of Aboriginal culture and history, as well as its exhibition record since reopening, reveal largely successful efforts to abide by task force recommendations. The museum now places more emphasis on its Aboriginal collections, hosts exhibitions mounted by Aboriginal groups and museums, and often works closely with consultants of Aboriginal ancestry.

Petit à Petit

Collaboration and integration remain, however, contentious issues at the McCord Museum. A comprehensive evaluation of the museum's accommodation of task force priorities reveals that it falls short in the area of integrating Aboriginal staff into its various levels of operation: little evidence exists to claim that the museum supports the inclusion of Aboriginal people into its systematic administrative framework. During her tenure at the McCord

Museum, Dolorès Contré Migwans was the only permanent staff member of Aboriginal heritage, even though many local Aboriginal people conduct workshops and cultural demonstrations on a contractual basis. Migwans' post, as assistant to Native Programs, did not fully define her role at the museum. Migwans was hired in 1999 in the Visitor Services Department to coordinate an outreach team that had a mandate to present aspects of Aboriginal cultures to youth groups and encourage young people to visit the museum. This initiative was one of the public programs designed in conjunction with "Across Borders." Migwans and her team participated in summer festivals, visited summer camps, and held youth workshops that featured dancing, crafts, singing, and storytelling at the museum.[65]

When the contract for her work with "Across Borders" was complete, Migwans was hired as an assistant in Cultural and Educational Programmes to run Aboriginal cultural workshops, train new guides, and give tours on aspects of Aboriginal culture and history represented in the museum's permanent and temporary exhibitions. In this capacity, Migwans noticed that the guides' script for the tour of "Simply Montreal," the McCord Museum's permanent exhibition, tended to objectify the Aboriginal cultures presented. The head of Cultural and Educational Programmes asked Migwans to revise and improve the guide material to provide more of an Aboriginal perspective, and this greater awareness, in turn, led to an increase in the number of workshops and school programs the museum provided with Aboriginal themes.[66] These changes have been wide-ranging and have broadly influenced school and Aboriginal groups that visit the museum and the museum's exhibition practices. Migwans worked on integrating interactive components into the permanent and temporary exhibitions, and museum visitors now have a chance to speak with people of Aboriginal ancestry or see how traditional artistic skills are practised today.

Migwans also acted as a cultural liaison officer to various Aboriginal communities. Her priority was to invite Elders to view the museum's collection to identify patrimonial objects that originated in their communities. This process enabled Elders to return information and knowledge to their communities and sensitize other community members to forgotten aspects of their heritage. This cooperation continues to benefit the McCord Museum, as Elders' memories are a tremendous source of oral history. This process has generated increasingly frequent and profound collaborations, and it has had a snowball effect on other communities with ties to the ethnographic collection at the McCord Museum.[67] Migwans advised educational programmers at the museum and also conducted studies for Research and Exhibitions and the Department of Ethnology. Working in close collaboration with Moira McCaffrey, Migwans developed an internal policy regarding Aboriginal issues that related to the ethnological and archaeological collection so that the museum would have a formal framework in place for the future.[68] Migwans' future hopes for the projected First Peoples Gallery rest upon the involvement of Aboriginal people in the gallery's research and development and the enlistment of Aboriginal businesspeople as investors. Migwans believes that integrating Aboriginal consultants and collaborators into the development, operation, and spiritual aspects of the First Peoples Gallery will give Aboriginal people a greater sense of ownership of their heritage, as it is presented at the McCord Museum.[69] When asked about her patience with the seemingly slow pace of change at the museum, and the diplomatic manner with which she brought about change, Migwans smiled and said that this is the way to change things: "Petit à petit; sans faire peur à personne" (Little by little, without frightening anyone).[70]

Recently, the McCord Museum has rendered part of its collection more accessible through the "Keys to History" project on its website. With financial support from Canadian Heritage, the McCord Museum is undertaking a large-scale digitization of its collection. To date, thousands of objects from the museum's ethnological and archaeological artifacts, as well as photographic records from the renowned Notman Photographic Archives, have been put online. "Keys to History" also includes online exhibitions, games, thematic tours, and educational tools for use in classrooms.[71] This project gives access to isolated communities whose members might otherwise never have the chance to view the museum's collection.

While the McCord Museum has increased its collaboration with Aboriginal community members in the presentation of individual exhibitions and modernized its development of educational programming, the paucity of Aboriginal staff and the absence of Aboriginal board members remain cause for concern. Almost two decades after the publication of the task force report, there is not one member of the board of trustees who is of Aboriginal ancestry.[72] If not one person of Aboriginal ancestry is a member of the museum's governance structure, it is difficult for the museum to guarantee a long-term commitment to safeguarding Aboriginal concerns.

According to Victoria Dickenson, executive director of the museum, the board of trustees recently established a governance working group, which has started to look at the museum's composition in relation to the community it serves. Dickenson writes: "The McCord is conscious not only of the question of representation from the Aboriginal community but also from cultural communities that are part of Montreal's and Canada's more recent history. It is something that we will be bringing to the governance working group ... The McCord Board is open to change and growth, but change in social institutions is often slower than many wish!"[73]

One of the main purposes of a museum's board of trustees is to raise funds. The McCord Museum's reflections on the representativeness of its board of trustees are frustrated by concurrent financial concerns that mirror those voiced by Trudy Nicks, curator of ethnology at the Royal Ontario Museum. Nicks implied at the annual conference of the Canadian Museums Association in 2002 that museums are placing more emphasis on recruiting potential board members with social connections and fundraising skills than potential members from under-represented communities.[74] Gerald Conaty, senior ethnology curator at the Glenbow Museum in Calgary, where representation of First Nations on the museum's board is actively encouraged, notes that fundraising for the Glenbow Museum is not often undertaken in Aboriginal communities because these communities usually have serious economic problems that must be their first consideration.[75] Yet many of Canada's Aboriginal communities have members with important ties to industry and influential professional, political, or cultural networking contacts.

Conclusion

Although the McCord Museum has not implemented every recommendation made by the Task Force on Museums and First Peoples, it has made significant alterations to its exhibition planning and has increasingly included the histories and cultural production of Aboriginal peoples in its permanent exhibition. The McCord Museum has also recruited visiting curators and First Nations consultants and instituted innovative and varied educational programs to provide Aboriginal perspectives on its collections. Canadian museums that have Aboriginal ethnographic collections but no Aboriginal involvement in them can now look to Dolorès Contré Migwans' work as a model for educational development, the establishment of liaisons with local Aboriginal communities, and the integration of different voices into the daily management of museums.

To return to the quotation from Jean Hamelin introduced at the outset of this chapter, the McCord Museum has realized that it cannot be an innocent, neutral institution that is capable of remaining outside sociopolitical imperatives. The museum has accepted the challenge to recognize its responsibility and adapt to the recommendations of the 1992 task force report.

Although the McCord Museum is not yet an ideal institution from the perspective of the task force, it is obvious that the museum has welcomed and internalized its recommendations and progressed far beyond former entrenched exhibition planning and display policies. There is still considerable antagonism between Indigenous groups and museums, however. A few years of goodwill cannot erase centuries of colonial collection practices. Much remains to be done to assuage worries of territorial encroachment on both sides. Museums must be sensitive to the needs of Aboriginal communities, and Aboriginal communities may have to be patient with the pace of change in museums and other cultural institutions, which at times is infuriatingly slow. This analysis of the influence and repercussions of the task force recommendations on the McCord Museum reveals that they had a timely and much-needed positive impact. The historical, cultural, and intellectual integrity of the McCord Museum has been greatly enriched as the accuracy of its representations of Aboriginal heritage and culture has improved.

NOTES

1   Jean Hamelin, *Le Musée du Québec: Histoire d'une institution nationale* (Québec: Musée du Québec, 1991), 9-10, translated by the author.

2   Glenbow Museum, *The Spirit Sings: Artistic Traditions of Canada's First Peoples* (Toronto: McClelland and Stewart, 1987).

3   Bruce Trigger, "A Present of Their Past? Anthropologists, Native People, and Their Heritage," *Culture* 8, 1 (1988): 71-79; Julia Harrison, "'The Spirit Sings' and the Future of Anthropology," *Anthropology Today* 4, 6 (1988): 6-10; Amnesty International, *"Time is Wasting": Respect for the Land Rights of the Lubicon Cree Long Overdue*, Amnesty International, 1 April 2003, http://www.amnesty.org; also see John Goddard, "Forked Tongues," *Saturday Night* 103, 2 (1988), 38-45, http://www.nisto.com/cree/lubicon/1988/forked_tongues.html. For more background information on this dispute, see Friends of the Lubicon, http://www.tao.ca/~FOL.

4   Transcripts of "Preserving Our Heritage: A Working Conference for Museums and First Peoples" can be found at Committees, Task Force on Museums and First Peoples of Canada, E1165-T9, Indian Art Centre Archives, Gatineau, Quebec.

5   Roberta Pearson, "Custer Loses Again: The Contestation over Commodified Public Memory," in *Cultural Memory and the Construction of Identity*, ed. Dan Ben-Amos and Liliana Weissberg (Detroit, MI: Wayne State University Press, 1999), 176-201.

6 James Anderson, "Nationalist Ideology and Territory," in *Nationalism, Self-Determination and Political Geography*, ed. R.J. Johnston, David B. Knight, and Eleonore Kofman (London: Croom Helm, 1988), 18-39.

7 George MacDonald, 3 November 1988, transcript, "Preserving Our Heritage" conference, 7.

8 Barbara Tyler, 5 November 1988, transcript, "Preserving Our Heritage" conference, 16.

9 See McCord Museum of Canadian History, *Schools Program 2004-2005: Preschool-Primary* (Montreal: McCord Museum of Canadian History, 2004) and *Schools Program 2004-2005: Secondary* (Montreal: McCord Museum of Canadian History, 2004).

10 Dolorès Contré Migwans, assistant to Native Progams, McCord Museum of Canadian History, interview with author, Montreal, Quebec, 18 May 2004. Migwans left employment at the McCord Museum in 2008 but maintains a connection with the museum as a consultant.

11 David Fleming, "Positioning the Museum for Social Inclusion," in *Museums, Society, Inequality*, ed. Richard Sandell (London: Routledge, 2002), 215-16.

12 Ibid.

13 See Alan Gordon, *Making Public Pasts: The Contested Terrain of Montreal's Public Memories, 1891-1930* (Montreal and Kingston: McGill-Queen's University Press, 2001).

14 Brian Young, *The Making and Unmaking of a University Museum: The McCord, 1921-1996* (Montreal and Kingston: McGill-Queen's University Press, 2000).

15 Pamela Miller, "David Ross McCord," in *The McCord Family: A Passionate Vision*, ed. Pamela Miller et al. (Montreal: McCord Museum of Canadian History, 1992), 85.

16 Georges Erasmus and John MacAvity to Barbara Tyler, 19 September 1988, Committees, Task Force on Museums and First Peoples of Canada, E1165-T9; Indian Art Centre Archives, Gatineau, Quebec.

17 Georges Erasmus, 3 November 1988, transcript, "Preserving Our Heritage" conference, 2.

18 Chris McCormick, 3 November 1988, transcript, "Preserving Our Heritage" conference, 12.

19 Tyler, 5 November 1988.

20 Lola Young, "Rethinking Heritage: Cultural Policy and Inclusion," in *Museums, Society, Inequality*, ed. Sandell, 204.

21 Lee-Ann Martin, curator of Contemporary Canadian Aboriginal Art, Canadian Museum of Civilization, interview with author, Gatineau, Quebec, 10 May 2004.

22 The task force members were Tom Hill and Trudy Nicks (co-chairs), Henri Dorion, Joanna Bedard, Andrea Laforet, Gloria Cranmer Webster, Michael Ames, Miriam Clavir, Robert Janes, Carol Geddes, Katharine Pettipas, Donna Augustine, Bob

McGhee, Gerald McMaster, Nicholas DeLeary, Dorothy Daniels, Bill Byrne, Cathy Martin, Alex Greyeyes, Marie Routledge, Ruth Phillips, Linda Jules, Chuck Arnold, David Miller, Nancy Hall, Liz Thunder, Karen Isaacs, John McAvity, Lance Belanger, and Lee-Ann Martin. Associate members were Deborah Smith, Moira McCaffrey, Gerald Conaty, Margaret Hanna, Reg Crowshoe, Phil Stepney, and Peter Christmas. Although every effort was made to create a fully representative task force, the chairpersons encountered some difficulty finding Inuit members. See meeting minutes, 8-9 November 1990, 2, Canadian Museum of Civilization Archives, Task Force on Museums and First Peoples, 1990, 2002.25 box 726f5. Lee-Ann Martin was the coordinator for the crucial first year of the task force, after which the post was taken up by Nancy Hall of the Canadian Museums Association and then by Lance Belanger, artist and curator.

23   Task Force on Museums and First Peoples, *Turning the Page: Forging New Partnerships between Museums and First Peoples* (Ottawa: Canadian Museums Association and Assembly of First Nations, 1992), 1. The task force report was edited by Tom Hill of the Woodland Cultural Centre and Trudy Nicks of the Royal Ontario Museum. It was based on two years of consultations and regional meetings with fifty members, associate members, and contributors.

24   Ibid., 4.

25   Collections were defined as "not only human remains and artifacts, but also information associated with these materials: research results, photographs, works of art, and any other information related to First Peoples culture and history held in cultural institutions." Ibid.

26   Ibid.

27   Canadian Museums Association, *Ethics Guidelines* (Ottawa: Canadian Museums Association, 1999), 1.

28   International Council of Museums, *ICOM '86: Proceedings of the 14th General Conference and 15th General Assembly of the International Council of Museums* (Budapest: International Council of Museums, 1989), 101. Note that the Lubicon Nation began their boycott of "The Spirit Sings" in 1986.

29   Canadian Museums Association, *Ethics Guidelines*, 6, 14.

30   Ibid., 1.

31   Canadian Museums Association, *A Guide to Museum Positions, Including a Statement on the Ethical Behaviour of Museum Professionals* (Ottawa: Canadian Museums Association, 1979), 22-25.

32   Canada, Communications Canada, *Canadian Museum Policy: Temples of the Human Spirit* (Ottawa: Communications Canada, 1990), 15, 43; Canada, National Museums Task Force, *Report and Recommendations of the Task Force Charged with Examining Federal Policy concerning Museums* (Ottawa: Communications Canada, 1986).

33   See Canada, Canada Council for the Arts, "A Framework for Action," 2005, Canada Council for the Arts, http://www.canadacouncil.ca, and Canada, Canadian

Heritage, "Museums Assistance Program," January 2007, Canada, Canadian Heritage, http://www.pch.gc.ca/progs/pam-map/index_e.cfm.

34 See Canada Council for the Arts, "Aboriginal Arts Secretariat," Canada, Canada Council for the Arts, http://www.canadacouncil.ca/aboriginal.

35 Lee-Ann Martin, "Wordplay: Issues of Authority and Territory," in *Making a Noise: A Discussion of Contemporary Art, Art History, Critical Writing and Community from Aboriginal Perspectives*, ed. Lee-Ann Martin (Banff, AB: Banff Centre Press, 2005), 102-7.

36 Craig McNaughton and Daryl Rock, *Opportunities in Aboriginal Research: Results of SSHRC's Dialogue on Research and Aboriginal Peoples* (Ottawa: Social Sciences and Humanities Research Council of Canada, 2003), 1, 3, http://www.sshrc.ca/web/apply/background/aboriginal_backgrounder_e.pdf.

37 In 2007-8 an evaluation was completed that recommended continuation of the program, with minor adjustments. For a summary of the evaluation results, see Social Sciences and Humanities Research Council of Canada, "Management Response Summary: Aboriginal Pilot Program," SSHRC, http://www.sshrc.ca/site/about-crsh/publications/arpp_evaluation_response_e.pdf.

38 Martin, interview with author, 10 May 2004.

39 Lee-Ann Martin, *The Politics of Inclusion and Exclusion: Contemporary Native Art and Public Art Museums in Canada* (Ottawa: Canada Council for the Arts, 1991), 29, 31.

40 Martin, interview with author, 10 May 2004.

41 Young, *The Making and Unmaking*, 49-60.

42 Ibid., 115-24, 129-47, 157-69.

43 Miller, "David Ross McCord," 85.

44 Bruce G. Trigger and Michael Ames, "Share the Blame," *Vanguard* 17, 2 (1988): 15; Trigger, "A Present of Their Past?" 71-79, "Reply to Michael Ames," *Culture* 8, 1 (1988): 87-88, and "Who Owns the Past?" *Muse* 5, 4 (1988): 13-15.

45 McCord Museum, *Annual Report 1985-1986*, 10; see also McCord Museum, *Annual Report, 1986-1987*.

46 Glenbow Museum, *The Métis: A Glenbow Museum Exhibition* (Calgary: Glenbow Museum, 1985) and Julia Harrison, *Métis: People between Two Worlds* (Vancouver: Douglas and McIntyre, 1985); Betty Issenman and Catherine Rankin, *Ivalu: Traditions du vêtement Inuit/Traditions of Inuit Clothing* (Montreal: McCord Museum of Canadian History, 1988).

47 Betty Issenman, research associate, Department of Ethnology and Archaeology, McCord Museum of Canadian History, interview with author, Montreal, Quebec, 12 May 2004.

48 Ibid., and personal communication with author, 19 July 2004.

49 Issenman, interview with author, 12 May 2004. See also Betty Issenman and Catherine Rankin, *Ivalu*, 16, and McCord Museum of Canadian History, "Communiqué," 28 March 1988.

50 Issenman, personal communication with author, 19 July 2004.

51 Issenman, interview with author, 12 May 2004.

52 Ibid. Northern representatives included delegates from the Avataq Cultural Institute in Inukjuaq (northern Quebec). The meeting between the McCord Museum and the Avataq Cultural Institute probably took place in 1984: Betty Issenman, personal communication with author, 27 March 2007.

53 Issenman, interview with author, 12 May 2004.

54 Ibid.

55 Ibid.; Betty Issenman and Catherine Rankin, memo to colleagues, 10 October 1988, courtesy of Betty Issenman; Betty Issenman and Catherine Rankin, letter to the editor, *Inuit Art Quarterly* 4, 3 (Summer 1989): 2, 40; David M. Lank, chairman of McCord Museum's board of directors, letter to B. Issenman, 4 October 1988, courtesy of Betty Issenman. Note that despite the curators' dissatisfaction with the "Ivalu" catalogue, public response to the exhibition was very positive, Issenman, personal communication with author, 19 July 2004.

56 Marcel Caya, McCord Museum director, in Issenman and Rankin, *Ivalu*, 12.

57 Moira McCaffrey, introduction to *Wrapped in the Colours of the Earth: Cultural Heritage of the First Nations*, ed. Moira McCaffrey et al. (Montreal: McCord Museum of Canadian History, 1992), 37. This catalogue includes all three exhibitions mentioned above.

58 Luke Rombout, preface to *Wrapped in the Colours of the Earth*, ed. McCaffrey et al., 11.

59 McCord Museum, *Annual Report, 1990-1991*, 14.

60 Please note that there is no catalogue for this exhibition.

61 Moira McCaffrey, "Crossing New Borders to Exhibit Iroquois Tourist Art," in *On Aboriginal Representation in the Gallery*, ed. Linda Jessup, with Shannon Bagg (Ottawa: Canadian Museum of Civilization, 2002), 73-92.

62 Ibid., 82-83.

63 Ibid., 83-84.

64 Ibid., 83.

65 Migwans, interview with author, 18 May 2004.

66 Ibid.

67 Migwans, personal communication with author, 22 March 2007.

68 Migwans, interview with author, 18 May 2004, and personal communication with author, 22 March 2007.

69 Migwans, interview with author, 18 May 2004, and personal communication with author, 8 July 2004.

70 Migwans, interview with author, 18 May 2004.

71 McCord Museum of Canadian History, "Keys to History," McCord Museum of Canadian History, http://www.musee-mccord.qc.ca/en/keys.

72 Victoria Dickenson, personal communication with author, 25 May 2004.

73 Ibid., 6 February 2009.

74 Quyen Hoang, "First Nations People Mining the Museum: A Case Study of Change at the Glenbow Museum" (Master's thesis, Concordia University, 2003), 31.

75 Ibid., 17.

WORKS CITED

Amnesty International. *"Time is Wasting": Respect for the Land Rights of the Lubicon Cree Long Overdue.* Amnesty International, 1 April 2003. http://www.amnesty.org.

Anderson, James. "Nationalist Ideology and Territory." In *Nationalism, Self-Determination and Political Geography*, ed. R.J. Johnston, David B. Knight, and Eleonore Kofman, 18-39. London: Croom Helm, 1988.

Canada. Canada Council for the Arts. "Aboriginal Arts Secretariat." Canada Council for the Arts. http://canadacouncil.ca/aboriginal (accessed 14 September 2006).

–. Canada Council for the Arts. "A Framework for Action," 2005. Canada Council for the Arts. http://www.canadacouncil.ca.

–. Canadian Heritage. "Museums Assistance Program," January 2007. Canadian Heritage. http://www.pch.gc.ca/progs/pam-map/index–e.cfm.

–. Communications Canada. *Canadian Museum Policy: Temples of the Human Spirit.* Ottawa: Communications Canada, 1990.

–. National Museums Task Force. *Report and Recommendations of the Task Force Charged with Examining Federal Policy Concerning Museums.* Ottawa: Communications Canada, 1986.

Canadian Museums Association. *Ethics Guidelines.* Ottawa: Canadian Museums Association, 1999.

–. *A Guide to Museum Positions, Including a Statement on the Ethical Behaviour of Museum Professionals.* Ottawa: Canadian Museums Association, 1979.

Fleming, David. "Positioning the Museum for Social Inclusion." In *Museums, Society, Inequality,* ed. Richard Sandell, 213-24. London: Routledge, 2002.

Glenbow Museum. *The Métis: A Glenbow Museum Exhibition.* Calgary: Glenbow Museum, 1985.

–. *The Spirit Sings: Artistic Traditions of Canada's First Peoples.* Toronto: McClelland and Stewart, 1987.

Goddard, John. "Forked Tongues." *Saturday Night* 103, 2 (1988): 38-45. http://www.nisto.com/cree/lubicon/1988/forked_tongues.html

Gordon, Alan. *Making Public Pasts: The Contested Terrain of Montreal's Public Memories, 1891-1930.* Montreal and Kingston: McGill-Queen's University Press, 2001.

Hamelin, Jean. *Le Musée du Québec: Histoire d'une institution nationale.* Québec: Musée du Québec, 1991.

Harrison, Julia. *Métis: People between Two Worlds.* Vancouver: Douglas and McIntyre, 1985.

–. "'The Spirit Sings' and the Future of Anthropology." *Anthropology Today* 4, 6 (1988): 6-10.

Hoang, Quyen. "First Nations People Mining the Museum: A Case Study of Change at the Glenbow Museum." Master's thesis, Concordia University, 2003.

International Council of Museums. *ICOM '86: Proceedings of the 14th General Conference and 15th General Assembly of the International Council of Museums.* Budapest: International Council of Museums, 1989.

Issenman, Betty, and Catherine Rankin. *Ivalu: Traditions du vêtement Inuit/Traditions of Inuit Clothing.* Montreal: McCord Museum of Canadian History, 1988.

–. Letter to the editor. *Inuit Art Quarterly* 4, 3 (Summer 1989): 2, 40.

Martin, Lee-Ann. *The Politics of Inclusion and Exclusion: Contemporary Native Art and Public Art Museums in Canada.* Ottawa: Canada Council for the Arts, 1991.

–."Wordplay: Issues of Authority and Territory." In *Making a Noise: A Discussion of Contemporary Art, Art History, Critical Writing and Community from Aboriginal Perspectives,* ed. Lee-Ann Martin, 102-7. Banff, AB: Banff Centre Press, 2005.

McCaffrey, Moira. "Crossing New Borders to Exhibit Iroquois Tourist Art." In *On Aboriginal Representation in the Gallery,* ed. Linda Jessup, with Shannon Bagg, 73-92. Ottawa: Canadian Museum of Civilization, 2002.

–. Introduction to *Wrapped in the Colours of the Earth: Cultural Heritage of the First Nations,* ed. Moira McCaffrey, Claude Chapdelaine, J. Bruce Jamieson, and Ruth Holmes Whitehead, 34-39. Montreal: McCord Museum of Canadian History, 1992.

McCord Museum of Canadian History. "Communiqué." 28 March 1988.

–. "Keys to History." McCord Museum of Canadian History. http://www.musee-mccord. qc.ca/en/keys.

–. *Schools Program 2004-2005: Preschool-Primary.* Montreal: McCord Museum of Canadian History, 2004.

–. *Schools Program 2004-2005: Secondary.* Montreal: McCord Museum of Canadian History, 2004.

McNaughton, Craig, and Daryl Rock. *Opportunities in Aboriginal Research: Results of SSHRC's Dialogue on Research and Aboriginal Peoples.* Ottawa: Social Sciences and Humanities Research Council of Canada, 2003. http://www.sshrc.ca/web/apply/ background/aboriginal_backgrounder_e.pdf.

Miller, Pamela. "David Ross McCord." In *The McCord Family: A Passionate Vision,* ed. Pamela Miller, Moria McCaffrey, Brian Young, Donald Fyson, and Donald Wright, 85-87. Montreal: McCord Museum of Canadian History, 1992.

Pearson, Roberta. "Custer Loses Again: The Contestation over Commodified Public Memory." In *Cultural Memory and the Construction of Identity,* ed. Dan Ben-Amos and Liliana Weissberg, 176-201. Detroit, MI: Wayne State University Press, 1999.

Rombout, Luke. Preface to *Wrapped in the Colours of the Earth: Cultural Heritage of the First Nations,* ed. Moira McCaffrey, Claude Chapdelaine, J. Bruce Jamieson, and Ruth Holmes Whitehead, 11. Montreal: McCord Museum of Canadian History, 1992.

Social Sciences and Humanities Research Council of Canada. "Management Response Summary: Aboriginal Pilot Program." SSHRC. http://www.sshrc.ca/site/about-crsh/publications/arpp_evaluation_response_e.pdf.

Task Force on Museums and First Peoples. *Turning the Page: Forging New Partnerships between Museums and First Peoples*. Ottawa: Canadian Museums Association and Assembly of First Nations, 1992.

Trigger, Bruce G. "A Present of Their Past? Anthropologists, Native People, and Their Heritage." *Culture* 8, 1 (1988): 71-79.

–. "Reply to Michael Ames." *Culture* 8, 1 (1988): 87-88.

–. "Who Owns the Past?" *Muse* 5, 4 (1988): 13-15.

Trigger, Bruce G., and Michael Ames. "Share the Blame." *Vanguard* 17, 2 (1988): 15-18.

Young, Brian. *The Making and Unmaking of a University Museum: The McCord, 1921-1996*. Montreal and Kingston: McGill-Queen's University Press, 2000.

Young, Lola. "Rethinking Heritage: Cultural Policy and Inclusion." In *Museums, Society, Inequality*, ed. Richard Sandell, 203-12. London: Routledge, 2002.

PART 4

Aboriginal Thought and Innovation in Subnational Governance

7
The Manitoba Government's Shift to "Autonomous" First Nations Child Welfare: Empowerment or Privatization?

Fiona MacDonald

In recent decades a group autonomy approach to cultural recognition and accommodation has found increased legitimacy in liberal democracies. This is especially true for groups designated as "national minorities," such as Canada's First Nations. Indigenous scholars, activists, and various "multiculturalism" theorists have made arguments in favour of autonomy for First Nations in Canada.[1] Family law – more specifically, child welfare – has been an area in which Canadian governments have appeared most willing to make concessions of autonomy to First Nation communities.

Various provinces across Canada have taken steps toward granting First Nations some autonomy over the provision of child welfare services for Indigenous families. This trend is consistent with broader trends in the accommodation of cultural group rights. As Ayelet Shachar notes, "In the growing age of diversity, the state is relatively receptive to minority cultures' requests for greater degrees of legal control over their [minority groups'] own family affairs," which results in what she refers to as "multicultural jurisdictions."[2]

This chapter identifies an overlap between the concerns of feminist scholars of political economy, who focus on issues of privatization, and some First Nations scholars' observations regarding the impact of current models of group autonomy. For some scholars, cultural group autonomy through group rights is an essential step toward obtaining a stable and just democratic state. The point of departure for this chapter is the recognition that the legal strategies and practices of *some* forms of group autonomy, though often empowering for groups on one level, bring about unintended negative consequences on another level. More specifically, an analysis focused on the welfare regime reveals that the group right to autonomy, generally viewed as a concession made by the state to meet the demands of groups, must also be evaluated as part of a broader governmental strategy of neoliberal restructuring.[3] This strategy is not simply about meeting the particular demands of groups but also about meeting the requirements of the contemporary governmental shift toward privatization within liberal democratic states. That being the case, particular manifestations of group autonomy are vulnerable to the same criticisms that are launched against practices of privatization. These practices include a variety of policies designed to shift contentious issues out of the public sphere, thereby limiting public debate and collective (i.e., state) responsibility.[4] Through a critical examination of the shift to "autonomous" First Nations child welfare services, this chapter demonstrates that the shift to group autonomy must include a strong materialist focus if it is to contribute to meaningful, transformative change. Consequently, this chapter highlights the need for advocates of autonomy to think more carefully about effective, devolved policy change regarding First Nations in Canada.

What Is Privatization?

Although the term "privatization" referred originally to the sale of government assets to the private sector, it has now come to refer to a tectonic shift in public policy and a movement within liberal democracies toward a particular political orientation.[5] Janine Brodie explains how "the politics of restructuring revolve around a multi-faceted contraction and re-regulation of the public and the political realms as they were constituted by the postwar welfare state, and the simultaneous expansion of the private whether defined as markets or the domestic sphere."[6] Thus, as Fudge and Cossman note, "a whole new set of assumptions about the role of government and the rights of citizens is emerging."[7] Restructuring involves a variety of practices that have come to dominate liberal democratic politics since the 1980s and which redraw the public-private boundaries in order to shrink some aspects of the public by granting autonomy to the market and the family. As Brodie and others have argued, this shift alters the political identities and public spaces of postwar Canadian politics and results in new forms of domination as well as the reshaping of more familiar ones that are rooted in gender, race, and class.[8]

First Nations and Autonomous Child Welfare: A Case Example

Indigenous scholars, activists, and various advocates of multiculturalism have made arguments in favour of some form of self-government or "independence" because of the unique "social facts" peculiar to the Indigenous experience.[9] While the meaning, and implications, of self-determination are contested both within and outside First Nations communities, many of the arguments that have dominated the discursive terrain focus on achieving self-determination for Indigenous peoples in Canada across a range of legal and social arenas, including family law.[10]

Given that various First Nations leaders have lobbied for autonomy in child welfare services, the establishment of First Nations jurisdictions in this policy area may appear to be a positive and transformative change in the policies of the Canadian state. Nevertheless, the case of autonomous child welfare services for First Nations in the Province of Manitoba demonstrates that, in practice, the establishment of these jurisdictions may not be the transformative concessions they are often conceived to be in theory. When these changes are assessed contextually through a lens that focuses on the welfare regime, the motivations, implications, and limitations of such "progressive" developments become more complex. Specifically, this analytical approach reveals that these kinds of jurisdictional changes must be considered as part of a broader shift in Canadian politics toward neoliberal political practice.[11] They are instances of neoliberal multiculturalism. Consequently, many of the negative and potentially dangerous trends associated with privatization – including reregulation, reprivatization, co-optation, depoliticization, and individualization – are also visible in the practical trend toward cultural group autonomy.[12] Overall, these processes lead us away from a holistic, transformative, capacity-building approach to political and social justice for autonomous groups and, in fact, may make it more difficult for groups to obtain truly progressive change, as these developments limit the legitimate discursive terrain and narrow the political-opportunity structure available to Indigenous social movements. As a result, it may be more difficult to achieve political and social justice for Indigenous peoples in Canada. The sense of mistrust among First Nations may also increase as promises made by the state once again fall short in terms of practical outcomes.

This chapter focuses primarily on changes in child welfare policy for First Nations in Manitoba. The majority of Manitoba's child welfare services have not typically been government services. Services in Winnipeg and southern Manitoba developed as children's aid societies, and they have remained private in this sense. The restructuring currently underway in Manitoba does not involve an all-encompassing shift from government service to private service but rather focuses exclusively on the growing First Nations population in the region.[13] The changes involved are unprecedented in Canada in that they include the development of First Nations agencies that will have jurisdiction for First Nations clients regardless of where they live, instead of only for those First Nations living on a reserve. As a result, other provinces are observing these changes as a potential template for reform.[14]

What Do First Nations Want?

Demands for autonomous child welfare services have been of central import-ance in the move toward independence for many Indigenous communities, scholars, leaders, and activists.[15] This sentiment was reflected in the 1991 *Report of the Aboriginal Justice Inquiry of Manitoba*, which noted, "If Aborig-inal people are correct, and we believe they are, part of the reason for the high numbers of Aboriginal people in correctional facilities is the fact that Aboriginal people still do not fully control their own lives and destinies, or the lives of their own children. Aboriginal people must have more control over the ways in which their children are raised, taught and protected."[16]

In the decade following the report, demands for autonomy have only increased, especially in regard to the need for Aboriginal governance in urban settings, rather than simply in reserve communities.[17] This strong consensus on the need for autonomy over family services is due largely to the historic-ally volatile, injurious, and colonial relationship between child welfare, education systems, and Indigenous peoples in Canada and the continued over-representation of First Nations children in mainstream child welfare.[18]

This over-representation is well documented across Canada. For example, the 2001 Manitoba government vision document *Promise of Hope: Commitment to Change* acknowledges that, despite significant reforms that have been introduced in recent years, high numbers of First Nations children, and fam-ilies, continue to be involved in the provincial child and family services system: "Currently, Aboriginal children make up about 21 percent of Mani-toba's population under the age of 15, but they account for 78 percent of children currently in care of the overall child and family services system."[19]

While Manitoba may present one of the most glaring examples of over-representation of First Nations children in child welfare, the problem of over-representation exists throughout Canada. For example, British Columbia also reported high numbers of First Nations children in care in the 1992 commissioned report *Liberating Our Children, Liberating Our Nations*. Accord-ing to the government's statistics, Aboriginal people made up less than 4 percent of the population of British Columbia; however, of the 3,393 children who were in care as a result of court orders under the *Family and Child Servi-ces Act*, 1,751 (51.6 percent) were Aboriginal.[20]

The number of children in care is not static. Children move in and out of the system as they are returned to their families, adopted by strangers, or reach the age of majority. The rate of new admissions, however, remains constant. In 1991-92, for instance, 952 Aboriginal children became wards of the superintendent. Over a single generation an average of more than one out of every five Aboriginal children became wards of the superintendent.[21]

There is also evidence to suggest that First Nations clients may present some of the most complex child welfare cases in regions where, as a result of past and present oppression, social problems – including poverty, suicide, substance abuse, domestic abuse, and sexual abuse – are strikingly more prevalent. As the Royal Commission on Aboriginal Peoples noted, abuse has "spilled back into communities," following colonial intervention and abuse in the form of residential schools and other destructive policies.[22] According to a 1989 study conducted by the Native Women's Association of the Northwest Territories, eight out of ten girls under the age of eight had already been victims of sexual abuse, and the same was true for 50 percent of boys of the same age. Social scientists have repeatedly argued that this abuse results largely from the destruction of traditional Indigenous culture.[23] Furthermore, as Patricia Monture notes, "not only are First Nations children more likely to be apprehended but, once they are taken into care, First Nations children are less likely either to be returned to their parents or placed for adoption."[24] In short, First Nations children present some of the hardest cases, statistically, for current child welfare practices. Moreover, when combined with the volatile historical record of state intervention experienced by First Nations, these numbers shed light on why so many First Nations communities have demanded autonomous control over child welfare services as part of the move toward self-determination. In a report written for the British Columbia government, Lavina White (Haida Nation) and Eva Jacobs (Kwakiutl Nation) explain how "the solutions [for the present problems we face] can only be found by our Nations and communities accepting these problems as theirs, and your government recognizing that the methods of resolving these problems must be ours. Your government must relinquish responsibility for resolving our problems, and support our Nations and communities as they identify and implement their solutions."[25] Autonomy in child welfare provision is often articulated as being central not only to the move toward political independence but also to the establishment of better services to meet the culturally specific needs of First Nations families, which are so vastly overrepresented within the existing system.

The Colonial Legacy

The demand for autonomous child welfare services by Indigenous peoples cannot be understood outside the particular historical context of colonialism and oppression that First Nations have experienced at the hands of the Canadian state. This history has included the Canadian state rejecting and, at times, criminalizing traditional ways of child rearing and family life, as was manifested in a number of legalistic interventions since the time of European settlement. Many of these interventions occurred in the era of residential schooling, when First Nations children were forcibly removed from their families and communities.[26] The legacy of this history is manifest in the continuing over-representation of First Nations children within provincial child and family services agencies. The vast over-representation of First Nations children and families in Canadian child welfare systems is, in part, explained by societal factors, including poverty, inadequate housing, and lack of a sufficient economic base.[27] These factors need to be considered in tandem with political factors such as gaps in jurisdictional accountability and, at times, a lack of due process in family courts.[28] Moreover, there is now a broad literature that has emerged from government reports and the work of Indigenous scholars, activists, and welfare practitioners themselves that acknowledges how the current situation of First Nations communities is a direct result of the rupturing of First Nations communities and families by state intervention, regardless of whether this intervention was justified as being in the best interests of the Canadian nation or the best interests of the child.[29]

While this intervention has taken many forms, perhaps none has been more detrimental than the placement of Indigenous children in residential schools across the country.[30] As stated in the 1992 report of the Aboriginal Justice Inquiry, the main goal of residential schools and their assimilation strategies was not to further education but rather "to remove Aboriginal children from the influences of their parents and communities, and to rid them of their languages and cultures."[31] In fact, the term "assimilationist" is in many ways too generous, as it downplays the genocidal aspect of these initiatives.[32]

It is now well known that the residential school environment was an atmosphere of woeful mistreatment, neglect, and profound abuse of children. It is even more troubling that these realities were known to government and church authorities throughout the history of the school system:

> At the heart of the vision of residential education – a vision of the
> school as home and sanctuary of motherly care – there was a dark

contradiction, an inherent element of savagery in the mechanics
of civilizing children. The very language in which the vision was
couched revealed what would have to be the essentially violent
nature of the school system in its assault on child and culture. The
basic premise of resocialization, of the great transformation from
"savage" to "civilized" was violent. "To kill the Indian in the child,"
the department aimed at severing the artery of culture that ran between generations and was the profound connection between parent and child sustaining family and community. In the end, at the
point of final assimilation, "all there is in the race should be dead."[33]

The long-term impact of these violent realities is undeniable. The Aboriginal Healing Foundation estimates that the number of residential school
attendees still living is about ninety thousand.[34] According to Statistics Canada's "Aboriginal People's Survey 2001," one-third of Aboriginal people aged
fifteen and over who lived off-reserve had family members who attended
residential schools.[35] The experiences these children endured have an impact
on their adult lives and the lives of their family and community members.
As Chief Ed Metatawabin of the Fort Albany First Nations community explains, "Social maladjustment, abuse of self and others and family breakdown
are some of the symptoms prevalent among First Nations babyboomers. The
'Graduates' of the era are now trying and often failing to come to grips with
life as adults after being raised as children in an atmosphere of fear, loneli-
ness, and loathing."[36]

In conjunction with the residential school program of eradicating "the
Indian problem," other strategies of civilization through dislocation were
being carried out. In a policy widely referred to as the "60s scoop," a large
number of Indigenous children were adopted out of Indigenous communities
into non-Indigenous homes. The children often crossed international borders,
which ensured that they were disconnected from community traditions,
cultural identities, and cultural practices.[37] Thus, while the over-representation
of First Nations children in child welfare continues today, the 1960s are often
referred to as the initial, and most culturally offensive, period of this type of
intervention.

Overall, the experience of intense intervention, forced assimilation, and
community fragmentation has left many scars on First Nations communities,
including a deep mistrust and resentment toward governmental child welfare services and the Canadian state in general. As Joyce Green observes: "In

Canada in the twenty-first century, the majority of people identify as citizens of the state, the human rights of which the government is expected to protect. For the most part, this is the happy norm for Canadians. Yet there are communities within the Canadian state who do not share this understanding or this experience. Among these, Aboriginal peoples are likely to understand the state as an oppressor that has been economically and politically strong at the direct expense of Aboriginal nations."[38] This history reinforced a deep commitment to cultural distinction and preservation among Indigenous communities. Indigenous familial and cultural breakdown, endorsed by the Canadian state, is repeatedly cited as being rooted in Canada's colonial history. The invocation of Indigenous tradition is often conceived of as a "powerful means of resisting colonialism."[39] It is not surprising, then, that First Nations autonomy in general and autonomous child welfare service in particular have become such central concerns in current debates. As White and Jacobs state, "In the long run, recognition of our inherent right to self-government and the paramountcy of our family law provide the only framework for dealing with the protection and strengthening of our families and children."[40] From this perspective, child welfare services must be community-centred because only the community has the cultural knowledge and capabilities required to work with First Nations children from an Indigenous worldview approach.[41]

Within this particular historical context, it is clear that autonomy is and will remain a central aspect of First Nations politics in Canada. Moreover, in the past decade this perspective appears to have gained increasing legitimacy outside of First Nations communities, a development that is reflected in the general discourses and specific policy shifts of various Canadian governments.[42] Although the meaning of the constitutionally entrenched right to self-government is still being contested, significant steps have already been taken in many provinces toward the delegation of authority over child welfare matters from the provincial government to agencies established by First Nations communities.

Over the last two decades, a number of incremental changes have been made regarding First Nations communities and child welfare authority. The Province of Manitoba is a forerunner in this regard. As was noted by the Aboriginal Justice Inquiry, "tremendous advances" had been made in the delivery of child and family services for Aboriginal families living in on-reserve communities.[43] These advances were initiated by First Nations in the early 1980s through the establishment of their own child and family service agencies. These agencies, however, only had jurisdiction on-reserve. Aboriginal children and families living off-reserve continued to be served by mainstream child and family service agencies.

Thus, in its 1991 report, the Aboriginal Justice Inquiry concluded that a number of changes were still required to serve First Nations families well. These recommendations included the following:

- Amend Principle 11 of the *Child and Family Services Act* to read: "Aboriginal people are entitled to the provision of child and family services in a manner which respects their unique status, and their cultural and linguistic heritage."
- Expand the authority of existing Indian agencies to enable them to offer services to band members living off reserve.
- Establish an Aboriginal child and family services agency in the city of Winnipeg to handle all Aboriginal cases.[44]

In 1999 the Government of Manitoba committed itself to responding to these recommendations. By August 2000 the provincial government, the Manitoba Metis Federation, the Assembly of Manitoba Chiefs, and Manitoba Keewatinowi Okimakanak (the northern Manitoba organization of First Nations chiefs) had signed agreements establishing a joint initiative to develop a plan to (1) "recognize a province-wide First Nations right and authority by extending and expanding off-reserve jurisdiction to First Nations," (2) "recognize a province-wide Metis right and authority," and (3) "restructure the existing child and family services system through legislation and other changes."[45]

These commitments culminated in the establishment of the Aboriginal Justice Inquiry – Child Welfare Initiative and the subsequent establishment of several committees to oversee the development of these changes. The vision statement and mission statement of the initiative reaffirm the espoused commitment to First Nations by focusing on the recognition of the "distinct rights" and "unique authority" of First Nations and Métis populations and by including repeated references to "child and family services" that are "community-based."[46] Furthermore, these developments received enthusiastic public support from high-profile Indigenous organizations. Upon signing the memorandum of understanding that supports the creation of this new child and family services system, David Chartrand, president of the Manitoba Metis Federation, stated, "Our people have waited generations to restore our responsibility and hope for our children ... We have lost thousands of our children from our families and because of this we risk losing our culture. We can even say that our children have lost their souls. The Metis Nation is family oriented. We are a proud people and continue to make a significant contribution in the building of this beautiful province. We can once more keep our children within our families and our culture. I must commend this government for taking action."[47] Similarly, the Assembly of Manitoba Chiefs has described the changes as "another step toward full jurisdiction over child welfare for First Nations people. It represents one step closer to self-government."[48]

The process of child welfare service delegation in Manitoba is currently in the implementation phase and centres on the creation of the following new authorities: the First Nations of Northern Manitoba Child and Family Services Authority, the First Nations of Southern Manitoba Child and Family Services Authority, the Metis Child and Family Services Authority, and the General Child and Family Services Authority.[49] Caseloads, resources, and assets are currently being transferred to the most "culturally appropriate authority" and its respective agencies. These transfers are currently being completed on a region-to-region basis. The magnitude of these transfers was apparent in the estimate that five thousand of the fifteen thousand Manitoba families that received child welfare services in 2003 would *choose* to transfer to one of the new Aboriginal agencies.[50]

Demands for autonomous child welfare have come from First Nations communities themselves as well as from other stakeholders.[51] However, when the over-representation of First Nations children in care is examined in combination with the particular forms of autonomy being offered by the state, a welfare regime analysis suggests that the state's willingness to meet First Nations demands for justice through decentralization may be more complex and potentially harmful than a direct response through community autonomy. In fact, this analysis reveals that this form of autonomy is, at best, a case of what Alan Noël aptly refers to as "autonomy with a footnote" – that is, "the *negative autonomy* of the non-participant."[52]

Assessing the Risks of Autonomy

REREGULATION

When assessing the shift in child welfare service provision, we need to consider how the new form of autonomy is manifest in practice. As has already been demonstrated, Manitoba's child welfare reform included the creation of new Aboriginal-controlled authoritative bodies with increased "rights" and "responsibilities." The bodies were endorsed by high-profile First Nations organizations because they promised to ensure that Aboriginal children would be cared for in a manner consistent with Aboriginal culture and philosophy.[53] Upon close examination, however, it is doubtful whether autonomy has increased. This is most obvious when the hierarchical structure of the new system is examined, for as White and Jacobs aptly note, in many cases that involve the creation of First Nations autonomy, the state remains the true centre of power. They observe: "Even in situations where a full delegation of decision-making has been made to the Aboriginal agency ... ministerial policies, based on Anglo-Canadian cultural values and assumptions, continue to play a major role in the provision of services to our children and families."[54]

This is the case in Manitoba. Despite claims of fundamental change, the provincial government remains the ultimate authority for the safety and protection of First Nations children.[55] The continuation of ministerial power limits the kinds of change that can take place and is a significant step away from the kinds of "self-defined autonomy" that are advocated by Joyce Green or a holistic fundamental change, which is advocated by Taiaiake Alfred and Patricia Monture-Angus.[56] Both Alfred and Monture-Angus argue that a meaningful change is not so much a change in who administers services but a complete overhaul of the value systems that lie beneath existing practices. It must be a decolonized autonomy. For Alfred, this kind of independence includes the complete rejection of Western assumptions, including Western notions of the state, executive authority, sovereignty, and citizenship. Instead, he argues: "In a very real sense, to remain Native – to reflect the essence of Indigenous North Americans – our politics must shift to give primacy to concepts grounded in our own cultures.[57]

Alfred observes that a failure to address the fundamental aspects of service provision risks reinscribing old values and, hence, old problems into the new system. He argues, "In this 'new' relationship [of "self-government"], indigenous people are still bound to another's power order. The rusty cage may be broken, but a new chain has been strung around the indigenous neck; it offers more room to move, but it still ties our people to white men pulling on the strong end."[58]

Alfred's words carry even more significance when the question of funding is added into the analysis. For in the case of child welfare, funding in the new system will also continue to be approved by the province. As is explained in the vision document *Promise of Hope: Commitment to Change*, "existing funds and resources will be transferred to the new authorities. In turn, the authorities will give funding and resources to the agencies."[59] This leaves First Nations communities dependent on the amount of funds that the province sees fit to provide, but with the increased responsibility of deciding how these fixed funds will be spent. What we see in this example, then, is not so much fundamental deregulation (that is, the withdrawal of the state from positions of power) but rather a kind of reregulation (that is, the state's power will now be wielded in new, less transparent, and more indirect ways). Such change gives the impression of vastly increased autonomy or empowerment for First Nations communities while actually maintaining the existing power order to a significant degree. The province not only appears to make fundamental concessions to the demands of First Nations but, in the eyes of the broader Canadian public, also distances itself from some of the hardest child welfare cases, thereby allowing the state to take credit and avoid blame.

What then of the increased rights gained by First Nations in Manitoba? One example of a new right granted to First Nations authorities is the authority's right to define for itself the criteria on which its workforce is hired. According to the province's strategic design principles, "Each CFS [Child and Family Service] Authority requires a skilled and appropriate workforce; and each has the right to define 'skilled,' and 'appropriate,' and the criteria through which the workforce is hired."[60] Prima facie, this change may appear to grant more autonomy, but when this change is considered in light of the fact that the province determines overall funding, the practical space in which to use this new-found autonomy is restricted significantly. Again, as White and Jacobs observe, this kind of shift may actually result in further inequalities between First Nations and non-First Nations in the provision of child welfare.[61] Mainstream child welfare across Canada is notoriously underfunded and understaffed, and these old difficulties will be transported to the new system along with the existing funds. However, new inequalities may also be created as a result of differential employment criteria for First Nations and mainstream agencies. First Nations communities will have to try to make the best use of the funding granted by the province while simultaneously dealing with some of the most difficult and extensive caseloads. Financial pressures, combined with increasing First Nations caseloads (the Aboriginal population in Canada is "young, growing and increasingly urbanized"), may result in fewer staff, heavier caseloads, or lower hiring standards for First Nations agencies.[62] Old problems of inadequate service provision and insufficient human resources will also continue to plague the new system. Furthermore, the transfer of existing funds does nothing to address substantial levels of material inequality between First Nations and non-First Nations communities in Canada. In fact, this shift allows the state to off-load the responsibility of staffing agencies with inadequate funding to First Nations communities, thus opening the possibility of having them participate in the maintenance, and potential increase, of their own disadvantage. This sets the stage for a "blame the victim" reaction if First Nations groups are subsequently unable to manage the issues within their autonomous administrative sphere.

Reprivatization and Individualization

The reregulation of child welfare culminates in both a reprivatization and individualization of First Nations child welfare issues as First Nations demands become subject to state manipulation. While the shift is not directly from the public to the market or the family (although these trends are also detectable), it is a movement away from the public domain to the private or domestic domain of a particular "minority" or "national" group. Group rights claims are often couched in the language of privacy, and this discourse has been co-opted by the state, fairly successfully, in the area of child welfare. Co-optation of First Nations discourses facilitates the removal of First Nations concerns regarding the safety and protection of their children out of the realm of the public and into the realm of the private under the pretence of "returning" the issue of First Nations child welfare to its rightful, "natural" place in First Nations communities.[63] At first this move seems to respond directly to First Nations' demands. In this case the state successfully fragments the statistically hardest child welfare cases from mainstream child welfare and, in so doing, distances itself and its mainstream practices from the situation of First Nations children. Because the responsibility of child welfare has now been "returned" to its "natural" place in First Nations communities, the state forces First Nations groups to accept responsibility for a set of issues that extend far beyond the jurisdiction, and decision-making power, they have been granted.

In a similar vein, the piecemeal strategy of the state and its incumbent practices of individualization also risk perpetuating the negative images that, historically, have been attached to individual First Nations communities. Once child welfare administration is relegated to the private jurisdiction of First Nations groups, the state distances itself from responsibility and narrows opportunities for political contestation. Conflict about resources, funding, and service provision are shifted out of the state's jurisdiction and into the hands of First Nations communities – they are individualized. At the same

time, however, the state continues to hold ultimate authority over funding
and the scope of service provision, which makes it difficult to address the
inherently linked issues of poverty, unemployment, health, and housing.

The opportunity to systemically address First Nations issues is further
reduced by the fact that the state is choosing to deal with each issue in an
artificially fragmented fashion. As has been discussed, issues of child welfare
cannot be separated from other issues of social concern. Nevertheless, the
state's strategy of dealing with each concern separately makes it extremely
difficult for First Nations groups to achieve a holistic response. The devolution of child welfare services to First Nations has produced a number of
targeted benefits, including "new, more culturally appropriate resources for
children ... better quality services, including more prevention and resource
development initiatives ... and healing programs based on a circle of caring
philosophy and medicine wheel teachings."[64] However, this approach has
also reduced fundamental holistic change by facilitating small, controlled
modifications that include enough of the old system to maintain current
power balances while giving the illusion of flexibility and progress.

CO-OPTATION

The processes of privatization, including depoliticization and individualization, are facilitated by the co-optation of progressive discourses. In this case
the state has successfully co-opted many dominant First Nations discourses,
including that of self-government, to encourage regressive policy changes.
This has been realized under the auspices of "progressively" returning the
care of First Nations children to the natural location of First Nations communities in order to facilitate the inevitable move toward self-government.

After decades of colonial intervention by the Canadian state, First Nations
groups have increasingly demanded various forms of self-determination.
Instead of self-determination in any meaningful sense, however, the state (in
this case the Government of Manitoba) has offered, and has now significantly implemented, an intermediary role for First Nations communities. As
Taiaiake Alfred and Jeff Corntassel have noted, this kind of concession is
insufficient for the First Nations goal of self-determination and may actually
threaten any future attempt to achieve this goal. They describe this process
as "Aboriginalism":

> In Canada today, many Indigenous people have embraced the
> Canadian government's label of "aboriginal," along with the

concomitant and limited notion of postcolonial justice framed within the institutional construct of the state. In fact, this identity is purely a state construction that is instrumental to the state's attempt to gradually subsume Indigenous existences into its own constitutional system and body politic ... Far from reflecting any true history or honest reconciliation ... "aboriginalism" is a legal, political and cultural discourse designed to serve an agenda of silent surrender to an inherently unjust relation at the root of the colonial state ... It must be understood that the aboriginalist assault takes place in a politico-economic context of historic and ongoing dispossession and of contemporary deprivation and poverty; this is a context in which Indigenous peoples are forced by the compelling needs of physical survival to cooperate individually and collectively with the state authorities to ensure their physical survival.[65]

Thus, as Alfred and Corntassel highlight, the welfare state context is useful for understanding state motivations and decision making as well as the motivations and compromises that some group members and leaders are "willing" to make.

Conclusion

This discussion is largely an exploratory analysis of the potential implications of changes that are, at present, still being defined and implemented. However, applying a welfare regime analysis to the case of autonomous First Nations child welfare helps to illuminate the potential dangers and negative implications that accompany demands for autonomy as Indigenous peoples seek meaningful independence and "multicultural citizenship." The discussion of this case underlines the significance that welfare regimes may hold in the politics of group accommodation and recognition. As the privatization literature suggests, welfare regime restructuring reconstitutes political spaces and identities, including "cultural" ones, thereby reconfiguring the opportunities for future developments. This case also demonstrates that discourse plays a primary role in this shift, as language facilitates current change through processes of co-optation and constrains future change through processes of depoliticization and individualization.

Once an issue is privatized through law in forms such as rights, it becomes increasingly difficult to get these same issues back into the public, political domain. This is because the demands appear to be met (i.e., autonomy has been granted) and, therefore, groups no longer appear to have a legitimate differentiated position from which to contest the position of the state. Groups are left negotiating within the entrenched status quo rather than contesting and rejecting it for something more suitable. In other words, this form of group autonomy does not encourage groups to combat ineffective policies through political participation and, in fact, may make it more difficult to do so. Consequently, some forms of group autonomy can *inhibit* rather than *contribute to* an emancipatory citizenship regime for Canada's Indigenous peoples.

Overall, a welfare regime perspective reveals new difficulties for the pursuit of social and political justice among national groups in Western liberal democracies such as Canada. It reveals that cultural communities and the social movements and leaders who act on their behalf must constantly reposition themselves in response to the state's concessions in order to bring their unresolved concerns out of the private, domestic sphere of the group and into a political space of public state accountability. Although a form of collective or group privacy is an important part of group autonomy and decolonization, it must, as Iris Marion Young suggested, come in the form of voluntary withdrawal as opposed to forced non-participation.[66] Moreover, this perspective reveals that during periods of change and negotiation groups may be required to give up some privacy in order to ensure a more robust form of autonomy. In turn, a more "public" practice of autonomy could enable such groups to hold other entities accountable, most notably the state. Given the complexities that come with Indigenous issues of justice and welfare, this period is likely to be quite lengthy and will require institutionalized avenues to ensure that the necessary mechanisms of accountability are available to groups.

Finally, the welfare regime perspective highlights the practical inadequacies of current theories of cultural group autonomy as put forward by dominant multicultural theorists. Although culture and identity are integral to the pursuit of a just form of autonomy for groups, the most important factor is the remaining, albeit at times more covert, power relations that exist between groups and the state. It follows from this observation that groups must be conceived of as being *political* as much as they are viewed as *cultural*. From this perspective, cultural performance may be an important political act, but it is also necessary to recognize that political performance is an important cultural act. The two are, in many ways, inseparable.

NOTES

1   Geoffrey York, *The Dispossessed: Life and Death in Native Canada* (Toronto: Lester and Orpen Dennys, 1989); Canada, Royal Commission on Aboriginal Peoples, *Report of the Royal Commission on Aboriginal Peoples*, vol. 5, *Renewal: A Twenty-Year Commitment* (Ottawa: Canada Communications Group, 1996), chap. 1, http://www.ainc-inac.gc.ca/ch/rcap/sg/sgmm_e.html; Taiaiake Alfred, *Peace, Power, Righteousness: An Indigenous Manifesto* (Don Mills, ON: Oxford University Press, 1999); Patricia Monture-Angus, *Journeying Forward: Dreaming First Nations Independence* (Halifax, NS: Fernwood, 1998); Patrick Macklem, *Indigenous Difference and the Constitution of Canada* (Toronto: University of Toronto Press, 2001); Charles Taylor, "The Politics of Recognition," in Charles Taylor et al., *Multiculturalism: Examining the Politics of Recognition*, ed. Amy Gutmann (Princeton, NJ: Princeton University Press, 1994), 25-73.

2   Ayelet Shachar, *Multicultural Jurisdictions: Cultural Differences and Women's Rights* (Cambridge: Cambridge University Press, 2001), 46-47.

3   In this chapter, the term "welfare regime" is used to denote the welfare state in its broadest sense. As Esping-Anderson observes, "To talk of 'a regime' is to denote the fact that in the relation between state and economy a complex of legal and organizational features are systematically interwoven." Thus, the welfare state context involves an ever-shifting constellation of social rights that are shaped by and, in turn, contribute to a policy paradigm that impacts not only the typical "welfare" policy areas themselves but also the overarching citizenship regime in which all matters of equality, autonomy, and accountability are interpreted, upheld, or dismantled. Gosta Esping-Anderson, *The Three Worlds of Welfare Capitalism* (Princeton, NJ: Princeton University Press, 1990), 2.

4   Janine Brodie, *Politics on the Margins: Restructuring and the Canadian Women's Movement* (Halifax, NS: Fernwood Publishing, 1995); Marlee Kline, "Blue Meanies in Alberta: Tory Tactics and the Privatization of Child Welfare," in *Challenging the Public/Private Divide: Feminism, Law, and Public Policy*, ed. Susan B. Boyd (Toronto: University of Toronto Press, 1997), 330-59; Brenda Cossman and Judy Fudge, "Introduction: Privatization, Law, and the Challenge to Feminism," in *Privatization, Law, and the Challenge to Feminism*, ed. Brenda Cossman and Judy Fudge (Toronto: University of Toronto Press, 2002), 3-37.

5   Fudge and Cossman, "Introduction," 1.

6   Brodie, *Politics on the Margins*, 11.

7   Fudge and Cossman "Introduction," 16.

8   Brodie, *Politics on the Margins*, 14. See also Kline, "Blue Meanies" and Cossman and Fudge, "Introduction."

9   Macklem, *Indigenous Difference*; Alfred, *Peace, Power, Righteousness*; Monture-Angus, *Journeying Forward*; Canada, Royal Commission on Aboriginal Peoples, vol. 5, *Renewal*, chap. 1; Will Kymlicka, *Multicultural Citizenship* (New York: Oxford

University Press, 1995). It must be acknowledged that the majority of Indigenous scholars and activists do not see themselves as part of the multiculturalism rubric; nor do they self-identify as a minority group. I wish to support the fact that Indigenous peoples self-identify as *nations*, and should be recognized as such. Nonetheless, the discourse of multiculturalism is sometimes invoked to reflect the dominant conception of Indigenous issues that is embedded in theories of multiculturalism and government practice, and also, at times, to contest it.

10 While the focus in this article is on child welfare, the implications demonstrated by this case extend into other policy areas – including First Nations health, policing, and education – where increased autonomy is being debated and implemented to varying degrees. For more on demands for autonomy in these other areas, see Manitoba, Aboriginal Justice Implementation Commission, *Report of the Aboriginal Justice Inquiry of Manitoba* (Winnipeg: Government of Manitoba, 1991), http://www.ajic.mb.ca/volumel/toc.html; Canada, Royal Commission on Aboriginal Peoples, vol. 5, *Renewal*, chap. 1; British Columbia, British Columbia Ministry of Children and Family Development, *Healing Ways: Aboriginal Health and Service Review* (Victoria: Government of British Columbia, 1999) and *The Mental Health and Well-Being of Aboriginal Children and Youth: Guidance for New Approaches and Services: A Report Prepared for British Columbia Ministry of Children and Family Development* (Victoria: Government of British Columbia, 2004).

11 As Marlee Kline notes in her critical analysis of the 1994 decision by the Alberta government to privatize the delivery of child welfare services, the movement toward "community-based" child welfare services may not be a simple case of progressive change. My analysis works in the same critical vein as Kline's work by examining the dynamic between these trends and the dominant multiculturalism/group autonomy discourse. See Marlee Kline, "Blue Meanies," 33.

12 While it is beyond the scope of this chapter, it is worth noting that although these trends have serious implications for all group members, they hold particular significance for First Nations women because the process of neoliberal restructuring is inherently gendered and often results in these women and their children falling through the cracks of the provincial child and family services system. See Brodie, *Politics on the Margins* and Brenda Cossman "Family Feuds: Neo-Liberalism and Neo-Conservative Visions of the Reprivatization Project," in *Privatization, Law, and the Challenge to Feminism*, ed. Cossman and Fudge, 169-217. See also Joyce Green, "Canaries in the Mines of Citizenship: Indian Women in Canada," *Canadian Journal of Political Science* 34, 4 (2001): 715-38, for an in-depth exploration of the unique issues confronting Canada's Indigenous women.

13 Recently, child welfare services in the Winnipeg region were taken over by the Manitoba government – ostensibly for fiscal reasons – with no explicit link made to current changes related to the restructuring of services for the First Nations population.

14   Manitoba, Aboriginal Justice Inquiry – Child Welfare Initiative, "Inter-Provincial Lessons on Child Welfare Governance? An Invitational Forum, 22 February 2002, Vancouver," Aboriginal Justice Inquiry – Child Welfare Initiative, http://www.aji-cwi.mb.ca.

15   York, *The Dispossessed*; Union of British Columbia Indian Chiefs, *Calling Forth Our Future: Options for the Exercise of Indigenous Peoples Authority in Child Welfare* (Vancouver: Union of British Columbia Indian Chiefs, 2002).

16   Manitoba, Aboriginal Justice Implementation Commission, *Report of the Aboriginal Justice Inquiry*, "Child Welfare," vol. 1, chap. 14.

17   For a comprehensive overview of these concerns, see United Native Nations, the Aboriginal Council of Winnipeg, and the Institute on Governance, *Aboriginal Governance in Urban Settings: Working Together to Build Stronger Communities*, conference report, 31 March 2002, Institute on Governance, http://www.iog.ca/publications/UNN_Conference_Report.pdf.

18   See Douglas Durst, *Self-Government and the Growth of First Nations Child and Family Services (FNCFS)* (Regina: Social Policy Research Unit, Faculty of Social Work, University of Regina, 2002).

19   Manitoba, Aboriginal Justice Inquiry – Child Welfare Initiative, *Promise of Hope: Commitment to Change*, August 2001, Aboriginal Justice Inquiry – Child Welfare Initiative, http://www.aji-cwi.mb.ca/eng/Phase3/promiseofhope.html. The Aboriginal Justice Inquiry (AJI) was established in the spring of 1988 to investigate the condition of Aboriginal people in the justice system of Manitoba. It was conducted by Justice Murray Sinclair and involved fairly extensive consultation with Aboriginal communities and a number of public hearings. The scope of the AJI encompassed all aspects of the system, including policing, courts, and correctional services. The findings and recommendations were released in a wide-ranging report in 1991. Aboriginal Justice Inquiry – Child Welfare Initiative, "Press Release," 17 April 2000, Aboriginal Justice Inquiry – Child Welfare Initiative, http://www.aji-cwi.mb.ca/eng/news_release_ajic.html.

20   Lavina White and Eva Jacobs, *Liberating Our Children, Liberating Our Nations* (Victoria: Government of British Columbia, Ministry of Social Services, 1992), 2.

21   White and Jacobs, *Liberating Our Children*, 2.

22   Canada, Royal Commission on Aboriginal Peoples, "Residential Schools," in *Report of the Royal Commission on Aboriginal Peoples*, vol. 1, *Looking Forward, Looking Back* (Ottawa: Canada Communications Group, 1996), pt. 2, chap. 10, http://www.ainc-inac.gc.ca/ch/rcap/sg/sgm10_e.html.

23   Ibid.; Joyce Timpson, "Four Decades of Literature on Native Canadian Child Welfare: Changing Themes," *Child Welfare* 74, 3 (1995): 525-46; Cindy Blackstock et al., *Keeping the Promise: The Convention on the Rights of the Child and the Lived Experiences of First Nations Children and Youth* (Ottawa: First Nations Child and Family Caring Society of Canada, 2004).

24   Patricia Monture, "A Vicious Circle," *Canadian Journal of Women and the Law* 3, 1 (1989): 3.

25   White and Jacobs, *Liberating Our Children*, v.

26   As stated in the report of the Aboriginal Justice Inquiry, the main goal of residential schools and their assimilation policy was not to further education but rather "to remove Aboriginal children from the influences of their parents and communities, and to rid them of their languages and cultures." See Manitoba, Aboriginal Justice Implementation Commission, *Report of the Aboriginal Justice Inquiry of Manitoba*, "Child Welfare," vol. 1, chap. 14.

27   As Augie Fleras and Jean Leonard Elliott note, Canada has been ranked at or near the top by the United Nations as the best place to live in the world, yet Aboriginal people on reserves are ranked 63rd on a human development index. See Augie Fleras and Jean Leonard Elliot, *Unequal Relations: An Introduction to Race, Ethnic, and Aboriginal Dynamics in Canada* (Scarborough ON: Prentice Hall, 1999), 49.

28   See Patrick Johnston, *Native Children and the Child Welfare System* (Ottawa: Canadian Council on Social Development, 1983); Brad McKenzie and Pete Hudson, "Native Children, Child Welfare, and the Colonization of Native People," in *The Challenge of Child Welfare*, ed. Kenneth L. Levitt and Brian Wharf (Vancouver: UBC Press, 1985), 125-41; Cheryl Avina, *Effects of Forced Removal from Family and Culture on Indian Children* (Twin Cities, MN: NAES College, 1993). Monture, "A Vicious Circle;" Timpson, "Four Decades of Literature"; Canada, Royal Commission on Aboriginal Peoples, "Residential Schools;" British Columbia Human Rights Commission, *Removal of Aboriginal Children from their Families by the Ministry of Children and Families* (Vancouver: British Columbia Human Rights Commission, 2001).

29   As is discussed in the *Report of the Royal Commission on Aboriginal Peoples*, residential schools were part of the process of "nation building" and were seen as contributing to "peaceful," stable conditions for the settler majority. The "best interest of the child" test (since modified) was used historically to impose standards developed by judges that ignored the importance of culture and heritage for Indigenous children and contributed, overall, to a racist, assimilationist system. Canada, Royal Commission on Aboriginal Peoples, "Residential Schools." See also Monture "A Vicious Circle" and Marlee Kline "Child Welfare Law, 'Best Interest of the Child' Ideology, and First Nations," *Osgoode Hall Law Journal* 30, 2 (1992): 375-425.

30   Residential schools reached their "high point," with eighty schools, in 1931 and grew again in the 1950s as part of Canada's postwar expansion into Inuit homelands. The residential school system was maintained until the 1980s, with schools built in every province and territory except Prince Edward Island, New Brunswick, and Newfoundland. Children from every Aboriginal group – Indian, Inuit, and Métis – were registered, although the federal government did not officially assume

constitutional responsibility for Métis people at the time. See Canada, Royal Commission on Aboriginal Peoples, "Residential Schools."

31 Manitoba, Aboriginal Justice Implementation Commission, *Report of the Aboriginal Justice Inquiry,* "Child Welfare".

32 The impact of these schools is in many ways immeasurable. In regard to the death rate of students, some ran as high as 47 percent. See Canada, Royal Commission on Aboriginal Peoples, "Residential Schools." See also Monture, "A Vicious Circle," 3.

33 Canada, Royal Commission on Aboriginal Peoples, "Residential Schools."

34 Aboriginal Healing Foundation, *The Healing Has Begun: An Operational Update from the Aboriginal Healing Foundation* (Ottawa: Aboriginal Healing Foundation, 2002).

35 Statistics Canada, "Aboriginal Peoples Survey 2001," Statistics Canada, http://www.statcan.ca/english/freepub/89-589-XIE/context.htm.

36 Canada, Royal Commission on Aboriginal Peoples, "Residential Schools."

37 Monture, "A Vicious Circle," 1-2, 8; Manitoba, Aboriginal Justice Implementation Commission, *Report of the Aboriginal Justice Inquiry,* "Child Welfare"; Canada, Royal Commission on Aboriginal Peoples, "Residential Schools."

38 Green, "Canaries in the Mines of Citizenship," 715-16.

39 Ibid., 726.

40 White and Jacobs, *Liberating Our Children,* 35.

41 Monture describes the Indigenous worldview approach as a need to recognize the "indigenous factor," which is "the unique character of First Nations children as members of a specific class." Monture traces most issues – child welfare, criminal justice, family violence, alcohol and drug abuse, or lack of education and employment – to a conflict in the basic values of Indigenous societies and the dominant Canadian society, a conflict characterized as "force and coercion" versus "consensus and cooperation": Monture, "A Vicious Circle," 3. For more discussion on the Indigenous worldview, see George Manuel and Michael Posluns, *The Fourth World: An Indian Reality* (New York: Collier Macmillan Canada, 1974) and Grace Ouellette, *The Fourth World: An Indigenous Perspective on Feminism and Aboriginal Women's Activism* (Halifax, NS: Fernwood Publishing, 2002).

42 See Douglas Durst, "The Circle of Self-Government: A Guide to Aboriginal Government of Social Services," in *Issues in Northern Social Work Practice,* ed. Roger Delaney, Keith Brownlee, and Kim M. Zapf, Northern Social Work Collection, vol. 2 (Thunder Bay, ON: Centre for Northern Studies, Lakehead University, 1996), 104-25.

43 Manitoba, Aboriginal Justice Inquiry – Child Welfare Initiative, *Promise of Hope.*

44 Ibid.

45 Ibid.

46 Ibid.

47   Manitoba, Aboriginal Justice Inquiry – Child Welfare Initiative, "Press Release,"
     22 February 2000, Aboriginal Justice Inquiry – Child Welfare Initiative, http://
     www.aji-cwi.mb.ca.

48   Assembly of Manitoba Chiefs, "First Nations Child and Family Services – Ogimaa-
     kaan 2001," Assembly of Manitoba Chiefs, http://www.manitobachiefs.com/
     index1.html.

49   Manitoba, Aboriginal Justice Inquiry – Child Welfare Initiative, "Proposed
     Changes," Aboriginal Justice Inquiry – Child Welfare Initiative, http://www.aji-cwi.
     mb.ca/eng/Phase3/pamphlet.html.

50   Manitoba, Aboriginal Justice Inquiry – Child Welfare Initiative, "Press Release,"
     24 November 2003, Aboriginal Justice Inquiry – Child Welfare Initiative, http://
     www.aji-cwi.mb.ca/eng/news_release_proclamation.html .

51   See Pete Hudson and Brad McKenzie, "Extending Aboriginal Control over Child
     Welfare Services: The Manitoba Child Welfare Initiative," *Canadian Review of Social
     Policy* 51, 4 (2003): 55.

52   Alain Noël, "Without Quebec: Collaborative Federalism with a Footnote?" *Policy
     Matters* 1, 2 (2000): 17 (emphasis added).

53   Manitoba, Aboriginal Justice Inquiry – Child Welfare Initiative, "Background,"
     Aboriginal Justice Inquiry – Child Welfare Initiative, http://www.aji-cwi.mb.ca/
     eng/background.html.

54   White and Jacobs, *Liberating Our Children*, 35.

55   Manitoba, Aboriginal Justice Inquiry – Child Welfare Initiative, "Background." For
     the Province of Manitoba, the restructuring currently underway does not exclude
     government more than its predecessor did. Instead, the development of the new
     authorities creates a new level of administration between agencies and government.
     See also Hudson and McKenzie, "Extending Aboriginal Control over Child Welfare
     Services," 49-66.

56   Green, "Canaries in the Mines of Citizenship"; Alfred, *Peace, Power, Righteousness*;
     Monture, *Journeying Forward*.

57   Alfred, *Peace, Power, Righteousness*, xiv.

58   Ibid., xiii.

59   Manitoba, Aboriginal Justice Inquiry – Child Welfare Initiative, *Promise of Hope*,
     27.

60   Manitoba, Aboriginal Justice Inquiry – Child Welfare Initiative "Background."

61   White and Jacobs, *Liberating Our Children*, 45.

62   The 2001 census showed that nearly half of the non-reserve Aboriginal population
     in Canada was under the age of twenty-five, compared to just under a third of the
     non-Aboriginal population. Statistics Canada, "Aboriginal Peoples Survey 2001."

63   The notion of "return" has been particularly prominent in the Manitoba case and
     is often invoked in various news releases and public documents. For example,
     statements such as "the proposed restructuring plan recognizes and respects

Manitoba's cultural diversity and returns to Metis and First Nations peoples the right to develop and control the delivery of their own child and family services" can be found throughout the Aboriginal Justice Inquiry – Child Welfare Initiative website: see "Background."

64   Hudson and McKenzie, "Extending Aboriginal Control," 50.

65   Taiaiake Alfred and Jeff Corntassel, "Being Indigenous: Resurgences against Contemporary Colonialism," *Government and Opposition* 40, 4 (2005): 599 (emphasis added).

66   Iris Marion Young, *Justice and the Politics of Difference* (Princeton, NJ: Princeton University Press, 1990).

WORKS CITED

Aboriginal Healing Foundation. *The Healing Has Begun: An Operational Update from the Aboriginal Healing Foundation.* Ottawa: Aboriginal Healing Foundation, 2002.

Alfred, Taiaiake. *Peace, Power, Righteousness: An Indigenous Manifesto.* Don Mills, ON: Oxford University Press, 1999.

Alfred, Taiaiake, and Jeff Corntassel. "Being Indigenous: Resurgences against Contemporary Colonialism," *Government and Opposition* 40, 4 (2005): 597-614.

Assembly of Manitoba Chiefs. "First Nations Child and Family Services – Ogimaakaan 2001." Assembly of Manitoba Chiefs. http://www.manitobachiefs.com.

Avina, Cheryl. *Effects of Forced Removal from Family and Culture on Indian Children.* Twin Cities, MN: NAES College, 1993.

Blackstock, Cindy, Sarah Clarke, James Cullen, Jeffrey D'Hondt, and Jocelyn Formsma. *Keeping the Promise: The Convention on the Rights of the Child and the Lived Experiences of First Nations Children and Youth.* Ottawa: First Nations Child and Family Caring Society of Canada, 2004.

British Columbia. British Columbia Human Rights Commission. *Removal of Aboriginal Children from Their Families by the Ministry of Children and Families.* Vancouver: British Columbia Human Rights Commission, 2001.

British Columbia. British Columbia Ministry of Children and Family Development. *Healing Ways: Aboriginal Health and Service Review.* Victoria: Government of British Columbia, 1999.

–. *The Mental Health and Well-Being of Aboriginal Children and Youth: Guidance for New Approaches and Services: A Report Prepared for British Columbia Ministry of Children and Family Development.* Victoria: Government of British Columbia, 2004.

Brodie, Janine. *Politics on the Margins: Restructuring and the Canadian Women's Movement.* Halifax, NS: Fernwood Publishing, 1995.

Canada. Royal Commission on Aboriginal Peoples. *Report of the Royal Commission on Aboriginal Peoples.* Vol. 5, *Renewal: A Twenty-Year Commitment.* Ottawa: Canada Communications Group, 1996. http://www.ainc-inac.gc.ca/ch/rcap/sg/sgmm_e.html.

–. "Residential Schools." In *Report of the Royal Commission on Aboriginal Peoples,* vol. 1, *Looking Forward, Looking Back,* pt. 2, chap. 10. Ottawa: Canada Communications Group, 1996. http://www.ainc-inac.gc.ca/ch/rcap/sg/sgm10_e.html.

Cossman, Brenda "Family Feuds: Neo-Liberalism and Neo-Conservative Visions of the Reprivatization Project." In *Privatization, Law, and the Challenge to Feminism,* ed. Brenda Cossman and Judy Fudge, 169-217. Toronto: University of Toronto Press, 2002.

Cossman, Brenda, and Judy Fudge. "Introduction: Privatization, Law, and the Challenge to Feminism." In *Privatization, Law, and the Challenge to Feminism,* ed. Brenda Cossman and Judy Fudge, 3-37. Toronto: University of Toronto Press, 2002.

Durst, Douglas. "The Circle of Self-Government: A Guide to Aboriginal Government of Social Services." In *Issues in Northern Social Work Practice,* ed. Roger Delaney, Keith Brownlee, and Kim M. Zapf, 104-25, Northern Social Work Collection, Vol. 2. Thunder Bay, ON: Centre for Northern Studies, Lakehead University, 1996.

–. *Self-Government and the Growth of First Nations Child and Family Services (FNCFS).* Regina: Social Policy Research Unit, Faculty of Social Work, University of Regina, 2002.

Esping-Anderson, Gosta. 1990. *The Three Worlds of Welfare Capitalism.* Princeton, NJ: Princeton University Press, 1990.

Fleras, Augie, and Jean Leonard Elliot. *Unequal Relations: An Introduction to Race, Ethnic, and Aboriginal Dynamics in Canada.* Scarborough, ON: Prentice Hall, 1999.

Green, Joyce. "Canaries in the Mines of Citizenship: Indian Women in Canada." *Canadian Journal of Political Science* 34, 4 (2001): 715-38.

Hudson, Pete, and Brad McKenzie. "Extending Aboriginal Control over Child Welfare Services: The Manitoba Child Welfare Initiative." *Canadian Review of Social Policy,* 51, 4 (2003): 49-66.

Johnston, Patrick. *Native Children and the Child Welfare System.* Ottawa: Canadian Council on Social Development, 1983.

Kline, Marlee. "Blue Meanies in Alberta: Tory Tactics and the Privatization of Child Welfare." In *Challenging the Public/Private Divide: Feminism, Law, and Public Policy,* ed. Susan B. Boyd, 330-59. Toronto: University of Toronto Press, 1997.

–. "Child Welfare Law, 'Best Interests of the Child' Ideology, and First Nations." *Osgoode Hall Law Journal* 30, 2 (1992): 375-425.

Kymlicka, Will. *Multicultural Citizenship.* New York: Oxford University Press, 1995.

Macklem, Patrick. *Indigenous Difference and the Constitution of Canada.* Toronto: University of Toronto Press, 2001.

Manitoba. Aboriginal Justice Implementation Commission. *Report of the Aboriginal Justice Inquiry of Manitoba.* Winnipeg: Government of Manitoba, 1991. http://www.ajic.mb.ca/volumel/toc.html.

Manitoba. Aboriginal Justice Inquiry – Child Welfare Initiative. "Background." Aboriginal Justice Inquiry – Child Welfare Initiative. http://www.aji-cwi.mb.ca/eng/background.html.

–. "Inter-Provincial Lessons on Child Welfare Governance? An Invitational Forum, 22 February 2002, Vancouver." Aboriginal Justice Inquiry – Child Welfare Initiative. http://www.aji-cwi.mb.ca.

–. "Press Release," 22 February 2000. Aboriginal Justice Inquiry – Child Welfare Initiative. http://www.aji-cwi.mb.ca/eng/news_release_mmf.html.

–. "Press Release," 17 April 2000. Aboriginal Justice Inquiry – Child Welfare Initiative. http://www.aji-cwi.mb.ca/eng/news_release_ajic.html.

–. "Press Release," 24 November 2003. Aboriginal Justice Inquiry – Child Welfare Initiative. http://www.aji-cwi.mb.ca/eng/news_release_proclamation.html.

–. *Promise of Hope: Commitment to Change*, August 2001. Aboriginal Justice Inquiry – Child Welfare Initiative. http://www.aji-cwi.mb.ca/eng/Phase3/promiseofhope.html.

–. "Proposed Changes." Aboriginal Justice Inquiry – Child Welfare Initiative. http://www.aji-cwi.mb.ca/eng/Phase3/pamphlet.html.

Manuel, George, and Michael Posluns. *The Fourth World: An Indian Reality*. New York: Collier Macmillan Canada, 1974.

McKenzie, Brad, and Pete Hudson. "Native Children, Child Welfare, and the Colonization of Native People." In *The Challenge of Child Welfare*, ed. Kenneth L. Levitt and Brian Wharf, 125-41. Vancouver: UBC Press, 1985.

Monture, Patricia. "A Vicious Circle." *Canadian Journal of Women and the Law* 3, 1 (1989): 1-17.

Monture-Angus, Patricia. *Journeying Forward: Dreaming First Nations Independence*. Halifax, NS: Fernwood, 1998.

Noël, Alain. "Without Quebec: Collaborative Federalism with a Footnote?" *Policy Matters* 1, 2 (2000): 1-26.

Ouellette, Grace. *The Fourth World: An Indigenous Perspective on Feminism and Aboriginal Women's Activism*. Halifax, NS: Fernwood Publishing, 2002.

Shachar, Ayelet. *Multicultural Jurisdictions: Cultural Differences and Women's Rights*. Cambridge: Cambridge University Press, 2001.

Statistics Canada. "Aboriginal Peoples Survey 2001." Statistics Canada. http://www.statcan.ca/english/freepub/89-589-XIE/context.htm.

Taylor, Charles. "The Politics of Recognition." In Charles Taylor, Kwame Anthony Appiah, Jürgen Habermas, Stephen C. Rockefeller, Michael Walzer, and Susan Wolf, *Multiculturalism: Examining the Politics of Recognition*, ed. Amy Gutmann, 25-73. Princeton, NJ: Princeton University Press, 1994.

Timpson, Joyce. "Four Decades of Literature on Native Canadian Child Welfare: Changing Themes." *Child Welfare* 74, 3 (1995): 525-46.

Union of British Columbia Indian Chiefs. *Calling Forth Our Future: Options for the Exercise of Indigenous Peoples Authority in Child Welfare*. Vancouver: Union of British Columbia Indian Chiefs, 2002.

United Native Nations, the Aboriginal Council of Winnipeg, and the Institute on Governance. *Aboriginal Governance in Urban Settings: Working Together to Build Stronger*

Communities. Conference report, 31 March 2002. Institute on Governance. http://www.iog.ca/publications/UNN_Conference_Report.pdf

White, Lavina, and Eva Jacobs. *Liberating Our Children, Liberating Our Nations*. Victoria: Government of British Columbia, Ministry of Social Services, 1992.

York, Geoffrey. *The Dispossessed: Life and Death in Native Canada*. Toronto: Lester and Orpen Dennys, 1989.

Young, Iris Marion. *Justice and the Politics of Difference*. Princeton, NJ: Princeton University Press, 1990.

8

Rethinking the Administration of Government: Inuit Representation, Culture, and Language in the Nunavut Public Service

Annis May Timpson

Aboriginal peoples in Canada have protracted histories of being managed by non-Aboriginal public servants who have often based their work on regulations that reflect dominant Canadian values. It is not surprising, therefore, that social movements to increase Aboriginal peoples' control over the governance of their communities have included calls for greater Aboriginal representation in the institutions that service them. Although initial efforts to achieve this objective focused on raising levels of Aboriginal employment in the public sector, more recent initiatives have taken account of institutional, cultural, and linguistic factors that shape Aboriginal participation in government employment.[1]

The creation and development of a public service for the new territorial government of Nunavut provides a key opportunity to consider how Aboriginal people in Canada have tried to rethink the administration of public government to increase Aboriginal representation and embed Aboriginal values, cultural perspectives, and languages in the public sector. When Nunavut was carved out of Northwest Territories in 1999, it was designed with the objective of establishing a population-reflective public service. Close to 85 percent of the territory's population is Inuit; as a result, Nunavut became the first Canadian jurisdiction to be established with the objective of building a public service that would be staffed predominantly by Aboriginal people. In this chapter I analyze how the public service project in Nunavut has tried to ensure Aboriginal representation in institutional, numerical, cultural, and linguistic terms. I also consider what might be learned from the Nunavut experience for the development of more Aboriginal-oriented public governments in other areas of Canada.

At the outset, it was envisaged that the Government of Nunavut (GN) would become the major employer of the territory's burgeoning Inuit population. It was critical, therefore, for its public service to offer a culturally familiar environment in which members of Nunavut's Indigenous community would want to work. However, the decision to create an Inuit-oriented public service in Nunavut also reflected the desire of Inuit in the eastern Arctic for a new territorial government that would be informed by Inuit culture and not simply modelled on the structure of governance in Northwest Territories.[2] As one trainee policy analyst in the new government reflected: "My understanding from hearing my mother's generation and other generations is that the past government, the Government of the Northwest Territories, wasn't reflective. It was an imposed government. The workforce was Southern based. So really who was working within the government and affecting Inuit lives and culture and policy didn't understand the culture ... In the long run in order to really have programs and policies that are reflective of what Inuit need you need Inuit working within the government that know the issues from the heart, that know them from experience."[3]

Designing an Inuit-Sensitive Public Service Infrastructure

Institutional representation of Aboriginal interests in the design of the new government resulted from the work of the Inuit-led Nunavut Implementation Commission (NIC), which was established by the 1993 *Nunavut Act* to "advise the Government of Canada, the Government of the Northwest Territories and Tungavik on the establishment of Nunavut ... [including] the administrative design of the first Government of Nunavut."[4] After extensive consultation across the Nunavut Settlement Area, the NIC produced a blueprint for the new territorial government that emphasized "the need to respect the unique culture, language and history of the aboriginal residents of Nunavut" in the design of the bureaucratic infrastructure of the new government.[5]

The NIC sought to achieve this objective in the design of core and program departments in the GN. Its proposal that the Department of Executive and Intergovernmental Affairs "coordinate relations with aboriginal organizations" encouraged new thinking about the way governments in Canada could conduct external relations. Similarly, its recommendation that the Department of Justice "provide a justice system relevant to the life style, customs and culture of Nunavut" marked a key stage in a much longer process of reconciling contemporary Canadian jurisprudence with traditional Inuit law.[6]

While designing the infrastructure of the new government, the NIC also recommended the creation of program departments that would sustain Inuit values in policy development. Its design of the Department of Sustainable Development (DSD) and the Department of Culture, Language, Elders and

TABLE 1

Departmental structure of the Government of Nunavut

	1999	2004
Core departments	Executive and Intergovernmental Affairs Finance and Administration Human Resources Justice	Executive and Intergovernmental Affairs Finance Human Resources Justice
Program departments (routine)	Health and Social Services Education Public Works and Telecommunications Community Government and Transportation	Health and Social Services Education Community and Government Services
Program departments (innovative)	Sustainable Development Culture, Language, Elders and Youth	Economic Development and Transportation Environment Culture, Language, Elders and Youth

SOURCE: Nunavut Implementation Commission, *Footprints in New Snow*, 28, and Nunavut, "Civil Service Changes Underline Government Commitment to Economic Prosperity and Inuit Qaujimajatuqangit," news release, 10 March 2004, http://www.gov.nu.ca.

Youth (CLEY) are of particular note (Table 1). The Department of Sustainable Development was established to bring issues of the environment, economy, and human development together to preserve Inuit knowledge of the land and to encourage the use of traditional knowledge alongside scientific approaches to resource management.[7] Initially, its mandate also included the management of social security payments in the territory – an indication of the importance of this source of income to many households in Nunavut.[8] The importance of connecting Elders and youth to preserve Inuit culture in a period of modernization was reflected in CLEY. This innovative department was created to "bring Inuit language and culture into the everyday lives and work of the residents of Nunavut," to preserve and promote Inuit culture and language, and to ensure that the youngest citizens of Nunavut acquired cultural wisdom from Elders in the territory.[9]

Although both departments were central to the creation of Inuit-sensitive institutions of government, only CLEY survived. Demands from within and outside the GN became so extensive that the DSD proved unsustainable as a

single department. In 2004 it was split to form the Department of Environment, on the one hand, and the Department of Economic Development and
Transportation, on the other (Table 1).

The experience of designing an Inuit-sensitive infrastructure for the GN
contains important messages for future initiatives to develop public governments that reflect Aboriginal values. While the design of the GN reinforced
the centrality of Inuit cultural priorities, the evolution of government infrastructure demonstrates how intergovernmental pressures can overwhelm
departments created with Aboriginal cultural priorities in mind, particularly
as senior officials in these units find themselves working on multiple intergovernmental files that in most other jurisdictions are serviced by separate
departments.[10] This suggests that when the departmental infrastructure of a
government is designed to reflect Aboriginal priorities, consideration must
be given not only to the cultural perspectives of the Aboriginal communities
that the government is designed to serve but also to extraneous factors that
may have an impact on the realization of these cultural objectives in the
operation of governance.

Strategies to Ensure Numeric Representation of Inuit within the GN

The vision of building a population-reflective public service in Nunavut to
ensure proportionate Inuit representation in government employment was
encoded within the 1993 Nunavut Land Claims Agreement (NLCA), which
preceded the creation of Nunavut. This was signed after some twenty-five
years of negotiation between the federal government, the Government of the
Northwest Territories (GNWT), and the Tungavik Federation of Nunavut (the
organization that was established by Inuit to negotiate the land claim and
reconstituted as Nunavut Tunngavik Incorporated (NTI) once the claim was
settled).

According to Article 23 of the NLCA, the federal and territorial governments and NTI were to "cooperate in the development and implementation
of employment and training" in order to "increase Inuit participation in
government employment in the Nunavut Settlement Area to a representative
level."[11] This obliged both governments to ensure that the level of Inuit employment in the public sector in Nunavut reflected "the ratio of Inuit to the
total population in the Nunavut Settlement Area ... within all occupational
groupings and grade levels."[12]

The first government of Nunavut committed itself to building "an effective, functional and skilled public service, which is responsible to the

public it serves and increasingly representative of the population of Nunavut" and to initiating processes that would ensure the development of a "representative workforce in all sectors" by 2020.[13] The GN's Inuit Employment Plan was to train Inuit for public service employment, increase awareness of Inuit culture in recruitment and personnel strategies, and monitor the ethnic composition of the public service on a quarterly basis to assess how effectively its goal of building a population-reflective public service in Nunavut was being met.[14]

Training Inuit for public service employment in Nunavut was addressed, initially, by the creation of a $39.8 million Nunavut Unified Human Resources Development Strategy, which was funded by the federal government as part of the $150 million start-up budget allocated for the creation of Nunavut. Designed to expand the pool of educated and skilled Inuit, the strategy developed training opportunities for unemployed Inuit who wished to enter the public service in Nunavut. It also provided in-service training for Inuit public servants who wanted to increase their responsibilities and remuneration.[15]

Training programs have been developed since the inception of Nunavut, including the Public Service Career Training Program; the Summer Student Employment Program for Inuit; the Public Service Inuit Training Program, which trains Inuit for positions in areas of the public service where they are under-represented; the Nunavut Senior Assignment Program, which was designed to enable land claim beneficiaries to "enhance their management, leadership and specialised skills" on the job and under the guidance of senior managers within the GN; and Sivuliqtiksat, "a two-year management development program to prepare beneficiaries [for] management roles in the GN's public service."[16]

The GN's culturally sensitive recruitment strategies include the development of competency-based job descriptions "to ensure that knowledge, skills and abilities form the basis of qualifications for positions rather than dependence on education and years of experience" and interviews that focus on "the skills, knowledge and attitudes required [to undertake a job] rather than on perceived academic credentials."[17] As a former deputy minister of human resources in the GN noted, "efforts have been made to ensure that applicants are interviewed in their own language and a behavioural model of interviewing is adopted so that the candidate can draw directly on their own experience to explain their capacity to undertake a particular job."[18]

Data on levels of Inuit and Qallunaat (non-Inuit) employment within the GN reveal the initial impact of these training and recruitment initiatives.

The GN was only 6 percent short of the target of 50 percent Inuit employment at the outset of Nunavut on 1 April 1999. Although the GN's public service expanded quickly after that, the overall proportion of Inuit employed within it declined marginally in the years that followed and reached a low point of 42 percent in June 2003 (see Table 2). Since then, there has been a gradual improvement in the representation of Inuit in the GN's professional, managerial, and executive posts. By 2007 the number of Inuit employees in the GN was greater than the number of Qallunaat employees. Nonetheless, the greatest increase in Inuit employment has been concentrated in the paraprofessional and administrative support categories of the territorial public service. Indeed, almost all posts in the lowest rung of the GN's six employment categories are filled by Inuit, and, I have observed, they are primarily filled by women.

Why has Inuit employment in the GN not accelerated more rapidly? The Nunavut Unified Human Resources Development Strategy may not have been developed soon enough to ensure a sufficient pool of skilled Inuit workers in the early years of Nunavut. In addition, the long tradition of hunting and gathering in Inuit society, and the continuing importance of these activities to the economies of many Inuit households, means that office work does not appeal to all Inuit.[19] Indeed, this partly accounts for the complexities of attracting young Inuit men into the territorial government's workforce.

The entry of Inuit into government employment is also affected by competition for skilled Inuit in Nunavut. The GN has to compete with the private sector and with a range of Inuit organizations that are affiliated with NTI and, in many respects, provide a more Inuit-oriented working environment.[20] Moreover, because the government is still operating around 20 percent below its planned staffing capacity, the demands of working for the GN can be stressful. As one Inuk trainee in the Department of Human Resources commented:

> It's just work overload – trying to get so many things done with
> short deadlines and trying to meet a lot of deadlines. And they
> seem to have to be done all at the same time. So, it's difficult to
> let go of something and just to do something well ... And when
> you're hired for a certain term, like myself, I can use myself as an
> example ... I was hired for six months, and it takes approximately
> six months to get used to a job. So, for me, it was quite challen-
> ging because I had specific tasks to do in this six month period,
> and it was almost like a very crash course in orientation, learning

TABLE 2

Percentage (and number) of Inuit (I) and Qallunaat (Q) employees in departments and boards of the Government of Nunavut, 1999-2008

	June 1999		June 2001		June 2003		June 2005		June 2007		June 2008	
	I	Q	I	Q	I	Q	I	Q	I	Q	I	Q
Executive	61	39	48	52	50	50	47	53	47	53	55	45
Senior management	22	78	20	80	18	82	25	75	28	72	26	74
Middle management	24	76	19	81	19	81	23	77	25	75	24	76
Professional	41	59	23	77	23	77	25	75	26	74	27	73
Paraprofessional	47	53	54	46	57	43	61	39	68	32	69	31
Administrative support	64	36	78	22	81	19	86	14	91	9	94	6
Overall percentage	44	56	43	57	42	58	47	53	51	49	52	48
Number of employees	220	280	925	1,243	1,014	1,395	1,414	1,506	1,499	1,466	1,517	1,425

SOURCE: Nunavut, Department of Human Resources, *Towards a Representative Public Service: Inuit Statistics as of June 2001*, 3, 18; *June 2003*, 3; *June 2006*, 3; *June 2007*, 2; *June 2008*, 2. Department of Human Resources, http://www.gov.nu.ca/hr/site/towardrepps.htm.

about the new government, the policies, and everything else included as to what I was doing ... And all the time I'm thinking and
speaking in Inuktitut, but I've got to transfer it into English because that's how we work right now.[21]

ADDRESSING THE SLOW RATE OF GROWTH OF INUIT EMPLOYMENT IN NUNAVUT

Frustration with the slow rate of growth of Inuit employment in Nunavut
was aired by Inuit leaders in the GN and NTI during lengthy negotiations
with the federal government to ensure that the initial ten-year planning period funding that underwrote the NLCA implementation contract was renewed
in 2003.[22] Negotiators from Nunavut argued that the federal government
needed to invest more heavily in Inuit employment training to meet its NLCA
commitments. Federal officials indicated that, without decisions by ministers
to respond positively to such calls for new initiatives, the only recourse to
support further training initiatives in Nunavut would be from existing sources
of funds.[23]

Problems in the negotiation of additional federal investment in training
led NTI and the GN to appoint the international accounting firm PricewaterhouseCoopers to assess the costs of not building a population-reflective
public service in Nunavut. In itself this decision is an interesting example of
Indigenous negotiators choosing to engage mainstream experts (in cost-
benefit analysis) to further their political objectives. The consultants' report
identified persistent barriers to Inuit employment in the GN, including Inuit
perceptions of limited work availability, low educational attainment among
Inuit, the absence of sufficient mentoring of Inuit within the public sector
workplace, and the prevalence of English as the language of work.[24] The
consultants also made a direct connection between a numerically representative public service and a culturally reflective public service by arguing
that "full implementation of Article 23 [in the NLCA] would ensure that Inuit
have the power to develop and administer government policies in a manner
consistent with Inuit values and culture, in direct proportion to the percentage of the population they represent."[25] In addition they advised that "full
implementation of Article 23 would ensure that Inuit receive their fair share
of Government funding resources, as per the requirement that the Representative Level be achieved at all occupational groups and grade levels."[26]

The report emphasized both the direct and indirect costs of not achieving
a population-reflective public service in Nunavut. It estimated that "Inuit

would have earned $258 million in compensation if Article 23 had been fully implemented ... [The consultants also argued that] Inuit under-representation in Government, particularly in the high paying positions [meant that] $123 million of this compensation [was] expected to go to non-Inuit in 2003 [and that] the total value of lost wages, if representation rates remain[ed] at their current level, [was] estimated to be $2.5 billion over the next 18 years."[27]

The report highlighted a range of indirect social and economic benefits for Nunavut that would ensue with increased Inuit representation in public service employment, including reduced expenditure on high-cost health care delivery and the potential reduction of alcohol abuse and crime levels.[28] It anticipated that additional benefits for Nunavut would accrue from economies of scale, including more training facilities and increased spending on goods and services (as Inuit would be more likely to spend a greater proportion of their income in Nunavut than employees from the South). The consultants also considered that more innovation would arise with greater Inuit representation, particularly as they anticipated that this would lead to more effective "leveraging of Government sustainable development initiatives and [greater recognition being accorded to] the value of Inuit knowledge."[29]

Significantly, the report concluded with the argument that "a coordinated and comprehensive strategy for the effective implementation of Article 23 should be developed – one that takes into account both short-term and long-term goals."[30] In particular, it recommended that the costs of focusing on quick-ramp-up strategies such as Inuit-sensitive advertising, interviewing, and training initiatives should be assessed together with the costs of developing a longer-term "Human Capital Strategy ... based on the theory that the fundamental barrier to employment is education."[31]

EXPANDING THE POOL OF EDUCATED INUIT FOR PUBLIC SECTOR EMPLOYMENT

The importance of education for longer-term human capital development in Nunavut was reinforced by Justice Thomas Berger's 2006 report, which was written in his capacity as the conciliator appointed to try to resolve the two-year deadlock in implementation contract negotiations between NTI, the GN, and the federal government.[32] Writing after extensive consultations across Nunavut and in Ottawa, Berger argued that the current range of training, scholarship, career development, and retention programs for Inuit had focused too much energy on the demand-side of realizing Article 23's objective and detracted attention away from the fundamental causes of the declining pool of educated Inuit available to take up employment in the GN's public service.

In his report Berger asserted that Article 23's objective would be realized only if questions about the supply and demand side of the development of a representative public service were addressed in tandem.[33] As he noted, "Today there are about 100 Inuit high school graduates every year. [Yet] the achievement of Article 23's objective of representative Inuit employment (i.e. 85 percent) would require the addition of something like 1500 Inuit to the workforce, over and above the number required to maintain current levels in the face of retirements and other departures from the public service."[34]

Berger reinforced arguments about the cultural importance for Inuit of increased educational investment in Nunavut. In the report he argued that "only a robust and effective system of bilingual education [in the Inuit language and English] can provide the foundation for the fulfillment of the objective of Article 23."[35] He also pointed out that, if "Nunavut students had first and second language skills by the time they complete their schooling, they would be able to maintain their identity and their culture, and at the same time be equipped to enter governmental or private sector employment."[36] He noted: "Nunavut needs a generation of executives and managers, computer software designers, architects, audiologists, nurses, doctors, lawyers, accountants, x-ray technicians, RCMP members and, of course, teachers. It is likely that few of them will receive their post-secondary education in Inuktitut ... A central objective of the Nunavut education system, therefore, must be to produce high school graduates whose ability to function in English enables them to enter colleges and universities in southern Canada and to achieve success in their chosen programs, so that they can qualify for responsible positions in their own public service."[37]

Berger recommended that the shift in language instruction in Nunavut's schools should be more gradual. He argued that when English becomes a language of instruction in Grades 4 and 5, Inuktitut should not be abandoned but should remain a language of instruction alongside it, with at least two periods a day being taught in Inuktitut (possibly with greater Inuinnaqtun immersion in the western Kitikmeot, where the regional dialect is endangered).[38] Given that "only 35 percent of teachers speak Inuktitut," Berger also recognized that there would be insufficient teachers in Nunavut to ensure a rapid promotion of bilingualism within the school system.[39] He therefore recommended that interim measures – such as fostering language nests in families and drawing Inuktitut speakers in the community into the school system – would need to accompany the training of potential teachers in both

Inuktitut and English.[40] Such initiatives would, of course, increase the inter-generational transmission of Inuit thought.

Berger acknowledged that "nothing quite like this has been undertaken in Canada in the past. There is no template for a jurisdiction-wide bilingual education program for all children."[41] Nonetheless, he argued that an additional investment of $20 million per annum would be essential to develop the teacher training and bilingual curriculum materials needed to lay the foundations of such an education system.[42] He also argued that the bulk of this funding would have to come from the federal government and would have to be "over and above what Nunavut receives through Territorial Formula Financing. It is funding that, like the federal funds that go to the provinces and territories to fund English and French, [would] have to be targeted funding, not devoted to any other territorial priorities."[43]

Although the federal government set up a working group to review Berger's recommendations, it would not agree to inject additional targeted funds into Nunavut over and above those contained in the territorial funding formula.[44] This impasse in implementation contract negotiations led NTI to file a $1 billion lawsuit against the federal government in December 2006 for breach of the NLCA implementation contract.[45] The suit included a claim against "the total salaries and benefits lost to Inuit amount[ing] to $123 million annually because the government has not implemented the land claim and continues to import a Southern workforce."[46]

While NTI's legal challenge clearly highlights the financial implications for Inuit if Article 23 of the NLCA is not fully implemented, the two external reports discussed in this section highlight the structural issues that make the achievement of a population-reflective public service in Nunavut so complex. Indeed, the Nunavut experience suggests that the creation of population-reflective public institutions in communities with significant Aboriginal populations cannot simply be considered a project to be addressed by those responsible for public sector workforce development. Only if such a project is underscored by well-funded, long-term, culturally sensitive education and training strategies can both the supply and demand side of creating representative public sector institutions be addressed.

Building a Culturally Conscious Bureaucracy
Rethinking the administration of government to take account of Aboriginal perspectives extends beyond the question of numerical representation. It also

involves building a culture of public government that reflects Aboriginal values.[47] In Nunavut this has taken two forms: identifying methods to embed Inuit cultural perspectives into the operation of government and developing policies to increase the use of the Inuit language as an official language of government.

The broader issue of how to embed Inuit cultural perspectives in public government in Nunavut was addressed in the early stages of developing the GN. The term *Inuit Qaujimajatuqangit (IQ)* (that which is long known by Inuit) was chosen by Inuit cultural experts to supersede the term "traditional knowledge" (as it was used in the GNWT) and ensure that Inuit values were placed front and centre in the GN.[48] This objective was reflected in the first government's strategic plan for the long-term development of Nunavut, which emphasized how *Inuit Qaujimajatuqangit* would "provide the context [for developing] an open, responsive and accountable government."[49]

The Department of Culture, Language, Elders and Youth, with support from activists in the departments of Sustainable Development and Justice, took the lead on developing *IQ* initiatives within the GN. A two-day workshop in Niaqunngut (also called Apex) in September 1999 was followed by *IQ* initiatives designed to raise awareness of Inuit culture and integrate Inuit knowledge into bureaucratic operations in all departments (Table 3). However, the process of embedding Inuit knowledge within the GN has proved to be complicated because understandings of *IQ* vary across communities, genders, and generations. Moreover, it is not straightforward to integrate cultural perspectives that have been developed over time, in a land-based culture, into the operation of a newly established, office-based government.

In November 2000 the minister of CLEY appointed an Inuit-only task force (made up of two GN employees, two members of the Nunavut Social Development Council, and two Elders) to consider the development of a government-wide strategy on *IQ*. Significantly, its 2002 report urged the GN to rethink its approach to *IQ* and "incorporate itself into Inuit culture," rather than merely seeking to "incorporate Inuit culture into itself."[50] In response, the GN began to connect the procedural orientation of early *IQ* initiatives to a policy-based analysis of *IQ*, which required government departments to evaluate policy objectives in their annual business plans in terms of *IQ*. Moreover, in 2003 the GN established Tuttarviit, an interdepartmental committee that operates solely in Inuktitut and brings together *IQ* representatives from different departments.[51]

TABLE 3

Key Inuit Qaujimajatuqangit initiatives in the Government of Nunavut, 1999-2006

	Department	*IQ* initiative
Core departments	Executive and Intergovernmental Affairs	Inuit-sensitive internal architecture Ceremonial events (drum dancing, etc.) Time out on the land
	Finance	Public servant responsible for *IQ*
	Human Resources	*IQ* committee
	Justice	*IQ* committee – Illinit Gatherings in Inuktitut Resident Inuit Elder for policy advice Time out on the land
Program departments	Culture, Language, Elders and Youth	*IQ* workshop 1999 *IQ* task force 2000 *IQ* coordinator appointed 2001 *IQ* advisor appointed 2003 Coordinate Tuttarviit Support Inuit Qaujimajatuqangit Katimajiit
	Education	Development of *IQ* curricular materials
	Health and Social Services	Elders brought in to advise on policy *IQ* advisor in department
	Community and Government Services (formerly Public Works and Telecommunications)	Public servant responsible for *IQ* *IQ* newsletter *IQ* suggestions box
	Economic Development and Transportation Environment (formerly Sustainable Development)	Research on *IQ* Elders brought in to advise on policy *IQ* committee

SOURCE: Material collated by author during fieldwork in Iqaluit, Nunavut, September 1999, April 2001, and June 2006.

One interesting example of the way departmental *IQ* committees are trying to incorporate the GN into Inuit culture is found in the Department of Justice, where the *IQ* committee has adopted the name Illinit to denote "trails created by dog teams," on which "Inuit journeyed confidently into unknown territory by following the paths left by dog team travellers who had gone ahead."[52] Illinit's terms of reference indicate that it is "to provide advice, direction, and assistance to the Department of Justice on all matters involving the use of Inuktitut in the workplace, on the incorporation of Inuit Qauji-majatuqangit (IQ) into the Department's programs and services, and on the incorporation of the Department into Inuit culture."[53] The committee's name, however, highlights the trail-blazing work involved in integrating Inuit cultural knowledge into the operations of a government department.

When the second government of Nunavut took office in 2004, it emphasized how the "important principles of Inuit Qaujimajatuqangit," transmitted intergenerationally through the advice of Elders, are "particularly relevant to the way [the GN] should deliver its services."[54] Its strategic plan disaggregated the principal components of IQ and identified how they could be transposed into government practice. Although many IQ principles, when transposed into bureaucratic objectives for territorial governance, reflect best-practice objectives that would ideally be found in any Canadian public service, others – such as *Aajiiqatigiinniq* (consensus-oriented decision-making), *Qanuqtuurniq* (survival-based resourcefulness), and *Avatittinnik Kamatsiarniq* (stewardship of the land, animals, and the environment) – are strongly rooted in Aboriginal priorities (Table 4).

The decision to address the issue of IQ within the GN has had important consequences. First, although there was significant debate in the early days of Nunavut about Elders not being integrated into governance of the new territory, IQ initiatives provided opportunities for Elders to advise officers in the GN on ways in which working practices and policies could reflect fundamental aspects of traditional Inuit culture. Elders were directly involved in the 1999 IQ workshop in Niaqunngut, and they were key members of the GN's IQ task force. In 2001 the Department of Justice created the post of Elder-in-residence to provide public servants and, more recently, Illinit with advice on how the department could take account of traditional Inuit law.[55] Moreover, in September 2003 the GN announced the creation of an eleven-person IQ advisory council, Inuit Qaujimajatuqangit Katimajiit (IQK), which ensures that Elders and community representatives advise government about the integration of IQ into its working practices and policy developments.[56] In order to reinforce connections between Elders and public servants in the design of the GN's policy on IQ, this council was reappointed in September 2005 with clearer links to Tuttarviit.[57]

Second, for an Inuit workforce operating in a government that functions primarily in English, the process of working on IQ – in committees with other Inuit – has provided a forum to raise consciousness about the broader position of Inuit within the GN and the potential experience of working in an Inuit-defined workplace. One senior public servant explained it this way:

TABLE 4

Guiding principles of Inuit Qaujimajatuqangit in the 2004-9 strategic plan of the Government of Nunavut

IQ principle	Government objective
Inuuqatigiitsiarniq Respecting others Caring for people	Respect others and treat others equally, as long advised by Elders; promote impartiality.
Tunnganarniq Fostering good spirit Being welcoming/ inclusive	Make workplace friendly, welcoming for Nunavummiut, Elders, colleagues, and others; remove language and cultural barriers to welcome people.
Pijitsirniq Serving and providing for family and community	Encourage staff to serve each other and the community to the best of their abilities.
Aajiiqaqigiinniq Making decisions through discussion and consensus	Reach important decisions with input from individuals, face-to-face meetings, direct communication, and consensus development; use the Inuit language widely as the primary language of communication; respect silence as part of communication and recognize that it does not necessarily signify agreement.
Pilimmaksarniq/ Pijariuqsarniq Skills development through practice, effort, and action	Develop a flexible, accommodating workplace for new ideas and practices that need to be implemented; give Inuit staff opportunities to develop skills on the job during regular hours through mentoring, in-service training, and professional development.
Piliriqatgiiniq/ Ikajuqtigiiniq Working together for a common cause	Encourage Inuit and non-Inuit staff to work together from the basis of their own knowledge to develop mutual understanding and a balanced approach to program and service provision; serve the public well through collaboration and mutual understanding in the workplace.
Qanuqtuurniq Being innovative and resourceful	Explore different opportunities for Inuit to move forward and survive.
Avatittinnik Kamatsiarniq Respect and care for the land, animals, and the environment	Foster *Avatittinnik Kamatsiarniq*, a strong Inuit value that has sustained Inuit for eons and is just as important today.

SOURCE: Nunavut, *Pinasuaqtavut: 2004-2009* (Iqaluit: Government of Nunavut, 2004), 3-4.

Its easier to understand the concept if you reverse the table. Let's say, for example, we were living in a totally Inuit society all across Canada. And here, in Nunavut, it was all Qallunaat, and everything has been running the Inuit way ... If you were going to make the government and all the systems more Qallunaat when it's been operating in a very Inuit way, how would you go about doing it? You wouldn't just set up an IQ committee or a Western Qaujimanatuqangit Committee ... you wouldn't just do that. You would look at all aspects of how people relate to each other – how people make decisions, how policies are made, what impact they have on the people – because policies are not just about things on paper. It's about how people operate and how they relate to each other and how decisions are made and how you service people and how you program things.[58]

The Nunavut experience highlights the complexities of transposing Aboriginal knowledge into the contemporary bureaucratic framework of public governance. At the same time, it reveals the importance of enabling Aboriginal public servants to work with Elders, thereby connecting the project of a new government with the body of Indigenous knowledge developed through intergenerational survival on the land. In addition, the Nunavut example shows how the provision of opportunities for Aboriginal public servants to work on a significant cultural project, such as embedding *IQ* within government practice, can provide key spaces in public government in which Aboriginal employees can work together entirely in their own language.

Aboriginal Languages and the Language of Work

Inuit politicians have long considered the development of the Inuit language as being central to their vision of Nunavut. As the Nunavut Constitutional Forum noted back in 1983, "Perhaps there is no more fundamental goal of a Nunavut government, nor one more essential to guarantee the survival and unique contribution of Inuit in Canada ... Official status for Inuktitut will hasten the full participation by Inuit in employment opportunities in Nunavut ... testify to the unique cultural nature of Nunavut and ... encourage other residents of Nunavut to learn the language of the majority."[59]

When the first elected government of Nunavut took office, it stated that the territory should become "a fully functional bilingual society, in Inuktitut and English, respectful and committed to the needs and rights of French speakers, with a growing ability to participate in French."[60] It also emphasized that efforts would be made to ensure that by 2020 "Inuktitut, in all its forms, [would become] the working language of the Government of Nunavut."[61]

More recently, the GN has adopted the phrase "the Inuit language" to take account of the seven different dialects spoken across the territory. Six of these dialects are collectively referred to as "Inuktitut," which is spoken throughout the Baffin and Keewatin regions and written using syllabic script. The seventh dialect – Inuinnaqtun – though severely endangered, is still spoken in the western Kitikmeot region of Nunavut and written using roman orthography.[62]

Developing the Inuit language as the working language of the GN is central to the full realization of the objectives of Article 23 of the NLCA and the integration of *Inuit Qaujimajatuqangit* into government operations. It is also important because most Inuit speak primarily Inuktitut or Inuinnaqtun at home but find themselves shifting between their Indigenous language and English in the workplace.[63] However, this project is complicated. Limited teaching of the Inuit language throughout the school system means that Nunavut's schools are "not producing graduates truly competent in Inuktitut" or, indeed, Inuinnaqtun.[64] As Jacques-Louis Dorais noted:

> Without having been schooled in the Inuit language until the end of high school, nobody possesses enough Inuktitut vocabulary and speaking habits to express him- or herself with ease in all fields of conversation in this language. Such vocabulary does exist in specialized lexicons, but it is not taught in school. For the time being, then, mastering a level of Inuktitut sophisticated enough for expressing oneself easily when speaking about administration, technical topics, or even everyday life in a modern community constitutes a professional skill which only interpreters and translators possess (and which most of them do not use outside their work).[65]

Moreover, as Berger noted, "Inuit of Nunavut have the lowest rate of literacy in English in the country" as the "'early exit immersion' model [of language training in the territorial school system] ... provides students with an insufficient foundation in their first language and too sudden an immersion in their second."[66] In short, not all Inuit working for the GN have complete communication skills either in the Inuit language or in English. Furthermore, most Qallunaat working for the GN have nothing more than rudimentary skills in the Inuit language.

Although the GN has always provided Qallunaat employees, on appointment to government employment, with a basic ten-week course in Inuktitut, very few Qallunaat employees have opted for more extensive language training.[67] Moreover, until recently the GN's focus on equipping Qallunaat staff with basic Inuit language skills detracted attention from the important issue of developing opportunities for Inuit public servants to upgrade their Indigenous language skills. Only since 2006, when the former premier of Nunavut, Paul Okalik, announced that fluency in the Inuit language would be a requirement for high office in the GN, have senior public servants focused systematically on language training.[68] Interestingly, this new expectation led to a program of intensive Inuit language training for key Inuit and Qallunaat public servants, which was headed by Eva Aariak at the Pirurvik language centre in Iqlauit after she completed her term of office as Nunavut's first languages commissioner.[69]

Eva Aariak's commitment to the protection and promotion of the Inuit language was demonstrated throughout her work as Nunavut's first languages commissioner and in her 2008 campaign for election to the Nunavut Legislative Assembly.[70] Aariak's subsequent success in being chosen as premier of Nunavut suggests that the implementation of new language legislation will be a priority for the third government of Nunavut.[71] Indeed, this commitment has been reinforced by the 2009 appointment of the experienced Inuit language advocate Alexina Kublu as the new languages commissioner of Nunavut.[72]

LANGUAGE LEGISLATION

In its recent development of language legislation for Nunavut, the GN has sought to move beyond the official language legislation it inherited from the GNWT at the time of territorial division. The first Legislative Assembly of Nunavut engaged in extensive consultation regarding the most appropriate way to revise this legislation for Nunavut.[73] The second Legislative Assembly developed and passed significant new legislation to recognize, protect, and promote the Inuit language in Nunavut.

Nunavut's new *Official Languages Act* was passed by the Legislative Assembly of Nunavut in June 2008 and, at the time of writing, is awaiting federal approval, as is required under the 1993 *Nunavut Act*.[74] This legislation seeks to place the Inuit language on par with English and French as one of the official languages of Nunavut and establish official language requirements for the Government of Nunavut, the Legislative Assembly, the Nunavut Court of Justice, and other judicial or quasi-judicial bodies and public agencies in Nunavut. The Act specifies that the new minister of languages will be expected to undertake a range of initiatives to promote the equal status of official languages of Nunavut, including the development of an official languages plan and an organizational strategy to ensure its implementation within relevant organizations.[75] The legislation also reinforces the powers of Nunavut's official languages commissioner to monitor and comment on the implementation of the Act. Interestingly, the legislation requires the commissioner to resolve any language-related disputes "through mediation and other methods consistent with Inuit Qaujimajatuqangit."[76]

The preamble to the legislation notes that "it is desirable that the Inuit Language be recognized as the indigenous language of Nunavut, the spoken and preferred language of a majority of Nunavummiut, [and] a defining characteristic of the history and people of Nunavut."[77] It also considers it desirable, "as contemplated by the Nunavut Land Claims Agreement," that the Inuit language be recognized as a necessary element not only "in the improvement of Inuit social, economic and cultural well-being" but also in "the development of the public service and ... government policies, programs and services."[78] However, it is the *Inuit Language Protection Act,* passed by the Legislative Assembly of Nunavut in September 2008, that seeks to ensure the broader retention, protection, and promotion of the Inuit language in Nunavut.[79]

The Inuit Language Protection Act is unique in Canada and does not require external approval by the federal government. It not only seeks to honour "as wise guardians, the Inuit Elders and the other Inuit Language speakers and educators who have sustained and developed the Inuit Language from time immemorial" but also to serve as a "foundation necessary to a sustainable future for the Inuit of Nunavut as a people of distinct cultural and linguistic identity within Canada."[80]

The Act sets out five key approaches to supporting "the more meaningful engagement of Inuit language speakers in all levels of governance and in socio-economic development in Nunavut."[81] First, it commits the GN to developing territorially based rights so that Nunavummiut can receive education in the Inuit language. It asserts that "every parent whose child is enrolled in the education program in Nunavut, including a child for whom an individual education plan has been proposed or implemented, has the right to have his or her child receive Inuit Language instruction."[82] Moreover, it specifies that "the Government of Nunavut shall, in a manner that is consistent with Inuit Qaujimajatuqangit, design and enable the education program to produce secondary school graduates fully proficient in the Inuit Language, in both its spoken and written forms."[83] Significantly, this approach not only espouses the core objectives of the 2006 Berger report, it also integrates language education with *IQ*.

Second, the Act focuses on the public sector workplace as a critical arena for Inuit language protection. It specifies that "the Inuit Language is a language of work in territorial institutions, and every employee of a territorial institution has the right to use the Inuit Language at work to the extent and in the manner provided in this Act and the regulations."[84] To this end, the territorial government is expected to "identify and implement measures to eliminate any barriers to inividuals who prefer to speak the Inuit Language during recruitment or in the workplace" and to "identify and implement measures to increase the use of the Inuit Language as a working language of the institution."[85] The Act requires the territorial government to ensure that ("except in cases where a language other than the Inuit Language is a bona fide requirement") individuals are informed that they "may submit an application entirely in the Inuit Language" and, "if selected for an interview, to have the job interview entirely in the Inuit Language."[86] The GN is also expected to "determine, through an active offer made at the commencement of employment, whether the new employee prefers the Inuit Language as his or her language of work" and ensure that management is able to communicate with, supervise, appraise, and mentor these employees in the Inuit language and accept grievances in the Inuit language.[87] Moreover, the Act requires the territorial government to offer training and upgrading in the Inuit language and assessments of employee competence in the Inuit language.[88]

Third, the legislation promotes the Inuit language in the broader civic society of Nunavut. It asserts that every public sector body, municipality, or private sector body in Nunavut should "display all its public signs in the Inuit Language ... together with any other language used" and ensure that the Inuit language is integral to any public communications.[89] The Act also requires these organizations to ensure that "the Inuit Language text of its public signs, posters and commercial advertising is at least equally prominent with any other language used" and that reception and customer services provided for the general public can be conducted in the Inuit language.[90]

Fourth, the Act establishes the Inuit Language Authority (Inuit Uqaus-inginnik Taiguusiliusqtiit) to expand knowledge and expertise in the Inuit language and "consider and make decisions about Inuit Language use, development and standardization."[91]

Finally, the legislation specifies the responsibilities and powers of both the minister of languages and the territory's languages commissioner. These specifications enable the minister to develop language policies, plans, and programs to "promote the use and development of the Inuit Language so that it can be used in the full range of activities and sectors of Nunavut society."[92] It also provides the official languages commissioner of Nunavut with a range of powers to ensure that both public and private sector organizations in Nunavut comply with the legislation. Once again, this legislation requires the languages commissioner to exercise these powers in accordance with general principles of *Inuit Qaujimajatuqangit*.[93]

The GN's approach to language policy development in Nunavut goes beyond that inherited from the GNWT. It seeks not only to integrate the Inuit language into the broader framework of official language recognition in Canada but also to make Indigenous language protection a priority for the territorial government. The emphasis on language rights in Nunavut's new legislation still leaves the fundamental problem of resources for Indigenous language education, training, and development unresolved. Nonetheless, the new language legislation in Nunavut emphasizes that the creation of a public service that is fully oriented toward Aboriginal cultural perspectives cannot be complete without measures to ensure that Aboriginal languages have official recognition and significant protection in the relevant jurisdiction.

Conclusion

Nunavut's example highlights some of the complexities of integrating Aboriginal values into public government. It shows that this process requires long-term strategies to improve Aboriginal representation at all levels of the public service. It also demonstrates the degree to which the improvement of Aboriginal representation in public sector employment cannot be divorced from the broader issue of investment in Aboriginal education. Questions of institutional design, cultural recognition, and language promotion interconnect in the development of an Indigenous-oriented public service. The Nunavut case study highlights the value of providing opportunities for Aboriginal public servants to work together and, in cross-cultural contexts, to design culturally sensitive procedures for government. It also shows that the development of public service institutions that reflect Aboriginal values needs to be underscored by consultation between Elders in the community and public servants who work for government. This consultation can ensure that the key people responsible for conveying Aboriginal thought and knowledge between generations are directly involved in the design and development of new approaches to public government.

Finally, Nunavut's example underlines that recognition of Aboriginal values, languages, and culture is central to the indigenization of public governance in areas that serve significant Aboriginal communities. It is far from easy to meld long-established Indigenous traditions with contemporary public governance, particularly when understandings of and the use of Indigenous languages, in which cultural ideas are embedded, have been eroded by settler education systems. Nonetheless, the process is critical to ensure that the structures and operation of new, Indigenous-oriented governments are fully informed by traditions of Indigenous thought. Moreover, the emphasis in Nunavut on identifying how core Indigenous values can inform public service operations is an innovation that could benefit the development of public governments in other jurisdictions.

ACKNOWLEDGMENTS
I thank all those who provided me with interviews and commented on earlier drafts of this chapter. I gratefully acknowledge research support from the Canadian Studies Faculty Research Award Program at Foreign Affairs and International Trade Canada. I also acknowledge funding received from the Social Sciences and Humanities Research Council of Canada through its Multilateral Collaborative Research Initiative on Indigenous Peoples and Governance.

NOTES
1 See Canada, Royal Commission on Equality in Employment, *Equality in Employment: A Royal Commission Report* (Ottawa: Minister of Supply and Services, 1984), 33-37; Canada, Human Resources and Social Development Canada, Employment Equity Act annual reports, 1999-2007, http://www.hrsdc.gc.ca/en/lp/lo/lswe/we/ ee_tools/reports/annual/index-we.shtml; and Annis May Timpson, "Expanding the Concept of Representative Bureaucracy: The Case of Nunavut," *International Review of Administrative Sciences* 72, 4 (2006): 517-30.
2 See Inuit Tapisarat of Canada, *Political Development in Nunavut*, a report prepared for the Board of Directors of Inuit Tapisarat of Canada, discussed at the annual

general meeting, Igloolik, 3-7 September 1979, 2. See also, Graham White, "Public Service in Nunavut and the Northwest Territories: Challenges of the Northern Frontier," in *Government Restructuring and Career Public Service,* ed. Evert Lindquist (Toronto: Institute of Public Administration of Canada, 2000), 112-47.

3 Siobhan Arnatsiaq-Murphy, trainee policy analyst, Department of Justice, Government of Nunavut, interview with author, Iqaluit, April 2001.

4 Nunavut Implementation Commission, *Footprints in New Snow: A Comprehensive Report from the Nunavut Implementation Commission to the Department of Northern Affairs and Northern Development, Government of the Northwest Territories and Nunavut Tunngavik Incorporated concerning the Establishment of the Nunavut Government,* (Iqaluit: Nunavut Implementation Commission, 1995), A-3.1. The 1993 *Nunavut Act* was a federal statute that enabled the territory of Nunavut to come into being and a public government to be established in the new territory, S.C. 1993, c. 28.

5 Nunavut Implementation Commission, *Footprints in New Snow,* 28.

6 Ibid.

7 Nunavut, Department of Sustainable Development, *2000/2001 Business Plan,* Legislative Assembly of Nunavut, Tabled Document no. 87, 19 April 2000, 1.

8 See Jack Hicks and Graham White, "Nunavut: Inuit Self-Determination through a Land Claim and Public Government?" in *Nunavut: Inuit Regain Control of Their Lands and Their Lives,* ed. Jens Dahl, Jack Hicks, and Peter Jull (Copenhagen: International Work Group for Indigenous Affairs, 2000), 41-42.

9 Nunavut Implementation Commission, *Footprints in New Snow,* 28.

10 See Annis May Timpson, "The Challenges of Intergovernmental Relations for Nunavut," in *Reconfiguring Aboriginal-State Relations – Canada: The State of the Federation 2003,* ed. Michael Murphy (Montreal and Kingston: McGill-Queen's University Press, 2005), 216.

11 Canada, Indian and Northern Affairs Canada and Tungavik Federation of Nunavut, *Agreement Between the Inuit of the Nunavut Settlement Area and Her Majesty the Queen in Right of Canada* (Ottawa: Minister of Indian Affairs and Northern Development and the Tungavik, 1993), 191, Nunavut Tunngavik Incorporated, http://www.tunngavik.com/category/publications/nunavut-land-claims-agreement.

12 Ibid. While Article 23 applied to all government operations in Nunavut, this chapter focuses on the development of Aboriginal representation in the territorial government's public service.

13 Nunavut, *Pinasuaqtavut: The Bathurst Mandate* (Iqaluit: Government of Nunavut, 1999), 6-7.

14 Nunavut, Department of Human Resources, *Inuit Employment Plan* (Iqaluit: Government of Nunavut, 2000).

15 Marcel Fortier and Francine G. Jones, "Engineering Public Service Excellence for Nunavut: The Nunavut Human Resources Development Strategy," *Arctic* 51, 2 (1998): 191-94.

16 Nunavut, Department of Human Resources, *Inuit Employment Plan,* 8, 89; Marion Ittinuar, "Working towards a Representative GN Workforce" (paper presented to the Indian and Northern Affairs Canada/Université Laval conference, "Building Nunavut," Université Laval, Quebec, March 2000), 2; and Nunavut, Department of Human Resources, *2002-2003 Public Service Annual Report* (Iqaluit: Government of Nunavut, 2002), 11, http://www.gov.nu.ca/hr/site/psannualreport.htm.

17 Nunavut, Department of Human Resources, *2002-2003 Public Service Annual Report,* 12; and Nunavut, Department of Human Resources, *Inuit Employment Plan,* 61.

18 David Omilgoitok, deputy minister, Department of Human Resources, Government of Nunavut, interview with author, Iqaluit, April 2001.

19 On the importance of hunting and gathering to Nunavut's economy, see Hicks and White, "Nunavut: Inuit Self-Determination," 37-38.

20 "Inuk Staffing Still Low," *Nunatsiaq News,* 8 June 2001, http://www.nunatsiaq.com.

21 Annie Gordon, wellness coordinator, Department of Human Resources, Government of Nunavut, interview with author, Iqaluit, March 2001.

22 Hugh Lloyd, director of Aboriginal and circumpolar affairs, Department of Executive and Intergovernmental Affairs, Government of Nunavut, interview with author, Iqaluit, September 2003. See also, Jim Bell, "Inuit Employment in Government Moving Backward," *Nunatsiaq News,* 2 May 2003, http://www.nunatsiaq.com.

23 David Baker, director general, Strategic Policy and Devolution, Northern Affairs Program, Department of Indian and Northern Affairs, interview with author, Hull, Quebec, October 2002.

24 PricewaterhouseCoopers, *The Cost of Not Successfully Implementing Article 23: Representative Employment for Inuit within the Government,* 17 February 2003, 15, Nunavut Tunngavik Incorporated, http://www.tunngavik.com/category/publications/implementation.

25 Ibid., 7.

26 Ibid., 15.

27 Ibid., 9.

28 Ibid., 54-59.

29 Ibid., 52.

30 Ibid., 12.

31 Ibid., 62.

32 Thomas R. Berger, *Nunavut Land Claims Agreement Implementation Contract Negotiations for the Second Planning Period 2003-2013: Conciliator's Final Report,* "The Nunavut Project," 1 March 2006, Nunavut Tunngavik Incorporated, http://www.tunngavik.com/category/publications/implementation.

33 Ibid., 55-58.

34 Ibid., 45.

35 Ibid., 46.

36 Ibid., 30.

37 Ibid., 23.

38 Ibid., 49.

39 Ibid., vii.

40 Ibid., 31-32.

41 Ibid., 30.

42 Ibid., 40.

43 Ibid., 41.

44 Jim Bell, "Harper on Berger: New School Funds outside TFF," *Nunatsiaq News,* 18 August 2006, http://www.nunatsiaq.com.

45 "NTI Hits Ottawa with $1 Billion Lawsuit," *Nunatsiaq News,* 8 December 2006, http://www.nunatsiaq.com.

46 Nunavut Tunngavik Incorporated, "NTI Launches Lawsuit Against Government of Canada for Breach of Contract," news release 06-24, 6 December 2006, 1.

47 See Ailsa Henderson, *Nunavut: Rethinking Political Culture* (Vancouver: UBC Press, 2007), 190-212.

48 See Nora Sanders, "Through Cultural Eyes: Perspectives on Aboriginal Governance" (keynote address, "First Nations, First Thoughts," 30th Anniversary Conference, Centre of Canadian Studies, University of Edinburgh, 5 May 2005), 8, http://www.cst.ed.ac.uk/Events/Conferences.

49 Nunavut, *Pinasuaqtavut: The Bathurst Mandate,* 4.

50 Nunavut, Department of Culture, Language, Elders and Youth, *The First Annual Report of the Inuit Qaujimajatuqangit (IQ) Task Force* (Iqaluit: Government of Nunavut, 2002), 1.

51 See Nunavut, Department of Culture, Language, Elders and Youth, *IQ Newsletter* 1, 1 (2004), http://www.gov.nu.ca/cley/english/newsletter.htm.

52 Nunavut, Department of Justice, *Illinit Newsletter* 1, 2 (April 2006): 1.

53 Ibid.

54 Nunavut, *Pinasuaqtavut: 2004-2009* (Iqaluit: Government of Nunavut, 2004), 3.

55 Sanders, "Through Cultural Eyes," 18-19.

56 "GN appoints IQ advisory council," *Nunatsiaq News,* 12 September 2003, http://www.nunatsiaq.com.

57 Nunavut, Department of Culture, Language, Elders and Youth, *Business Plan 2005-06* (Iqaluit: Government of Nunavut, 2005), F-4.

58 Naullaq Arnaquq, assistant deputy minister, Department of Education, Government of Nunavut, interview with author, Iqaluit, April 2002.

59 Nunavut Constitutional Forum, *Building Nunavut: A Working Document with a Proposal for an Arctic Constitution,* 18, tabled in the Legislative Assembly of the Northwest Territories, 17 May 1983.

60 Nunavut, *Pinasuaqtavut: The Bathurst Mandate,* 7.

61 Ibid., 4.

62 See Hicks and White, "Nunavut: Inuit Self-Determination," 100n48.

63   See Nunavut, Nunavummit Kiglisiniartiit/Nunavut Bureau of Statistics, "Language Data from the 2001 Nunavut Household Survey," PowerPoint presentation, March 2003, slides 10, 25, 27, 30, 36, 69, 102, and 106, Nunavut Tunngavik Incorporated, http://www.tunngavik.com/documents/publications/2001-Language-data-Nunavut-Household-Survey.pdf.

64   Berger, *Conciliator's Final Report*, iv.

65   Jacques-Louis Dorais, "Inuit Language Protection Law Isn't Feasible," *Nunatsiaq News*, 13 April 2007, http://www.nunatsiaq.com.

66   Berger, *Nunavut Land Claims Agreement Implementation Contract*, iv and 28-9.

67   Nunavut, Department of Human Resources, *Combined 1999-2000 and 2000-2001 Public Service Annual Report* (Iqaluit: Government of Nunavut, 2001), 15, http://www.gov.nu.ca/hr/site/psannualreport.htm.

68   CBC News, "Learn Inuktitut or *iqqanaijaaqajjaagunniiqtutit*, Mandarins Told," CBCnews.ca, 7 June 2006, http://www.cbc.ca/canada/story/2006/06/07/inuktitut-language.html.

69   Jane Cooper, assistant deputy minister, Department of Environment, Government of Nunavut, inteview with author, Iqaluit, June 2006. See also the websites for the Pirurvik Centre and Tusaalanga Inuktitut.

70   See Nunavut, Office of the Languages Commissioner, annual reports, 1999-2004, http://langcom.nu.ca/index.html; Jim Bell, "It's Seven Against One on Oct. 27," *Nunatsiaq News*, 24 October 2008, http://www.nunatsiaq.com.

71   Nunavut, Legislative Assembly, Members, "The Honourable Eva Aariak, Premier of Nunavut," Legislative Assembly of Nunauvut, http://www.assembly.nu.ca/english/members/bios/Eva_Aariak.html.

72   Nunavut, Legislative Assembly, "Speaker of the Legislative Assembly Announces Designation of New Languages Commissioner of Nunavut," news release, 7 January 2009.

73   Nunavut, Legislative Assembly, Special Committee to Review the Official Languages Act, *Interim Report*, Fifth Session, First Legislative Assembly, March 2002; Nunavut, Legislative Assembly, Special Committee to Review the Official Languages Act, *Final Report*, Sixth Session, First Legislative Assembly, December 2003.

74   Nunavut, Legislative Assembly, *Official Languages Act*, S.Nu. 2008, c. 10; see also Nunavut, "Nunavut Legislative Assembly Approves the *Official Languages Act*," news release, 5 June 2008, http://www.gov.nu.ca/english/news/2008.shtml; *Nunavut Act*, S.C. 1993, c. 28, s. 38.

75   *Official Languages Act*, s. 13(2).

76   Ibid., s. 22.2(b)

77   Ibid., Preamble.

78   Ibid.

79   *Inuit Language Protection Act*, S.Nu. 2008, c. 17.

80   Ibid., Preamble.

81   Ibid.
82   Ibid., s. 8.1.
83   Ibid., s. 8.2(a).
84   Ibid., s. 12.1.
85   Ibid., ss. 12.2(a)-(b).
86   Ibid., ss. 12.2(d) (i)-(ii).
87   Ibid., s. 12.2(f).
88   Ibid., s. 12.2(g).
89   Ibid., s. 3.1(a), s. 3.2.
90   Ibid., ss. 3.1(c)-(d).
91   Ibid., s. 15; s. 16(1).
92   Ibid., s. 24(2), s. 25(2).
93   Ibid., s. 27.1.

WORKS CITED

Bell, Jim. "Harper on Berger: No New School Funds Outside TFF." *Nunatsiaq News*, 18 August 2006. http://www.nunatsiaq.com.

–. "Inuit Employment in Government Moving Backward." *Nunatsiaq News*, 2 May 2003. http://www.nunatsiaq.com.

–. "It's Seven Against One on Oct. 27." *Nunatsiaq News*, 24 October 2008. http://www.nunatsiaq.com.

Berger, Thomas R. *Nunavut Land Claims Agreement Implementation Contract Negotiations for the Second Planning Period 2003-2013: Conciliator's Final Report, "The Nunavut Project."* 1 March 2006. Nunavut Tunngavik Incorporated. http://www.tunngavik.com/category/publications/implementation.

Canada. Human Resources and Social Development Canada. Employment Equity Act annual reports, 1999-2007. http://www.hrsdc.gc.ca/en/lp/lo/lswe/we/ee_tools/reports/annual/index-we.shtml.

Canada. Indian and Northern Affairs Canada and Tungavik Federation of Nunavut. *Agreement Between the Inuit of the Nunavut Settlement Area and Her Majesty the Queen in Right of Canada.* Ottawa: Minister of Indian Affairs and Northern Development and the Tungavik, 1993. Nunavut Tunngavik Incorporated. http://www.tunngavik.com/category/publications/nunavut-land-claims-agreement.

Canada. Royal Commission on Equality in Employment. *Equality in Employment: A Royal Commission Report.* Ottawa: Minister of Supply and Services. 1984.

CBC News. "Learn Inuktitut or *iqqanaijaaqajjaagunniiqtutit*, Mandarins Told." CBCnews.ca, 7 June 2006. http://www.cbc.ca/canada/story/2006/06/07/inuktitut-language.html.

Dorais, Jacques-Louis. "Inuit Language Protection Law Isn't Feasible." *Nunatsiaq News*, 13 April 2007. http://www.nunatsiaq.com.

Fortier, Marcel, and Francine G. Jones. "Engineering Public Service Excellence for Nunavut:

The Nunavut Human Resources Development Strategy." *Arctic* 51, 2 (1998): 191-94.

"GN Appoints IQ Advisory Council." *Nunatsiaq News,* 12 September 2003. http://www. nunatsiaq.com.

Henderson, Ailsa. *Nunavut: Rethinking Political Culture.* Vancouver: UBC Press, 2007.

Hicks, Jack, and Graham White. "Nunavut: Inuit Self-Determination through a Land Claim and Public Government?" In *Nunavut: Inuit Regain Control of Their Lands and Their Lives,* ed. Jens Dahl, Jack Hicks, and Peter Jull, 30-115. Copenhagen: International Work Group for Indigenous Affairs, 2000.

Inuit Tapisarat of Canada. *Political Development in Nunavut.* A Report prepared for the Board of Directors of Inuit Tapisarat of Canada, discussed at the annual general meeting, Igloolik, 3-7 September 1979.

"Inuk Staffing Still Low." *Nunatsiaq News.* 8 June 2001. http://www.nunatsiaq.com.

Ittinuar, Marion. "Working Towards a Representative GN Workforce." Paper presented to Indian and Northern Affairs Canada/Université Laval conference "Building Nunavut," Université Laval, Quebec, March 2000.

"NTI Hits Ottawa with $1 Billion Lawsuit." *Nunatsiaq News,* 8 December 2006. http:// www.nunatsiaq.com

Nunavut. "Civil Service Changes Underline Government's Commitment to Economic Prosperity and Inuit Qaujimajatuqangit." News release, 10 March 2004. http:// www.gov.nu.ca/english/news/2004.shtml.

–. "Nunavut Legislative Assembly Approves the Official Languages Act." News release, 5 June 2008. http://www.gov.nu.ca/english/news/2008.shtml.

–. *Pinasuaqtavut: 2004-2009.* Iqaluit: Government of Nunavut, 2004.

–. *Pinasuaqtavut: The Bathurst Mandate.* Iqaluit: Government of Nunavut, 1999.

Nunavut. Department of Culture, Language, Elders and Youth. *Business Plan 2005-06.* Iqaluit: Government of Nunavut, 2005.

–. *The First Annual Report of the Inuit Qaujimajatuqangit (IQ) Task Force.* Iqaluit: Government of Nunavut, 2002.

–. *IQ Newsletter* 1, 1 (2004). http://www.gov.nu.ca/cley/english/newsletter.htm.

Nunavut. Department of Human Resources. *2002-2003 Public Service Annual Report.* Iqaluit: Government of Nunavut, 2002. http://www.gov.nu.ca/hr/site/psannualreport.htm.

–. *Combined 1999-2000 and 2000-2001 Public Service Annual Report.* Iqaluit: Government of Nunavut, 2001. http://www.gov.nu.ca/hr/site/psannualreport.htm.

–. *Inuit Employment Plan.* Iqaluit: Government of Nunavut, 2000.

–. *Public Service Annual Report 2002-3.* Iqaluit: Government of Nunavut, 2002. http:// www.gov.nu.ca/hr/site/index.htm.

–. *Towards a Representative Public Service: Inuit Statistics as of June 2001; June 2003; June 2006; June 2007; June 2008.* Department of Human Resources. http://www.gov. nu.ca/hr/site/towardrepps.htm.

Nunavut. Department of Justice. *Illinit Newsletter* 1, 2 (April 2006).

Nunavut. Department of Sustainable Development. *2000/2001 Business Plan.* Legislative Assembly of Nunavut, Tabled Document no. 87, 19 April 2000.

Nunavut. Legislative Assembly. Members. "The Honourable Eva Aariak. Legislative Assembly of Nunavut. http://www.assembly.nu.ca/english/members/bios/Eva_Aariak. html.

–. "Speaker of the Legislative Assembly Announces Designation of New Languages Commissioner of Nunavut." News release, 7 January 2009.

–. Special Committee to Review the Official Languages Act. *Final Report.* Sixth Session, First Legislative Assembly, December 2003.

–. Special Committee to Review the Official Languages Act. *Interim Report.* Fifth Session, First Legislative Assembly, March 2002.

Nunavut. Nunavummit Kiglisiniartiit/Nunavut Bureau of Statistics. "Language Data from the 2001 Nunavut Household Survey." PowerPoint presentation, March 2003. Nunavut Tunngavik Incorporated. http://www.tunngavik.com/documents/ publications/2001-Language-data-Nunavut-Household-Survey.pdf.

Nunavut. Office of the Languages Commissioner. Annual reports, 1999-2004. http:// langcom.nu.ca/index.html.

Nunavut Constitutional Forum. *Building Nunavut: A Working Document with a Proposal for an Arctic Constitution.* Tabled in the Legislative Assembly of the Northwest Territories, 17 May 1983.

Nunavut Implementation Commission. *Footprints in New Snow: A Comprehensive Report from the Nunavut Implementation Commission to the Department of Northern Affairs and Northern Development, Government of the Northwest Territories and Nunavut Tunngavik Incorporated concerning the Establishment of the Nunavut Government.* Iqaluit: Nunavut Implementation Commission, 1995.

Nunavut Tunngavik Incorporated. "NTI Launches Lawsuit Against Government of Canada for Breach of Contract." News release 06-24, 6 December 2006.

PricewaterhouseCoopers. *The Cost of Not Successfully Implementing Article 23: Representative Employment for Inuit within the Government,* 17 February 2003. Nunavut Tunngavik Incorporated. http://www.tunngavik.com/english/publications.php.

Sanders, Nora. "Through Cultural Eyes: Perspectives on Aboriginal Governance." Keynote address, "First Nations, First Thoughts" 30th Anniversary Conference, Centre of Canadian Studies, University of Edinburgh, 5 May 2005. http://www.cst.ed.ac.uk/ Events/Conferences.

Timpson, Annis May. "The Challenges of Intergovernmental Relations for Nunavut." In *Reconfiguring Aboriginal-State Relations – Canada: The State of the Federation 2003,* ed. Michael Murphy, 207-35. Montreal and Kingston: McGill-Queen's University Press. 2005.

–. "Expanding the Concept of Representative Bureaucracy: The Case of Nunavut." *Inter-*

national Review of Administrative Sciences 72, 4 (2006): 517-30.

White, Graham. "Public Service in Nunavut and the Northwest Territories: Challenges of the Northern Frontier." In *Government Restructuring and Career Public Service*, ed. Evert Lindquist, 112-47. Toronto: Institute of Public Administration of Canada, 2000.

9
A Fine Balance? Aboriginal Peoples in the Canadian North and the Dilemma of Development

Gabrielle A. Slowey

Pressure for Canadian resources drives Canada's national development, but does it also drive Aboriginal development? With more land claims settlements and self-government arrangements being negotiated across the country, the debate about whether to engage in resource development as a strategy to promote economic development and exercise political power is important. It is a debate that is tied intimately to issues of culture and framed in terms of a choice: capitalism or traditionalism, assimilation or fossilization? The dilemma of development that faces many northern Aboriginal communities is real, but is it really a matter of choosing one path over another? And do new institutions of governance provide Aboriginal communities with the economic tools they require to realize their economic *and* cultural goals? Although Aboriginal communities are overwhelmed by Western institutions and materialism, this chapter argues that framing development as a choice between culture and modernity posits a false dichotomy, as development is not about choosing one or the other but rather about how to secure the best of both worlds. This has become increasingly evident as many Aboriginal communities in Canada's North have embraced resource development as an economic strategy to balance culture and capitalism. They have done so because Aboriginal culture consists not only of hunting, trapping, and fishing but also of politics and economy.

Considering that communities experience self-government and self-sufficiency (the two mutually reinforcing components of self-determination) differently across northern Canada, it is possible that economic development is critical, and not antithetical, to the project of cultural preservation (for instance, money is essential for those who continue traditional pursuits, whether it be for gas and snowmobiles or bullets and rations). That is, although it challenges some of the traditional dimensions of Aboriginal culture (i.e., land use and the animal resource base), economic self-determination does not necessarily signal the destruction of Aboriginal culture; rather, it can provide space in which Aboriginal communities can exercise agency through the design of new programs, services, and businesses that reflect or even enshrine cultural values, norms, and expectations.

Aboriginal culture is constant and forms the basis for political and economic development in a contemporary neoliberal context. Culture is not, however, rigid. Regardless of whether a community chooses to engage in resource development, the underlying fact remains that Aboriginal culture is dynamic, not static, and, thus, capable of adaptation and change. Moreover, if a community does choose to engage in resource extraction, the degree to which it is able to maximize its opportunities for economic development and cultural preservation is critical to its perceived success. As Frances Abele explains, rather than judging them for their choice, "we need to recognize and understand the aspirations of those who seek change to protect their future and their way of life."[1] Indeed, the ability to adapt has been the key to the survival of Aboriginal cultures.

The Parallels and Perils of Development

To understand the dilemma that Aboriginal communities confront, it is necessary to recognize their historical condition of dependence and dispossession, which is tied to Canada's capitalist development in the global political economy. Canada's economic growth has long depended on the extraction of staples (or resources), a demand driven by global market forces. The linking of remote production areas with external markets, therefore, was critical to the formative development of the state. Hence, for the Canadian north, a region predominantly inhabited by Aboriginal peoples (First Nations, Inuit, and Métis), resource development is an age-old project that has transformed their culture and tied their own development and growth to resource exports and state policies.[2]

In the postwar era, the Canadian government began institutionalizing the notion of state planning and intervention in the economic and social spheres to regulate the economy in accordance with the tenets of Keynesian economics. Changes in the global economic order required changes in government responsibilities. To that end, a new era in government expansion led to new ideas about the role of Aboriginal policy. For example, the federal government extended social policy and programming to include First Nations communities. At the same time, the exploration of oil and gas deposits across northern Canada led governments, at both the federal and provincial levels, to promote northern development as a mechanism for Aboriginal development. However, the state's assumption that resource development would lead to Aboriginal development proved erroneous: Aboriginal peoples instead became increasingly reliant on state assistance.

It was during this time that the concept of development, like the kindred concepts of growth and modernization, first emerged, with its historical and intellectual roots located in periods of social change.[3] Theories of development sought to explain the political and economic problems of poorer nations and devise strategies to alleviate poverty and elevate standards of living.[4] To that end, development and progress were portrayed as linear processes, with cultures passing through phases of development associated with modernization and capitalism. As products of a particular time and place, however, development theories were tied to a historical moment and used primarily to explain material relations between the global North and South (or "third world"). Given these narrow parameters, it was of great value when contributors to Mel Watkins' edited volume on the Dene Nation drew upon theories of development and notions of dependency to capture the nature of relations between the first and fourth worlds. More specifically, they drew on concepts associated with development to articulate the challenges confronting the Dene community of Northwest Territories in the context of looming oil and gas development.[5] This work was significant because it demonstrated that Dene dependency and underdevelopment were based on state interventionism and First Nations dispossession. It also highlighted the deficiency of government policy of the day and exposed potential pitfalls associated with First Nations development predicated on resource development.

Since that time there has been a shift in the global political economy and, with it, a shift in government policy. Neoliberal globalization and international pressure for access to Canada's natural resources have, once again, converged to transform the role of the state. Consequently, major changes have occurred in the state's policy direction, or development strategy, with respect to Aboriginal peoples.[6] This is in large part evident in the "shift away from [a] tightly controlled and hierarchical relationship toward greater recognition of Aboriginal communities with rights of jurisdiction."[7] More specifically, government policy on the administration of Aboriginal peoples, the settlement of land claims, and the negotiation of self-government has ushered in a new period in Aboriginal development. Clearly these events have shaped the ability of First Nations to assert greater political autonomy, achieve greater economic control over land and resources, and ensure the retention and affirmation of First Nations culture. The extent to which the concept of development has (re-)emerged to become intertwined with notions of self-determination is, therefore, of note; that is, the discourse and language of development is now used by many Aboriginal groups to describe their goal of self-determination.

The term "globalization," a euphemism for development in the contemporary context, invokes the rhetoric of progress and growth to legitimate systems of power and domination. It suggests that increased market freedoms and decreased government intervention will improve the lives and fortunes of individuals. Interestingly, instead of seeing globalized "development" as a force of domination and disempowerment, many Aboriginal communities are seizing upon it as a potential source for liberation and empowerment, particularly as the state has now devolved many of the responsibilities for program design and delivery into the hands of Aboriginal communities and stands in support of Aboriginal development. In the wake of these changes, Aboriginal groups are taking the reins and transforming the way business is being done, thereby raising the standard for Aboriginal involvement. As the chair of the Aboriginal Pipeline Group, Fred Carmichael, points out, "The Mackenzie gas project is setting the standard for how business will be done in the future in the North. It is an example of a unique partnership between Aboriginal people, government and industry. Aboriginal people will share in the ownership and benefits of the proposed project."[8] Change has been most remarkable, therefore, in the attitude of the many Aboriginal groups that now seek to participate in, and also guide, development projects in the region.

Aboriginal communities now recognize the value of being involved in the process of resource development, as opposed to remaining on the sidelines. Self-determination provides these communities with a new-found sense of agency. Given the reality that development will occur with or without them, Aboriginal peoples confront a dilemma: choose to be part of development or have it done to them. In the face of this predicament, self-determination can be an important building block to more equitable power sharing and a means to ensure the inclusion and influence of Aboriginal peoples in the development process, if only to safeguard their cultural norms and practices.

Not all communities embrace or support resource development. Sometimes it depends on the community and sometimes it depends on the project. Whether it is the First Nations of northern Ontario declaring a moratorium on mining exploration and forestry on their traditional territories or Arctic communities, like the Dehcho in the Mackenzie Valley, challenging gas pipe-line construction, some Aboriginal communities continue to voice their opposition to resource development projects operating on their traditional land.[9] The Dehcho leader, Herb Norwegian, has been quoted as saying: "This so-called 'development' project is out of control and we have to tell the pol-iticians that it is like a cancerous tumour and that the Mackenzie Gas Project is designed to feed that tumour."[10] Similarly, for its part, the Vuntut Gwitchin First Nation (VGFN) of Old Crow, in Yukon, has launched an international challenge to prevent the development of oil and gas in the Arctic National Wildlife Refuge (ANWR) located in Alaska. Although the potential area for resource extraction lies in another country, the Vuntut Gwitchin argue that the development of the ANWR would disrupt the migration of the Porcupine caribou and disturb their calving grounds. This is critical because the com-munity continues to depend on the caribou for cultural and practical subsist-ence. Hence, these communities stand at the crossroads of development. Their opposition reinforces the supposition that development leads to assimilation; therefore, those who choose to oppose development for cultural reasons are considered noble and viewed as more firmly rooted in tradition. However, as the case of the Vuntut Gwitchin demonstrates, the line between cultural protection and economic development is increasingly blurred. As Chief Linklater explains, "the Vuntut Gwitchin people are not opposed to oil and gas development, per se. The development of oil and gas is not the focus of opposition but the negative effects it has on the community [certainly are]."[11]

The VGFN's vision for a healthy community drives its antidevelopment position. First and foremost, the Vuntut Gwitchin stand opposed to the ANWR development for social, cultural, and environmental reasons. They are still suffering the effects of the last oil boom, which saw a dramatic rise in fetal alcohol syndrome and the abuse of drugs. The Vuntut Gwitchin also see the environmental threats of development. Yet, at the same time, they do not exist purely as a traditional society, living exclusively off the land or in isola-tion from the rest of the world, nor are they against self-determination. Indeed, the Vuntut Gwitchin are leaders in the development of self-government. In fact, when negotiating its land claim, the VGFN took out a bank loan with significant interest in order to negotiate self-government. Chief Linklater explains that "you can always make money grow. So you can earn it back. But you can't make land grow."[12] To that end, the VGFN uses self-government as a way to protect land, devolve hierarchical decision-making processes, and empower community members. It operates for-profit companies. But, with members of the US government consistently focused on opening Alaska's Arctic refuge for drilling, the inability of the VGFN to prevent resource development reinforces the notion that development is imminent and capitalism unstoppable.[13] Consequently, the Vuntut Gwitchin recognize that the day will soon come when they will have to make the decision whether to support resource development that may occur on their land. They suggest that the key to survival is to be prepared and to strive for balance.

The desire to protect the land, values, and traditional activities remains at the heart of Aboriginal culture and strength. Indeed, Aboriginal culture remains strong and firmly rooted in people, the territory of the communities, and the hands of the leaders. Although differences over development necessarily exist in Aboriginal communities (both between communities and between members and leaders within those communities), the elites who drive development (or antidevelopment) positions do so based on their role as elected leaders who represent their community's interests. In essence, the elites, or leaders, are the voice of the community-development position. Visitors to these communities are not always privy to internal or local critiques of development (even though in some cases community members can be quite frank in their discussions with researchers about their feelings on these matters). Nonetheless, it is poignant to observe the extent to which members of Aboriginal communities in the Far North continue to use their informal networks to express their opinions to leaders. Whether in favour of specific decisions and actions or opposed to them, leaders are more accessible to community members, and are available to meet with them, because of the small size of most northern communities. For instance, it is quite common to go "visiting" with representatives of chief and council, whether in their homes, in members' homes, or within the community. In the community of Old Crow, the government office is located in the middle of town, which means Elders and members of the general community can access, or "visit," leaders, which they do. This practice reflects the extent to which the community at large feels it can monitor the actions of its leadership; in turn, the leaders feel accountable to anyone who drops by.

In many instances self-government has simply "formalized" these informal mechanisms. Aside from the actual election of leaders, formal mechanisms in the community of Old Crow include an annual assembly in which community leaders, and government workers, present annual reports to

Vuntut Gwitchin community members and, in exchange, the membership has an opportunity to vet government activity and express concern or differing viewpoints. The annual General Assembly of the Vuntut Gwitchin is held at Tlo-Kut, located on the banks of the Porcupine River six miles upstream from Old Crow, usually at the beginning of August. It is a forum in which presentations are made and resolutions are passed that direct the government of the VGFN. As Chief Linklater acknowledges, "Communication is the key. If good information is continuously flowing between the Government and the People, the people are giving good feedback and the government is making decisions in a timely manner."[14] While no political system is perfect and the voice of all citizens is never adequately represented, the voices of the Aboriginal nations appear to be encapsulated in the leaders selected to represent them.

Despite growing pressure to modernize institutions and develop land and resources – on top of increasing pressures associated with materialism, urbanization, alienation, and dispossession – the foundations of Aboriginal cultures appear to be unlikely to disappear anytime soon. This is not to suggest that these cultures remain intact or unaltered. Indeed, Aboriginal cultures have been changing constantly since first contact with European fur traders. They have been shaped and influenced by external events, including shifts in the broader political economy and in state policy. Aboriginal cultures are now being shaped internally through self-determination and demands to safeguard culture and create more economic opportunities. The challenge now is how best to preserve the cultural foundations, and communities differ in the strategies they choose to accomplish this goal.

Strategies for Political Development

Like the global South or third world in the 1960s, Aboriginal peoples today are involved in the processes of decolonization and development.[15] In seeking self-determination, different Aboriginal groups also seek to remove themselves from the domination and oppression of the colonizing state. However, by virtue of engaging in self-government negotiations and land claims settlements, Aboriginal governments appear to be capitulating rather than furthering the process of decolonization, in the sense that they are normalized within the existing relations of the state. This is because decolonization requires a reordering of political power and jurisdictional control and authority, which cannot really be achieved under the limited parameters of self-government. What can be achieved, however, is a delinking or detaching of Aboriginal governance from the clutches of Canada's federal government; in other words, an important measure of independence, if not decolonization per se.

The political nature of development reveals itself in the struggle for control of resources, which is influenced not only by geography but also by Aboriginal goals and strategies. As the Assembly of First Nations has argued, "especially important is the right to natural resources and the ability to initiate economic development that generates wealth and keeps it in native hands."[16] In other words, if Aboriginal communities have any hope of ending their dependency on the state, they need to develop the capacity for autonomous growth. This requires political authority, jurisdictional control, and the relevant authority to exercise their independence. Unfortunately, the transfer of control and authority over non-renewable resources, such as oil and gas or diamonds, is not, in general, forthcoming. However, limited control over resources such as fisheries and forests are more likely because these are traditional resources and not nearly as lucrative for the state in terms of profit and royalties.

Self-government and the integration of Aboriginal peoples into the Canadian socio-economic fabric, in whatever form or dimension, do not sound the death knoll for Aboriginal people or their cultures. In fact, they may mean just the opposite. There are various expressions of Aboriginal autonomy and authority in Canada. What appears to be consistent, however, is that self-government enables Aboriginal peoples not only to secure influence in resource development and the benefits that arise from it but also to achieve greater jurisdiction over the language, customs, and cultural practices they seek to protect. As Nellie Cournoyea explains: "The Inuvialuit Final Agreement of 1984 provided us with the tools to assert our interests within a specified region, in particular three goals: (1) to preserve Inuvialuit cultural identity and values within a changing northern society, (2) to enable Inuvialuit to be equal and meaningful participants in the northern and national economy and society; and (3) to protect and preserve the Arctic wildlife, environment and biological productivity."[17] In northern Yukon the VGFN is now able to control access to, and development within, its traditional territory and is working to protect the Porcupine caribou, upon which its members still depend. The James Bay Northern Quebec Agreement provides compensation to traditional trappers who spend time on the land each year.[18] In varying ways and degrees, Aboriginal peoples are using land claims and self-government to gain a measure of control over the protection and perpetuation of traditional activities and pursuits.

Although geography is not the only determining factor, the settlement of claims and the negotiation of self-government are most likely to occur in communities that exist on or near resource development projects.[19] As a consequence, northern communities most often wrestle with the possibilities and pitfalls of resource development. Since First Nations began to enter into agreements with the state, several models for more effective participation in policy making and decision making have emerged. For instance, one need only consider the numerous environmental co-management boards and advisory councils that emerged as a consequence of the 1984 Inuvialuit Final Agreement for evidence of this dimension of development.[20] Specifically, the settlement of this claim led to the formation of numerous consultative bodies and agencies that exist to monitor and review resource development project proposals. The creation of new bodies, including the Wildlife Management Advisory Council, the Environmental Impact Review Board, and the Environmental Impact Screening Committee, reflects an important shift in governance in terms of power, relationships, and accountability. These boards provide the Inuvialuit with a place to bring their concerns and values into the decision-making process. They reconfigure relations between Aboriginal people and the state not only in terms of influence and accountability but also in terms of cultural dynamics, especially with respect to issues surrounding resources and their development.

Although Western institutions, processes, and ideas of development dominate resource development, Canada can no longer proceed without taking into account Aboriginal culture, ideas, and issues. Consultation and cooperation remain an important step in resource development projects as the state and corporations are forced to engage with, listen to, and, at times, yield to Aboriginal demands. As one executive at Syncrude put it: "Having bad relations with local Aboriginal people in this area would just be a nightmare. You don't want the expense [of a hearing] but the expense of the hearing is not the thing. The expense of the delay of approval – that is the thing."[21] As resource development companies seek to increase profits, they also seek to avoid costly hearings and protests that interrupt potential resource extraction. Even when these processes are required, as is the case with the Mackenzie Valley Environmental Impact Review Board in Northwest Territories, gaining the consent of local Aboriginal communities is critical.[22] Consequently, the prevailing approach has been to develop long-term relationships with Aboriginal peoples so that grievances can be addressed on an ongoing basis.

Influence over development is one thing; self-governance is also promoted as a way to "indigenize" Aboriginal governance. In most cases, however, self-government is a reflection of the reproduction and modernization of social and political infrastructures. That is, self-government exists largely in a Weberian sense as communities build up infrastructure and highly organized bureaucracies. Self-government also centres on the implementation of procedures and regulations intended to bring about economic growth efficiently and effectively. In this way the political dimension of development is tied to a general movement toward a more modern, bureaucratic, technological, and economically advanced society, which is perceived to be incompatible with traditional Aboriginal culture. Moreover, self-government is viewed as a form of modernization because it entails the transition from traditional to modern forms of social organization, both in cultural terms and in terms of political practice. The concept of self-determination anticipates that Aboriginal peoples will adapt Western-style governments and, hence, privileges one culture over another. Yet many Aboriginal people are not deterred. They remain focused on the objective of regaining control over cultural programming.[23] Thus, Aboriginal peoples may come to embrace government and even dimensions of Western culture as part of a broader plan to balance culture and capitalism.

One criticism of Aboriginal governance may be that such a balance cannot occur because capitalism subsumes culture for profit; by taking on the responsibilities of self-government and resource development, many Aboriginal communities will become accessories to this process. Indeed, in many ways self-government undermines and even oppresses traditional forms of governance because it is based upon non-Aboriginal concepts of economic growth and institutional development. At a fundamental level, with the alliance of big business and government, most band councils can be more appropriately characterized as neocolonial regimes. As multinational corporations seek to further exploit the resources located on or near Indigenous lands, they encroach even more upon Aboriginal territories. In this context the transition to self-governance can more accurately be described as a transition from traditional colonial domination to neocolonialism or economic colonialism. At the same time, Tony Mercredi, a former chief of the Athabasca Chipewyan First Nation, reminds us that many of the problems currently plaguing First Nations stem from the power imbalance inherent in the current Aboriginal-state relationship: "By having the institutions and regulations of the Euro-Canadian society imposed upon us, our sense of balance is lost."[24] Countering colonial dominance and restoring balance requires that self-government be rooted in traditional concepts and values of governance.

Although Michael Asch maintains that the ideological premise of universalism produces an "inexorable force towards the assimilation of minorities into the culture of the majority," many Aboriginal groups are working consciously to take the best from both worlds.[25] The challenge is daunting; Aboriginal language usage and knowledge is diminishing. Material, corporate culture is growing. This does not mean that Aboriginal culture no longer exists. It persists, but as has happened since the fur trade, it is constantly changing, not necessarily by its own design but by virtue of external forces that seek to destroy it. The key to self-government, therefore, is managing change by designing programs that preserve as much of the culture as possible so that Aboriginal communities can chart their own course and, in the process, challenge the ever-narrowing boundaries of the Western development paradigm.

As land claims have been settled, different communities have introduced different cultural policies as they struggle to impart their cultural values to youth. For instance, the Mikisew Cree First Nation has introduced a program that involves young people returning to the land to learn traditional hunting techniques and traditional modes of living. Youth are taught important skills such as how to track, hunt, kill, and clean moose. When successful, they are required to bring the meat back to the community to share with the Elders. They also have an Elders' program, which plans trips and events for Elders living within the community. In many ways Elders remain an important part of the community, even going into schools to teach youth language and cultural skills such as tufting and how to make moccasins.[26] Programs like these suggest that cultural programming is an integral part of self-government and indicate the extent to which the connection to culture remains intact, even if it is somewhat changed and, in many ways, challenged. That is, although the land base is shrinking as the animal stocks diminish, the traditional connection to the land and to traditional economic activities endures. Fortunately, there exists a clear and conscious effort on the part of Aboriginal peoples to protect and maintain that which remains and to ensure its continuity into the future.

The Economics of Development

During the 1970s many Arctic Aboriginal groups opposed resource development because they feared an increase in social, political, and economic
problems and environmental degradation. However, current economic interests and the needs of Aboriginal peoples appear to be responsible for
changing this opposition. The North is considered the land of opportunity
for resource extraction and development. Many Aboriginal groups, especially those living along the Mackenzie Delta or near Yellowknife in Northwest Territories, want the opportunities that accompany resource
development. The desire to engage in development, in many cases, represents
a change of heart. For example, although Richard Nerysoo, the president of
the Gwich'in Tribal Council, once argued against a pipeline, telling the
Mackenzie Valley Pipeline Inquiry that "white people push the Indian aside
and take over everything," he now says that having a settled land claim will
give his region more economic clout and hope for new jobs. As he told CBC
News: "I think there's a whole series of opportunities. We can start with basic
employment opportunities, the idea of training for long-term jobs. Not just
the construction initiatives, but the other aspect, of course, is the issue of
spin-off opportunities that really result from any kind of revitalization of the
economy."[27] What Aboriginal groups do not want are the socio-economic
problems, increased drug and alcohol abuse in particular, that often accompany development. Regardless, resource development remains the economic engine of the North, not to mention the spin-off industries. In this region,
most Aboriginal groups are all too familiar with the boom and bust cycle
attached to resource development and exploration. Yet land claims are being
settled and companies are exploring new avenues for economic development,
all of which may result in the transformation of the current state of socio-
economic disparity.

Archie Waquan, the former chief of the Mikisew Cree First Nation, con-
cedes that new avenues for economic development are necessary because "the
sad reality of it all is everything has been affected with no hope of recovering
or healing."[28] There is a sense that it is impossible to live a traditional lifestyle,
as First Nations did years ago, "because there has been too much development
and globalization."[29] Despite what some might consider a sudden leap into
the modern world, First Nations like the Mikisew Cree First Nation have
neither forfeited nor forgotten their cultural heritage or their responsibilities
to this legacy as stewards of the land. Their Cree identity is not lost in the
pragmatic recognition that it is impossible to recapture or live exclusively by

traditional means. Instead, economic development strategies encompass Cree values while recognizing the importance of being able to compete and participate in the global economy. The key to balancing these two elements lies in their choice of activity.

Aboriginal economic development is not just about economic growth: it includes strategies designed to reduce inequality (including poverty and unemployment) and ensure that people prosper, benefit, and participate. It reflects the adaptive nature of and flexibility inherent in Aboriginal culture. Many Aboriginal communities are actively engaged in the practical business of trying to solve concrete problems. High rates of unemployment, poor housing stocks, above-average suicide and incarceration rates, and below-average health and socio-economic status are just some of the problems currently confronting Aboriginal peoples. Changing tactics and changing social values reflect changing material circumstances. With land claim settlement dollars in the bank and powers of governance in their hands, Aboriginal groups are engaging in resource development as a way to achieve important economic objectives. The economic objectives of self-determination are most often tied to improving material circumstances, not simply the accumulation of wealth but also the provision of basic needs such as housing, health, and education. Reduction of poverty, unemployment, and inequality are also important areas of development. As claims are settled, development strategies tend toward the creation of new economic opportunities as well as the preservation of traditional activities.

Aboriginal development strategies differ between communities. Some choose to take advantage of resource development occurring on or near their land. Some choose to reject it. And some, like the Mikisew Cree, focus on the creation of companies that exist primarily to service local development initiatives. With its own capital and initial assistance from oil sands producers, the Mikisew Cree First Nation has created a host of financially successful companies that service neighbouring oil and gas giants. These companies, in turn, invariably employ band members in an effort to provide employment opportunities and alleviate welfare dependence. However, the Mikisew Cree recognize that dependence upon a finite resource is an act of folly and, consequently, seek to diversify their economic portfolio by expanding their economic enterprises beyond the local oil sands community.[30]

In other communities, such as the Oujé-Bougoumou First Nation of James Bay, Quebec, the band does not engage directly in resource development. Instead, nearby resource development provides the catalyst for treaty negotiation and self-government implementation. It also creates an environment conducive to entrepreneurial activity. This includes First Nations community governments providing loans to individual band members with sound business proposals. If approved, it is the individual who opens up a business and repays the loan with proceeds from the business. In this scenario, the development strategy is targeted at improving the socio-economic prospects of individuals while also improving the overall health of the community.

What is interesting about these two examples is that they are both entrepreneurial in nature. Firt Nations community governments promote business development and employment opportunities as part of a strategy to improve the socio-economic status of their members. Even though these communities may suffer criticism of their actions from other, more "traditional," groups, the fact remains that both groups recognize the importance of First Nations participation in the market economy and neither would concede that they have abandoned their culture in exchange for jobs and wages. Just the opposite. Self-sufficiency is promoted as an integral component of First Nations culture, as it exists today, and, consequently, forms an important part of any community development strategy.[31]

Conclusion

Development is more than a theoretical construct or synonym for self-determination: it is a way of conceptualizing the world in normative ways. Historically, it was assumed that development was good and, hence, shaped practical paths to growth and modernization. Development was tied intimately to the capitalist regime of accumulation and worked to transform traditional cultures that challenged its proliferation. Today, while the concept of development retains its traditional principles, it is promoted (even if it is not always viewed) as "good."[32] Contemporary theories of development are increasingly informed by development paths and practices. Rethinking development in light of emerging development strategies and empirical experience is necessary because development itself has moved from the realm of theory to become a practical part of self-determination in the Canadian north.

While political and economic development is important, "self-determination is a shallow goal if identity and culture are not part of the equation."[33] Increasingly, development strategies adopted by different Aboriginal communities are focused on managing cultural change as it is shaped and transformed by the political and economic demands of resource development. Although the goal of advancing as an Aboriginal person or community may well be the most challenging, the goal of preserving collective and individual identities drives development. This is because Aboriginal cultural identity is tied intimately to Aboriginal development, cultural institutions, and resources such as land and language. Although self-determined development can be viewed as a perversion of the inherent right to self-determination and as the reflection of the assimilation of Aboriginal peoples into "Western civilization," it can also be viewed as a mechanism through which to exert agency. To people of the North, resource development cannot continue forever and success is not measured solely by profits. Ultimately, they seek to preserve their right to live on their land on their own terms.

ACKNOWLEDGMENTS
I thank Annis May Timpson for her editorial suggestions and Emily Rozitis for research support. I also thank all the people who shared their time and perspectives with me.

NOTES
1   Frances Abele, "Understanding What Happened Here: The Political Economy of Indigenous Peoples," in *Understanding Canada: Building on the New Canadian Political Economy*, ed. Wallace Clement (Montreal and Kingston: McGill-Queen's University Press, 1997), 124.
2   Harold Innis, *The Fur Trade in Canada: An Introduction to Canadian Economic History* (1930; repr., Toronto: University of Toronto Press, 1999), x.
3   Norman Long, "Development Studies," in *Social Science Encyclopedia*, ed. Adam Kuper and Jessica Kuper (London: Routledge, 1989), 198.
4   Works by theorists of development include Fernando H. Cardoso, "The Consumption of Dependency Theory in the United States," *Latin American Research Review* 12, 3 (1977): 7-24; André Gunder Frank, *Capitalism and Underdevelopment in Latin America: Historical Studies of Chile and Brazil* (New York: Monthly Review Press, 1967); Walter W. Rostow, *The Stages of Economic Growth: A Non-Communist Manifesto* (Cambridge: Cambridge University Press, 1960).
5   Watkins writes that "large-scale resource projects are said by their proponents to create 'development.' In fact, for native people what has resulted is properly characterized as 'underdevelopment.'" In Mel Watkins, "From Underdevelopment to Development," in *Dene Nation: The Colony Within*, ed. Mel Watkins (Toronto: University of Toronto Press, 1977), 91.
6   A development strategy is defined as an "effort to change existing economic and social structures and institutions in order to find enduring solutions to the problems facing decision-makers." Moreover, the term "development strategy" implies an actor, normally the state. In the context of this chapter, the First Nation is also

suggested as an actor. See Robert B. Potter, "Theories, Strategies and Ideologies of Development," in *The Companion to Development Studies*, ed. Vandana Desai and Robert B. Potter (London: Arnold, 2002), 61.

7   Michael J. Prince and Frances Abele, "Paying for Self-Determination: Aboriginal People, Self-Government, and Fiscal Relations in Canada," in *Reconfiguring Aboriginal-State Relations – Canada: The State of the Federation, 2003*, ed. Michael Murphy (Montreal and Kingston: McGill-Queen's University Press, 2005), 245.

8   Imperial Oil, *A Partner in the Community: 2005 Corporate Citizenship Report*, 33, Imperial Oil, http://www.imperialoil.ca/Canada-English/Files/Corporate_Citizenship/2005citizenship.pdf.

9   Mining Watch Canada, "First Nations Declare a Moratorium on Mining Exploration and Forestry in the Far North: No Means No," 5 April 2007, Mining Watch Canada, http://www.miningwatch.ca.

10 Polaris Institute, "Deh Cho Leader Calls for Tar Sands Moratorium," *Canadian Dimension*, 2 February 2007, http://www.canadiandimension.com/articles/2007/02/08/896.

11 Joe Linklater, Vuntut Gwitchin Chief, interview with author, Toronto, 11 February 2005.

12 Ibid.

13 Alan Freeman, "U.S. Senate Opens Alaska's Arctic Refuge for Drilling," *Globe and Mail*, 17 March 2005: A3.

14 Linklater, e-mail communication with author, 16 January 2008.

15 Another study that also links the Aboriginal issue with dependency theory is Marie-Anik Gagné, *A Nation within a Nation: Dependency and the Cree* (Montreal: Black Rose Books, 1994), 148.

16 Phil Fontaine, "Indian Act Is Racist: Fontaine," *Globe and Mail*, 3 June 2004: A11.

17 Nellie Cournoyea, "The Challenge of Natural Resource Development in Canada's North" (2001 Donald Gow Memorial Lecture, Queen's University, Kingston, Ontario, 27 April 2001), 2.

18 Grand Council of the Crees, "Section 30: Income Security Program for Cree Hunters and Trappers," *James Bay and Northern Quebec Agreement*, 1975, http://www.gcc.ca.

19 See Gabrielle A. Slowey, *Navigating Neoliberalism: Self-Determination and the Mikisew Cree First Nation* (Vancouver: UBC Press, 2008), 17.

20 See Graham White, "Treaty Federalism in Northern Canada: Aboriginal-Government Land Claims Boards," *Publius* 32, 3 (2002): 89-116.

21 Syncrude executive, interview with author, Fort McMurray, Alberta, 5 May 2000.

22 According to the board's website, "The Mackenzie Valley Environmental Impact Review Board was established in 1998 under the Mackenzie Valley Resources Management Act. This federal legislation came about as a result of commitments

made by the federal government when it settled the Gwich'in and Sahtu land claims in the Northwest Territories. The Canadian Environmental Assessment Act no longer applies in the Mackenzie Valley. The Review Board is a co-management Board which means that half of the board members are nominated by First Nations, while the federal and territorial governments nominate the other half." See Mackenzie Valley Environmental Impact Review Board, "About the Review Board," http://www.mveirb.nt.ca/about/.

23 See Annis May Timpson, "Stretching the Concept of Representative Bureaucracy: The Case of Nunavut," *International Review of Administrative Sciences* 72, 4 (2006): 517-30.

24 Canada, Royal Commission on Aboriginal Peoples, *Report of the Royal Commission on Aboriginal Peoples*, vol. 2, *Restructuring the Relationship* (Ottawa: Canadian Communications Group, 1996), 20, http://www.ainc-inac.gc.ca/ch/rcap/sg/sgmm_e. html.

25 Michael Asch, "The Dene Economy," in *Dene Nation*, ed. Watkins, 47. In his research White cites an interviewee from Nunavut Tunngavik Incorporated who says that "bridging the two worlds of Inuit ways and Western ways is the real challenge" and that success results in the average person, or "little guy" in the community, having an impact on decision-making processes. See White, "Treaty Federalism in Northern Canada," 89.

26 This information is derived from personal observations when the author worked in the community of Fort Chipewyan, Alberta, the home of the Mikisew Cree First Nation, in the summer of 1997.

27 CBC News, "Gwich'in President Supports Pipeline," 27 January 2000, CBC News, http://www.cbc.ca/news/story/2000/01/27/yk_nerysoo270100.html.

28 Canada, Royal Commission on Aboriginal Peoples, "Presentation by Mikisew Cree First Nation, Chief Archie Waquan, Fort Chipewyan, ALTA 92-06-18," *For Seven Generations: An Information Legacy of the Royal Commission on Aboriginal Peoples*, CD-ROM (Ottawa: Libraxus Inc., 1997), 17.

29 Author interview with Mikisew Cree member no. 27, Edmonton, 27 May 2000.

30 Slowey, *Navigating Neoliberalism*, 64.

31 Again, this information is derived from personal observations and communications received while the author was visiting the community of Oujé-Bougoumou, Quebec, in 2004.

32 See Robert B. Anderson, Leo Paul Dana, and Teresa E. Dana, "Indigenous Land Rights, Entrepreneurship and Economic Development in Canada: 'Opting-in' to the Global Economy," *Journal of World Business* 41, 1 (2006): 45-55.

33 Mason Durie, *Te Mana, Te Kawanatanga: The Politics of Maori Self-Determination* (Melbourne: Oxford University Press, 1998), 79.

WORKS CITED

Abele, Frances. "Understanding What Happened Here: The Political Economy of Indigenous Peoples." In *Understanding Canada: Building on the New Canadian Political Economy,* ed. Wallace Clement, 118-40. Montreal and Kingston: McGill-Queen's University Press, 1997.

Anderson, Robert B., Leo Paul Dana, and Teresa E. Dana. "Indigenous Land Rights, Entrepreneurship and Economic Development in Canada: 'Opting-in' to the Global Economy." *Journal of World Business* 41, 1 (2006): 45-55.

Asch, Michael. "The Dene Economy." In *Dene Nation: The Colony Within,* ed. Mel Watkins, 47-61. Toronto: University of Toronto Press, 1977.

Canada. Royal Commission on Aboriginal Peoples. *Report of the Royal Commission on Aboriginal Peoples.* Vol. 2, *Restructuring the Relationship.* Ottawa: Canadian Communications Group, 1996. http://www.ainc-inac.gc.ca/ch/rcap/sg/sgmm_e.html.

–. "Presentation by Mikisew Cree First Nation, Chief Archie Waquan, Fort Chipewyan, ALTA 92-06-18." *For Seven Generations: An Information Legacy of the Royal Commission on Aboriginal Peoples.* Ottawa: Libraxus Inc., 1997, CD Rom.

Cardoso, Fernando H. "The Consumption of Dependency Theory in the United States," *Latin American Research Review* 12, 3 (1977): 7-24.

CBC News. "Gwich'in President Supports Pipeline," 27 January 2000. CBC News. http://www.cbc.ca/news/story/2000/01/27/yk_nerysoo270100.html.

Cournoyea, Nellie. "The Challenge of Natural Resource Development in Canada's North." 2001 Donald Gow Memorial Lecture, Queens University, Kingston, Ontario, 27 April 2001.

Durie, Mason. *Te Mana, Te Kawanatanga: The Politics of Maori Self-Determination.* Melbourne: Oxford University Press, 1998.

Fontaine, Phil. "Indian Act Is Racist: Fontaine," *Globe and Mail,* 3 June 2004: A11,

Frank, André Gunder. *Capitalism and Underdevelopment in Latin America: Historical Studies of Chile and Brazil.* New York: Monthly Review Press, 1967.

Freeman, Alan. "U.S. Senate Opens Alaska's Arctic Refuge for Drilling." *Globe and Mail,* 17 March 2005: A3.

Gagné, Marie-Anik. *A Nation within a Nation: Dependency and the Cree.* Montreal: Black Rose Books, 1994.

Grand Council of the Crees. "Section 30: Income Security Program for Cree Hunters and Trappers." *James Bay and Northern Quebec Agreement,* 1975. http://www.gcc.ca.

Imperial Oil. *A Partner in the Community: 2005 Corporate Citizenship Report.* Imperial Oil. http://www.imperialoil.ca/Canada-English/Files/Corporate_Citizenship/2005citizenship.pdf.

Innis, Harold. *The Fur Trade in Canada: An Introduction to Canadian Economic History.* 1930. Reprint, Toronto: University of Toronto Press, 1999.

Long, Norman. "Development Studies." In *Social Science Encyclopedia,* ed. Adam Kuper and Jessica Kuper, 198. London: Routledge, 1989.

Mackenzie Valley Environmental Impact Review Board. "About the Review Board." Mackenzie Valley Environmental Impact Review Board. http://www.mveirb.nt.ca/about/.

Mining Watch Canada. "First Nations Declare a Moratorium on Mining Exploration and Forestry in the Far North: No Means No," 5 April 2007. Mining Watch Canada. http://www.miningwatch.ca.

Polaris Institute. "Deh Cho Leader Calls for Tar Sands Moratorium." *Canadian Dimension*, 2 February 2007. http://www.canadiandimension.com/articles/2007/02/08/896/.

Potter, Robert B. "Theories, Strategies and Ideologies of Development." In *The Companion to Development Studies*, ed. Vandana Desai and Robert B. Potter, 61-64. London: Arnold, 2002.

Prince, Michael J., and Frances Abele. "Paying for Self-Determination: Aboriginal Peoples, Self-Government, and Fiscal Relations in Canada." In *Reconfiguring Aboriginal-State Relations – Canada: The State of the Federation, 2003*, ed. Michael Murphy, 237-63. Montreal and Kingston: McGill-Queen's University Press, 2005.

Rostow, Walter W. *The Stages of Economic Growth: A Non-Communist Manifesto*. Cambridge: Cambridge University Press, 1960.

Slowey, Gabrielle A. *Navigating Neoliberalism: Self-Determination and the Mikisew Cree First Nation*. Vancouver: UBC Press, 2008.

Timpson, Annis May. "Stretching the Concept of Representative Bureaucracy: The Case of Nunavut." *International Review of Administrative Sciences* 72, 4 (2006): 517-30.

Watkins, Mel. "From Underdevelopment to Development." In *Dene Nation: The Colony Within*, ed. Mel Watkins, 84-99. Toronto: University of Toronto Press, 1977.

White, Graham. "Treaty Federalism in Northern Canada: Aboriginal-Government Land Claims Boards." *Publius* 32, 3 (2002): 89-116.

PART 5

Thinking Back, Looking Forward: Political and Constitutional Reconciliation

10

Civilization, Self-Determination, and Reconciliation

Michael Murphy

Reconciliation speaks to the past, present, and future of Aboriginal-state relations in Canada. Perhaps nowhere was this message more clearly articulated than in the final report of the Royal Commission on Aboriginal Peoples (RCAP). As was nicely encapsulated in the title of the opening volume – *Looking Forward, Looking Back* – the commissioners recommended an honest and open confrontation with the history of colonization, concrete measures to address the contemporary legacy of injustice, and the forging of a new relationship built on the foundations of mutual recognition, respect, and trust.[1] First Nations have articulated their own visions of reconciliation, and many of their voices were instrumental in shaping the recommendations of the RCAP. Although there is no grand, unified First Nations perspective on reconciliation, there is widespread agreement that it encompasses a forward-looking relationship among equals who will seek to establish bonds of trust and mutual respect by working to rectify the injustices of the past and who are committed to governing the terms of their coexistence in a spirit of reciprocity and mutual consent.[2]

The response from non-Aboriginal Canada has been slow, and somewhat muted, but reconciliation has inexorably found its way onto the policy agenda. The Supreme Court of Canada has located reconciliation at the heart of its jurisprudence on Aboriginal rights. Thus, it describes section 35 of the Canadian Constitution as the "framework through which the fact that aboriginals lived on the land in distinctive societies, with their own practices, customs and traditions, is acknowledged and reconciled with the sovereignty of the Crown" and as a solid foundation for negotiating fair and sustainable terms of existence between governments and First Nations.[3] In spite of its regrettable decision to ignore the RCAP's broader vision of reconciliation, the federal government has taken steps in the right direction through its efforts to deal with the legacy of residential schools.[4] The Government of

British Columbia has also signalled its intention to shift the relationship between the province and First Nations onto a new footing, one based on the principles of mutual respect, the recognition and accommodation of Aboriginal rights, and a commitment to a just and sustainable reconciliation of Crown-Aboriginal claims to title and political jurisdiction.[5]

Although most close observers would agree that bridging the distance between the Crown's and First Nations' visions of reconciliation remains a very challenging work in progress – burdened as it is by a legacy of conflict and mistrust and the troubling persistence of Indigenous disadvantage and disempowerment – there has at least been a degree of convergence on the idea that the way forward requires a break with historical policies of assimilation and the denial of fundamental Aboriginal rights. Yet this convergence is anything but complete, and for some it is this very attempt to break decisively with Canada's assimilationist history that is most responsible for the current state of crisis in many First Nations communities and the conflictual nature of Aboriginal-state relations in Canada. One of the most articulate exponents of this point of view is political scientist Tom Flanagan, whose influential book *First Nations? Second Thoughts* is animated by its own very distinctive vision of reconciliation. Flanagan's book delivers an impassioned defence of the assimilation agenda that is grounded in a conscious and unapologetic effort to rehabilitate the concept of civilization that captured the imagination of so many European intellectuals in the Age of Empire.[6] Reconciliation in this new civilizationist paradigm is predicated on the acceptance that the colonization of the Americas was historically inexorable and, ultimately, justifiable as a means of spreading the scientific, technological, and material benefits of modernity. This alternative agenda for the future carries a clear message for First Nations: abandon the quixotic quest for self-determination that forms the core of Aboriginal nationalism and embrace the inevitability, and multiple advantages, of assimilation.

The object of this chapter is to highlight the failure of Flanagan's position both as a moral and a practical vision of reconciliation. The major weaknesses of his vision are its characterization of Aboriginal nationalism as an obstacle rather than a key contributor to the reconciliation agenda and its tendency to marginalize First Nations voices rather than calling for their inclusion in Canada's ongoing political conversation. As in the past so in his vision of the future, First Nations are expected to live their lives according to an agenda established predominantly by others, rather than being accorded a place as full and equal partners in the negotiation of their relationships with the peoples and governments of Canada. The argument of this chapter proceeds in three parts. The first section examines the historical roots of civilizationist thinking in the works of several influential political theorists who wrote in the Age of Empire. The second section examines Flanagan's efforts to resurrect and rehabilitate this concept of civilization as a foundation for Crown–First Nations reconciliation in Canada. The third section offers a critique of Flanagan's project, focusing in particular on his mischaracterization of Aboriginal nationalism and on the moral and practical weaknesses of his civilizationist paradigm of reconciliation.

Historical Civilizationism

A broad spectrum of European political theorists in the Age of Empire shared a perspective I call civilizationism. Civilizationists ranked societies on a scale of human development that measured their degree of material and moral-intellectual progress, the template for which was provided by the highly advanced societies of Europe. Civilizationism encompassed two interdependent strands of development: one scientific, the other humanistic. In scientific terms "civilization" referred to a society's technological and organizational capacity to dominate its environment, thereby increasing its security, power, and prosperity. In its humanistic sense, it referred to the cultivation of those traits considered to be uniquely human or definitive of human excellence. Following John Stuart Mill's classic distinction, civilization in a narrow sense served to distinguish wealthy and powerful nations from underdeveloped or barbarian societies, whereas civilization in a broader sense referred to the cultivation of our most cherished human capacities such as nobility, wisdom, individuality, and morality.[7]

At the heart of the civilizationist paradigm was the assumption that non-European peoples are generally inferior to their European counterparts. European superiority was commonly expressed in terms of the stages theory of human advancement, according to which human societies pass through a series of phases of historical development during their transition from a barbarous to a fully civilized mode of existence. At the pinnacle of this evolutionary model were placed the states and peoples of Europe, whereas non-European societies were placed at various lower stages of the process.[8] Most civilizationists held to some version of the stages theory, but they frequently disagreed on whether civilization would ever emerge in its fullest sense in non-European societies and whether the process of civilizing the uncivilized should be achieved by incentive, coercion, or consent; in other words, they varied somewhat in their assessments of the justifiability of colonialism.

THE SCIENTIFIC DIMENSION

The greatest similarities among civilizationist thinkers related to the scientific dimensions of the doctrine. The central emphasis was on technological advancement and the development of more effective means of organizing economy, society, and the polity. A central theme in most civilization theory was the power that comes from coordinated, collective enterprise. What is it, Mill asked, that "makes all savage communities poor and feeble? The same cause which prevented the lions and tigers from long ago extirpating the race of men – incapacity of co-operation. It is only civilized beings who can combine."[9] Marx and Engels expressed a similar view in seeking to reconcile the necessity of dissolving premodern and precapitalist societies in the colonies. Speaking specifically of the Iroquois, Engels concluded: "Impressive as the people of this epoch may appear to us ... they are still bound, as Marx says, to the umbilical cord of the primordial community. The power of these communities had to be broken, and it was broken."[10] According to Marx, it was only by organizing themselves (or being organized by others) into a capitalist mode of existence that these societies could move from a position of domination *by* their environment to domination *of* their environment.[11] We see this view again in the work of social contractarians such as Hobbes and Locke who describe Indians wandering wild in the woods of America, lacking in the fundamentals of agricultural, economic, and political organization, divided from one another by fear and suspicion, and living brutish, wretched, and needy lives.[12] As Hobbes wrote to his contemporaries, the state of nature – the war of all against all – is no mere fiction. "For the savage people in many places of *America*, except the government of small Families, the concord whereof dependeth on naturall lust, have no government at all; and live at this day in a brutish manner, as I said before."[13]

This general power of combination and cooperation is articulated across a range of specific activities, including the institutionalization of regimes of land enclosure and private property, which in tandem with the development of commercial agriculture and resource extraction industries, was designed to increase productivity and the accumulation of wealth. In the eighteenth and nineteenth centuries, wealth production and accumulation increasingly came to incorporate urbanization, large-scale mechanized industrialization, a complex division of labour, and networks of domestic and international commerce and trade. Other standard elements of civilization included institutionalized mass education (what Mill called "the diffusion of intelligence"); the flourishing of arts, letters, and architecture; advances in the human and natural sciences, the arts of navigation, and networks of transportation and communication; and, generally, the comforts and refinements of a well-ordered and highly cultured mass society, including increased leisure time and relative freedom from the tyranny of menial or crushing labour.[14]

The central organizational element for the civilizationist was, of course, the modern state. In contrast to savages, who were generally understood to live in a lawless condition – likened by Hobbes to the state of nature – and characterized by only the most rudimentary form of sociopolitical organization, civilized societies were marked by the presence of a highly institutionalized and centralized political authority that exercised sovereignty and enforced the rule of law within clearly delimited borders. Thus, the sovereign was considered the ultimate expression of a civilized society's power to combine. As Hobbes concluded: "The Greatest of humane Powers, is that which is compounded of the Powers of most men, united by consent, in one person, Naturall, or Civill, that has the use of all their Powers depending on his will; such as is the Power of a Commonwealth."[15] The sovereign head of the modern state was therefore granted the authority to represent, exercise, and enforce the collective agency or will of society. The ultimate end of this established and institutionalized political order was the guarantee of safety, security, and organizational resources essential to economic, cultural, scientific, and moral progress.

THE HUMANISTIC DIMENSION

The humanistic dimension of civilization, as understood by theorists such as Locke and Mill, encompassed the development of certain character traits or habits of mind such as self-discipline, reasonableness, respect for authority, industriousness, a capacity for mutual accommodation, and a willingness to recognize others as our equals.[16] Mill in particular is famous for emphasizing the importance of individuality – our capacity (and willingness) to engage in original or independent thought – which for him was the hallmark of a truly free and self-governing individual.[17] Things worked a little differently for Kant. In the Kantian worldview, civilized societies achieve progress by means of their unsocial sociability: the tendency of their inhabitants to be simultaneously drawn into society while their natural competitiveness, glory seeking, and relentless desire for possessions and power continually threaten its dissolution. Nevertheless, it is precisely their asocial tendencies that push civilized beings beyond a life of complacent self-sufficiency to ever greater deeds and accomplishments, both material and moral-intellectual. In the absence of these asocial traits (in themselves mostly deplorable), Kant concluded that humanity's true potential would remain forever unrealized, and our fate would be to live an existence more worthy of sheep, or savages.[18]

Despite their unanimity in judging non-European societies inferior to their European counterparts, civilization theorists varied with respect to their assessment of the degree and relative duration of this inferiority. Mill and Marx, for example, took the view that less civilized non-European societies were by no means devoid of admirable qualities (e.g., strength, intelligence, bravery) and were perfectly capable of achieving levels of moral and scientific excellence comparable to Europeans; but, ultimately, they were dependent for their progress upon European guidance or, in Marx's view, interference and disruption – which is to say, they were incapable of progressing fully on their own.[19] Locke took an even dimmer view of the character and capacities of non-Europeans. In *An Essay concerning Human Understanding*, he describes American Indians as ignorant and childlike – as lacking in industry, discipline, and rationality – and places them on a level with children, idiots, the illiterate, and other savages. They were perhaps even akin to animals, living a brutish and meagre existence in the wilderness areas of America.[20] Yet, as Bikhu Parekh tells us, Locke believed that these differences were determined by the influences of climate and geography, rather than inalterable biology, and, thus, the deficiencies of the uncivilized could ultimately be overcome, though, again, not without the guiding hand of Europeans.[21]

Given Kant's reputation as a founder of modern liberalism, many find it bewildering and counterintuitive that he held, by far, the most disparaging view of non-European peoples. Kant firmly believed in a hierarchy of races, with white Europeans at its apex. To quote from his *Physical Geography*: "Humanity is at its greatest perfection in the race of whites. The yellow Indians do have a meagre talent. The negroes are far below them and at the lowest point are a part of the American peoples."[22] Kant reserved his greatest contempt for American Indians, whom he described elsewhere as weak, passive, lacking in industry, incapable of any culture, and deficient in their rational and moral faculties. In his opinion, they occupied the very bottom of the racial hierarchy.[23] Kant may have also doubted the capacity of the uncivilized races to transcend their inferior natures. Although he shared Locke's view that different physical, intellectual, and moral traits crystallized under the influence of different climates and geographies, his feeling was that once these characteristics and dispositions took hold, they would strongly resist further alteration. This would seem to suggest that in Kant's opinion civilizing missions had their inherent limits.[24]

Civilizationism and Colonialism

The moment of truth for any theory of civilization is its orientation toward European colonialism, and in this regard we encounter some unexpected but revealing differences among this group of theorists. Locke is well known for his supportive stand on colonial policy in the Americas, the centrepiece of which was his theory of property. In Lockean terms, North American Indians merely roamed over their territories and thus were derelict in their natural duty to make productive use of the land via European modes of cultivation. It followed that any such unproductive lands could be said to be in the so-called state of nature and thus subject to appropriation without consent by the first European to use them in a truly civilized and productive manner.[25] Moreover, since Locke also deemed the Indians to be in a prepolitical stage of development, it follows that they could not legitimately claim sovereignty over their lands and thereby defend themselves against such confiscations.[26] While analysts seem to agree that Locke did not support the colonists' right to hunt, arbitrarily kill, or enslave the Indigenous inhabitants, Tully notes that, in Lockean terms, any attempt by the Amerindians to defend their territories from European enclosure could justifiably have been repelled by the appropriators under conditions of self-defence and just war.[27] Locke did believe that the Indigenous peoples of America were entitled to rights and protections as individuals but not as autonomous, or self-governing, political societies. Indeed, he argued that with European assistance they could be assimilated and civilized, which, in his view, would ultimately be to their benefit.[28]

Mill and Marx, though perhaps somewhat less disparaging of non-European societies than Locke, were no less willing to condone colonialism. Although both theorists were prepared to acknowledge the many good qualities displayed by non-European peoples, on the whole they considered these societies to be stagnant, incapable of self-improvement, and capable of achieving civilization only through external intervention and direction. In Mill's view, people who had not yet achieved the maturity of their faculties must, like children, be improved through compulsion. Stated bluntly: "Despotism is a legitimate mode of government in dealing with barbarians, provided the end be their improvement, and the means justified by actually effecting that end. Liberty, as a principle, has no application to any state of things anterior to the time when individuals or societies have become capable of improvement by means of free and open discussion."[29] Mill referred to this state of affairs as a gentle or parental despotism – a government of leading strings – whose core principle should be one of guidance, not force. Backward societies that had been guided to a higher stage of development could, and in Mill's view should, be granted self-government or perhaps absorbed and assimilated by a more civilized nation.[30]

Marx's theory is a little more complex. He was simultaneously one of the fiercest critics and greatest defenders of European colonialism. Marx and Engels both documented the unparalleled destruction, brutality, and hypocrisy of colonialism – a system that in their view pretended to be of benefit to all but in fact only enriched the capitalist classes at the expense of increasingly impoverished colonized populations. As Marx wryly observed in *Capital:* "The discovery of gold and silver in America, the extirpation, enslavement and entombment in mines of the aboriginal population, the beginning of the conquest and looting of the East Indies, the turning of Africa into a warren for the commercial hunting of black-skins, signalised the rosy dawn of the era of capitalist production."[31] Yet, for Marx, colonialism was also essential and, in historical materialist terms, inevitable. It was essential in order to explode the stagnant and inefficient economies of the colonies, to lay the foundations for an industrial society capable of conquering material scarcity, and to thereby provide the material conditions for a world free of the necessity of crushing and exploitative labour. It was also necessary as a means to uproot and dissolve semi-civilized societies in the colonies, whose social structures and norms restrained human excellence and creativity and artificially divided men from one another by means of tradition, superstition, and the perpetuation of parochial communal identities. The increasing immiseration of the overseas colonial proletariat was also, in Marx's view, a cruel but essential pathway to the development of revolutionary consciousness, and to the social revolution that would eventually see the transcendence of capitalist civilization in both Europe and the colonies. Distressing though it may be to compassionate observers, Marx exhorted people to reconcile themselves to this harsh reality, for colonialism was an essential and unavoidable link in the historical chain of human emancipation.[32]

Kant took the most unexpected position of all. Given the depth of his contempt for the non-white races, one might expect a vigorous defence of colonialism, but Kant in fact rejected the practice of European imperialism, along with its various pragmatic and moral justifications. Kant's views are encapsulated in his theory of cosmopolitan right. At the core of Kantian cosmopolitanism is the insight that, since the earth is a globe with a necessarily limited space, peaceful relations among peoples can only be maintained if we learn to tolerate one another's company. On this basis Kantian theory supports the right of any nation to move around the globe in search of trade and peaceful interaction with other nations. And, so long as we approach others in a spirit of goodwill and accommodation, other nations are under a corresponding moral duty to receive us cordially in their midst. The right of visitation is, therefore, balanced by the duty of hospitality.[33]

Kant was nevertheless adamant that the right to visitation did not automatically confer the right to settle on another nation's territory: this latter move required a special contract and the explicit consent of the people in question. Kant took particular pains to emphasize the interests of pastoral or hunting peoples, such as the Indigenous inhabitants of the Americas, who relied on large tracts of wasteland for their sustenance. Unlike Locke, he rejected the argument that such lands were open to European expropriation, arguing instead for a more limited European right to settle in these territories, and only after the negotiation of treaties with the existing inhabitants, whose interests were not to be exploited by means of deception or sharp dealing.[34] Kant also saw little merit in the many popular justifications for bypassing these standards of conduct, including the duty to spread the gift of culture or civilization or the objection that the world would still be in a lawless condition had mankind held any reservations about using violence to achieve law-governed states.[35] Although, in Kant's view, Europeans could justifiably look with contempt upon the manner in which savages clung to their lawless freedom, neither their contempt nor their desire to improve the lot of barbarians could serve as a justification for their subjugation.[36]

All the same, Kant never swayed from being convinced of both the comprehensive superiority of European civilization and the historical inevitability of European global dominance. Indeed, he is famous for remarking that "our continent [Europe] ... will probably legislate eventually for all other continents."[37] Exactly how this state of affairs was to be squared with his emphasis on consent and the moral equality of every member of the human race Kant did not say. Regardless, his final conclusion was that we must reconcile ourselves to this distasteful reality and take comfort in the conviction that European domination would ultimately serve the broader cause of human advancement.

As a rule, civilization theorists focused intensively on the radical differences between European and New World societies, and these differences (be they scientific and material or moral-intellectual in nature) were generally greeted as evidence of the inferiority of non-European peoples. Yet civilizationists disagreed in their assessments of the degree and permanence of non-European inferiority, and there seems to be no necessary connection between the assumptions made about a society's level of advancement and the justifiability of its colonial subjection. In Locke this relationship is fairly predictable, while in Kant there is a surprising disjuncture between his racist views and his condemnation of the colonial policies of his day. Marx, on the other hand, was characteristically ambivalent. Yet, in spite of these differences, civilizationists were in agreement on the desirability of transcending uncivilized forms of life, even if they deplored, as did Kant and Marx, the means by which this was sometimes accomplished. Perhaps more significantly, they all accepted the inevitability of Europe's domination of the uncivilized parts of the globe, a conclusion that takes on a quasi-mystical tone in Kant and Marx when it is described as one element in the hidden plan of history.

Rehabilitating Civilizationism:
Flanagan's *First Nations? Second Thoughts*

More than a century and a half later, in an age in which civilizationist thinking has been widely discredited for its narrow, ethnocentric, and frequently racist biases, Tom Flanagan set himself the ambitious and controversial task of rehabilitating civilizationist thought as part of a radical critique of the prevailing trajectory of Crown–First Nations reconciliation in Canada.[38] Flanagan contends that at the time of first contact European cultures were several thousand years more advanced along the path of civilization than the Aboriginal cultures they encountered in the Americas. In addition, he argues that this massive civilization gap has been ignored by contemporary analysts of Aboriginal-state relations, who instead emphasize a historical relationship of equals and nation-to-nation partnerships. A more open and honest assessment of the past must, in his view, lead to the conclusion that the colonization and conquest of First Nations was inevitable and, if we accept the arguments of John Locke and others, justifiable.[39]

The target of Flanagan's book is a position he defines very broadly as the Aboriginal orthodoxy, whose adherents have built their notions of reconciliation around concepts of Aboriginal sovereignty and nationhood, the inherent right to Aboriginal self-government, ancient territorial rights, and Crown-Aboriginal relationships grounded in treaties of mutual recognition and respect. Flanagan rejects this vision of the future as unrealistic (it refuses to countenance the inevitability of First Nations assimilation) and reactionary (it turns its back on progress and the undeniable benefits that civilization and modernity have to offer). He also argues that this vision's moral foundation is profoundly illiberal in its desire to ground collective Aboriginal rights in immutable racial differences and historical privilege.[40] Reconciliation, in Flanagan's view, will only be possible when First Nations are ready to cease dwelling on the past and begin envisioning a future in which they are fully assimilated citizens of Canada, a future that offers them the security and high standard of living that only a highly civilized society makes possible.

Flanagan recognizes that "civilization" has become something of a dirty word in contemporary academic circles, for good reason, and his intention is to jettison its pejorative connotations and apply the term more objectively to mean the progressive betterment of the human condition by scientific, technological, and organizational means. His vision of civilization seeks to retain what he takes to be the more neutral and scientific elements of the concept – including an emphasis on agriculturalism, the division of labour, and centralized political authority – found in theorists such as Mill and Locke while shedding the parochial and ethnocentric assumption that Europe was the only really civilized part of the world. Flanagan uses the term "civilization" (as he believes archaeologists still do) to refer to societies or cultures that have passed a certain threshold of technological and organizational development. This threshold is crossed once a society acquires attributes such as intensive and mechanized agriculture; large-scale urbanization; a complex division of labour; intellectual advances such as record keeping, writing, and astronomy; advanced technology; and formalized and hierarchical government (e.g., the modern state).[41] In Flanagan's view it makes no sense to conclude that a society is either wholly civilized or wholly savage, for civilization is a feature that cultures exhibit to varying degrees. He is, therefore, happy to include Old World cultures such as those of Egypt, China, and India among the ranks of the civilized, cultures that a more rigid civilizationist such as Mill would be inclined to classify as barbarian.[42]

Whereas Flanagan accepts the relativity of concepts such as goodness and beauty, he maintains that civilization is an objectively definable way of life whose application is universal across time and cultures. Human history, moreover, is a story of the progressive and inexorable domination of the uncivilized by the civilized: societies that adopt the attributes of civilization acquire increasing and demonstrative power over nature and, crucially, over uncivilized societies. To be clear, Flanagan is not suggesting that individuals in uncivilized societies are less intelligent, wise, kind, or courageous than their counterparts in civilized societies – on the contrary, they may even be superior in their possession of these virtues.[43] Within his framework, all cultures (or races) are capable of civilization; what explains the varied speed and timing of their move toward civilization are differences not in the inherent characteristics or abilities of individuals but in the environments and geographies in which the societies took root. Following Jared Diamond, Flanagan argues that the rapid advance of European civilizations can be explained by the natural advantages they enjoyed as a result of their geographical and environmental circumstances.[44] To summarize briefly: a particular distribution and variation of domesticated species of plants and animals in Europe facilitated the rapid development of agricultural societies, which in turn facilitated the rapid acquisition of technological, organizational, and material commodities essential to power and conquest. From this perspective, European domination of the New World came about not as a result of the inherent inferiority of Aboriginal peoples but, instead, as a result of bad timing. The comparatively less fruitful environments in which Aboriginal societies took root entailed a slower pace of civilization, which, in turn, meant Aboriginal societies simply could not compete with the more advanced nations of Europe when these societies came to the New World.[45]

Viewed from this perspective, the conquest and absorption of uncivilized peoples by the civilized is such a dominant and inevitable part of human history it seems almost pointless to raise questions about its morality. "It is like asking whether it is right or wrong that childbirth is painful, or that everyone eventually has to die, or that floods and droughts occur."[46] Nevertheless, if a moral justification is desired, Flanagan finds one readily available in Locke's conclusion that Europeans established a superior claim to uncultivated lands in the New World by putting them to more productive economic use, thereby laying the foundations for a large and prosperous agricultural society. This justification is worth quoting at length:

> Initially, all people, whether hunters or farmers, have an equal right
> to support themselves from the bounty of the earth. But the hunt-
> ing mode of life takes up a lot of land, while agriculture, being

more productive, causes population to grow and leads to civilization. As their numbers increase, civilized peoples have a right
to cultivate the additional land necessary for their support. If the
hunters deny them that opportunity ... they impede the equal
access of the farmers to the bounty of the earth ... The farmers are
justified in taking land from the hunters and defending it as long
as they make the arts of civilization available to the hunters.[47]

The assertion of European sovereignty in the Americas was an essential part
of the process of opening up productive land and providing a framework of
law and order to protect property rights and other liberties essential to a
progressive and prosperous social order.[48] To the argument that such actions
constituted an infringement of the pre-existing sovereignty and nationhood
of the Indigenous inhabitants, Flanagan's response is that these societies never
achieved the level of political organization – statehood in the European sense
– for these arguments to carry any legal or moral weight. Aboriginal sovereignty, he claims, is a fiction: "Sovereignty in the strict sense exists only in
the organized states characteristic of civilized societies."[49]

Indeed, to strive for the recognition and implementation of Aboriginal
sovereignty and nationhood is, in Flanagan's view, an unrealistic and reckless
attempt to swim against the tide of history. In practical terms, this Aboriginal orthodoxy promises only to prolong the immiseration of First Nations
by rationalizing their attachment to a backward, and backward-looking,
model of socio-economic and political development. In moral terms, moreover, the Aboriginal orthodoxy is grounded in a fundamentally illiberal effort
to establish race as the "constitutive factor of the political order" by assigning
a privileged set of rights to Aboriginal peoples on the grounds of their biological difference from other Canadians. "It would redefine Canada as an
association of racial communities rather than a polity whose members are
individual human beings."[50] Flanagan therefore advises First Nations to
abandon the struggle for sovereignty, give up their less civilized (meaning
less successful) cultures, embrace assimilation, and avail themselves of the
wealth of benefits that flow from a highly civilized mode of existence.[51]

The Moral and Practical Sterility of Civilizationism
Critical voices are essential to any debate about reconciliation with First Nations, regardless of whether these voices belong to moderate reformers or
more radical rejectionists such as Flanagan.[52] The particular value of radical

critiques is that they challenge us to articulate and defend first principles – the very foundations of our preferred visions of reconciliation. In the following section, I offer a critique of the moral and practical underpinnings of Flanagan's analysis and explain, in the process, how he misconceives the character and the significance of First Nations voices, particularly those speaking the language of nationalism and self-determination, in the reconciliation debate.

The central moral failing of Flanagan's civilizationist paradigm of reconciliation is its unsatisfactory engagement with the question of consent. Flanagan's attention is so tightly focused on what he thinks Aboriginal peoples *should* choose that he rarely considers the question of their *right to make their own choices*. Flanagan is not entirely unaware of this problem, and he acknowledges that critics will object strongly to his invocation of the Lockean defence of land and sovereignty acquisition in the Americas. In fact, Flanagan expresses his own reservations about this argument, given that it requires hunter-gatherers to give up a mode of life to which they have become deeply attached. "By what right [he asks] do the civilized require the uncivilized to renounce their ancient way of life?"[53] In fact, he sees no such moral justification, but neither does he see any moral justification for telling agriculturalists they must give up *their* way of life. Flanagan makes an intriguing point here, but the point rings a somewhat false note because agriculturalists were not, as Flanagan knows, required to give up their mode of life. Quite the opposite: their mode of life came to dominate at the expense of hunter-gatherers in the Americas. Flanagan's remarks do, nevertheless, suggest the possibility of a compromise position, which is to work toward a *mutually* acceptable reconciliation of the rights and interests of Aboriginal and non-Aboriginal peoples in Canada. Unfortunately, as a result of his tendency to see the relationship between Native peoples and newcomers as a kind of zero-sum game, Flanagan is either unable or unwilling to see the merits of this alternative course of action.[54] Rather than explore the possibilities of such an ethical compromise, Flanagan resorts to the empirical rejoinder that normative questions of this sort have simply been superseded by the facts. Questions of morality or immorality aside, Flanagan argues that it is simply an unavoidable fact of human history that "civilized societies are so much more powerful than uncivilized [sic] that it is only a matter of time until the former extend their sway over the latter."[55]

A similar equivocation between facts and norms pervades Flanagan's analysis of Aboriginal sovereignty claims. To dismiss these claims on the basis that First Nations did not measure up to European definitions of statehood is simply to substitute fact for justification and, therefore, miss the point spectacularly. Regardless of whether they met the factual criteria of sovereignty or statehood – a question that is itself the subject of some debate – First Nations on a more fundamental level question the morality of the process whereby Europeans denigrated and displaced Indigenous systems of self-rule during the process of colonial state formation.[56] Of course, early European intellectual and political elites had their own justifications for defining the pre-existing rights of First Nations out of existence, or for ignoring them in practice, but surely it is the responsibility of contemporary analysts to subject such justifications to some sort of critical analysis, particularly in cases where the link between moral principle and self-interest is so clearly problematic? Although sensitive to this moral controversy, Flanagan is unwilling to devote any moral resources to its resolution, preferring instead the empirical argument that, like it or not, the assertion of European sovereignty in the Americas is an irreversible fact that no amount of moral hand-wringing is going to change.[57]

It is no small irony that Flanagan's classical liberal attitude toward colonialism bears such a striking resemblance to the Marxian project of reconciling us to the necessary evils of capitalist imperialism, one of the only differences being that Marx was much more critical of the self-serving nature of colonial subjugation and its human costs. Apart from a few minor reservations about the loss of the Aboriginal way of life, Flanagan is confident that European dominance in North America "was, for the most part, established peacefully and humanely," a conclusion that sits uncomfortably beside the histories of residential schools, the targeted destruction of Aboriginal economies and cultures, forced community relocations, and the denial of fundamental civil and political rights such as mobility, freedom of association, and the franchise.[58] Ultimately, Flanagan's unwillingness to question the moral legitimacy of North American colonialism has the unintended effect of placing Aboriginal peoples not only in the position of technological subordinates but also in the position of moral subordinates whose right to decide their own fate is counted as less than that of European newcomers. In fairness to Flanagan, he never explicitly endorses the position that Aboriginal peoples should be forcibly assimilated or that existing self-government agreements should be unilaterally abrogated. He goes only so far as to encourage the Canadian government not to transfer additional energy and resources in directions that would slow or inhibit the process of civilization and assimilation that is already, in his view, well under way.[59] Nevertheless, by steadfastly refusing to engage with the moral legacy of Canada's colonial past, he fails to transcend the more parochial and ethnocentric assumptions of his civilizationist predecessors. Just like Locke and Mill before him, Flanagan is able to view Aboriginal citizens as suitable *objects* for assimilation, but he is unable, or unwilling, to see these same citizens as fit *subjects* for self-government.

Flanagan does, on the other hand, have something to say about the moral failings of Aboriginal nationalism and the assertions of an inherent right to self-government. He sees in these claims a form of racism that assumes that rights to land and self-government should be assigned on the basis of genetic differences. One of the difficulties in assessing this criticism is that Flanagan groups a very broad and diverse array of academic and political perspectives in support of Aboriginal rights and self-government under a catchy, but hopelessly vague, slogan: the Aboriginal orthodoxy. Nevertheless, one is hard pressed to locate anywhere in this broad spectrum of opinion an argument that First Nations enjoy rights to territory and self-government because they are racially distinct from other Canadians.[60] What one does encounter, time and again, is an argument that links the rights of First Nations to their *political* distinctiveness, to their prior status as independent, self-governing, political communities.[61]

While this argument has numerous variations, and theorists differ substantially with regard to its precise institutional implications, Aboriginal nationalism almost invariably expresses a desire for political self-determination. According to Taiaiake (Gerald) Alfred, Aboriginal nationalism is a movement in favour of political and cultural autonomy whose institutional expression encompasses collective forms of self-government and a relationship of equals among Aboriginal and non-Aboriginal nations.[62] Self-determination encompasses the right of First Nations to choose how and by whom they will be governed and to determine the nature and extent of their relationships with other self-determining peoples in the absence of external interference and domination. For some, like John Borrows, self-government and control over Aboriginal affairs must also be joined with a measure of Aboriginal control over Canadian affairs through participation in shared institutions such as courts, legislatures, universities, and public media.[63] Whatever the specific institutional variation on self-determination, the underlying message, as Dale Turner reminds us, is the same: Aboriginal voices must be included in any democratic dialogue on the meaning and content of Aboriginal rights.[64] Viewed in this light, Aboriginal nationalism and the underlying claim to self-determination looks nothing at all like a kind of racist special pleading or a demand for extra rights that are denied to non-Aboriginal peoples. Instead, it looks everything like a demand for equality, for an equal right to exercise choices and make decisions that for too long have been the exclusive privilege of non-Aboriginal peoples through their control of the modern state.

Like so many of his civilizationist predecessors, Flanagan appears incapable of seeing Aboriginal peoples as anything other than objects of radical difference – exotic cultural grist for the mill of liberal assimilationism. This obsession with Aboriginal difference ultimately leads him to misrepresent Aboriginal nationalism as a yearning for some authentic cultural past, a rejection of cultural change and adaptation, and a refusal to acknowledge the kinds of socio-economic, material, and other benefits that cultural modernization may bring.[65] What Flanagan is in fact describing is one choice an Aboriginal nation *might* make with its right to self-determination, but, again, he ignores the more fundamental issue, which is the right of First Nations to make autonomous choices in the first place. Aboriginal nationalists seek to carve out a political space in which Indigenous peoples can make their own choices about the character of their cultures and the pace and direction of cultural change, rather than having these changes dictated or imposed by others.[66] And again, it is difficult to think of any representatives of Flanagan's Aboriginal orthodoxy who view the relationship between Aboriginal and non-Aboriginal cultures in such a zero-sum manner. Instead, what one commonly encounters is an ethic of cultural revision and reinvention – a celebration of creative borrowing and a judicious mixture of the best that Aboriginal and non-Aboriginal cultures have to offer each other.[67] As Joyce Green emphasizes in the context of reforms to Canadian federalism: "The processes and institutions of a reimagined political order must be a representation of indigenous aspirations, symbols, and practices as well as those of the colonizers."[68]

My last set of comments speaks to the practical dimensions of Flanagan's vision of reconciliation. First, regarding his confident prediction of the inevitability of Aboriginal assimilation, we have every reason to be skeptical. A similar aura of confidence accompanied the release of the White Paper on Indian policy of 1969, the very document that did so much to inspire the resurgent Aboriginal nationalism that remains such a prominent feature of the Canadian political landscape.[69] If the White Paper was a failure then, the chance of an updated version of its assimilationist message succeeding in today's even more highly politicized environment is, in the words of Alan Cairns, "close to zero."[70] The more recent failure of the Chrétien government's

First Nations Governance Act, which many saw as a successor to the White Paper, is perhaps the most recent testament to that fact.[71] As students of nationalism have long observed, once national identities take hold in a population, they prove to be tremendously resilient and resist destruction, even after decades of the most repressive measures or attempts at benign assimilation.[72] Flanagan himself admits that "in the case of aboriginal peoples, the political aspect of the identity seems to have enlarged as the cultural differences have shrunk," a statement that at best sits uneasily beside his confident prediction of the inevitability of assimilation.[73] All this suggests that, instead of waiting in vain for Aboriginal nationalism simply to fade away, our energies would be better spent searching for the means by which Aboriginal and non-Aboriginal identities can be brought into some form of mutual accommodation in Canada. This process has already been joined, in fits and starts, by governments and First Nations in Canada.[74]

A more serious concern is that Flanagan's uncompromising vision of reconciliation is a recipe for increased conflict and confrontation between the Crown and First Nations. Canada has been fortunate enough to have avoided the violence and bloodshed that frequently attends nationalist competition in other parts of the globe. Much of this good fortune stems from the patience shown by First Nations as they press their claims in the face of persistent public apathy and government intransigence. Yet our history also teaches us that, in the absence of a spirit of compromise and conciliation, the tensions underlying Crown–First Nations relationships can boil over into angry protests. This became apparent during the dispute at Caledonia in 2007 and when tragic violence erupted during conflicts at Oka in 1990 and Ipperwash in 1995. One of the clearest messages to emerge from the public inquiry into the death of Dudley George at Ipperwash is that behind most confrontations, such as those involving the Kettle and Stony Point First Nations, lies a long history of government failure to acknowledge, negotiate, or respond constructively to unresolved claims for the recognition of Aboriginal rights.[75] Viewed in this light, Flanagan's preferred vision of the future looks less like a constructive path toward mutual trust and reconciliation than a green light to continue down an already well-travelled route toward mutual hostility and bitter confrontation.

Conclusion

Reading Flanagan's account of colonialism in the Americas, one might easily get the impression that political domination happens of its own accord, rather than as a result of deliberate human choice and agency. Written out of the story is any sense of respect for the anguish or the agency of those who were subjected to colonial rule or any sense that those who were responsible for their subjection have a moral case to answer. At the heart of *First Nations? Second Thoughts* is a narrow and morally impoverished vision of the past whose shortcomings are equalled, if not exceeded, by the folly of its practical recommendations for the future. Ironically, Flanagan presents his civilization-ist model of reconciliation to us as a radical vision for the future of Canada's First Nations. Nonetheless, it is difficult to disagree with Alan Cairns' obser-vation that it is more "a revival of yesterday's settled understanding of where our non-Aboriginal predecessors thought we were heading ... that is only radical because it now attracts fewer supporters than in its heyday."[76] Canada can still choose this backward-looking vision, anchored in the assumptions of a distant age, or it can continue to work with First Nations toward a just and lasting vision of reconciliation built on principles of mutual respect, mutual accommodation, and consent. On such a path, there is still hope that this country can gradually move out from under the long shadow of its col-onial past.

ACKNOWLEDGMENTS

The author would like to thank Annis May Timpson for helpful comments on an ear-lier draft. Thanks also to Karl Beckert, Melanie Bunce, and Pam Prior for valuable research assistance. Financial assistance from the Social Sciences and Humanities Research Council of Canada is gratefully acknowledged.

NOTES

1   Canada, Royal Commission on Aboriginal Peoples, *Report of the Royal Commission on Aboriginal Peoples,* 5 vols. (Ottawa: Canada Communications Group, 1996), see especially 1:675-94 and 2:38.

2   See Ovide Mercredi and Mary Ellen Turpel, *In the Rapids: Navigating the Future of First Nations* (Toronto: Viking Press, 1993); John Borrows, *Recovering Canada: The Resurgence of Indigenous Law* (Toronto: University of Toronto Press, 2002); Joyce Green, "Self-Determination, Citizenship, and Federalism: Indigenous and Can-adian Palimpsest," in *Reconfiguring Aboriginal-State Relations – Canada: The State of the Federation 2003,* ed. Michael Murphy (Montreal and Kingston: McGill-Queen's University Press, 2005), 329-52; and Dale Turner, *This Is Not a Peace Pipe: Towards a Critical Indigenous Philosophy* (Toronto: University of Toronto Press, 2006).

3   *R. v. Van der Peet,* [1996]] 2 S.C.R. 507 at para. 31. For a critical discussion of the court's reconciliation jurisprudence, see John Borrows, "Uncertain Citizens:

Aboriginal Peoples and the Supreme Court," *Canadian Bar Review* 80, 1 (2001): 32-37. For the court's emphasis on negotiation, see *Delgamuukw v. British Columbia,* [1997] 3 S.C.R. 1010 at para. 186.

4   See the "Statement of Reconciliation," in Canada, Indian and Northern Affairs, *Gathering Strength: Canada's Aboriginal Action Plan* (Ottawa: Indian Affairs and Northern Development, 1997), 4-5. This policy was in stark contrast with the Harper government's initial decision not to issue an apology as part of its settlement with residential school survivors. See Bill Curry, "No Residential School Apology, Tories Say," *Globe and Mail,* 27 March 2007, http://www.theglobeandmail. com. The Conservative government later changed track on this policy, delivering an official public apology for the residential schools policy in the House of Commons on 11 June 2008. That year it also established the Truth and Reconciliation Commission, an initiative launched under the leadership of the former Liberal government, with a five-year mandate to probe this chapter in Canadian history.

5   British Columbia, Ministry of Aboriginal Relations and Reconciliation. "The New Relationship with First Nations and Aboriginal People," Government of British Columbia, http://www.gov.bc.ca/arr/newrelationship/default.html.

6   Tom Flanagan, *First Nations? Second Thoughts* (Montreal and Kingston: McGill-Queen's University Press, 2000).

7   John Stuart Mill, "Civilization," in *Collected Works of John Stuart Mill,* vol. 18, ed. J.M. Robson (Toronto: University of Toronto Press, 1977), 119-47.

8   James Tully, "Rediscovering America: The Two Treatises and Aboriginal Rights," in *An Approach to Political Philosophy: Locke in Contexts,* by James Tully (Cambridge: Cambridge University Press, 1993), 137-71, and *Strange Multiplicity: Constitutionalism in an Age of Diversity* (Cambridge: Cambridge University Press, 1995), 64-66, 71-72. For a particularly detailed version of the stages theory, see Frederick Engels, "The Origin of the Family, Private Property and the State," in *Selected Works,* vol. 3, by Karl Marx and Frederick Engels (Moscow: Progress Publishers, 1977), 193-334.

9   Mill, "Civilization," 121-22.

10 Engels, "The Origin of the Family," 267.

11 See, for example, Marx's essay "On Imperialism in India," in *The Marx-Engels Reader,* ed. Robert C. Tucker (New York: Norton, 1978), 653-58. Of course, for Marx and Engels these processes of coercive capitalist development were merely the necessary historical precursors of communist revolution. In the same sense, the liberal capitalist states of Europe represented only the penultimate stage of human development. Human history and human progress would only truly begin after the transition to a communist society.

12 John Locke, *Second Treatise of Government,* ed. C.B. Macpherson (Indianapolis: Hackett, 1980), s. 41.

13 Thomas Hobbes, *Leviathan,* ed. Richard E. Flathman and David Johnston (New York: Norton, 1997), 71.

14 Mill, "Civilization," 120-25; see also Hobbes, *Leviathan*, chap. 13; Engels, "The Origin of the Family," passim; and Locke, *Second Treatise of Government*, chap. 5.

15 Hobbes, *Leviathan*, 48.

16 See Bhikhu Parekh, "Liberalism and Colonialism: A Critique of Locke and Mill," in *The Decolonisation of Imagination: Culture, Knowledge and Power*, ed. Jan N. Pieterse and Bhikhu Parekh (London: Zed Books, 1995), 81-98.

17 John Stuart Mill, *On Liberty*, ed. Elizabeth Rapaport (Indianapolis, IN: Hackett, 1978), 53-71.

18 Immanuel Kant, "Idea for a Universal History with a Cosmopolitan Purpose," in *Kant's Political Writings*, ed. Hans Reiss (Cambridge: Cambridge University Press, 1991), 41-53.

19 See John Stuart Mill, *Utilitarianism, Liberty, Representative Government*, Everyman's Library edition (London: J.M. Dent and Sons, 1954), 363-64; and Marx's two essays on British imperialism in India:, "On Imperialism in India" and "The Future Results of British Rule in India," in *The Marx-Engels Reader*, ed. Tucker, 653-64.

20 John Locke, *An Essay concerning Human Understanding* (New York: Prometheus, 1994), bk. 1, chap. 2, para. 27 and bk. 2, chap. 11, para. 10. For discussion, see Kathy Squadrito, "Locke and the Dispossession of the American Indian," in *Philosophers on Race: Critical Essays*, ed. Julie K. Ward and Tommy L. Lott (Oxford: Blackwell, 2002), 102-4.

21 Parekh, "Liberalism and Colonialism," 87. For a more skeptical view on this point, see Squadrito, "Locke and the Dispossession of the American Indian," 117.

22 Quoted in Robert B. Louden, *Kant's Impure Ethics: From Rational Beings to Human Beings* (New York: Oxford University Press, 2000), 99.

23 For more on Kant's racism toward Native Americans, see Robert Bernasconi, "Kant as an Unfamiliar Source of Racism," in *Philosophers on Race*, ed. Ward and Lott, 148-49.

24 See Emmanuel Chukwudi Eze, "The Color of Reason: The Idea of 'Race' in Kant's Anthropology," in *Postcolonial African Philosophy: A Critical Reader*, ed. Emmanuel Chukwudi Eze (Oxford: Blackwell, 1997), 103-40; and Robert Bernasconi, "Who Invented the Concept of Race? Kant's Role in the Enlightenment Construction of Race," in *Race*, ed. Robert Bernasconi (Oxford: Blackwell, 2001), 11-36.

25 See Locke, *Second Treatise of Government*, 18-30. For discussion, see Tully, "Rediscovering America," 137-71.

26 See Locke, *Second Treatise of Government*, 52-65, particularly 58. See also Parekh, "Liberalism and Colonialism," 84-86.

27 Tully, "Rediscovering America," 144-45. For a more ambivalent position on Locke's attitude toward forcible dispossession, see Squadrito, "Locke and the Dispossession of the American Indian," 106-11.

28 See Parekh, "Liberalism and Colonialism," and Tully, "Rediscovering America," 162.

29   Mill, *Utilitarianism*, 73, 382. My discussion of Locke and Mill in this section owes much to Parekh's excellent essay "Liberalism and Colonialism."

30   Mill, *Utilitarianism*, 199, 363-64. Thus, Mill castigates colonial despotism in civilized colonies such as America and Australia while championing it in less civilized colonies such as India (376-77).

31   Karl Marx, "Genesis of the Industrial Capitalist," in *On Colonialism*, Karl Marx and Frederich Engels (Moscow: Foreign Languages Publishing House, 195?), 289.

32   Marx, "On Imperialism in India," 657-58.

33   Immanuel Kant, "The Metaphysics of Morals," in *Kant's Political Writings*, ed. Hans Reiss (Cambridge: Cambridge University Press, 1991), 172.

34   Ibid., 172-73. See also Immanuel Kant, "Perpetual Peace: A Philosophical Sketch," in *Kant's Political Writings*, ed. Reiss, 105-8.

35   Kant, "The Metaphysics of Morals," 173.

36   Kant, "Perpetual Peace," 102-3. For a darker view of Kant's colonial theorizing, see James Tully, *Public Philosophy in a New Key*, vol. 2, *Imperialism and Civic Freedom* (Cambridge: Cambridge University Press, 2008).

37   Kant, "Idea for a Universal History," 52.

38   For critiques of civilizationist thinking, see Darlene Johnston, "First Nations and Canadian Citizenship," in *Belonging: The Meaning and Future of Canadian Citizenship*, ed. William Kaplan (Montreal and Kingston: McGill-Queen's University Press, 1996), 349-67; John L. Tobias, "Protection, Civilization, Assimilation: An Outline History of Canada's Indian Policy," in *Sweet Promises: A Reader on Indian-White Relations in Canada*, ed. J.R. Miller (Toronto: University of Toronto Press, 1991), 127-44; and Canada, Royal Commission on Aboriginal Peoples, *Report*, 1:137-99.

39   Flanagan, *First Nations? Second Thoughts*, 6, 35-39.

40   Ibid., 6, 25, 194.

41   Ibid., 9, 29, 33.

42   Ibid., 25, 34.

43   Ibid., 33-34, 46.

44   Jared Diamond, *Guns, Germs, and Steel: The Fates of Human Societies* (New York: Norton, 1999).

45   Flanagan, *First Nations? Second Thoughts*, 46. Cf. William Uzgalis, "An Inconsistency Not to Be Excused: On Locke and Racism," in *Philosophers on Race*, ed. Ward and Lott, 95-97.

46   Flanagan, *First Nations? Second Thoughts*, 39.

47   Ibid., 42-43. I discuss Flanagan's caveats to this argument in the next section.

48   Ibid., 39-44, 59.

49   Ibid., 59. See also 6, 22-23, 67-88.

50   Ibid., 194. See also 6, 8-9.

51   Ibid., 43, 60.

52　For a moderate reformer, see Alan Cairns, *Citizens Plus: Aboriginal Peoples and the Canadian State* (Vancouver: UBC Press, 2000). Additional radical voices belong to Melvin H. Smith, *Our Home or Native Land? What Governments' Aboriginal Policy Is Doing to Canada* (Victoria: Crown Western, 1995); and Albert Howard and Francis Widdowson, "The Disaster of Nunavut," *Policy Options* (July-August 1999): 58-68.

53　Flanagan, *First Nations? Second Thoughts*, 59. See also 43-44.

54　This spirit of compromise is a pervasive feature of the contemporary literature on Aboriginal-state relations in Canada. See, for example, Peter Ittinuar, "The Inuit Perspective on Aboriginal Rights," in *The Quest for Justice: Aboriginal Peoples and Aboriginal Rights*, ed. Menno Boldt and J. Anthony Long (Toronto: University of Toronto Press, 1985), 47-53; Canada, Royal Commission on Aboriginal Peoples, *Treaty Making in the Spirit of Coexistence: An Alternative to Extinguishment* (Ottawa: Canada Communications Group, 1995); Borrows, *Recovering Canada*, 138-58; and Tony Penikett, *Reconciliation: First Nations Treaty Making in British Columbia* (Vancouver: Douglas and McIntyre, 2006).

55　Flanagan, *First Nations? Second Thoughts*, 60.

56　See, for example, the debate between Green and Dickason in L.C. Green and Olive P. Dickason, *The Law of Nations and the New World* (Edmonton: University of Alberta Press, 1989)

57　Flanagan, *First Nations? Second Thoughts*, 43-44, 60-61.

58　Ibid., 25.

59　Ibid., 45, 192-98.

60　Questions of territory and self-government are distinct from questions of membership. As Flanagan is undoubtedly aware, race-based membership codes were imposed on First Nations as part of the Canadian government's historical assimilation policy. See, for example, Bonita Lawrence, "Gender, Race, and the Regulation of Native Identity in Canada and the United States: An Overview," *Hypatia* 18, 2 (2003): 3. For a discussion of the contemporary echoes of this policy in a First Nations community, see E.J. Dickson-Gilmore, "*Iate-Onkwehonwe*: Blood Quantum, Membership and the Politics of Exclusion in Kahnawake," *Citizenship Studies* 3, 1 (1999): 27-44.

61　See Gerald Alfred, *Heeding the Voices of Our Ancestors: Kahnawake Mohawk Politics and the Rise of Native Nationalism in Canada* (Oxford: Oxford University Press, 1995); James Tully, "The Struggles of Indigenous Peoples for and of Freedom," in *Political Theory and Indigenous Rights*, ed. Paul Patton, Duncan Ivison, and Will Saunders (Cambridge: Cambridge University Press, 2000), 36-59; and Kiera Ladner, "Treaty Federalism: An Indigenous Vision of Canadian Federalism," in *New Trends in Canadian Federalism*, ed. François Rocher and Miriam Smith (Peterborough, ON: Broadview Press, 2003), 167-94.

62　Alfred, *Heeding the Voices of Our Ancestors*, 98, 185. See also Ladner, "Treaty Federalism," 184-87; James (Sákéj) Youngblood Henderson, "Empowering Treaty Federalism," *Saskatchewan Law Review* 58, 2 (1994): 326; Wendy Moss, "Inuit

Perspectives on Treaty Rights and Governance Issues," in Canada, Royal Commission on Aboriginal Peoples, *Aboriginal Self-Government: Legal and Constitutional Issues* (Ottawa: Canada Communications Group, 1995), 59-139; and Philip Awashish, "From Board to Nation Governance: The Evolution of Eeyou Tapay-Tah-Jeh-Souwin (Eeyou Governance) in Eeyou Istchee," in *Reconfiguring Aboriginal-State Relations – Canada: The State of the Federation 2003*, ed. Michael Murphy (Montreal and Kingston: McGill-Queen's University Press, 2005), 165-83.

63 Borrows, *Recovering Canada*, 138-41.

64 Turner, *This Is Not a Peace Pipe*, 5, 121.

65 For another example of this sort of approach, see Howard and Widdowson, "The Disaster of Nunavut."

66 See Alfred, *Heeding the Voices of Our Ancestors*, 103, 178-79; Mary Ellen Turpel, "Indigenous Peoples' Rights of Political Participation and Self-Determination: Recent International Legal Developments and the Continuing Struggle for Recognition," *Cornell International Law Journal* 25, 3 (1992): 593; and Ittinuar, "The Inuit Perspective on Aboriginal Rights," 50-51.

67 See, for example, Borrows, *Recovering Canada*; Tully, *Strange Multiplicity*; Turner, *This Is Not a Peace Pipe*; Patrick Macklem, *Indigenous Difference and the Constitution of Canada* (Toronto: University of Toronto Press, 2001); and Tim Schouls, *Shifting Boundaries: Aboriginal Identity, Pluralist Theory, and the Politics of Self-Government* (Vancouver: UBC Press, 2003).

68 Green, "Self-Determination, Citizenship and Federalism," 334.

69 Canada, *Statement of the Government of Canada on Indian Policy, 1969* (Ottawa: Queen's Printer, 1969). For background on this period, see Sally Weaver, *Making Canadian Indian Policy* (Toronto: University of Toronto Press, 1981).

70 Alan Cairns and Tom Flanagan, "An Exchange," *Inroads* 10 (2001): 110.

71 See Michael Murphy, "Looking Forward without Looking Back: Jean Chrétien's Legacy for Aboriginal-State Relations," in "The Chrétien Legacy," special issue, *Review of Constitutional Studies* 9, 1 and 2 (2004): 151-69.

72 See Walker Connor, "National Self-Determination and Tomorrow's Political Map," in *Citizenship, Diversity, and Pluralism: Canadian and Comparative Perspectives*, ed. Alan C. Cairns et al. (Montreal and Kingston: McGill-Queen's University Press, 1999), 202-30; and Donald Horowitz, *Ethnic Groups in Conflict* (Berkeley: University of California Press, 1985).

73 Cairns and Flanagan, "An Exchange," 117.

74 See, for example, the various essays in Michael Murphy, ed., *Reconfiguring Aboriginal-State Relations*.

75 Ontario, *Report of the Ipperwash Inquiry*, Ipperwash Inquiry, Honourable Sydney B. Linden, Commissioner, http://www.attorneygeneral.jus.gov.on.ca/inquiries/ipperwash/.

76 Cairns and Flanagan "An Exchange," 110.

WORKS CITED

Alfred, Gerald. *Heeding the Voices of Our Ancestors: Kahnawake Mohawk Politics and the Rise of Native Nationalism in Canada.* Oxford: Oxford University Press, 1995.

Awashish, Philip. "From Board to Nation Governance: The Evolution of Eeyou Tapay-Tah-Jeh-Souwin (Eeyou Governance) in Eeyou Istchee." In *Reconfiguring Aboriginal-State Relations – Canada: The State of the Federation 2003,* ed. Michael Murphy, 165-83. Montreal and Kingston: McGill-Queen's University Press, 2005.

Bernasconi, Robert. "Kant as an Unfamiliar Source of Racism." In *Philosophers on Race: Critical Essays,* ed. Julie K. Ward and Tommy L. Lott, 145-66. Oxford: Blackwell, 2002.

–. "Who Invented the Concept of Race? Kant's Role in the Enlightenment Construction of Race." In *Race,* ed. Robert Bernasconi, 11-36. Oxford: Blackwell, 2001.

Borrows, John. *Recovering Canada: The Resurgence of Indigenous Law.* Toronto: University of Toronto Press, 2002.

–. "Uncertain Citizens: Aboriginal Peoples and the Supreme Court." *Canadian Bar Review* 80, 1 (2001): 15–41.

British Columbia. British Columbia Ministry of Aboriginal Relations and Reconciliation. "The New Relationship with First Nations and Aboriginal People." Government of British Columbia. http://www.gov.bc.ca/arr/newrelationship/default.html.

Cairns, Alan. *Citizens Plus: Aboriginal Peoples and the Canadian State.* Vancouver: UBC Press, 2000.

Cairns, Alan, and Tom Flanagan. "An Exchange." *Inroads* 10 (2001): 103-23.

Canada. *Statement of the Government of Canada on Indian Policy, 1969.* Ottawa: Queen's Printer, 1969.

–. Indian and Northern Affairs. "Statement of Reconciliation." In *Gathering Strength: Canada's Aboriginal Action Plan,* 4-5. Ottawa: Indian Affairs and Northern Development, 1997.

Canada. Royal Commission on Aboriginal Peoples. *Report of the Royal Commission on Aboriginal Peoples.* 5 vols. Ottawa: Canada Communications Group, 1996.

–. *Treaty Making in the Spirit of Coexistence: An Alternative to Extinguishment.* Ottawa: Canada Communications Group, 1995.

Connor, Walker. "National Self-Determination and Tomorrow's Political Map." In *Citizenship, Diversity, and Pluralism: Canadian and Comparative Perspectives,* ed. Alan C. Cairns, John C. Courtney, Peter MacKinnon, Hans J. Michelmann, and David E. Smith, 202-30. Montreal and Kingston: McGill-Queen's University Press, 1999.

Curry, Bill. "No Residential School Apology, Tories Say." *Globe and Mail,* 27 March 2007. http://www.theglobeandmail.com.

Diamond, Jared. *Guns, Germs, and Steel: The Fates of Human Societies.* New York: Norton, 1999.

Dickson-Gilmore, E.J. "*Iate-Onkwehonwe:* Blood Quantum, Membership and the Politics of Exclusion in Kahnawake." *Citizenship Studies* 3, 1 (1999): 27-44.

Engels, Frederick. "The Origin of the Family, Private Property and the State." In *Selected Works*, vol. 3, by Karl Marx and Frederick Engels, 193-334. Moscow: Progress Publishers, 1977.

Eze, Emmanuel Chukwudi. "The Color of Reason: The Idea of 'Race' in Kant's Anthropology." In *Postcolonial African Philosophy: A Critical Reader*, ed. Emmanuel Chukwudi Eze, 103-40. Oxford: Blackwell, 1997.

Flanagan, Tom. *First Nations? Second Thoughts*. Montreal and Kingston: McGill-Queen's University Press, 2000.

Green, Joyce. "Self-Determination, Citizenship, and Federalism: Indigenous and Canadian Palimpsest." In *Reconfiguring Aboriginal-State Relations – Canada: The State of the Federation 2003*, ed. Michael Murphy, 329-52. Montreal and Kingston: McGill-Queen's University Press, 2005.

Green, L.C., and Olive P. Dickason. *The Law of Nations and the New World*. Edmonton: University of Alberta Press, 1989.

Henderson, James (Sákéj) Youngblood. "Empowering Treaty Federalism." *Saskatchewan Law Review* 58, 2 (1994): 241-329.

Hobbes, Thomas. *Leviathan*. Ed. Richard E. Flathman and David Johnston. New York: Norton, 1997.

Horowitz, Donald. *Ethnic Groups in Conflict*. Berkeley: University of California Press, 1985.

Howard, Albert, and Frances Widdowson. "The Disaster of Nunavut." *Policy Options* (July-August 1999): 58-68.

Ittinuar, Peter. "The Inuit Perspective on Aboriginal Rights." In *The Quest for Justice: Aboriginal Peoples and Aboriginal Rights*, ed. Menno Boldt and J. Anthony Long, 47-53. Toronto: University of Toronto Press, 1985.

Johnston, Darlene. "First Nations and Canadian Citizenship." In *Belonging: The Meaning and Future of Canadian Citizenship*, ed. William Kaplan, 349-67. Montreal and Kingston: McGill-Queen's University Press, 1996.

Kant, Immanuel. "Idea for a Universal History with a Cosmopolitan Purpose." In *Kant's Political Writings*, ed. Hans Reiss, 41-53. Cambridge: Cambridge University Press, 1991.

–. "The Metaphysics of Morals." In *Kant's Political Writings*, ed. Hans Reiss, 131-75. Cambridge: Cambridge University Press, 1991.

–. "Perpetual Peace: A Philosophical Sketch." In *Kant's Political Writings*, ed. Hans Reiss, 93-130. Cambridge: Cambridge University Press, 1991.

Ladner, Kiera. "Treaty Federalism: An Indigenous Vision of Canadian Federalism." In *New Trends in Canadian Federalism*, ed. François Rocher and Miriam Smith, 167-94. Peterborough, ON: Broadview Press, 2003.

Lawrence, Bonita. "Gender, Race, and the Regulation of Native Identity in Canada and the United States: An Overview." *Hypatia* 18, 2 (2003): 3-31.

Locke, John. *An Essay concerning Human Understanding*. New York: Prometheus, 1994.

–. *Second Treatise of Government*. Ed. C.B. Macpherson. Indianapolis, IN: Hackett, 1980.

Louden, Robert B. *Kant's Impure Ethics: From Rational Beings to Human Beings*. New York: Oxford University Press, 2000.

Macklem, Patrick. *Indigenous Difference and the Constitution of Canada*. Toronto: University of Toronto Press, 2001.

Marx, Karl. "The Future Results of British Rule in India." In *The Marx-Engels Reader*, ed. Robert C. Tucker, 659-64. New York: Norton, 1978.

–. "Genesis of the Industrial Capitalist." In *On Colonialism*, Karl Marx and Frederich Engels, 288-302. Moscow: Foreign Languages Publishing House, 195?.

–. "On Imperialism in India." In *The Marx-Engels Reader*, ed. Robert C. Tucker, 653-58. New York: Norton, 1978.

Mercredi, Ovide, and Mary Ellen Turpel. *In the Rapids: Navigating the Future of First Nations*. Toronto: Viking Press, 1993.

Mill, John Stuart. "Civilization." In *Collected Works of John Stuart Mill*, vol. 18, ed. J.M. Robson, 119-47. Toronto: University of Toronto Press, 1977.

–. *On Liberty*. Ed. Elizabeth Rapaport. Indianapolis: Hackett, 1978.

–. *Utilitarianism, Liberty, Representative Government*. Everyman's Library Edition. London: J.M. Dent and Sons, 1954.

Moss, Wendy. "Inuit Perspectives on Treaty Rights and Governance Issues." In Canada, Royal Commission on Aboriginal Peoples, *Aboriginal Self-Government: Legal and Constitutional Issues*, 59-139. Ottawa: Canada Communications Group 1995.

Murphy, Michael. "Looking Forward without Looking Back: Jean Chrétien's Legacy for Aboriginal-State Relations." In "The Chrétien Legacy," special issue, *Review of Constitutional Studies* 9, 1 and 2 (2004): 151-69.

–, ed. *Reconfiguring Aboriginal-State Relations – Canada: The State of the Federation 2003*. Montreal and Kingston: McGill-Queen's University Press, 2005.

Ontario. *Report of the Ipperwash Inquiry*. The Ipperwash Inquiry, Honourable Sydney B. Linden, Commissioner. http://www.attorneygeneral.jus.gov.on.ca/inquiries/ipperwash/.

Parekh, Bhikhu. "Liberalism and Colonialism: A Critique of Locke and Mill." In *The Decolonisation of Imagination: Culture, Knowledge and Power*, ed. Jan N. Pieterse and Bhikhu Parekh, 81-98. London: Zed Books, 1995.

Penikett, Tony. *Reconciliation: First Nations Treaty Making in British Columbia*. Vancouver: Douglas and MacIntyre, 2006.

Schouls, Tim. *Shifting Boundaries: Aboriginal Identity, Pluralist Theory, and the Politics of Self-Government*. Vancouver: UBC Press, 2003.

Smith, Melvin H. *Our Home or Native Land? What Governments' Aboriginal Policy Is Doing to Canada*. Victoria: Crown Western, 1995.

Squadrito, Kathy. "Locke and the Dispossession of the American Indian." In *Philosophers on Race: Critical Essays*, ed. Julie K. Ward and Tommy L. Lott, 102-4. Oxford: Blackwell, 2002.

Tobias, John L. "Protection, Civilization, Assimilation: An Outline History of Canada's Indian Policy." In *Sweet Promises: A Reader on Indian-White Relations in Canada*, ed. J.R. Miller, 127-44. Toronto: University of Toronto Press, 1991.

Tully, James. *Public Philosophy in a New Key*. Vol. 2, *Imperialism and Civic Freedom*. Cambridge: Cambridge University Press, 2008.

–. "Rediscovering America: The Two Treatises and Aboriginal Rights." In *An Approach to Political Philosophy: Locke in Contexts*, by James Tully, 137-71. Cambridge: Cambridge University Press, 1993.

–. *Strange Multiplicity: Constitutionalism in an Age of Diversity*. Cambridge: Cambridge University Press, 1995.

–. "The Struggles of Indigenous Peoples for and of Freedom." In *Political Theory and Indigenous Rights*, ed. Paul Patton, Duncan Ivison, and Will Sanders, 36-59. Cambridge: Cambridge University Press, 2000.

Turner, Dale. *This Is Not a Peace Pipe: Towards a Critical Indigenous Philosophy*. Toronto: University of Toronto Press, 2006.

Turpel, Mary Ellen. "Indigenous Peoples' Rights of Political Participation and Self-Determination: Recent International Legal Developments and the Continuing Struggle for Recognition." *Cornell International Law Journal* 25, 3 (1992): 579-602.

Uzgalis, William. "An Inconsistency Not to Be Excused: On Locke and Racism." In *Philosophers on Race: Critical Essays*, ed. Julie K. Ward and Tommy L. Lott, 81-100. Oxford: Blackwell, 2002.

Weaver, Sally. *Making Canadian Indian Policy*. Toronto: University of Toronto Press, 1981.

11
Take 35:
Reconciling Constitutional Orders

Kiera L. Ladner

For Indigenous peoples, the story of Canada is one of myth, magic, deceit, occupation, and genocide. For Canadians, the story is one of discovery, lawful acquisition, and the establishment of peace, order, and good governance. These conflicting stories of Canadian history are representative of historical narratives of the colonized and the colonizer. But they are not just matters of historical perspective or concern: they define and frame how the colonized and the colonizer explain the past, understand the present, and envisage the future. These conflicting historical narratives are the first thoughts and principles that define (and confine) the perspectives and the political realities of both Indigenous nations and the Canadian nation(s).

My article, "Up the Creek: Fishing for a New Constitutional Order" in the *Canadian Journal of Political Science* explores both Mi'kmaq and Canadian historical narratives in an attempt to explain the claims of each nation within the same fishery and the resulting jurisdictional quagmire and contestation of sovereignties.[1] The article discusses how each nation claims to have gained jurisdiction over Mi'kma'ki (Mi'kmaq territory) and the salmon within this territory; how neither sees its jurisdiction as being circumvented, eliminated by, or ceded to the other; and how both claim some semblance of jurisdiction today. In short, the federal government bases its jurisdictional claims on an act of "legal magic," on the incantation of the European explorers who proclaimed the lands "discovered" and established the sovereignty of the Crown.[2] This act of legal magic was accomplished specifically through the *Magna Carta, 1215*, which established a common fishery and a public right to fishing, and the *Constitution Act, 1867*, which provided the Canadian federal government with the responsibility for maintaining the public fishery. Meanwhile, Mi'kmaq base their claims on their own constitutional order, which defines and regulates fishing as both a right and a responsibility of Mi'kmaw within Mi'kma'ki. From this perspective Mi'kmaq have a right to fish and a responsibility for the salmon, rights and responsibilities that have never been ceded to the Crown (or any of its representatives) but were instead recognized, and affirmed, in the treaties that established Mi'kmaw's constitutional relationship with the Crown and recognized the Crown's ability to govern its own subjects within Mi'kma'ki.

As both the story of Canada and the case of this jurisdictional quagmire illustrate, the roots of these competing constitutional orders run deep and are not likely to be uprooted without tremendous upheaval and the prioritization of reconciliation. Reconciliation is required if Canadians and their governments are to come to terms with these competing constitutional orders and if these contested sovereignties are to be resolved peacefully. Reconciliation is required because Indigenous constitutional orders and the resulting disputes over Canadian sovereignty are not only the root cause of most contemporary disruptions in Indian country, they are also the foundation upon which the growing unrest in Indian country – particularly among youth – is built. While such movements are gaining momentum, similar needs, demands, and unrest are being expressed in multiple forums and by a multiplicity of actors, including both *Indian Act* leaders and traditional leaders.

It is becoming increasingly apparent in Indigenous politics that it is necessary to find a way to live together and reconcile competing stories of Canada, competing constitutional orders, and contested sovereignties. The problem, however, is that this is not becoming increasingly obvious in mainstream Canadian politics. In fact, most would argue that reconciliation is not even on the political map for most Canadians and most Canadian leaders, as is evident in the reaction I receive from scholars working on issues of justice and reconciliation and from students of Canadian politics. This is extremely problematic. However, it is a situation that is likely to change as Indigenous unrest grows and as Indigenous communities simply begin dismantling the colonial order within their communities, regardless of the reaction of the Canadian government.

As change erupts reconciliation will become increasingly necessary. Reconciliation will be necessary given that the stories of Canada that define and confine perspectives, and political realities, make it impossible to engage in any meaningful conversation that would resolve unrest and address Indigenous demands for the dismantlement of the colonial order. There is no starting point or common position from which to begin, because the first thoughts and principles of Indigenous nations run contrary to the first thoughts and principles of the Canadian nation(s). Worse yet, each group contests the sovereignty and constitutional claims of the other. As unrest grows and reconciliation becomes increasingly necessary, it becomes more and more obvious that how to start the process of reconciliation is unknown, as is the vision of what reconciliation will look like. Luckily, the courts and scholars have been somewhat proactive in this visioning process. By stepping beyond questions of necessity, the Supreme Court and scholars such as John Borrows, and myself, have turned their attention to questions of possibility and process.

In "Up the Creek" I examined the contestation of sovereignty in Mi'kma'ki by way of Mi'kmaw perspectives on Canadian history, politics, and constitutional law. In this chapter I continue this exploration of Indigenous political and constitutional thought in order to understand those first thoughts, and principles, that define (and confine) Indigenous understandings of contemporary political reality and the relationship with Canada. My purpose in so doing is to consider the possibility of reconciling Aboriginal and non-Aboriginal perspectives and constitutional orders. More specifically, by giving voice to Aboriginal perspectives and Indigenous constitutional orders, I seek to understand how two constitutional orders and their contested sovereignties can be reconciled and to determine whether reconciliation is indeed possible. In so doing, I look to the courts to determine if there is an existing vision of reconciliation that would allow these contested sovereignties to be reconciled, and I begin the process of addressing the possibilities for reconciliation that were created by section 35 of the *Constitution Act, 1982* by offering up a new understanding of the Canadian Constitution and constitutional reconciliation that is grounded in indigenist thought. It should be noted that what follows are my ponderings on reconciliation, decolonization, section 35, and constitutional pluralism at this point in time. I am quite certain that I will continue to think about and write on these matters for years to come.

The Courts and Reconciliation

While many Canadians may not be cognizant of their history and may choose to ignore the realities of the present, reconciliation is necessary. It is a necessity for Indigenous peoples as they seek to realize their goals of self-determination, cultural renewal, and economic independence; it is also a necessity for Canadians as they grapple with demands for a new, or renewed, relationship between Indigenous peoples and the settler nation(s). It is a necessity that has been recognized and advocated by the courts in several decisions that pertain to Aboriginal rights. The Supreme Court of Canada has argued that the purpose of recognizing and affirming Aboriginal (and treaty) rights in section

35(1) of the *Constitution Act, 1982* was to "achieve a reconciliation of the pre-existence of Aboriginal societies with the sovereignty of the Crown."[3]

It can be easily argued that the treaties achieved a reconciliation of Aboriginal and Crown sovereignties (or claims thereof). This manner of understanding the treaties is commonly referred to as "treaty federalism" or "treaty constitutionalism."[4] Treaty constitutionalism suggests that treaties between Indigenous nations and colonial nations were not only negotiated on a nation-to-nation basis but also entailed mutual recognition of nationhood and affirmations of commitment to a nation-to-nation relationship. These nation-to-nation agreements allowed the newcomers (and their perpetual offspring) and Indigenous peoples to coexist peacefully as autonomous nations within the same territory. Treaties recognize and affirm a right to self-government and sovereignty for each nation (alien and Indigenous) within Indigenous territories, and they do not limit such rights, except in areas of jurisdiction that are explicitly delegated or dealt with in each specific treaty.[5]

While I acknowledge that many nations did not negotiate treaties with the Crown, most had normalized and/or formal relationships defined by a mutual recognition of nationhood. These relationships typically affirmed and/or defined the right of each nation to govern itself – though not necessarily within the occupied territory – and such relationships did not typically provide any recognition or rights to the occupiers within a territory vis-à-vis the resources of a territory. Most importantly, in situations in which such relationships were not formalized and treaties were not negotiated, no areas of jurisdiction were explicitly delegated to the Crown and, thus, Indigenous nations maintained all rights and responsibilities within their territory. However, the rights and responsibilities of Indigenous nations still needed to be formally reconciled with the Crown's assertion of sovereignty as justified by its legal magic – which is inherent in the act of discovery and the legal system that colonial nations created to justify and legitimize their occupation and destruction of "other" nations.[6]

Some scholars have argued that section 35(1) recognizes and affirms the treaties (and the constitutional orders and relationships that they recognized and affirmed) and Indigenous constitutional orders that were not limited by any treaty relationship (Aboriginal rights) as part of the Canadian constitutional order.[7] The Supreme Court, however, has not taken this approach. Rather than recognizing the supremacy of Indigenous constitutional orders, as James (Sákéj) Youngblood Henderson advocates, the court has instead viewed Aboriginal and treaty rights as creations of the Canadian constitutional order that is subject to judicial interpretation and parliamentary supremacy.[8] The court has therefore framed reconciliation in a manner that is inconsistent with principles of treaty constitutionalism, and it has done so in a way that disregards Indigenous constitutional orders (regardless of treaty) and subjects Indigenous nations and their "sovereign" constitutional orders to the sovereignty of the Crown.

For former Chief Justice Lamer, achieving such a reconciliation meant recognizing that Aboriginal rights could be limited by Canadian sovereignty and that divisive rights had to be balanced or weighed against the rights of Canadians and the "public interest" (of which they are a part). In rendering its decision in *Gladstone* (1996), the court argued that it had a responsibility to limit the First Nations fishery to subsistence fishing in order to protect the public interest and the rights of "all Canadians."[9]

Using similar (il)logic to decide *Mitchell v. MNR* (2001), a case regarding the transporting of goods across the imaginary line (international border) that runs though the reserve of Akwesasne, Chief Justice McLachlin provided further justification for Canada's limitation of Aboriginal rights. She stated:

> Since s. 35(1) is aimed at reconciling the prior occupation of
> North America by aboriginal societies with the Crown's assertion
> of sovereignty, the test for establishing an aboriginal right focuses
> on identifying the integral defining features of those societies.
> Stripped to essentials, an aboriginal claimant must prove a modern practice, tradition or custom that has a reasonable degree of
> continuity with the practices, traditions and customs that existed
> prior to contact. The practice, custom or tradition must have been
> "integral to the distinctive culture" of the aboriginal peoples, in
> the sense that it distinguished or characterized their traditional
> culture and lay at the core of the peoples' identity. It must be a
> "defining feature" of the aboriginal society, such that the culture
> would be "fundamentally altered" without it. It must be a feature
> of "central significance" to the peoples' culture, one that "truly
> made the society what it was." This excludes practices, traditions
> and customs that are only marginal or incidental to the aboriginal
> society's cultural identity, and emphasizes practices, traditions and
> customs that are vital to the life, culture and identity of the aboriginal society in question.[10]

As McLachlin's explanation of the court's "Aboriginal rights test" demonstrates, the court's understanding of reconciliation has little to do with reconciling or working out a mutually agreeable relationship between the competing constitutional orders. It pertains more clearly to the interests of Canadians, to limiting the rights of Indigenous peoples by freezing them in some perpetual "permafrost" and incorporating any remnants of a separate constitutional order into Canada.

Reconciliation has not been a point of consideration in Supreme Court decisions that pertain to treaty rights because the court has not applied its Aboriginal rights test to cases involving treaty rights. Instead, the court has developed a separate set of methods and tests to validate the existence of claimed treaty rights and to ascertain the meaning and justifiable limitations of such rights. That said, I would argue that the court's understanding of reconciliation (and reconciliation as the purpose of section 35) is implicit in, or at the very least consistent with, the court's understanding of, and justification for, infringement. Developed in cases such as *Sparrow* (1990), the infringement test recognizes the ability of governments to restrict or interfere legitimately with constitutionally recognized and protected rights when the limitation is reasonable, does not pose "undue hardship," and does not deny holders the ability to exercise their rights.[11] While this test does not speak directly to the court's understanding of reconciliation and section 35(1), the manner in which it was transformed and expanded in *Marshall II* (1999) does so. *Marshall II* removes the necessity of justification from the infringement test and creates the opportunity for "unjustified infringement" in such a way that a government is now able to impose, unilaterally, regulations and restrictions that may not need to meet any standard or justification at all.[12] In short, *Marshall II* subjects the constitutionally recognized rights of treaty nations to considerations of "compelling public purpose," parliamentary supremacy, and Canadian sovereignty.[13] In essence, it is as former Chief Justice Lamer argued in the *Van der Peet* and *Gladstone* decisions. In these decisions he not only suggested that the purpose of section 35(1) was to "reconcile the pre-existance of Aboriginal society with the sovereignty of the Crown," he also asserted that reconciliation meant recognizing that section 35 rights could be limited by Canadian sovereignty and had to be balanced against the rights of Canadians and the public interest.[14]

This discussion of the court's framing of reconciliation, Aboriginal rights, and treaty rights demonstrates how the judiciary has proved to be ineffective in (1) providing Indigenous peoples with the opportunities and means to decolonize themselves and their relationship with the colonial state and (2) addressing competing constitutional orders and the resulting disputes of sovereignty. That the judiciary has been ineffective in dealing with these matters is not simply a matter of the courts finding against First Nations. They have not simply failed to understand Indigenous perspectives and realities or acknowledge the different stories of Canada and the magic of colonialism, which are grounded in (and continue to define) the perspectives and political realities of Indigenous nations. The courts have, much like scholars such as Tom Flanagan, decided to ignore Indigenous perspectives and to perpetuate colonialism and its hierarchy of knowledge, histories, and peoples.[15]

In short, the ineffectiveness of the judiciary in its dealings with Indigenous nations is the result of the courts' colonial mentality and their position as defenders of the interests of the colonial state and the colonial paradigm. Their rationalization of, or test for, Aboriginal rights (including the underlying idea that Aboriginal rights must be compatible with Canadian sovereignty) and their understanding of treaty rights and infringement (both pre- and post-*Marshall II*) obfuscate and deny Aboriginal peoples the right and the opportunity to exercise sovereignty, engage in a nation-to-nation relationship, and govern within their territory (i.e., manage their resources) in accordance with their own constitutional order (as is possibly recognized and affirmed in treaties). The manner in which the Supreme Court obfuscates and denies First Nations their rights and the opportunity to re-establish their own constitutional orders (as well as the ability to realize the nation-to-nation relationship agreed upon) can be demonstrated with reference to the key components of the Aboriginal rights and infringement tests: reconciliation and sovereignty.

As Russel Barsh and James (Sákéj) Youngblood Henderson explain, the idea that the purpose of section 35(1) of the Constitution is reconciliation is "a doctrine plucked from thin air."[16] Nevertheless, the implications of such a doctrine are enormous: "Taken to its logical extreme, the 'reconciliation' test has the effect of extinguishing everything that had not already been judicially recognized prior to 1982."[17] This is because the test implies that an Aboriginal right "may have been circumscribed or extinguished prior to 1982 by the mere existence of British settlement."[18] I concur with Barsh and Henderson's characterization of the implications of this test. Even if the test is not taken to its logical extreme, it is extremely problematic. By requiring the reconciliation of that which is inconsistent with Canadian law and/or the "collective interests" or the "common good," the court is recognizing the supremacy of the laws, rights, and interests of non-Aboriginal Canadians. Since the court views Indigenous nations as Canadians and as part of the common or collective, it has defined the "common good" and the "collective interest" (as represented by the federal government) as the middle ground.

Reconciliation

Given the parameters and limitations of the Supreme Court's view of reconciliation and its understanding of Aboriginal rights and treaty rights (and the judiciary's respective tests and methods of interpretation), it is easy to understand why the court's vision, and judicial action itself, would be ineffective for Indigenous peoples seeking to reconcile competing constitutional orders and contested sovereignties. After all, in its framing of reconciliation and Aboriginal and treaty rights, the court has chosen to ignore the contemporary manifestations of precolonial societies, to deny the treaty order or the nation-to-nation relationships established previously, to negate Indigenous sovereignty by requiring compatibility with Canadian sovereignty, and to relegate discussions of decolonization and reconciliation to a consideration of what benefits the common good (read: the colonial state). How can reconciliation between co-sovereigns be attained through judicial action when the court is a colonial institution that is charged with the responsibility of defending the Crown's sovereignty? The constitutional order itself denies the treaty order, Indigenous sovereignty, Indigenous constitutional orders, and Aboriginal and treaty rights. Still, although the courts are not the vehicle in which to pursue reconciliation, it is possible that they have opened a doorway to a future of reconciliation within Canada, a future in which reconciliation and the processes of reconciliation (such as truth commissions) are envisioned outside of the box, as it has been defined by the courts.

It appears to be impossible. Reconciliation has not been framed in a manner that gives a voice to the big political issues of colonialism and decolonization or in a way that facilitates (or even calls for) political reconciliation. The court's attempts at reconciliation have "sustained and legitimated inequalities" to such a degree that in both *Van der Peet* and *Marshall II* the court limited economic development on the ground that Aboriginal and treaty rights had to be weighed against the rights of other Canadians to sustain or develop a public fishery. Simply put, the court avoided the bigger issue of competing constitutional orders and advanced a doctrine of homogeneity in which Aboriginals and non-Aboriginals constitute a "people" unified by the collective interest or common good and the unequivocal sovereignty of the Crown.

Still, as Henderson reminds us, Canada has, by and large, already reconciled the two constitutional orders in the treaty process.[19] As I have written elsewhere and alluded to in my discussion of treaty constitutionalism (or treaty federalism) earlier in this chapter, the treaties created a constitutional order that recognized and affirmed the rights of each nation to govern its own people within a given territory and facilitated the delegation of certain responsibilities to the colonial Canadian government (typically as mutual jurisdictions).[20] Jurisdictions not specifically delegated to the colonial government remain the exclusive domain of the Indigenous constitutional order. Thus, in the event that no treaty was negotiated, all jurisdictions remain in the Indigenous constitutional order because the relationship between the nation and its jurisdiction was never reconciled.

Whichever the case may be, both situations of competing constitutionalism (treaty and non-treaty) were further reconciled in 1982 with the inclusion of Aboriginal and treaty rights in the Canadian Constitution. In fact, many have argued that the *Constitution Act, 1982* in effect represented a gesture toward political reconciliation because Indigenous constitutional orders were recognized implicitly. Nonetheless, the Canadian government's efforts have focused on dismantling Indigenous constitutional orders and maintaining a system of colonial administrators (manifest in the *Indian Act* band council system of government). As a result, formal political reconciliation continues to be necessary because Indigenous constitutional orders continue to be the object of oppression and domination.

We need to acknowledge that reconciliation – particularly political reconciliation – is the necessary first step. This step has been taken at several different points in time by the treaty makers, the judiciary, and those politicians (and academics) who patriated the Constitution in 1982. To go beyond this first step and to succeed in meaningful political reconciliation, we must begin to entertain questions of possibility. As James Henderson, Marjorie Benson, and Isobel Findlay note:

> The challenge is to make the present and the future an enabling
> environment for all peoples, and to promote a fair and just society
> by respecting the treaty reconciliations and creating new reconciliations where needed. As the Lamer Court said, "we are all here to

stay." The courts should not, through narrow interests or neglect, compromise the future. The future is the only heritage that remains uncontaminated by colonial thinking and laws ... When all Canadians start to conceive a way to restore our environment, to cleanse our legislative and judicial systems, and to imagine a pluralistic future of fresh chances and unlimited possibilities, we shall begin to share our future. The crucial question is how do we get there?[21]

For legal scholars such as Henderson, Benson, Findlay, Barsh, Borrows, and Macklem, the answer lies in the Canadian constitutional order.[22]

Constitutional Ponderings Take 35

The inclusion of Aboriginal and treaty rights in the Canadian Constitution in 1982 ushered in great possibilities for Indigenous peoples and their constitutional orders. It offers the possibility of decolonizing Canada and creating a postcolonial country based on the recognition and affirmation of Indigenous constitutional orders in section 35 as part of the rubric of Aboriginal and treaty rights. Indeed, as Henderson, Benson, and Findlay argue, the recognition and affirmation of Aboriginal and treaty rights in the *Constitution Act, 1982* further reconciled the Aboriginal constitutional order with the Canadian constitutional order (and its claims of sovereignty) by placing Indigenous constitutional orders within the framework of constitutional supremacy:

> Section 35(1) expressly affirms Aboriginal and treaty rights in the constitutional supremacy of Canada ... The Constitution Act, 1982 has reconciled Aboriginal peoples with constitutional supremacy, the structural division of the imperial sovereignty. It vests their constitutional rights in the constitution of Canada, which is different than the Lamer Court's interpretation of constitutional rights reconciliation of Aboriginal peoples with the sovereignty of the Crown. While treaty relationships still remain vested with the imperial Crown, the treaty and Aboriginal rights are now vested in the Aboriginal peoples of Canada. The constitution of Canada replaces the indivisible sovereignty.[23]

This is essentially an argument in favour of treaty constitutionalism, post-1982. It is a logical method of constitutional analysis that interprets section

35 and the Canadian Constitution from the vantage point of treaty constitutionalism or treaty federalism. It is an understanding that is both historically grounded and widely held (as it was in 1982) because it honours the spirit and the intent of the treaties, does not deny or obfuscate Indigenous constitutional orders, and provides a foundation for decolonization. Furthermore, it is an understanding of the Canadian Constitution that speaks of political reconciliation and, thus, the formal reconciliation of Indigenous and Canadian constitutional orders in a manner that does not avoid the big issues of sovereignty, colonial legacies, decolonization, constitutional pluralism, and the non-necessity of homogeneity.

Understood in this light, section 35(1) is an affirmation of treaty constitutionalism. As explained previously, treaty constitutionalism contends that treaties recognized and affirmed Indigenous constitutional orders, delegated certain powers and responsibilities to the Crown, and provided colonial orders with the ability to govern their own people within the shared territories. In cases where no such treaty was negotiated, the prerogatives of both "sovereigns" remain intact because neither constitutional order has ever been subsumed by, limited by, or incorporated into the other. Whereas Indigenous constitutional orders exist under the rubric of treaty rights for treaty nations; in cases where no treaty exists, these constitutional orders give meaning to the nation's Aboriginal rights because they frame and define the rights and responsibilities of both citizens and the nation. Thus, regardless of whether a treaty exists, Indigenous rights and responsibilities are vested in and limited by Indigenous constitutional orders; whereas they are merely "recognized and affirmed," not created or vested in, section 35(1) of the Canadian constitutional order. Still, Canadian governments (and their courts) claim exclusive jurisdiction over Indigenous nations and their territories and claim Aboriginal and treaty rights as a mere burden on the Crown's sovereignty.

To entertain questions of Canadian sovereignty and the resulting claims of exclusive jurisdiction (divided between Canadian governments and excluding Indigenous nations) or to suggest that Indigenous claims of rights and responsibilities (framed as an Aboriginal or treaty right) must be reconciled with the sovereignty of the Crown is wrong. This treatment denies and obfuscates the history of colonization and the rights of Indigenous nations (as established in the colonial period). The presumption of sovereignty and exclusive jurisdiction has been challenged in Canadian law and in legal and constitutional scholarship.[24] As Patrick Macklem explains:

How is it that the settling nations were able to make claims of
sovereignty over these people, claims that form the historical
backdrop to contemporary assertions of Canadian sovereignty
over Canada's First Nations? In the debates surrounding
Confederation, there was no discussion whatsoever about the
propriety of asserting Canadian sovereignty over Canada's
indigenous population. Sovereignty was assumed, and its
assumption is basic to the Canadian legal imagination.
Aboriginal peoples in Canada are currently imagined in law
to be Canadian subjects, or Canadian citizens. Parliament is
imagined to possess the ultimate law-making authority over all
its citizens. A fundamental assumption underpinning the law
governing Native people is that Parliament has the authority to
pass laws governing Native people without their consent.[25]

As Macklem argues, such assumptions are extremely problematic and their
legitimacy and legality are questionable in international and domestic law
and in legal doctrines (constitutional and otherwise). Macklem is not alone
in questioning and challenging these assumptions that form the bedrock of
the Canadian constitutional order because Indigenous nations neither sur-
rendered their sovereignty nor provided their consent. In raising such questions, scholars such as Borrows argue that Indigenous sovereignty and
constitutional orders continue to exist in an altered form as they become a
part of the Canadian constitutional order (an "amalgam of different ... orders"), thus necessitating the incorporation of Aboriginal ideals and principles into the Canadian constitutional order.[26] Meanwhile, others such as
James Tully see the continuance of Indigenous sovereignty and constitutional orders as the basis for Aboriginal self-determination and even treaty
constitutionalism.[27]

    The fact is that Indigenous people never ceded their rights and respon-
sibilities (collective sovereignty) under their own constitutional order; nor
did they consent to be ruled by the Crown or its operatives (such as Parliament). These claims are simply historical myths that were created for the
benefit of the colonizers; they are legal conventions that were created by
colonial authorities to legitimate European expansion and its territorial claims
vis-à-vis other would-be colonizers. But while the legal magic of Europe and
its colonial offspring claims to have made the rights and responsibilities of
the "other" vanish, the actions of colonial authorities tell a different story,

one that recognizes and affirms Indigenous nationhood, rights, and responsibilities through the treaty process and beyond. Most importantly, the legal magic did not eliminate the Indigenous constitutional orders, for they continue to exist in accordance with their own legal and political traditions to this day, though in an altered form that is limited by treaty and colonial or Canadian policies.

Sidestepping the matter of legal magic and accepting that Indigenous constitutional orders exist as part of the Canadian constitutional order in section 35(1) leads one to question the meaning of political reconciliation (particularly constitutional reconciliation). Section 35, as so many have argued, contains within it the inherent right to self-government (not simply self-administration), a right that is recognized in but not created by the Canadian Constitution. Self-governance is a right and a responsibility vested in Indigenous constitutional orders, and as such it contains all jurisdictions essential for contemporary Indigenous governance in Canada. In other words, vested as it is in "Aboriginal legal orders, laws and jurisdictions and unfolded through Aboriginal and treaty rights," the section 35(1) right to self-determination contains all matters of jurisdiction, subject to the limitations agreed to in each nation's treaty (in the past or the future).[28]

While there is no need to engage in a discussion with Canadian governments on the matter of self-governance insofar as jurisdictional matters, legal orders, laws, and structures of governance are concerned, such a need may exist within each nation. As a result of colonization and federal policies of political genocide, Indigenous peoples will need to engage in processes of decolonization. As they rekindle and empower Indigenous constitutional orders, Indigenous peoples will likely need to engage in discussions about renewing, and possibly even recreating, Indigenous legal and political systems.

No matter what the courts think, Indigenous nations do not exist in a state of permafrost. Legal, jurisdictional, and administrative necessities that did not exist at the time of contact, or when the Canadian government engaged in political genocide through the *Indian Act*, are now a reality and will continue to emerge from time to time. Constitutional orders need to adapt and evolve to respond to modern necessities such as the regulation of motor vehicles and traffic, environmental protection, emergency preparedness, and power delivery. These processes of constitutional renewal have to be engaged, just as the Canadian constitutional order is continuously renewed through constitutional interpretation; executive, legislative, or judicial action; and intergovernmental relations.

Regardless of how these Indigenous constitutional orders are renewed, there is no need to negotiate self-government so far as jurisdictional matters are concerned. However, a need may exist to reconcile and coordinate competing jurisdictions, and shared jurisdictional areas, and also to address the sharing of traditional territories and their resources. Indeed, many treaties address matters of shared jurisdiction, as was the case with education in the numbered treaties.[29] In these instances Indigenous and Canadian governments will need to engage in some semblance of political reconciliation to coordinate their policies and programs or agree upon a division of responsibility in shared areas, as has been done in areas of jurisdiction that are shared by the provincial and federal governments (either directly or by way of the federal spending power). Furthermore, in areas where Indigenous and Canadian governments both claim the same jurisdiction and the corresponding right and/or responsibility, reconciliation may be necessary to coordinate jurisdictions and avoid confrontation. This is the case in the matter of the salmon fishery in Mi'kma'ki, where provincial, federal, and Mi'kmaq authorities all claim to have jurisdiction.

Constitutional reconciliation need not be doomed because of avoidance and homogeneity. Recognition of each nation's constitutional order automatically sidesteps issues of homogeneity, for it acknowledges the political diversity of nations and their treaty relationships and fails to support the existing homogeneity of the colonial nation, its vision of reconciliation, and its claims of sovereignty and exclusive jurisdiction. Instead of avoiding pertinent issues that underlie the need for reconciliation, recognition offers an opportunity to achieve a mutually agreeable political reconciliation of the primary issues resulting from colonialism (land rights, sovereignty, and self-determination).

Reconciliation of these competing constitutional orders by means of consultation, coordination, intergovernmental negotiation, and judicial interpretation would not necessarily force Indigenous nations to reconcile their existence with the sovereignty of the Crown. According to Chief Justice McLachlin in the decision of *Haida Nation v. British Columbia:*

> The government's duty to consult with Aboriginal peoples and accommodate their interests is grounded in the honour of the Crown, which must be understood generously. While the asserted but unproven Aboriginal rights and title are insufficiently specific for the honour of the Crown to mandate that the Crown act

as a fiduciary, the Crown, acting honourably, cannot cavalierly run roughshod over Aboriginal interests where claims affecting these interests are being seriously pursued in the process of treaty negotiations and proof ... The controlling question in all situations is what is required to maintain the honour of the Crown and to effect reconciliation between the Crown and Aboriginal people with respect to the interests at stake. The effect of good faith consultation may reveal a duty to accommodate.[30]

Although McLachlin goes on to suggest that the "Crown must balance Aboriginal concerns reasonably with ... other societal interests," the emphasis remains on acting in accordance with the honour of the Crown, even when rights have not been demonstrated fully.[31] Moreover, reconciliation between Aboriginal people and the Crown involves and necessitates the honour of the Crown and, thus, the accommodation of Aboriginal interests without the Crown "cavalierly running roughshod over Aboriginal rights."

This is a bold statement that involves the interpretation and protection of Aboriginal rights and Crown responsibility from a court that seemed set upon curtailing Aboriginal rights in cases such as *Van der Peet* and *Mitchell* and intent on providing governments with every opportunity to forgo treaty rights in favour of societal interests and Crown sovereignty in cases such as *Marshall II*. That said, in some respects *Haida* represents a return to the past as well as a new treatment of Aboriginal rights and a more nuanced, Aboriginal-friendly understanding of reconciliation. Perhaps *Haida* represents a partial acknowledgement of this understanding of Aboriginal rights (and, thus, those rights protected by treaty) and the need to accommodate and reconcile these competing orders in a manner consistent with the honour of the Crown, the treaties, and a contextualized understanding of these *sui generis* rights. Although the federal government is claiming otherwise, *Haida* does indeed represent a shift in the court's understanding of both Aboriginal rights and the Crown's responsibilities (its honour), which may open the door more widely for a discussion of reconciliation. This discussion would facilitate a step toward a meaningful and mutually beneficial reconciliation of the competing constitutional orders, a reconciliation in which absolute primacy would not be given to assumptions of Crown sovereignty or Canadian interests, in so far as accommodation of Aboriginal interests is necessary to maintain the honour of the Crown.

Regardless of the judiciary's understanding of Aboriginal and treaty rights or the opportunities and protections that have been created by the courts, scholars will continue to think about questions of reconciliation and the meaning of section 35(1). Conversations with Henderson and Leroy Little Bear have led me to move beyond the current thinking about reconciliation; Aboriginal rights as understood, defined, and confined by the courts; and current understandings (in the literature and elsewhere) of treaty constitutionalism.

Henderson and Little Bear have encouraged me to think about the reconciliation of competing constitutional orders and what section 35(1) means for Indigenous constitutional orders and the Canadian constitutional order. To understand the meaning of section 35(1), reconciliation, and the implications of my ponderings thus far, one has to understand how it is that we came to need reconciliation to address contested sovereignties and competing constitutional orders. According to Henderson,

> These Aboriginal orders and treaties had the force of imperial law within North American colonies. The remarkable thing is that, despite this, the British imperial order forgot about reconciling them until 1982. The imperial statutes that established delegated self-rule and responsible government for the colonies never sought to reconcile these new powers with the pre-existing Aboriginal orders or with the empire's treaty obligations to Aboriginal peoples ...
> The constitutional affirmation of treaty and Aboriginal rights was designed to prevent the federal and provincial orders of government, as well as the judiciary, from flouting or overlooking Aboriginal rights or their underlying principles ... The ultimate purpose of these reforms was to create constitutional conditions – a legal and epistemic pluralism protected by the constitutional order from pragmatic, majoritarian politics – within which Aboriginal peoples and Canadians could rediscover good relations and live together on the shared land more compatibly.[32]

In creating this "legal and epistemic pluralism," section 35(1) constitutionalized Indigenous political orders and made them part of the Canadian Constitution. In so doing it reconciled what Henderson terms provincial federalism with treaty federalism or treaty constitutionalism. To take this one step further (as conversations with Henderson and Little Bear have urged), the rights and responsibilities vested in these Indigenous constitutional orders were not only recognized and affirmed within section 35(1) but also, through the process of constitutional renewal in 1982, reconciled with those rights and responsibilities (jurisdictions) that are vested within sections 91, 92, and 93 of the Canadian constitutional order. As a result of this constitutional pluralism, and because both sets of jurisdictions exist within the (implicitly recognized or explicitly established) Canadian constitutional order, there is no need to reconcile these rights with the sovereignty of the Crown. The process of constitutional renewal did just that as it recognized two sources of political authority: rights and responsibilities, on the one hand, and sovereignty, on the other. Regardless of this recognition and its implications, both forms of federalism exist as part of the Canadian Constitution and, thus, are the subject of constitutional supremacy rather than unconstitutional intrusions that are legitimized through the use of claims of parliamentary supremacy or even judicial supremacy.[33]

While I agree with Henderson and Little Bear to the extent that section 35(1) recognizes and affirms Indigenous constitutional orders as separate yet equal constitutional orders within the Canadian Constitution, I would argue that further reconciliation is necessary. Recognition – explicit or implicit – does not make for good governance and smooth transitions between jurisdictions, especially when jurisdictions will continue to be claimed by a number of different constitutional orders, which will increase the likelihood of multiple spheres of jurisdiction occupying the same territory. Constitutional orders will have to be accommodated and jurisdictions will need to be reconciled through negotiation, judicial interpretation, constitutional dialogues between governments and the courts, and consensual constitutional change or deviation. Legal and political dialogue will be necessary, as will a formal process of constitutional reconciliation. To this end, despite my disagreement with the judiciary's understanding of reconciliation (to reconcile the pre-existence of Aboriginal peoples with Canadian sovereignty), I would argue that the courts have opened the door in making reconciliation a constitutional requirement, especially when the requirement of reconciliation is paired with the constitutional requirement to uphold not only the honour of the Crown but also indigenist understandings of the Canadian Constitution, Indigenous constitutional orders, Indigenous history, and the principles of treaty constitutionalism. It is now for the courts to remember the principles of constitutional law that are to guide their decisions: "It is a basic rule, not disputed in this case, that one part of the Constitution cannot be abrogated or diminished by another part of the Constitution."[34]

Cut: Final Thoughts on Rethinking Our Future Together

Given that they exist as part of the Canadian Constitution, the courts cannot abrogate or diminish Indigenous constitutional orders. Still, while constitutional recognition may provide for the legal reconciliation of the two orders, it does not provide for political reconciliation. It is a situation that, if taken to its logical conclusion, accounts for the lack of substantive change in Aboriginal politics since 1982. This is because it is the very institutions that see themselves as the defenders of the Crown's sovereignty that are being asked to denounce this sovereignty and recognize the sovereignty of Indigenous peoples within both Indigenous and Canadian constitutional structures. Thus, given that the courts have been, and are likely to be, quite useless as an arena in which these constitutional orders can be reconciled (unless the court's interpretation of reconciliation holds), some alternative mechanism of reconciliation needs to be developed. This mechanism needs to be developed not only because of the courts' inabilities but also because the political relationship between Indigenous nations and the Canadian government needs to be reconciled to ensure that the ripples caused by overlapping and contradictory jurisdictions are smoothed over. The issue is political because, as the courts have said, "we are all here to stay"; thus, as interdependent and intertwined people and nations, we have to find a way to live here together in a mutually agreeable and mutually beneficial manner.

Finding our way will take time, discussion, and education. After all, how can Canadians begin to engage in a discussion of reconciliation or reconcile constitutional orders when most are ignorant about the real constitutional history of this land, when most are unaware of the need for reconciliation or emphatically deny it? Before any discussion occurs, we need to acknowledge and understand Indigenous perspectives, renderings of history, and dreams of the future. Canada needs to come to terms with the first thoughts, the principles and understandings of history, that guide Indigenous political and constitutional thought today. Canadians need to step beyond the myth of lawful acquisition and sovereignty to understand that the true magic lies in the relationships that were established between Indigenous peoples and the Crown that recognized and affirmed the sovereignty and rights of both nations and, in so doing, enabled the creation of Canada. If it is to move beyond the logic of Tom Flanagan's *First Nations? Second Thoughts*, then Canada will need to understand these original relationships, treaties, and Indigenous constitutional orders, which will continue to define and confine perspectives and political realities for Indigenous nations.

If we can come to terms with our constitutional histories and begin to understand the perspectives and visions of the other, then reconciliation may be possible. Still, a means of reconciliation that adequately addresses the competing constitutional orders (now unified under Canada's constitutional order) will need to be developed. Although finding our way and constructing a postcolonial polity will take time, time is of the essence, for while the relationship between these constitutional orders has yet to be fully realized, one thing is clear: Indigenous peoples have the ability to engage their governments in the range of jurisdictions that are explicit within their own constitutional orders, protected in the treaty order (regardless of treaty), and recognized and affirmed in section 35(1) of Canada's *Constitution Act, 1982.*

ACKNOWLEDGMENTS
I wish to thank Annis May Timpson and Peter Russell for their comments on versions of this chapter. I also wish to thank (Sákéj) Henderson, Leroy Little Bear, Fred Metallic, and Michael McCrossan for sharing their ideas and inspiration. I also acknowledge support received from the Social Sciences and Humanities Research Council and the Canada Research Chairs program.

NOTES

1   Kiera L. Ladner, "Up the Creek: Fishing for a New Constitutional Order," *Canadian Journal of Political Science* 38, 4 (2005): 923-55.

2   Peter H. Russell, *Recognizing Aboriginal Title: The Mabo Case and Indigenous Resistance to English-Settler Colonialism* (Toronto: University of Toronto Press, 2005), 30-50.

3   *R. v. Van der Peet,* [1996] 2 S.C.R. 508 at 31.

4   For a more thorough discussion of treaty federalism or treaty constitutionalism, see James (Sákéj) Youngblood Henderson, "Empowering Treaty Federalism," *Saskatchewan Law Review* 58, 2 (1994): 243-329; Kiera L. Ladner, "Treaty Federalism: An Indigenous Vision of Canadian Federalisms," in *New Trends in Canadian Federalism,* ed. François Rocher and Miriam Smith (Peterborough, ON: Broadview Press, 2003), 167-94.

5   Stephen Cornell, *The Return of the Native: American Indian Political Resurgence* (New York: Oxford University Press, 1988), 45-50.

6   See Russell, *Recognizing Aboriginal Title,* 42-46; Antony Anghie, "Finding the Peripheries: Sovereignty and Colonialism in Nineteenth-Century International Law," *Harvard International Law Journal* 40, 1 (1999): 1-80.

7   James (Sákéj) Youngblood Henderson, "First Nations Legal Inheritances in Canada: The Mikmaq Model," *Manitoba Law Journal* 23, 1 (1995): 1-31; Kiera Ladner, "Treaty Federalism," 167-94.

8   James (Sákéj) Youngblood Henderson, "Constitutional Powers and Treaty Rights," *Saskatchewan Law Review* 62, 2 (2000): 719-49.

9   *R. v. Gladstone*, [1996] 2 S.C.R. 723 at 73-75.

10   *Mitchell v. M.N.R.*, 2001 SCC 33, [2001] 1 S.C.R. 911 at 22.

11   *R. v. Sparrow*, [1990] 1 S.C.R. at 411.

12   Henderson, "Constitutional Powers and Treaty Rights," 728.

13   For a discussion of considerations of compelling public purpose, see Margaret E. McCallum, "Rights in the Courts, on the Water, and in the Woods: The Aftermath of *R. v. Marshall* in New Brunswick," *Journal of Canadian Studies* 38, 3 (2004): 211. For a discussion of parliamentary supremacy, see Russel Lawrence Barsh and James (Sákéj) Youngblood Henderson, "Marshalling the Rule of Law in Canada: Of Eels and Honour," *Constitutional Forum* 11, 1 (1999): 17. For a discussion of considerations of Canadian sovereignty, see John Borrows, *Recovering Canada: The Resurgence of Indigenous Law* (Toronto: University of Toronto Press, 2002), 99.

14   *R. v. Van der Peet*, [1996] 2 S.C.R. 508 at 31; *R. v. Gladstone*, [1996] 2 S.C.R. 723 at 73-75.

15   Tom Flanagan, *First Nations? Second Thoughts* (Montreal and Kingston: McGill-Queen's University Press, 2000).

16   Russel Lawrence Barsh and James (Sákéj) Youngblood Henderson, "The Supreme Court's Van der Peet Trilogy: Naive Imperialism and Ropes of Sand," *McGill Law Journal* 42, 4 (1997): 998.

17   Ibid., 999.

18   Ibid., 998.

19   Ibid.

20   Ladner, "Treaty Federalism," 167-94.

21   James (Sákéj) Youngblood Henderson, Marjorie Benson, and Isobel Findlay, *Aboriginal Tenure in the Constitution of Canada* (Scarborough, ON: Carswell Thomson Professional Publishing, 2000), 428.

22   See Henderson, Benson, and Findlay, *Aboriginal Tenure*; James Henderson and Russel Lawrence Barsh, *The Road Indian Tribes and Political Liberty* (Los Angeles: University of California Press, 1980); John Borrows, *Recovering Canada*; and Patrick Macklem, *Indigenous Difference and the Constitution of Canada* (Toronto: University of Toronto Press, 2001).

23   Henderson, Benson, and Findlay, *Aboriginal Tenure*, 433-34.

24   *Mitchell v. M.N.R.*, [2001] S.C.R. 911; *R. v. Pamajewon*, [1996] 2 S.C.R. 821; Henderson, "First Nations Legal Inheritances in Canada," 1-31.

25   Patrick Macklem, "Ethnonationalism, Aboriginal Identities, and the Law," in *Ethnicity and Aboriginality: Case Studies in Ethnonationalism*, ed. Michael D. Levin (Toronto: University of Toronto Press, 1993), 13.

26   Borrows, *Recovering Canada*, 139-44.

27   James Tully, *Strange Multiplicity: Constitutionalism in an Age of Diversity* (Cambridge: Cambridge University Press, 1995), 124-26.

28 Henderson, Benson, and Findlay, *Aboriginal Tenure*, 433.

29 Ladner, "Treaty Federalism," 178.

30 *Haida Nation v. British Columbia (Minister of Forests)*, 2004 SCC 73 at 5-6.

31 Ibid., at 6.

32 James (Sákéj) Youngblood Henderson, "Aboriginal Jurisprudences and Rights," in *Advancing Aboriginal Claims: Visions, Strategies, Directions*, ed. Kerry Wilkins (Saskatoon: Purich Publishing, 2004), 75-76.

33 Henderson, Benson, and Findlay, *Aboriginal Tenure*, 433.

34 *New Brunswick Broadcasting Co. v. Nova Scotia (Speaker of the House of Assembly)*, [1993] 1 S.C.R. 373.

WORKS CITED

Anghie, Antony. "Finding the Peripheries: Sovereignty and Colonialism in Nineteenth-Century International Law." *Harvard International Law Journal* 40, 1 (1999): 1-80.

Barsh, Russel Lawrence, and James (Sákéj) Youngblood Henderson. "Marshalling the Rule of Law in Canada: Of Eels and Honour." *Constitutional Forum* 11, 1 (1999): 1-18.

–. "The Supreme Court's Van der Peet Trilogy: Naive Imperialism and Ropes of Sand." *McGill Law Journal* 42, 4 (1997): 994-1009.

Borrows, John. *Recovering Canada: The Resurgence of Indigenous Law*. Toronto: University of Toronto Press, 2002.

Cornell, Stephen. *The Return of the Native: American Indian Political Resurgence*. New York: Oxford University Press, 1988.

Flanagan, Tom. *First Nations? Second Thoughts*. Montreal and Kingston: McGill-Queen's University Press, 2000.

Henderson, James (Sákéj) Youngblood. "Aboriginal Jurisprudences and Rights." In *Advancing Aboriginal Claims: Visions, Strategies, Directions*, ed. Kerry Wilkins, 67-90. Saskatoon: Purich Publishing, 2004.

–. "Constitutional Powers and Treaty Rights." *Saskatchewan Law Review* 62, 2 (2000): 719-49.

–. " Empowering Treaty Federalism." *Saskatchewan Law Review* 58, 2 (1994): 243-329.

–. "First Nations Legal Inheritances in Canada: The Mikmaq Model." *Manitoba Law Journal* 23, 1 (1995): 1-31.

Henderson, James, and Russel Lawrence Barsh. *The Road Indian Tribes and Political Liberty*. Los Angeles: University of California Press, 1980.

Henderson, James, Marjorie Benson, and Isobel Findlay. *Aboriginal Tenure in the Constitution of Canada*. Scarborough, ON: Carswell Thomson Professional Publishing, 2000.

Ladner, Kiera L. "Treaty Federalism: An Indigenous Vision of Canadian Federalisms." In *New Trends in Canadian Federalism*, ed. François Rocher and Miriam Smith, 167-94. Peterborough, ON: Broadview Press, 2003.

–. "Up the Creek: Fishing for a New Constitutional Order." *Canadian Journal of Political Science* 38, 4 (2005): 923-55.

Macklem, Patrick. "Ethnonationalism, Aboriginal Identities, and the Law." In *Ethnicity and Aboriginality: Case Studies in Ethnonationalism*, ed. Michael D. Levin, 9-28. Toronto: University of Toronto Press, 1993.

–. *Indigenous Difference and the Constitution of Canada*. Toronto: University of Toronto Press, 2001.

McCallum, Margaret E. "Rights in the Courts, on the Water, and in the Woods: The Aftermath of *R. v. Marshall* in New Brunswick." *Journal of Canadian Studies* 38, 3 (2004): 204-18.

Russell, Peter H. *Recognizing Aboriginal Title: The Mabo Case and Indigenous Resistance to English-Settler Colonialism*. Toronto: University of Toronto Press, 2005.

Tully, James. *Strange Multiplicity: Constitutionalism in an Age of Diversity*. Cambridge: Cambridge University Press, 1995.

Contributors

STEPHANIE BOLTON works at Indian and Northern Affairs Canada. She is a member of the Métis Nation of British Columbia.

ALISON K. BROWN is an academic fellow in the Department of Anthropology, University of Aberdeen. Her current research uses artifacts and photographs in museums and family homes to explore the interconnected relationships of Scots fur traders and Aboriginal peoples in northern Canada. Her publications include *Museums and Source Communities: A Routledge Reader* (edited with Laura Peers) and *Pictures Bring Us Messages/Sinaakssiiksi aohtsimaahpihkookiyaawa: Photographs and Histories from the Kainai Nation* (with Laura Peers and members of the Kainai Nation). She is currently co-editing *Reinventing First Contact: Expeditions, Anthropology, and Popular Culture* (with Joshua Bell and Robert Gordon).

ROBIN JARVIS BROWNLIE is an associate professor of history at the University of Manitoba and the author of *A Fatherly Eye: Indian Agents, Government Power, and Aboriginal Resistance in Ontario, 1918-1939*.

MARGARET KOVACH is Plains Cree and Saulteaux. She is assistant professor in educational foundations, University of Saskatchewan. Her research interests include the application of Indigenous epistemologies in Indigenous research designs within interdisciplinary contexts. She has extensive experience with community-based and academic Indigenous curriculum development, with a particular focus on distance education.

KIERA LADNER is associate professor and Canada Research Chair in Indigenous Politics and Governance, University of Manitoba. Her research interests include treaty constitutionalism, indigenist theory and methodology, decolonization, constitutional politics, and Indigenous governance ("traditional," *Indian Act*, and self-government).

FIONA MACDONALD is assistant professor, Department of Political Studies, University of Manitoba. Her research interests include critical multiculturalism, Indigenous politics, and feminist political thought.

LESLIE MCCARTNEY is a former executive director of the Gwich'in Social and Cultural Institute, Northwest Territories, where she was also the lead researcher in the Gwich'in Elders Biographies Research Project. She subsequently worked as project coordinator of the King's Cross Voices Oral History Project in London, England, and has recently become research officer for the Trinity Immigration Initiative at Trinity College, Dublin.

MICHAEL MURPHY is associate professor and Canada Research Chair in Comparative Indigenous State Relations at the University of Northern British Columbia. His research interests include citizenship and democratic theory, Indigenous rights and governance, multiculturalism, and the political philosophy of nationalism and self-determination. His recent publications include *Reconfiguring Aboriginal-State Relations – Canada: The State of the Federation, 2003* and *In Defence of Multinational Citizenship*.

TIM PATTERSON is a member of the Nlaka'pamux Nation (Lower Nicola Indian Band), British Columbia. He is coordinator of the Aboriginal Health Program at the University of Calgary's Faculty of Medicine. He has a long history of working with Aboriginal programming and research through Health Canada, Statistics Canada, the Calgary Board of Education, and the Canadian Unity Council. He also held child welfare positions at a number of First Nations communities in Alberta. His research interests and knowledge of Aboriginal issues focus primarily on First Nations oral narrative and tradition, as well as First Nations ways of knowing.

LAURA PEERS is reader in material anthropology and curator (Americas), Pitt Rivers Museum, University of Oxford. She is interested in the meanings that historical artifacts hold, for First Nations peoples and in relations between Indigenous groups and museums. In addition to her publications with Alison K. Brown, her recent work includes *Playing Ourselves: Native American and First Nations Interpreters at Historic Reconstructions* and "On the Treatment of Dead Enemies: Indigenous Human Remains in Britain in the Early 21st Century," in Helen Lambert and Maryon Macdonald, eds., *Social Bodies*.

GABRIELLE A. SLOWEY is an assistant professor in the Department of Political Science at York University. Her community-based research considers the ways in which neoliberal globalization, self-government, land claims, and resource development (specifically oil and gas extraction) intersect. Her previous projects focused on northern Alberta; James Bay, Quebec; and New Zealand. She is the author of *Navigating Neoliberalism: Self-Determination and the Mikisew Cree First Nation.*

ANNIS MAY TIMPSON is director of the Centre of Canadian Studies, University of Edinburgh. Her current research focuses on Aboriginal representation in public governments and on developing methods of governance and public policies that reflect Aboriginal values. She is author of *Driven Apart: Women's Employment Equity and Child Care in Canadian Public Policy* and a range of articles on the politics of embedding Inuit culture in the governance of Nunavut.

MARTIN WHITTLES is a social anthropologist and dean of the Williams Lake Campus, Thompson Rivers University, Kamloops. He has published extensively on numerous topics, including circumpolar ethnography, the Inuvialuit, Indigenous knowledge, ecology, customary and traditional economies, and Aboriginal narratives.

Index

Printed and bound in Canada by Friesens

Set in Giovanni and Scala Sans by Artegraphica Design Co. Ltd.

Copy editor: Lesley Erickson

Proofreader: Jean Wilson

Indexer: Annette Lorek